I0763239

DOING DOUBLE DUTCH

THE INTERNATIONAL CIRCULATION OF LITERATURE FROM THE LOW COUNTRIES

DOING DOUBLE DUTCH

THE INTERNATIONAL CIRCULATION OF LITERATURE FROM THE LOW COUNTRIES

Edited by
Elke Brems, Orsolya Réthelyi and Ton van Kalmthout

LEUVEN UNIVERSITY PRESS

This publication was made possible by financial support
of the Netherlands Organization for Scientific Research

ISBN 978 94 6270 097 0
D / 2017 / 1869 / 3
NUR: 621

Layout: Frederik Danko
Cover design: Frederik Danko

CONTENTS

Introduction

CHAPTER 1

Dutch on the Move

Studying the Circulation of Smaller Literatures

Elke Brems (University of Leuven, Belgium),
Orsolya Réthelyi (Eötvös Loránd University Budapest, Hungary / Huygens ING, Amsterdam, The Netherlands),
Ton van Kalmthout (Huygens ING, Amsterdam, The Netherlands)

Trying to divide the languages of the world into categories of 'large' and 'small' is necessarily a perilous undertaking. There are at this moment 7105 languages according to a study by Dahl, of which 200 are an official language of a given country. However, 94 % of the world population gets by using a mere 5.5 % of this enormous diversity of languages. It is, therefore, no surprise that Dahl concludes his analysis thus: 'It appears safe to say that however we define "major" and "minor", the overwhelming majority of the world's languages will end up on the minor side.'[1] De Swaan goes even further by categorizing 98 % of the world's languages as 'peripheral languages'.[2] Several languages are considered not only as 'minor', but as endangered languages. Jansson considers the fate of endangered languages 'one of humanity's major challenges'.[3] While most European languages do not belong to this group, not all of them are dominant or central languages. Ronen *et al.* start from a premise that one single language, English, acts as a 'global hub', which is surrounded by a group of languages regarded as 'intermediate global hub languages' (Spanish, German, French, Russian, Portuguese, and Chinese). De Swaan, on the other hand, uses the term 'hypercentral language' to describe English as 'the pivot of the world language system' and further classifies eleven other 'supercentral languages' (Arabic, Chinese, German, French, Hindi, Japanese, Malaysian, Portuguese, Russian, Spanish, Swahili).[4]

However, the influence of languages worldwide is not only governed by the number of people speaking a given language, or the global supremacy and power of the users of that language. An important role is also played by 'how connected the speakers of that language are'.[5] Evidence shows clearly that networks of interconnection, communication and mobility play a very important role in making a language influential. As Leerssen puts it: '(a) language is not a geographical fixture [...] it moves wherever its speakers move'.[6] And 'movement' can of course be virtual, as shown by the research of Ronen *et al.*, who study the connectivity of language users 'by mapping their networks of multilingual coexpressions', meaning book translations, use of Twitter and Wikipedia.[7] The connectivity of a language in the global language network is a more important predictor of both a language's influence and the international popularity of the cultural content produced in it. Within the structure of the networks connecting multilingual speakers and translated texts used in this research, Dutch plays a more important role than is usually assumed. The Low Countries are strong and active when it comes to cultural exchange, which positions the Dutch language firmly in the global language network. Ronen *et al.* were not the first research team to emphasize the relationship between languages from this perspective. As far back as two decades ago, Heilbron argued that the centrality of a language is not solely defined by the number of native speakers, but is also influenced by the number of speakers as a second language and the number of book translations.[8]

In 2001, De Swaan introduced the Q-value of a language to indicate its capacity for communication. In his definition, the Q-value of a given language is 'the product of the "prevalence" of a language, that is the percentage of speakers of a language within the constellation of languages, and its "centrality", that is the percentage of its *multilingual* speakers among all multilinguals in the constellation'.[9] It is interesting to observe how multilingualism – alongside translation – is also increasingly regarded as a way of bringing languages in contact with each other. De Swaan pointed to the importance of multilingualism in 2001: 'It is multilingualism that has kept humanity, separated by so many languages, together'.[10] Multilingualism also provides an opportunity for smaller languages to manifest and maintain themselves, and to gain influence. English is preferred in our times worldwide by learners of a foreign language, which means that 71% of all English users do not speak it as mother tongue. Nevertheless, with regard to the above observations about multilingualism, this phenomenon should not form a threat to smaller languages, but a springboard to give them more influence.

In the work of Heilbron and others on the global language network, the focus is placed emphatically on the export of books: a language can be regarded as important if it exports many books. Research results such as those of Ronen *et al.* substantially modify the picture; if all forms of contact (connectivity) are significant, import also plays an important role. Wilterdink and his fellow researchers consider the global language network as influenced by more than just one-way traffic. Influence from the center would not be possible without the presence of the periphery in the center: 'the movement from the semi(periphery) to the centre is not an exception, but a characteristic of the system'.[11]

THE DUTCH LANGUAGE

It is clear that at this moment the Dutch language, with more than twenty-three million native speakers, is not an endangered language. Dutch is spoken in two European countries (Belgium and the Netherlands), where it is the official language (in Belgium, Dutch shares this status with French and German). In his book *The World's Major Languages*, Comrie includes Dutch among the world's 44 major languages (together 0.5% of the world's languages). Dahl gives an inventory of the languages that have published more than 100,000 articles on Wikipedia and calculates the overlap with Comrie's results: twenty-nine languages appear in both lists, again, including Dutch.[12]

To use the words of De Swaan: there are plenty of specialized bilinguals in the Netherlands and Belgium, as well as an important foreign audience that has become proficient in the Dutch language.[13] According to figures of the Dutch Language Union, Dutch as a foreign language is taught worldwide by approximately 700 academics at 175 universities in 40 countries. In addition, as many as 6,000 Dutch teachers give classes at hundreds of non-academic institutions to some 400,000 learners of the language. There are more than 15,000 academic students learning the Dutch language internationally. This international context is reason enough for literary scholars to focus on both the national and the international circulation of Dutch-language literature.

LITERATURE AND TRANSLATION

The transnational circulation of literature often requires translation, which is costly in both time and money. Translation costs puts literature at a significant disadvantage in comparison to other border-crossing cultural goods. 'For language-bound culture to transcend linguistic barriers requires the services of specialized bilinguals, that is, translators, or a foreign audience that has learned the language of the original version.'[14]

The most obvious form of contact between languages and literatures is through translation. However, while multilingualism presupposes the simultaneous presence of both source and target languages, in the case of translation the target language replaces the source language and makes it invisible; rarely are readers confronted by both outside the classroom setting. In the field of Translation Studies, this ambiguous relationship is traditionally denoted with the terms 'foreignization' and 'domestication'. Can a book in the target language still be recognized as a product from a different culture, or are these traces erased and the book 'domesticized' to conform to the target culture? 'Translating can be a useful resource for promoting linguistic and cultural imposition, and, therefore, translation can also be useful to prevent it,' observes Diaz Fouces. This latter approach 'considers translation as an instrument to maintain diversity, i.e. the wealth of the ecolinguistic system, and, therefore, to resist the centripetal socioeconomic and sociocultural tensions'.[15]

To avoid the problematic question of 'major' and 'minor' languages, the term used by Branchadell *et al.* is 'less translated languages', which they define as 'all those languages that are less often the source of translation in the international exchange of linguistic goods, regardless of the number of people using these languages'.[16] The use of the comparative degree in this term leaves sufficient scope for relative interpretations. Whether one regards a language as more or less frequently translated depends on the material being compared. The label of 'less translated' also offers a number of Western languages a chance to escape the (ideologically tinted) role of dominant languages. The discussion then is not about how Western languages dominate other languages, but strives to reveal the relationships within the West, within which certain languages are overshadowed by others. D'haen states that smaller European literatures are generally not included when discussing 'eurocentrism' and the forming of a European identity. He calls this the 'semi-peripherialization' of most minor European languages. Terms such as center and periphery, major and minor, dominant and subordinate should be put into perspective in a similar fashion. It is, however, important to realize that these terms are not only relative (such as 'less translated languages'), but also dynamic. The relation undergoes constant change. As De Swaan rightly argues, a country can successfully elevate the international position of its language (and culture) by providing subsidies for internationalizing its cultural and/or literary field, thus advancing the centrality of its language and culture. Heilbron and Van Es also place great emphasis on the role of the government in facilitating translation flows.[17]

DUTCH LITERATURE IN TRANSLATION AND ADAPTATION

Dutch literature does have a significant international circulation, as shown for instance by the recent calculations of Heilbron and Van Es. Though the absence of reliable sources and databanks make precise comparisons difficult, it is visible that from 1800 onward, there has been a slow but constant growth in the amount of Dutch literature published in translation. Up to 1960, annual production remains under 100 titles per year, peaking in the beginning of the twenty-first century with approximately 600 literary translations annually.[18]

In the same study, Heilbron and Van Es differentiate between literature from Flanders and the Netherlands. They conclude that in the modern period translations of Flemish books into French were more prevalent, while the opposite can be said of literature from the Netherlands. For both Flemish and Dutch literature, the German language area remains the most important market. Heilbron and Van Es give the following explanation for this phenomenon: 'the smaller the socio-cultural difference between the two countries is, the larger the susceptibility to the literature from the other's country'.[19] They define the factors, which are advantageous for the intensive cultural exchange as 'geographical proximity, related languages, extensive trade transaction and professional contacts (including contact between publishers), tourism and migration across borders'.[20]

The difference between literature from Flanders and the Netherlands is in itself a construct worth scholarly attention. Modern European nation states are often constructed on the premises of the inseparable unity between a nation and a language. In the nineteenth century language came to be seen as one of the crucial markers of the (unique) cultural identity of the nation. At the same time, this historically rooted equalization of language and national identity has caused much criticism from different sides. Interesting critique is voiced by Emily Apter, who fulminates against 'the celebration of nationally and ethnically branded "differences" that have been niche-marketed as commercialized "identities"'.[21] She sees this type of identity as a commercial construct, not an ideological one. The same marketing logic plays an important role in the process of exporting literature to another country. Sometimes it boils down to putting a specific type of (stereotypical) cultural identity on the market. Here also the processes of domestication and foreignization often play a role; in certain cases it helps to promote the product as a form of 'exoticism', in others it does not.

It is important to realize that translation, or what is usually understood under this term, is not the only form of transfer by which literature can circulate. Adaptation is also an important vehicle for linguistic, geographical and intermedial transfer. Taking adaptations of literary works into account alongside translations expands the possibilities for studying the reception of literature of a certain language, in this case of Dutch, in a broader sense. Studying the emergence of new artistic products (theatrical performances, graphic novels, films, etc.) adapted from Dutch source texts can provide useful insights and comparisons about how these works circulate, both inside and outside the Dutch language area.

More than half a century ago, the linguist Roman Jakobson made the following threefold classification of translation in his seminal article from 1959:

1. Intralingual translation or *rewording* is an interpretation of verbal signs by means of other signs of the same language.
2. Interlingual translation or *translation proper* is an interpretation of verbal signs by means of some other language.
3. Intersemiotic translation or *transmutation* is an interpretation of verbal signs by means of signs of nonverbal sign systems.[22]

For this last term, Naaijkens has suggested the alternative term 'intermedial translation', but it is usually referred to as 'adaptation', which does not make the complexity of the terminology more transparent. [23] Adaptations can thus be seen as intersemiotic, or intermedial translations, but the reverse is also true:

one can look at translation as a specific form of adaptation. Much of what has been said so far about translations is also true for (other types of) adaptations, though some obvious differences between textual and non-textual adaptations also exist. To make this clear, the literary scholar Linda Hutcheon differentiates between three ways of narrating a story in her book *A Theory of Adaptation*, which require three *modes of engagement* from the public. These are:

1. telling, in written texts
2. showing, in performative genres, such as theatre and film
3. physical and kinesthetic interaction, in which the consumer participates in the story, such as video games and theme parks.[24]

Hutcheon shows how literary texts adapted into different products find new audiences time and time again. She defines an adaptation as 'an extended, deliberate, announced revisitation of a particular work of art', the product of which is not merely an inferior derivative of the 'original' text.[25] On the contrary, the adaptation sets the tone in cultural life: 'In the workings of the human imagination, adaptation is the norm, not the exception', as Hutcheons concludes in the final sentence of her book.

Translations and adaptations are therefore not secondary versions of the source text. Rather the process of adaptation into another language or into another form produces independent, new cultural products, which are often better suited to their new environment. Hutcheon goes as far as using a Darwinian metaphor to describe the process: 'Sometimes, like biological adaptation, cultural adaptation involves migration to favorable conditions: stories travel to different cultures and different media. In short, stories adapt just as they are adapted'.[26]

METHODOLOGICAL AND THEORETICAL APPROACHES

The methodology of cultural transfer studies has proven to be one of the most fruitful approaches for research into the circulation of literature. In this context Michel Espagne and Michael Werner, the pioneers of the study of *transferts culturels*, must be mentioned. They first started publishing on the subject in the 1980's and 90's and went on to apply this approach predominantly from a national perspective. For them, cultural transfer

> involves moving an object in space. It focuses on human movements, on travel, on the transport of books, art or utensils for purposes that were not necessarily intellectual. It implies a profound transformation linked to the changing conditions of the receiving culture. [...] The concept of cultural transfer arises from the linkage of two autonomic and asymmetric systems.[27]

Espagne & Werner prefer this term because it is neutral. In contrast to the term 'appropriation', for instance, it has the same meaning in different languages, and refers to the import and export side of cultural exchange, as well as the dynamics of the process. Armin Paul Frank, applying the term to the field of literary production, defines it as 'all kinds of literary and cultural border crossing: the concrete importation respectively exportation of literary and other cultural goods, but also the transportation of ideas and experiences by immigrants or travelers'.[28]

The concept of cultural transfer developed by Espagne and Werner offers a framework to look at the translation, including the adaptation, or using an overarching term, the 'transfer' of texts within a broader framework of cultural transfer. In an effort to include the dynamics of the original and target cultures, as well as the process of transmission into one concept, Espagne and Werner pleaded for a framework expressing the complexity, processuality and reciprocity of intercultural exchange relations.[29] This means that the cultural transfer model presupposes the permeable nature of national, cultural and linguistic boundaries. It also replaces the reception and influence-oriented approach with one analyzing the selection, reception and acculturation integrated with an analysis of the transformation processes accompanying these. Thirdly, the model involves a comprehensive concept of culture, including both objects and immaterial artefacts.[30]

Since the literary system includes not only the production of literature but also its disseminations and the reception, including in the form of translations and adaptations, Itamar Even-Zohar and others have repeatedly drawn attention to the crucial role of translators and other agents of transfer, as well as the circumstances of the receiving culture. Gideon Toury regards this as the most important aspect of the system of translating, because 'translations are facts of target cultures; on occasion facts of a special status, sometimes even constituting identifiable (sub)systems of their own, but of the target culture in any event.'[31] The circumstances of the receiving culture often cause the crucial transformation of the imported products, according to Espagne and Werner, under the influence of the so-called conjuncture of this system, not only with regard to its economical, but also its political, ideological and other aspects. The adjustments made to a foreign cultural product by an adapter, to harmonize it with the constellation, and the appropriation by the new public results in a so-called 'acculturation' of the cultural product.[32] In the process, the original meaning shifts, even if this is only visible in the aspect of 'foreignness', which intrudes into the configuration. To put it in other terms, in a new social-historical context the readers of adapted literary texts approach these works with new horizons of expectations, as Hans-Robert Jauss described it, with their own models, paradigms, convictions and values.[33] There are different methods to conceptualize this acculturation. In the following paragraphs we will mention a few possibilities.

Mona Baker, for instance, argues for a narrative approach. Interferences between sub-systems are created through different channels. These include art and literature, but also migration, for instance, or travel accounts and the international exchange of ideas. Baker adds narratives to this list, stories that are incorporated in a scientific theory, a literary text, a cartoon or any other artefact. She defines a narrative as 'a concrete story of some aspect of the world, complete with characters, settings, outcomes or projected outcome, and plot'.[34] It can materialize in widely divergent, textual and non-textual guises and is always part of a larger system of narratives.

Narratives control the behavior of people, claims Baker, as they construct a world around us and determine how we experience reality. Narratives constantly change through new experiences and different stories. This also happens intentionally, through the interpretive activity of translators: 'Translators and interpreters play a crucial role in both disseminating and contesting public narratives within and across national boundaries.'[35] They accentuate, change and undermine specific aspects of a narrative and thus contribute to the design of a social reality. Baker therefore sees adaptations and translations as narratives, as 'a form of (re)narration that *constructs* rather than *represents* the events and characters it narrates in another language'.[36] She regards translators as influential actors in global literary production since they are in the position to intervene in the process of receiving and passing down narratives: 'The narrative approach thus grants translators and interpreters considerable agency and acknowledges the decisive and highly complex role they play in their own societies [...] as well as globally [...].'[37]

Another way of conceptualising the process of acculturation is offered by Itamar-Even Zohar. Even-Zohar argues for viewing the literary field as a polysystem, or a universe – in the words of Pascale Casanova the *république mondiale des lettres*, the *world republic of letters* or: the *international literary space*[38] – which is made up of different subsystems. These subsystems represent different social groups, for instance national communities or cultural participants belonging to the populations of a specific language. These groups construct their identity from their cultural repertoire, 'the aggregate, or the accepted stock of options utilized by a group, and by its individual members, for the organization of life'.[39] The options refer to instructions on how to perceive the world and how to act within it. Applied to the literary domain, this refers to the entire knowledge about literary works, values, instruments, etc. shared by the members of the group. The repertoire stands for a collection of contextual factors, which determine the reception of a work. According to Even-Zohar, the making of a repertoire takes place through two procedures, *invention* and *import*.[40] He emphasizes not only the interaction, but also the hierarchical relationship between these two.

A third approach can be derived from Cultural Memory Studies as applied by Ann Rigney. She also regards literary texts as instruments of constructing and discussing cultural identity. Whenever these texts cross borders it is not only the texts themselves that change, but also the values and identities coded in them. She investigates 'the persistence of [...] texts across time, but above all in their reappearance in new guises in different places and media; in their capacity to move, mobilize, and generate new cultural activities.'[41] Translations and adaptations can be seen as forms of productive remembrance: a combination of repetition and innovation. Texts that are passed down through the ages must be continuously re-inscribed to remain readable and relevant.[42]

Recent research has focused in many aspects on the mediators of literature and placed great emphasis on the individual as a cultural transmitter. This shift within Translation Studies emphasizes the role of cultural transmitters as cultural actors reaching over the linguistic, artistic and geographical barriers, and thus as instruments of cultural transfer. Though the outcome and effects of the activities of mediators can differ greatly as a result of their social characteristics and position within the literary field, detailed research and case studies have brought new insights to the study of the circulation of literature, especially regarding peripheral literatures.[43]

Not only translators and interpreters, but the whole community of 're-creators' of a text come into view through the concept of the *fluid text*, introduced by John Bryant. In his book published under the same title, he argues that a literary work does not exist in the form of a single unchanging text, but is a narrative complex, made up from a series of progressive text-versions. Bryant sees a literary work as having a fluid structure: 'Simply put, a fluid text is any literary work that exists in more than one version. It is "fluid" because the versions flow from one to another.'[44] The author may be the perpetrator of this creative process, but is not necessarily the only one, since the creation of a literary text is a communal activity: family members, friends, editors and other parties also interfere with the text, subject it to what Bryant calls *cultural revision*.

This cultural revision can also take place in other historical and geographical dimensions, that is, in a new target culture. This is the kind of cultural revision on which this book focuses. Cultural revision can also take place in non-textual media. In his recent book, *Convergence Culture*, Jenkins discusses 'transmedia storytelling': 'A transmedia story unfolds across multiple media platforms, with each new text making a distinctive and valuable contribution to the whole.'[45] This is also an aspect, which receives attention in the following pages.

THE CODL PROJECT

This book is the result of an effort to discuss the international dissemination of Dutch literature through translations and adaptations and to provide insight into the position of a smaller, less-translated language within the field of world literature. The paradigm of national languages has long structured our thinking of culture and literature and is still dominant in disciplines such as literary theory (and even comparative literature). But research into literature has recently abandoned its national perspective to a significant extent. As a result of internationalizing tendencies and insights from field and systems theories, national literatures are no longer considered as more or less autonomous systems, but as parts of an international literary space. These tendencies are also apparent in the study of Dutch literature, which is increasingly regarded as a network of texts and poetics connected to other languages and literatures through a number of different channels.

The international polysystem consists of (cultural) subsystems in which all kinds of dynamic types of coherence and exchange can be distinguished. Much has been published about the import of foreign literary works in minor linguistic areas, mostly by means of translations.[46] In these studies, major literatures such as the English, French and German appear to play a mainly exporting role, while minor literatures such as the Dutch represent the receiving party. On this basis, it is assumed that those importing literatures are compromised and displaced to the margins of the literary system. However, in the course of time, many literary works from minor language areas have crossed borders, be it through translation, adaptation or another form of transfer. This transfer has occurred from the periphery to the center, and from periphery to periphery. In both cases, translation and adaptation play an important role in the perpetuation of these literary works. It is probable that they have remained present more frequently, in more varied forms, and for a lengthier period in the periphery of the literary system than has been assumed until now. This reservoir of untapped material is another reason we have chosen to concentrate on the export of Dutch literature in this book.

The Circulation of Dutch Literature Project (CODL), financed by a grant from the Netherlands Organisation for Scientific Research (NWO), ran from 2012 to 2015 and had a double objective. It combined infrastructural aims (the strengthening and expansion of the network of international Dutch Studies) with intrinsic goals to stimulate research into literary history, methodology and theory. One of the practical difficulties of studying the pathways of the international circulation of literature is the knowledge of languages necessary for this. Either the individual scholar has to be proficient in an extremely high number of languages, or alternatively he/she should have a large international network. CODL aimed to solve this challenge by consolidating a network of people who possess a knowledge of the Dutch language and expertise in at least one other target language and culture. Cooperation was one of the most important aspects of this research project. Approximately 140 researchers from 21 countries participated in the network.

In terms of its literary-historical objectives, CODL was not oriented towards compiling an exhaustive inventory of translations and adaptations of Dutch literature. Using a diachronic approach, it focused on a selection of thirteen canonical focus-texts from the Middle Ages to the present day in order to plot out and analyze their circulation history in a broad sense, including through translations and adaptations, inside and outside the Dutch-speaking area.

Our inquiry was guided by questions such as: What are the characteristics of Dutch literary texts that cross linguistic, historical, geophysical, political, religious or disciplinary borders, taking into account that the borders themselves are also due to change in the course of time? How do Dutch literary texts cross these borders? How are they translated and/or adapted? Who are the mediators (translators, editors, critics, teachers, readers, private and governmental organizations)? What role does adaptation into another genre or medium play in the transfer process? Why do these texts cross borders? Which poetical, biographical, societal, ideological factors influence the transfer? How and why do canons of Dutch literature differ in different areas, periods and social groups? A final objective of the CODL project was to focus on a number of theoretical and methodological approaches to the circulation of literature on the one hand, and to investigate their applicability in given cases on the other. It is, therefore, not surprising that this volume shows a wide range of approaches to the process of the international circulation of literature. Four articles address broader issues of theory and methodology.

Nico Wilterdink shows how a sociological approach can shed light on the ways the production, distribution and reception of literature is embedded in wider social relations and networks. Focusing on the international reception of contemporary Dutch literature in translation, he situates the growing international attention to Dutch literature within the context of transnational communication. In their article, **Reine Meylaerts**, **Maud Gonne**, **Tessa Lobbes** and **Diana Sanz Roig** utilize quite a different approach by focusing on the cultural mediators within the multilingual literary field of interwar Belgium. By investigating the whole range of official, semi-official and hidden transfer activities, they demonstrate the complexity of the process of cultural transfer and the shortcomings of traditional methodological concepts. **Herbert Van Uffelen** discusses the dynamic concept of reception studies in an essay focusing on interaction taking place on the borderline between source and target cultures. He emphasizes the importance of the selection of the corpus when studying the reception of literature. In his contribution, **Gillis Dorleijn** formulates twelve considerations for research of cultural transfer, as employed in this project. Among other things, he discusses the advantages and disadvantages of the descriptive approach and the pitfalls of metaphors as theoretical concepts. His other considerations concern the effect of institutional factors and cultural policy on the circulation of texts. He also emphasizes the importance of the local dimension in studying the international dissemination of literature.

The second section of this book comprises eleven articles ordered according to the chronology of the focus-texts. The section presents detailed case studies about the international dissemination of Dutch literary works in translations and adaptations. The case studies, though sharing an attitude of product- and process-orientation characteristic of the overarching CODL project, show great diversity regarding research questions and methods. One can find contributions by individual authors beside the articles written as a collaboration of a group of authors. The latter form reflects the scholarly cooperation within the CODL working groups investigating the international dissemination of a specific focus-text, which is in itself an act of transcending borders.

A number of articles address the reception of one of the CODL focus-texts in a certain language or culture. Such are the articles by **Michel De Dobbeleer** and **Wilken Engelbrecht** tracing the translation of Willem Elsschot's *Cheese* in Soviet Russian and Czech translations, respectively. The article by **Caroline de Westenholz**, in which she discusses the English reception of *The Hidden Force* by Louis Couperus, and the article by **Natalia Stachura** that deals with the Polish reception of Vondel's *Lucifer* also belong in this category. The article by **Peter Kegel**, **Marion Prinse**, **Matthieu Sergier** and **Marc van Zoggel** discusses the translation and reception of Willem Frederik Hermans' *The Dark Room of Damocles* and combines it with a text-internal approach. A similar approach is also used by **Jan Urbaniak** in his discussion of cultural stereotyping in the eighteenth-century novel *Sarah Burgerhart* by E. Wolff and A. Deken. Other articles focus on intermedial adaptation of a Dutch literary work, such as the articles by **Veerle Fraeters**, **Christine Hermann**, and the collaboration of **Elke Brems**, **Pieter Boulogne** and **Stéphanie Vanasten**. Two of CODL's focus-texts belong to the dramatic genre. The specific performance-driven reception and translation history of historical drama is discussed in the contributions of **Chiara Beltrami Gottmer**, **Marijke Meijer Drees**, **Marco Prandoni** and **Rita Schlusemann** (for Vondel's seventeenth-century play *Lucifer*) and **Orsolya Réthelyi** (for the medieval play *Elckerlijc*). Finally, **Suzanne van Putten-Brons** and **Peter Boot** chose several CODL texts in order to illustrate how literary criticism on the internet provides a new means for mediating Dutch literature.

The title of this volume, *Doing Double Dutch*, evokes a popular rope-skipping game in which two people turn two long jump ropes in opposite directions while a third person jumps them. A fitting metaphor for how literature circulates internationally: two dynamic spheres, the source culture and the target culture, engage one another in a complex pattern of movement resulting in a new literary work, translation, or adaptation formed somewhere in the middle.

NOTES

1 Ö. Dahl, 'The "minor language" perspective', in Th. D'haen, I. Goerlandt and R.D. Sell (eds.), *Major versus Minor? Languages and Literatures in a Globalized World* (Amsterdam/ Phildalphia: John Benjamins Publishing Company, 2015), pp. 15-24 (17).

2 A. De Swaan, *Words of the World: The Global Language System* (Cambridge: Polity Press, 2001), p. 4.

3 J. Jansson, 'The Language Milieu of the Old Order Amish: Preserving Pennsylvania Deitsch', in D'haen, Goerlandt and Sell (eds.), *Major versus Minor*?, pp. 25-42 (27).

4 De Swaan, *Words of the World*, p. 6.

5 S. Ronen *et al.*, 'Links that Speak: The Global Language Network and its Association with Global Fame', in *PNAS*, 15 December 2014, www.pnas.org/cgi/doi/10.1073/pnas.1410931111, p. 5616.

6 J. Leerssen, *National Thought in Europe: A Cultural History* (Amsterdam: Amsterdam University Press, 2006), p. 176.

7 Ronen *et al.*, 'Links that speak', p. 5616.

8 J. Heilbron, 'Nederlandse vertalingen wereldwijd: Kleine landen en culturele mondialisering', in J. Heilbron, W. de Nooy, and W. Tichelaar (eds.), *Waarin een klein land. Nederlandse cultuur in internationaal verband* (Amsterdam: Prometheus, 1995), pp. 206-253.

9 De Swaan, *Words of the World*, p. 178.

10 De Swaan, *Words of the World*, p. 1.

11 T. Bevers, J. Heilbron and N. Wilterdink, 'Inleiding', in T. Bevers *et al.*, *Nederlandse kunst in de wereld. Literatuur, architectuur en beeldende kunst 1980-2013* (Nijmegen: Vantilt, 2015), pp. 8-19 (14): 'de beweging van (semi)periferie naar centrum is geen uitzondering, maar kenmerkend voor het stelsel'. All English translations are by the authors.

12 Dahl, 'The "minor language" perspective'.

13 De Swaan, *Words of the World*, p. 41.

14 De Swaan, *Words of the World*, p. 41.

15 O. Diaz Fouces, 'Translation Policy for Minority Languages in the European Union: Globalisation and Resistance', in A. Branchadell and L. Margaret West (eds.), *Less Translated Languages* (Amsterdam/Philadelphia: John Benjamins Publishing Company, 2005.) pp. 95-104 (99).

16 A. Branchadell, 'Introduction: Less Translated Languages as a Field of Inquiry', in Branchadell and West (eds.), *Less Translated Languages*, pp. 1-23 (1).

17 J. Heilbron and N. van Es, 'In de wereldrepubliek der letteren', in T. Bevers *et al.*, *Nederlandse kunst in de wereld. Literatuur, architectuur en beeldende kunst 1980-2013* (Nijmegen: Vantilt, 2015), p. 43.

18 Heilbron and Van Es, 'In de wereldrepubliek der letteren', pp. 27-28.

19 Heilbron and Van Es, 'In de wereldrepubliek der letteren', p. 81: 'hoe kleiner de sociaal-culturele afstand tot een gegeven land, hoe groter de ontvankelijkheid voor literatuur uit dat land'.

20 Heilbron and Van Es, 'In de wereldrepubliek der letteren', p. 82. 'Geografische nabijheid, taalverwantschap, omvangrijk handelsverkeer en vele zakelijke contacten (waaronder contacten tussen uitgevers), toerisme en migratie over de grenzen heen' (our translation).

21 E. Apter, *Against World Literature. On the Politics of Untranslatability* (New York: Verso, 2013), p. 2.

22 R. Jakobson, 'On linguistic Aspects of Translation', in R.A. Brower (ed.), *On Translation* (Cambridge, Massachusetts: Harvard University Press, 1959), pp. 232-239 (233).

23 T. Naaijkens, 'Min no meer dijn ghelike: Over het circuleren van literatuur door middel van vertalingen, in het bijzonder die van de *Beatrijs*', in T. van Kalmthout, O. Réthelyi, and

R. Sleiderink (eds.), *Beatrijs de wereld in: Vertalingen en bewerkingen van het Middelnederlandse* verhaal (Gent: Academia Press, 2013), pp. 29-39 (34).

24 L. Hutcheon, *A Theory of Adaptation* (New York-London: Routledge, 2006), p. 13.

25 Hutcheon, *A Theory of Adaptation*, p. 170.

26 Hutcheon, *A Theory of Adaptation*, p. 31.

27 M. Espagne and M. Werner, *Transferts: Les relations interculturelles dans l'espace franco-allemand (XVIIIe et XIXe siècle)*. Textes réunis et présentés par – (Paris: Editions Recherche sur les Civilisations, 1988), p. 5: 'implique le déplacement materiel d'un objet dans l'espace. Il met l'accent sur des mouvements humains, des voyages, des transports des livres, d'objets d'art ou de biens d'usage courant à des fins qui n'étaient pas nécessairement intellectuelles. Il sous-entend une transformation en profondeur liée à la conjoncture changeante de la culture d'accueil. [...] C'est donc la mise en relation de deux systèmes autonomiques et asymétriques qu'implique la notion de transfert culturel'.

28 Cited by E. Andringa and S. Levie, 'Transfer and Integration: Foreign Literatures in National Contexts', in E. Andringa, and S. Levie (eds.), *Transfer and Integration. Foreign Literatures in National Contexts,* special issue of *Arcadia* 44: 2 (2009), pp. 229-236 (232).

29 M. Espagne and M. Werner, 'Deutsch-Französischer Kulturtransfer im 18. und 19. Jh.: Zu einem neuen interdisziplinären Forschungsprogramm des C.N.R.S.', in *Francia* 13 (1985), 502-510; M. Espagne, *Les transferts culturels franco-allemands* (Paris: PUF, 1999), p. 38.

30 S. Stockhorst. 'Introduction', in S. Stockhorst (ed.), *Cultural Transfer Through Translation: The Circulation of Enlightened Thought in Europe by Means of Translation* (Amsterdam/New York: Rodopi, 2010), p. 20.

31 G. Toury, *Descriptive Translation Studies and Beyond* (Amsterdam-Philadelphia: John Benjamins, 1995), p. 29.

32 Espagne & Werner, *Transferts*, pp. 5-6, 21-22.

33 J.L. Machor and Ph. Goldstein, *Reception Studies: From Literary Theory to Cultural Studies* (New York-London: Routledge, 2001), p. XI.

34 M. Baker, 'Translation as Re-narration', in J. House (ed.), *Translation: A Multidisciplinary Approach* (Basingstoke: Palgrave Macmillan, 2014), pp. 158-177 (159).

35 M. Baker, *Translation and Conflict: A Narrative Account* (London-New York: Routledge, 2006), p. 4.

36 Baker, 'Translation as Re-narration', p. 159.

37 Baker, 'Translation as Re-narration', p. 159.

38 P. Casanova, *The World Republic of Letters*, translated by M.B. DeBevoise (Cambridge, MA - London: Harvard University Press, 2004).

39 I. Even-Zohar, 'The Making of Culture Repertoires and the Role of Transfer', in I. Even-Zohar, *Papers in Culture Research* (Tel Aviv: Unit of Culture Research, Tel Aviv University, 2010), p. 70-76 (70), http://www.tau.ac.il/~itamarez/works/books/EZ-CR-2005_2010.pdf.

40 Even-Zohar, 'The Making of Culture Repertoires', p. 72.

41 A. Rigney, *The Afterlives of Walter Scott: Memory on the Move* (Oxford: Ofxord University Press, 2012), p.12.

42 Rigney, *The Afterlives of Walter Scott*, pp. 220-221.

43 See e.g. T. Lobbes and R. Meylaerts, 'Cultural Mediators and the Circulation of Cultural Identities in Interwar Bilingual Belgium: The Case of Gaston Pulings (1885-1941)', in *Orbis*

Litterarum 70: 5 (2015), pp. 405-436, and P. Broomans and M. Ronne, 'In the Vanguard of Cultural Transfer', in P. Broomans and M. Ronne (eds.), *In the Vanguard of Cultural Transfer: Cultural Transmitters and Authors in Peripheral Literary Fields*, pp. 1-12 (Groningen: Barkhuis Publishing, 2010).

44 John Bryant, *The Fluid Text: A Theory of Revision and Editing for Book and Screen* (Ann Arbor: The University of Michigan Press, 2002), p. 1.

45 H. Jenkins, *Convergence Culture: Where Old and New Media Collide* (New York: New York University Press, 2007), p. 98.

46 E.g. E. Andringa, 'Penetrating the Dutch Polysystem: The Reception of Virginia Woolf, 1920–2000', in *Poetics Today* 27: 3 (2006), pp. 501-568.

BIBLIOGRAPHY

Andringa, E., 'Penetrating the Dutch Polysystem: The Reception of Virginia Woolf, 1920–2000', in *Poetics Today* 27: 3 (2006), pp. 501-568.

Andringa, E. and S. Levie, 'Transfer and Integration: Foreign Literatures in National Contexts', in E. Andringa & S. Levie (eds.), *Transfer and Integration: Foreign Literatures in National Contexts,* special issue of *Arcadia* 44: 2 (2009), pp. 229-236.

Apter, E., *Against World Literature: On the Politics of Untranslatability* (New York: Verso, 2013).

Baker, M., *Translation and Conflict: A Narrative Account* (London/New York: Routledge, 2006).

Baker, M., 'Translation as Re-narration', in J. House (ed.), *Translation: A Multidisciplinary Approach* (Basingstoke: Palgrave Macmillan, 2014), pp. 158-177.

Bevers, T., J. Heilbron and N. Wilterdink, 'Inleiding', in T. Bevers *et al.*, *Nederlandse kunst in de wereld: Literatuur, architectuur en beeldende kunst 1980-2013* (Nijmegen: Vantilt, 2015), pp. 8-19.

Branchadell, A., 'Introduction: Less translated languages as a field of inquiry', in A. Branchadell and M. West (eds.), *Less Translated Languages* (Amsterdam/Phildalphia: John Benjamins Publishing Company, 2005), pp. 1-23.

Broomans, P. and M. Ronne (eds.), *In the Vanguard of Cultural Transfer: Cultural Transmitters and Authors in Peripheral Literary Fields* (Groningen: Barkhuis Publishing, 2010).

Bryant, J., *The Fluid Text: A Theory of Revision and Editing for Book and Screen* (Ann Arbor: The University of Michigan Press, 2002).

Casanova, P., *The World Republic of Letters,* translated by M.B. DeBevoise (Cambridge, MA / London: Harvard University Press, 2004).

Dahl, Ö., 'The "minor language" perspective', in Th. D'haen, I. Goerlandt and R.D. Sell (eds.), *Major versus Minor? Languages and Literatures in a Globalized World* (Amsterdam/Phildalphia: John Benjamins Publishing Company, 2015), pp. 15-24.

De Swaan, A., *Words of the World: The global Language System* (Cambridge: Polity Press, 2001).

Diaz Fouces, O., 'Translation Policy for Minority Languages in the European Union: Globalisation and Resistance', in A. Branchadell and L.M. West (eds.), *Less Translated Languages* (Amsterdam/Philadelphia: John Benjamins Publishing Company, 2005), pp. 95-104.

Espagne, M., *Les transferts culturels franco-allemands* (Paris: PUF, 1999).

Espagne, M. and M. Werner, 'Deutsch-Französischer Kulturtransfer im 18. und 19. Jh.: Zu einem neuen interdisziplinären Forschungsprogramm des C.N.R.S.', in *Francia* 13 (1985), pp. 502–510.

Espagne, M. and M. Werner, *Transferts: Les relations interculturelles dans l'espace franco-allemand (XVIIIe et XIXe siècle)*. Textes réunis et présentés par – (Paris: Editions Recherche sur les Civilisations, 1988).

Even-Zohar, I., 'The Making of Culture Repertoires and the Role of Transfer', in I. Even-Zohar, *Papers in Culture Research* (Tel Aviv: Unit of Culture Research, Tel Aviv University, 2010), pp. 70-76, http://www.tau.ac.il/~itamarez/works/books/EZ-CR-2005_2010.pdf.

Heilbron, J. 'Nederlandse vertalingen wereldwijd: Kleine landen en culturele mondialisering', in J. Heilbron, W. de Nooy and W. Tichelaar (eds.), *Waarin een klein land: Nederlandse cultuur in internationaal verband* (Amsterdam: Prometheus, 1995), pp. 206-253.

Heilbron, J. and N. van Es, 'In de wereldrepubliek der letteren', in T. Bevers *et al.* (eds.), *Nederlandse kunst in de wereld: Literatuur, architectuur en beeldende kunst 1980-2013* (Nijmegen: Vantilt, 2015).

Hutcheon, L., *A Theory of Adaptation* (New York/London: Routledge, 2006).

Jakobson, R., 'On Linguistic Aspects of Translation', in R.A. Brower (ed.), *On Translation* (Cambridge, Massachusetts: Harvard University Press, 1959), pp. 232-239.

Jansson, J., 'The Language Milieu of the Old Order Amish: Preserving Pennsylvania Deitsch', in T. D'haen, R. Goerlandt and R.D. Sell (eds.), *Major versus Mino*r? (Amsterdam/Phildalphia: John Benjamins Publishing Company, 2015), pp. 25-42.

Jenkins, H., *Convergence Culture: Where Old and New Media Collide* (New York: New York University Press, 2007).

Leerssen, J., *National Thought in Europe: A Cultural History* (Amsterdam: Amsterdam University Press, 2006).

Lobbes, T. and R. Meylaerts, 'Cultural Mediators and the Circulation of Cultural Identities in Interwar Bilingual Belgium: The case of Gaston Pulings (1885-1941)', in *Orbis Litterarum* 70: 5 (2015), pp. 405-436.

Machor, J.L. and Ph. Goldstein, *Reception Studies: From Literary Theory to Cultural Studies* (New York/London: Routledge, 2001).

Naaijkens, T., 'Min no meer dijn gehelike: Over het circuleren van literatuur door middel van vertalingen, in het bijzonder die van de *Beatrijs*', in T. van Kalmthout, O. Réthelyi and R. Sleiderink (eds.), *Beatrijs de wereld in: Vertalingen en bewerkingen van het Middelnederlandse verhaal* (Gent: Academia Press, 2013), pp. 29-39.

Rigney, A., *The Afterlives of Walter Scott: Memory on the Move* (Oxford: Oxford University Press, 2012).

Ronen, S. *et al.*, 'Links that Speak: The Global Language Network and its Association with Global Fame', in *PNAS*, 15 December 2014, www.pnas.org/cgi/doi/10.1073/pnas.1410931111, pp. 5616-5622.

Stockhorst, S., 'Introduction', in S. Stockhorst (ed). *Cultural Transfer through Translation: The Circulation of Enlightened Thought in Europe by Means of Translation* (Amsterdam/New York: Rodopi, 2010).

Toury, G., *Descriptive Translation Studies and Beyond* (Amsterdam/Philadelphia: John Benjamins Publishing Company, 1995).

Theoretical and Methodological Chapters

CHAPTER 2

Studying the Circulation of Dutch Literature

Some Considerations

Gillis Dorleijn (University of Groningen, The Netherlands)

This volume presents various contributions to the fascinating field of Cultural Transfer research. Notwithstanding the clear differences in approach, focus, and theoretical or conceptual orientation, a common ground can be found in the results. The study of the circulation of Dutch literature as conducted in this book produces valuable general insights that might warrant further reflection. I will try to tease out a handful of common strands, on the object level, regarding the specific processes studied, but also on the level of approach and methodology. In considerations like these, it is probably most appropriate to focus on the later, so I will take methodological considerations as a starting point and intersperse the discussion with specific observations drawn from the topics addressed in the papers compiled in this volume. For the sake of clarity and brevity, I will proceed point-by-point.

THE PROBLEM OF DESCRIPTION

Research on cultural transfer, including within Translation Studies, has the tendency to limit itself to pure description. That is understandable because processes of cultural transfer can only be studied if the data have been carefully assembled through archival work (publisher archives, correspondence between intermediaries, translators, authors, critics – all addressing the question 'what are the mediation processes?'), library searches, newspaper depositories and other databases ('what are the reception patterns?'), or comparisons between the source text and adaptations ('what is left out, added, rearranged?' paying special attention to the paratexts and the material presentation). But such dry descriptions of intermediary and reception situations in diverse contexts of the adaptation mechanism, as useful as they may be in themselves, ring somewhat hollow if no effort is made to formulate broader and interesting research questions or to posit a guiding hypothesis.[1]

The problem is of course that without description the researcher is left empty-handed. This is why collecting many descriptions together can be productive: it allows us to inductively discern broad patterns that say something about transfer processes in general, or about the specific characteristics of particular cultural settings. Take, for example, the various articles about how Elsschot's *Kaas* [*Cheese*] found its way to the former Soviet countries. Together, they give a broader perspective of the general mechanisms of and prerequisites for the process of intermediation and provide analogues of how the work was presented and received in Communist nations, whether it was to support the regime of the target culture or function as a horrific example of 'capitalist decline'. These cues are made available to the reader via paratexts. (Indeed, we learn that the mediator (translator) and readers in the target culture were accustomed to taking these ideological 'additions' with a grain of salt, sometimes to the extent of mentally dismissing them entirely.)

A case study can also be a way of providing a concrete illustration of a more expansive research project. Or both types of research (macro and micro) can enhance one another in fruitful ways. Wilterdink formulates a hypothetical insight (one of his 'five hypothetical explanations' for the growing interest in contemporary Dutch literature abroad) about translation success thus: a flourishing domestic market is 'an important condition for literary export'. Does Wilterdink's hypothesis hold when confronted with Engelbrecht's findings on the Czech book market before the war and the not-insignificant place Dutch literature held in it? It appears so. In the 1930s, literary production in the Netherlands flourished – certainly where the novel (and especially popular fiction) is concerned – partially thanks to an avid middle-class reading public. This in itself supports Wilterdink's observation, but there is more. Thanks to a flourishing reading culture among the 'stable middle class' at the time, Czechoslovakia also enjoyed a robust book market, including strong sales of popular books. There is an evident homology between the two markets and reading cultures, which likely was a factor contributing to the success of Dutch literature in Czech translation.

As far as the methodological status of descriptions and case studies is concerned, they should ultimately be understood as works-in-progress to be refined in subsequent academic work, or as preliminary studies in route to more problem-driven and hypothesis-driven research. As Wilterdink puts it, his research 'could serve as a framework for more detailed research'. But the opposite is also true: the detail-oriented research compiled here inspires us precisely to reach towards larger, broader research questions (and to find suitable methods to do so).

THE PROBLEM OF THEORY (AND METAPHOR)

Alongside the danger of getting bogged down in description and case studies is the threat of 'theory'. In Cultural Studies, and thus also in the study of cultural transfer, there is a tendency to introduce a (novel) collection of concepts that serves to shed light on a certain cultural situation. This situation is presented, as it were, in terms of theoretical concepts. The danger with this is that we remain stuck in a restatement of something we already know in other terms. The theory serves only as a rubber stamp and fails to fulfill its essential function, namely, to be an instrument for formulating questions or hypotheses that respond to or can be tested against the data under scrutiny. Luckily, the contributions in this book are largely free of this purely conceptual use of 'theory'.

Some contributions, however, do show a tendency to use metaphors that seem to want to function as a theoretical notion. The question is how advantageous this really is. Walter Benjamin's image of the 'afterlife' of a text is a case-in-point, as are André Lefevere's 'channel' and 'window' metaphors with respect to translations. Within the essays of both cultural philosophers, these metaphors function well enough. But one could ask how wise it is to use them outside the context of an essay, particularly when the metaphor creates the suggestion of a theoretical concept. The 'afterlife' of a text, separated from the original, can only live as a concept if it has been undergirded with theoretical and empirical insights from Adaptation Studies, which, among other things, teaches us that each reception context transforms a (translated, modified, adapted) text according to the rules that apply to that particular circuit. This volume contains excellent examples of such research (and I will soon return to them). Concerning the 'window' and 'channel' metaphors, Lefevere himself deemed the 'translation as a window opened to another world' metaphor to be a pious platitude, preferring 'channel' instead: 'foreign influences can penetrate the native culture, challenge it, and even contribute to subverting it'.[2] This speaks to a sympathetic vision of the critical function of (translated) literature. But how to determine this critical effect (of a foreign work) remains altogether unclear. Using 'window' and 'channel' metaphors implies a value judgment and at the very least a general (operationalized) measure by which to determine the nature of cultural penetration. (The fact that cultural import in totalitarian states was surveilled with Argus-like rigor for possible subverting effects, as De Dobbeleer in this volume shows so well, is another, empirical question.)

OBJECT LEVEL AND META-LEVEL

The points in the above heading call out a two-part division in research levels which lies, in fact, at the basis of all research in the study of culture. Culture (processes, interactions, participants' discourse, text revisions made by an adapter and all kinds of other phenomena) is the *object* of research. The researcher then makes claims about these things at the *meta-level.* There is thus a fundamental difference between statements (originating from the cultural participants) at the object level and statements at the meta-level (originating from the researcher, informed by his theoretical framework, about the object). Building on this thought, one must also be aware that all kinds of cultural divisions, classifications, characterizations, hierarchies, genres – literature versus non-literature, for example – are constructions produced by the culture (i.e. the cultural participants) one is studying. They are thus to be situated at the object level. As mentioned, these differentiations are made by those participating in a culture; they must not be adopted as self-evident by the researcher. Rather, an effort must be made to study how they function in the object culture. The object, in other words, is a socio-cultural practice around which the researcher constructs his research questions and hypotheses (which, again, are also constructions but then on the meta-level).

CULTURE AS A SET OF SOCIAL-CULTURAL PRACTICES

The contributions in this book provide many good examples of the aspects of socio-cultural practices: the behavior and motivations of bloggers writing on Dutch literature and their networks; the quantitative patterns in translation flows; the transmission processes and the intermediaries involved in these flows; adaptations of Dutch works in diverse cultures – all of which have their own (political, economic, religious and literary) context and reception, which are largely determined by the perception patterns and interests of the actors and institutions involved (see the contribution by Hermann on Conscience's *De Vlaamse leeuw* [*The Lion of Flanders*]); the niches of Christian spirituality and poststructuralist philosophy (Hadewijch alternatively as 'orthodox nun' and 'free-spirited heretic', as described by Fraeters). Researchers no longer ask whether an adaptation has done justice to its source text, as was once fashionable in Translation Studies, nor whether its reception was justified. Rather, as in the cases of Conscience and Hadewijch, they explore the behavior and motivations of the adapters or critics in the adaptation and reception process and the contextual factors that affect them.

These socio-cultural practices comprise all actions, including actors' speech acts. These actors form a community and can be explicitly linked to one another as part of a network, or indirectly associated in some way through the positions they occupy in the field and through the relations these positions entail. That is, a translator can have no actual contact with another translator but the two can still be linked because both find themselves in a particular position as translators (in relation to writers, publishers and literature foundations). And yet when it comes to prestige they may find themselves in different positions (one may have won a prestigious prize for translators, the other may have only just debuted or may translate exclusively for Harlequin's

Romances). Another dimension must be added to this conception of network relationships and so-called objective relations, namely, the perceptions of the actors and their accompanying logics of action (which could also be called their 'conceptions of literature'). Depending on their position and associated relations, actors perceive reality in a certain way and make certain distinctions that are brought into interaction with the world in which they circulate. A translator makes a distinction between various types of publishers – publisher A, which has a well-regarded literary backlist and publisher B, which publishes exclusively commercial titles in translation – a distinction that the average reader probably would not be so quick to make. Cognition and action are thus closely connected with one another. And the actors are connected with one another, too, in what we call a world (or a field). In brief, a culture is thus understood as a collection of social-cultural practices expressed through actors that are connected to one another in a world, or field, and whose cognition and logics of action (or their conceptions of art) are determined by schemata that interact with these practices.

INSTITUTIONAL STRUCTURES

To this we must add the idea of institutions as conglomerates of actors with shared practices, logics and cognitive schemata. In the literary world, this refers to such literary institutions as the (literary) publishing house (not just one specific publisher but the whole branch), the book market, literary criticism, literary education, the literary agency, etc. In the history of the literary world from the late-eighteenth century onward, we can speak of an increasing autonomy combined with an increase of structuring and differentiation, according to which institutional roles are divided. Early on, the publishing house, publisher and book store were one single entity; later they became separate institutions. Likewise, while publishing houses once published literary work alongside textbooks or juridical titles, they later gave way to specialized literary publishing houses. Thus, the literary world and the extent to which it is institutionalized is dynamic and in permanent development, even if some measure of institutionalization exerts a stabilizing effect. The literary world is an order which is determined by institutions. Actors act within (and between) these institutions and are always influenced by institutional logics.

In the useful methodological comments made by Meylaerts *et al.* on the analysis of cultural transfer, the institutional dimension of culture (and cultural transfer) are thematized clearly, especially when the 'different levels of analysis' are discussed. One of these levels concerns networks and the actor's place within it (in this case, the mediator), whose transfer activities are facilitated or controlled by these networks. The characteristics of the actors (the mediators) are also analyzed in an institutional light: in this analysis, the focus is not on their broader biographical traits but rather on a 'socio-biography' or better, their 'social and biographic trajectories' – the successive positions of a mediator and his perceptions in the various fields. Wilterdink approaches the transmission and reception of Dutch literature from a sociological perspective by which 'the production, distribution and reception of literature is seen as being part of, and embedded in social relations or social networks of different scope, ranging from micro to macro'. In these networks (including those that are connected with organizational structures and policies), translators, publishers, literary agents, booksellers, literary critics and academic literary specialists all participate. Many of these actors and institutional settings are addressed in other contributions in this volume. Engelbrecht, for instance, provides a sort of social biography of two translators who did much to expand Dutch literature in Czechoslovakia. The 'social' characteristics he calls out for one of them include her education (which provides her with cultural capital), and her contacts via a small national network around an important Czech writer, which in turn fed into a larger international network of like-minded Francophone writers including Maurice Maeterlinck and Emile Verhaeren, both from Flemish households, which in turn led to contact with Dutch (and which provide her with symbolic capital). Her marriage to a leading politician and her decision to relocate to the political and cultural capital city of Paris further increased her status. Her relationships with the most prominent publishing houses and the (commercial) success of her translations meant that whatever she put forward to translate was easily accepted for publication. In this way, positions, behavior and the habitus of the translator can be interpreted from an institutional perspective.

EMBEDDEDNESS OF THE CULTURAL FIELDS

The literary (or cultural) field exists within other fields, particularly within the so-called fields of power: politics, state, market, religion. Despite the cultural world being relatively autonomous, with its own institutions, logics and even classification and value criteria and so forth, it is always embedded in fields of power. These fields exert influence (via rules, laws, financial constraints or subsidies and ideological or religious norms),[3] which in turn can be affected by all kinds of cultural-identity conglomerates (variables such as nation, religion, gender and ethnicity).[4] We can also appropriate the general institutional systems used by Patricia Thornton, William Ocasio and Michael Lounsbury from a more abstract Institutional Logics perspective: family, religion, state, market, profession and corporation.[5] An important consequence of this is that cultural worlds usually have a *national* basis. Of course, there is also a transnational cultural world – the World Republic of Letters, for example, in which international streams of cultural (literary) goods are mediated. There are transnational cultural networks just as there are language-linked worlds that transcend the nation – such as the Netherlands and Flanders – or various language-linked cultures within a nation – such as Belgium (see Meylaerts *et al.*). But even in these translational or transcultural structures, the national perspective plays a role. I will return to this point later in this article.

Subsidies for translators or translation projects are an important factor in the transfer of a book or an author to a new language area and can in large part be held responsible for the success of Dutch literature abroad at the end of the twentieth and beginning of the twenty-first century (see, for instance, Wilterdink). At the same time, the publically-funded foundation that provides these subsidies is dependent on the government for its financing and general policy goals. Censorship is another known phenomenon in which governments take part in a regulating capacity, this time in a negative sense. Legitimization of the norms of a totalitarian regime via paratexts in a published translation – for instance quoting Lenin in the introduction to a Soviet publication of *Cheese* (see De Dobbeleer in this volume) – is discussed in a number of contributions in this volume. The open approach to the translation of popular literature in the Czech market by which names were replaced with their Czech equivalents and the story was even resituated in Czech surroundings was undoubtedly meant to reach a broader readership and thus served economic purposes (Engelbrecht). The contributions on Vondel's *Lucifer* show just how much the reception of a work varies across nationally-embedded frames. In this sense, in Poland we can speak of misreading *Lucifer* as 'non-fiction literature'; through the mediation of a study about the figure of Lucifer, Vondel's play is read as 'a theological work' popular in Catholic internet portals and Jesuit magazines, but also finds currency in 'Satanist' circles (as Stachura states in this volume). In Germany, Vondel appears as part of a broader German literature and as a proponent of the universalization of the national: he functions as an example of a 'genuine central European dramatist' and thus as an example of *Weltliteratur*. In South Africa, Vondel is woven into the (racist and politicized) discourse of 'family kinship' between South Africa and Afrikaans on the one hand and the Netherlands, Flanders and the Dutch language on the other (Beltrami Gottmer *et al.*). It is clear in all this that factors are in play from external fields (politics, state, religion, economy), all of which exert influence on the cultural and literary field.

SEGMENTATION OF A CULTURAL (OR LITERARY) FIELD

The above title focuses attention on the notion that a culture, but also each cultural segment within it (the cultural or literary field), is not homogenous. This is the case in two respects: 1.) Each field is a world of mutual cooperation, negotiation, competition, struggle. 2.) Within a field, various subfields can be found – individual circuits with their own logics and their own conceptions of art. These circuits can come into relation with one another and have permeable walls, or be relatively autonomous. This touches once again on the notion of institutional structures. Moreover, it is clear that at this point there is still much conceptual work to be done: How do we delineate subsystems, subfields, discourse segments? What are their internal structures? How are they related to other circuits? Transmission of culture or literature is not carried out so much from country A to country B (for instance, from the Netherlands or Flanders to Germany), but, where the source culture is concerned, to and from a specific segment within those cultures. Meylaerts *et al.*'s criticism that 'actual studies in cultural transfer mostly focus on exchanges between two national cultures [...] thus reproducing the idea of "static" national entities' touches on this same point. Other articles in this volume also speak to the idea that each culture (and within it, each cultural or literary field) has segments with their own behavioral norm patterns, value hierarchies and conceptions of literature: Jesuits and Satanists in Poland (see Stachura in this volume); different norms around a translation's fidelity to the source text for highbrow versus popular literature sectors (Engelbrecht); the various specific niches – Catholic spirituality and poststructuralist philosophy – in which the reception of Hadewijch was inscribed in France (Fraeters); or the circuit of the subfield of young adult literature, which has its own history altogether (Hermann).

DIMENSIONS OF CULTURAL INTERACTION: BELIEF, JUSTIFICATION, IDENTITY

Not all actions involved in cultural transfer are spontaneous or undirected, of course. Rather, they are motivated by various substantively grounded impetuses (cultural or ideological ideals, etc.) and are channeled by certain mechanisms. This involves the very complex question of identifying the relevant moving parts in the cultural world, or in the worlds between actors. When we apply this perspective to culture and literature – acknowledging that similar mechanisms are at work in other areas – then at least three related concepts become relevant. The first involves belief. Participants in a culture (for example, those active in the literary world or sub-world) share a belief in the values they speak of and act on, within the construction we just discussed. This involves a fundamental cultural, sociological and anthropological insight[6] that emphasizes once again the difference between object level and meta-level. At the object level, belief in distinctions, hierarchies, classifications, genres, values and ideals reigns. Researchers study these classifications, statements, behaviors, etc., at the meta-level (which, of course, is itself not unproblematic in that we researchers also are implicated in our own value-laden beliefs.)

The second concept is justification (or legitimization or consecration). Cultural actions are aimed at the justification of cultural products ('this text is valuable'), the justification of specific ways of reading ('this text should be read in this way') and the justification of the right to make authoritative statements about valuable texts and about the right modes of reading. Within culture, it is clear that there are various value regimes with their own justifications.[7]

The third concept is comprised of norms and identity. Belief in values and the justification of values paired with this are so important because actors use them as a basis for establishing norms that go to the essence of what they *are* in their own eyes, what their community is, what their attitude to life is – in short, their personal and collective identity. This goes beyond the purely literary, of course, and has to do with gender, family, regional, social and ethnic origins and religious or ideological views.

This point certainly deserves further explanation, but treating even the smallest part of the expansive literature on the topic would bring us too far afield. At the same time, the contributions collected in this volume are full of illustrations of such concepts and mechanisms.

CULTURAL TRANSFER: THE WORLD-SYSTEM OF CULTURES

The eight interrelated methodological and theoretical points described above, when taken together with the various contributions in this book, are fundamental to the practice of cultural transfer research. There are other approaches, of course. For instance, the contributions by Meylaerts *et al.* and Wilterdink put forward essential insights from Cultural Transfer Studies and a cultural-sociological approach respectively, both of which are derived from the theory of the literary world-system. Building on their useful remarks, I would like to emphasize two aspects. Firstly, that each world is structured according to the eight points mentioned above. For the study of cultural transfer on the level of target culture or receiving culture, the goal is to examine all relevant factors. Characteristics of a world can explain the nature of the transfer within that world, or even its very existence. Secondly, the relationship between the two or more worlds must be taken into account. The theory of the world system of cultures or literatures, with its centrality hypothesis positing the unequal distribution of cultural power between central, semi-peripheral and peripheral cultural areas, is indispensable in this regard.[8] This transnational space is actually a world of its own. To be clear, the Dutch-language language area has been peripheral or semi-peripheral for centuries, which implies that there is a relatively large amount of import and little export. In this transnational perspective as well, the concept of 'world' or 'field' maintains its justification through socio-cultural practices and all manners of field-specific and general societal obstacles and advantages.[9]

THE TENACITY OF LOCAL/NATIONAL PERSPECTIVES

Moreover, the transnational perspective can easily lead to misunderstandings. It is often said that globalization has shifted academic research and education into a post-national context and that the nation-state is losing its unique position as a benchmark.[10] That may be so, but we must not allow ourselves to be swept away by an unchecked post-nationalist idealism. The article in this volume by Beltrami Gottmer *et al.* seems to speak to this phenomenon. In it, the argument is made that cultural transfer 'analyses the non-national aspects of culture and in fact denies the concept of the national'. Cultural transfer, according to these authors, must be described as 'border-free', which implies 'thinking beyond or outside of national categories'. It is obvious that cultural transfer should not be seen solely as a nationally-embedded object. As Meylaerts *et al.* point out, it is crucial to take 'the reciprocity of transfers on all the cultures, including the source culture' into account. Meanwhile, most of the contributions collected here show that it is the national context – particularly when it comes to the context of reception, and thus also national (and nationalistic) parameters – that is most important, and that it engenders all kinds of material, political and symbolic borders. The irony is that Beltrami Gottmer *et al.* confirm this in the cases they choose to highlight: their analyses of the reception of Vondel in Germany, South Africa and the Dutch East Indies are all situated within locally-rooted frames.

Recognizing that the national or local perspective is operative is of utmost importance when studying cultural transfer. The well-known paradox of globalization is at work here as well: globalizing tendencies also exert a localizing effect. Cultural globalization may be a fact, but cultures differ in the extent to which they process these effects.[11] It is precisely the local processing mechanisms that are most important in much of transcultural research, and that is the case for this volume, too. Despite the increasing international orientation of the last half century, cultural practices (including the media) remain strongly tied to national institutions. The perceptions of actors are also determined by this local perspective, *inter alia* through the media and through national cultural and education policy. Additionally, the national frame of reference determines to a large extent the perspective with which many actors approach literature: the selection of external elements (brought in from foreign literatures) and their functioning in a target culture depend on local classification and hierarchization strategies.[12] Paradoxically, a transnational or transcultural approach forces us to look very closely at local mechanisms, actors, networks and institutions.

Likewise, Wilterdink's contribution shows how the reception of Dutch literature differs strongly per (national or language) area. He provides an explanation for this on the basis of the specific characteristics of each receiving area (Germany, France, the United Kingdom and the United States) and on the basis of the characteristics of the relationship between the source and target culture in terms of their different positions in the world system of cultures and their shared 'specific social (cultural, economic, political) relations'. Instances of reception are social facts; they are part of cultural exchange and must be understood in terms of power relations both an intercultural/transnational respect (the prestige of the source culture) and in a national respect, because upon arrival in a target country, a certain *re*-presentation of the source country takes place, to which local perceptions, conceptions and positions then respond. The field – the local literary world – is thereby a national entity that is crucial in transnational processes of mediating, processing and assigning meaning and value.[13]

The logic of reception in a target culture is thus once again dependent on specific groups in specific sub-segments of the cultural world (see point 7). To speak of the 'reception' of a foreign work in a national culture – reception is often spoken of in such broad terms, e.g. 'Dutch literature in Germany' – is thus inadequate. Among whom, in which segment, in which group, in which institutional setting precisely does the reception take place, and what are the interests of the receiving group and the intermediary actors? In this respect, it is important to distinguish three circles in which the reception and visibility of migrating cultural products (including authors, or literature) takes place in the target culture. This is what Bevers, Heilbron and Wilterdink do when they speak of the Netherlands: the protected Dutch circuit abroad (Dutch actors take the lead here), the broader circle of the art world (which includes the literary world) in the receiving country (local actors in a sphere of limited production take the lead here) and, finally, the broader public in the receiving country that welcomes a writer or a book into its fold (the national media in the target culture take the lead here).[14] Meanwhile, specific consecration agents (or justification agents) are also involved (reputable or niche publishers, university Dutch departments with a limited impact, a television show with a broad appeal, etc.). The mediators and their often-overlapping roles: translator, critic, agent, lecturer, editor (see Meylaerts *et al.* in particular) deserve special attention in this respect. Additionally, the mediator must adjust to the dominant norms of the field or subfield into which he is introducing the foreign author, and adapt to these norms when acting strategically. Here we converge once again with the local perspective, or a crossway of local perspectives.[15]

POLICY

This volume illustrates the richness of a programmatic approach. By compiling studies on the circulation of Dutch literature (and grouping them together in this volume), new academic insights and new research questions emerge (see point 1 above). The nice thing about this is that the research results presented here can also be used to inform policy. Here, the national perspective comes to the forefront once again. Take, for example, the contribution by Wilterdink. His findings show how a targeted cultural policy on the 1993 Frankfurter Buchmesse was an important factor for the success of Dutch literature abroad, particularly for the 'Dutch wave' in Germany.[16] But the study also signals a 'recent tendency of declining foreign interest in Dutch literature'.[17] The focus in this volume on the ways in which Dutch literature circulates abroad, the prerequisites for success that held in the past, and a comparison of the conditions then and now all can provide lessons for a targeted policy, the goal being to make a new Dutch wave possible. The importance of studying the circulation of Dutch literature extends beyond academics.

And let us not forget that many cultural transfer researchers are also lecturers and are engaged in one way or another in literary life (and are thus themselves actors at the object level). They lecture, for instance, on Dutch literature at universities abroad, compile reading lists, select works to be discussed, provide interpretation frameworks, invite literary authors as guest speakers, translate Dutch works with students or on their own, involve themselves in national (and foreign) debates on Dutch literature, and so forth. In other words, they make normative choices and become mediators themselves. Insights gained from research – always keeping in mind the approach described in the points above and maintaining a strict distinction between the two levels in order to separate normativity from objective analysis as much as possible – can also be put to use when acting as a mediator.

REVERSING THE PERSPECTIVE

Another lesson that can be drawn from the study of the circulation of Dutch literature once again has to do with the national perspective. Research on the dissemination of one literature (Dutch literature) shows time and again how the characteristics of the receiving national, local contexts constitute the frames within which (and provide the rules by which) Dutch literature is produced, processed, adapted and received (or rejected). This volume focuses *inter alia* on Germany, France, the United Kingdom, the United States, Poland, the former Soviet Union, Czech/Czechoslovakia, Hungary, South Africa, and the Dutch East Indies, and there is currently also research available on Italy, Spain, Portugal and the Scandinavian countries. As mentioned, this has produced interesting scholarship. But taken as a whole, the image of Dutch literature in the world remains fragmented, unfocused or even quasi non-existent. In the final analysis, Dutch literature maintains its peripheral (or at best semi-peripheral) status and its visibility in the world system of cultures is negligible.

Nevertheless, the fact that foreign literature, including Dutch literature, is always processed according to the rules of the receiving culture (or a segment within it) leads us to a turn in perspective for transcultural research. The focus of this kind of research then shifts to transcultural exchange *within* a culture or cultural field (even more radically than what Meylaerts *et al.* call for). Dirk de Geest once noted that scholars of Dutch should not study and teach Dutch literature but rather should study, as their object, what he calls 'literature in the Netherlands and Flanders'. This implies studying translated literature (and the way in which it is brought in by mediators) alongside non-translated literature in order to tease out how it functions in the process of literary negotiations, for instance with reference to conceptions of literature.[18] This, again, concerns the national prospective, but also includes an analysis of the role of transcultural processes, which are also multicultural. Such an approach, as all transcultural research, will hopefully be well-served by the modest considerations presented here and find application as the interesting research program initiated by CODL moves forward.

NOTES

1 Cf. J. Oosterholt, 'Ter inleiding', in *Tijdschrift voor Nederlandse Taal en Letterkunde* 128 (2012), pp. 185-191.

2 Cited in this volume by Michel De Dobbeleer in his article 'A Communist Compromise: Introducing Willem Elsschot's *Kaas* Soviet Style'.

3 See for instance K. van Rees, 'Field, Capital and Habitus: A Relational Approach to "Small" Literatures'. In G.-B. Kohler, P.I. Navumenka and R. Grüttemeier (eds.), *Kleinheit als Spezifik: Beiträge zu einer feldtheoretischen Analyse der belarussischen Literatur im Kontext 'kleiner' slavischer Literaturen* (Oldenburg: BIS-Verlag der Carl von Ossietzky Universität, 2012), pp. 1-43.

4 Compare with D. Cannadine, *The Undivided Past: History Beyond Our Differences* (London: Allen Lane, 2013), which calls into question these variables (to which clan and civilization are added), particularly when they are used by historians to legitimize (politically-motivated) differences between 'them and us'.

5 P.H. Thornton, W. Ocasio and M. Lounsbury, *The Institutional Logics Perspective: A New Approach to Culture, Structure, and Process* (Oxford: Oxford University Press, 2012).

6 M. Douglas, *How Institutions Think* (New York: Syracuse University Press, 1986).

7 See, for example, L. Boltanski and L. Thévenot, *De la justification: Economies de grandeur* (Paris: Gallimard, 1991).

8 Wilterdink infra; Heilbron, 'Towards a Sociology of Translation: Book Translations as a Cultural World-System', in *European Journal of Social Theory* 2 (1999), pp. 429-444; T. Bevers *et al.*, *Nederlandse kunst in de wereld: Literatuur, architectuur en beeldende kunst 1980-2013* (Nijmegen: Vantilt, 2015).

9 J. Heilbron and G. Sapiro, 'Outline for a Sociology of Translation: Current Issues and Future Prospects', in M. Wolf and A. Fukari (eds.), *Constructing a Sociology of Translation* (Amsterdam: John Benjamins, 2007), pp. 93-107.

10 E. Besamusca, A.J. Gelderblom and J.D. ten Tije, 'Transnationale neerlandistiek: taal zonder natie, culturen zonder muren', in *Internationale Neerlandistiek* 48 (2010), December, pp. 5-10.

11 D. Crane, 'Culture and Globalization: Theoretical Models and Emerging Trends', in D. Crane, Nobuko Kawashima and Ken'ichi Kawasaki (eds.): *Global Culture: Media, Arts, Policy, and Globalization* (London: Routledge, 2002), pp. 1-25.

12 P. Verstraeten, 'Het buitenland als referentiekader: De casus van het literaire expressionisme in Vlaanderen', in *Tijdschrift voor Nederlandse Taal en Letterkunde* 128 (2012), pp. 194-211.

13 For a good example of transnational reception from a field-theory prospective, see I. Kalinowski, 'Der französische Hölderlin: Theorie des literarischen Feldes und Rezeptionsforschung', in M. Joch and N.Chr. Wolf (eds.), *Text und Feld: Bourdieu in der literaturwissenschaftlichen Praxis* (Tübingen: Niemeyer, 2005), pp. 247-260.

14 Bevers *et al.*, *Nederlandse kunst in de wereld*, pp. 15-16.
15 Kalinowski, 'Der französische Hölderlin'.
16 See also J. Heilbron and N. van Es, 'In de wereldrepubliek der letteren', in Bevers *et al.*, *Nederlandse kunst in de wereld*, pp. 20-54.
17 See also N. Wilterdink, 'Schrijvers en hun reputaties', in Bevers *et al.*, *Nederlandse kunst in de wereld*, pp. 96-146 (p. 145).
18 G.J. Dorleijn and D. de Geest, 'Een of twee Nederlandse literaturen? Is dat wel de goede vraag? Enkele methodologische kanttekeningen', in R. Grüttemeier and J. Oosterholt (eds.), *Een of twee Nederlandse literaturen? Contacten tussen de Nederlandse en Vlaamse literatuur sinds 1830* (Leuven: Peeters, 2008), pp. 197-221.

BIBLIOGRAPHY

Besamusca, E., A.J. Gelderblom and J.D. ten Tije, 'Transnationale neerlandistiek: Taal zonder natie, culturen zonder muren', in *Internationale Neerlandistiek* 48 (2010), pp. 5-10.

Bevers, T., B. Colenbrander, J. Heilbron and N. Wilterdink, *Nederlandse kunst in de wereld: Literatuur, architectuur en beeldende kunst 1980-2013* (Nijmegen: Vantilt, 2015).

Boltanski, L. and L. Thévenot, *De la justification: Economies de grandeur* (Paris: Gallimard, 1991).

Cannadine, D., *The Undivided Past: History Beyond Our Differences* (London: Allen Lane, 2013).

Crane, D., 'Culture and Globalization: Theoretical Models and Emerging Trends', in D. Crane, Nobuko Kawashima and Ken'ichi Kawasaki (eds.), *Global Culture: Media, Arts, Policy, and Globalization* (London: Routledge, 2002), pp. 1-25.

Dorleijn, G.J. and D. de Geest, 'Een of twee Nederlandse literaturen? Is dat wel de goede vraag? Enkele methodologische kanttekeningen', in R. Grüttemeier and J. Oosterholt (eds.), *Een of twee Nederlandse literaturen? Contacten tussen de Nederlandse en Vlaamse literatuur sinds 1830* (Leuven: Peeters. 2008), pp. 197-221.

Douglas, M., *How Institutions Think* (New York: Syracuse University Press, 1986).

Heilbron, J. and G. Sapiro, 'Outline for a Sociology of Translation: Current Issues and Future Prospects', in M. Wolf and A. Fukari (eds.), *Constructing a Sociology of Translation* (Amsterdam: John Benjamins, 2007), pp. 93-107.

Heilbron, J., 'Towards a Sociology of Translation: Book Translations as a Cultural World-System', *European Journal of Social Theory* 2 (1999), pp. 429-444.

Heilbron, J. and N. van Es, 'In de wereldrepubliek der letteren', in T. Bevers, B. Colenbrander, J. Heilbron and N. Wilterdink, *Nederlandse kunst in de wereld: Literatuur, architectuur en beeldende kunst 1980-2013* (Nijmegen: Vantilt, 2015), pp. 20-54.

Kalinowski, I., 'Der französische Hölderlin: Theorie des literarischen Feldes und Rezeptionsforschung', in M. Joch and N.Chr. Wolf (eds.), *Text und Feld: Bourdieu in der literaturwissenschaftlichen Praxis* (Tübingen: Niemeyer, 2005), pp. 247-260.

Oosterholt, J., 'Ter inleiding', in *Tijdschrift voor Nederlandse Taal en Letterkunde* 128 (2012), p. 185-191.

Thornton, P.H., W. Ocasio and M. Lounsbury, *The Institutional Logics Perspective: A New Approach to Culture, Structure, and Process* (Oxford: Oxford University Press, 2012).

Van Rees, K., 'Field, Capital and Habitus: A Relational Approach to "Small" Literatures', in G.-B. Kohler, P.I. Navumenka and R. Grüttemeier (eds.), *Kleinheit als Spezifik: Beiträge zu einer feldtheoretischen Analyse der belarussischen Literatur im Kontext 'kleiner' slavischer Literaturen* (Oldenburg: BIS-Verlag der Carl von Ossietzky Universität, 2012), pp. 1-43.

Verstraeten, P., 'Het buitenland als referentiekader: De casus van het literaire expressionisme in Vlaanderen', in *Tijdschrift voor Nederlandse Taal en Letterkunde* 128 (2012), pp. 194-211.

Wilterdink, N., 'Schrijvers en hun reputaties', in T. Bevers, B. Colenbrander, J. Heilbron, and N. Wilterdink, *Nederlandse kunst in de wereld: Literatuur, architectuur en beeldende kunst 1980-2013* (Nijmegen: Vantilt, 2015), pp. 96-146.

CHAPTER 3

Breaching the Dyke

The International Reception of Contemporary Dutch Translated Literature

Nico Wilterdink (University of Amsterdam, The Netherlands)

On the 15th of July 2000, the English newspaper *The Independent* published an article on recently translated Dutch literature under the heading 'Hail the New Orange Order'. The article starts with a reference to a current exhibition of Dutch paintings in the Golden Age, in the Amsterdam Rijksmuseum, and in particular to a painting by Rembrandt shown in this exhibition, which is 'as expressive today as it was 370 years ago.' And then it is asked: 'Why has that same quality so rarely been visible in Dutch literature?' One answer is that 'Dutch writing did not have the art's advantages of an international language.' However, the article continues, this situation has started to change:

> A few Dutch novelists made it into English in the early 1990s, the scholarly Cees Nooteboom at their head. And, over the past couple of years, a growing stream has been breaching the dyke. Hugo Claus, Renate Dorrestein, Arnon Grunberg, Tessa de Loo, Margriet de Moor, Marcel Möring, Harry Mulisch and Connie Palmen may not be brand names to British readers, but at last some of their work is available in English.[1]

'Breaching the dyke': the metaphor is clear. It connects a well-known image of the Dutch landscape with the characterization of the international position of Dutch literature as historically isolated, obscure and invisible to the outside world. Only recently this isolation has diminished, it is suggested – a growing stream has been breaching the dyke.

This newspaper article is representative of the manner in which journalists and critics in different countries have, in the past few decades, written about Dutch literature. A recurrent observation is that this literature is largely unknown outside the Dutch-speaking population and does not play any significant role in the rest of the world. Sometimes it is added, as in the article just quoted, that this is beginning to change.

To give another example of this perception: just before the opening of the Frankfurt Book Fair of 1993, which placed Dutch and Flemish literature at the center of attention, the *Frankfurter Allgemeine Zeitung* (10 October 1993) published an overview article of the history and current situation of this literature. 'The Netherlands in not a country of great writers', is the opening sentence of the second paragraph. In contrast to other small countries like Norway, Denmark and Portugal, the Netherlands did not bring forward literary authors who acquired real international fame, nor had its literature any foreign impact:

> It sounds incredible, but a neighboring nation of fifteen million people – to which five million people from Flanders should be added – has not exerted any appreciable influence on the German literature.[2]

This perception of Dutch literature, however, is not constant over time and not everywhere the same. In this paper I will describe in broad outlines how the international perception and reception of Dutch literature (defined as literature from the Netherlands) changed since the 1980s, and how this varies among receiving nations, in particular the larger nations with which the Netherlands continues to have the strongest social and cultural relations: Germany, France, Britain and the United States. I will try to explain differences in the reception of Dutch literature between these nations from a sociological perspective. Furthermore, I will deal with the question to what extent and how Dutch literature is defined by non-Dutch reviewers as typically Dutch, and what meanings are attached to Dutchness in this context.[3]

The three main questions of this article are then:

1. How did the degree and nature of international attention to Dutch contemporary literature change since the 1980s, and what are the possible explanations for the observed change?
2. What are salient differences in the reception – attention, interpretation, appreciation – of Dutch contemporary literature between Germany, France, Britain and the USA, and how can these differences be explained?
3. To what extent and how is Dutch literature in translation defined by reviewers as typically Dutch, and which attributions of Dutchness are involved in these definitions?

DATA

These questions will be answered on the basis of articles about contemporary Dutch literature (including book reviews, written portraits of individual authors, and general overviews) in German, French, English and American newspapers between 1980 and 2012. The selected newspapers and the corresponding numbers of articles are specified in Table 1.

Source	Book reviews	Portraits	Overviews	Total
FAZ	202	47	26	275
BZ	31	9	0	40
Other German	11	7	4	22
Total German	*244*	*63*	*30*	*337*
M	60	26	7	93
F	24	8	4	36
Other French	5	1	1	7
Total French	*89*	*35*	*12*	*136*
T/ST	62	10	0	72
G	47	10	4	61
I	61	3	4	68
Other British	6	1	1	8
Total British	*176*	*24*	*9*	*209*
NYT	53	6	1	60
WP	33	3	1	37
Other American	11	1	2	14
Total American	*97*	*10*	*4*	*111*
Total	**606**	**132**	**55**	**793**
fiction	*460*	*86*	*37*	*583*
poetry	*7*	*0*	*2*	*9*
nonfiction	*133*	*12*	*0*	*145*
mixed	*6*	*34*	*16*	*56*

Table 1: Numbers of articles on Dutch literature (book reviews, authors' portraits, overviews) in German, French, British and American newspapers, and by genre, 1980-2012

FAZ: *Frankfurter Allgemeine Zeitung* (1993-2012). BZ: *Berliner Zeitung* (2000-2012). M: *Le Monde* (1990-2012). F: *Le Figaro* (1997-2012). T/ST: *The Times* and *The Sunday Times* (1985-2012). G: *The Guardian* (1980-2012). I: *The Independent* (1988-2012). NYT: *The New York Times* (1980-2012). WP: *The Washington Post* (1980-2012).

'Dutch contemporary literature' is defined here as literature (mainly fiction, but also poetry and literary nonfiction, broadly conceived[4]) which is originally written in Dutch by authors born and/or living in the Netherlands, who were productive in the period under investigation, 1980-2012. Flemish authors are not taken into account. The genre of children's literature, in which Dutch authors have been internationally quite successful in recent years, has also been left out.

Despite these restrictions, this is a broad explorative investigation, which does not go into the details of the international reception of specific authors or specific books. Its primary aim is to gain insight into the changing position of one, relatively small, national literature in what may be called the world-system of literature, or in other terms, the global literary field.

THE GROWING FOREIGN ATTENTION TO DUTCH LITERATURE IN TRANSLATION

The number of books translated from the Dutch has increased during the past fifty years. This can be seen in Figure 1, which shows the average annual number of book translations over five or ten years' periods since 1958.[5] The growth accelerated in the 1990s and reached a peak at the beginning of this century, followed by a slight decrease since 2007.

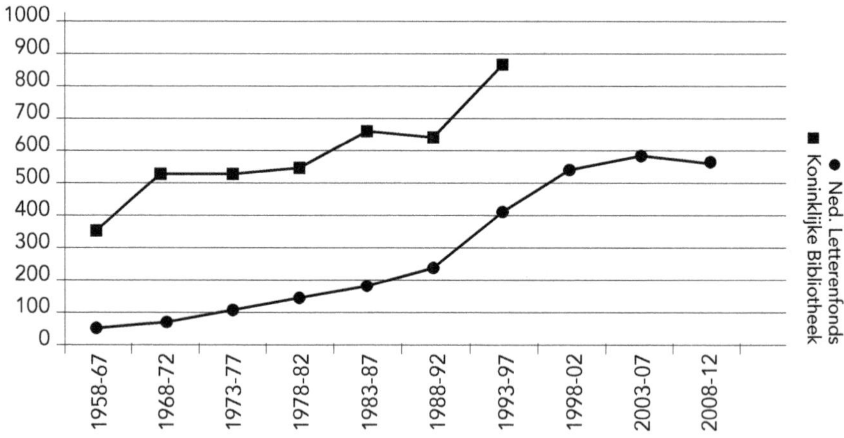

Figure 1. Annual number of book translations from Dutch, 1958-2012

This growth in translations corresponds more or less with the development of the *attention* to Dutch literature as indicated by the annual number of articles in the selected newspapers. This is represented by Figure 2, showing the annual total number of articles on Dutch literature in the English and American sources from 1980 to 2012. As the graph shows, there is an overall tendency

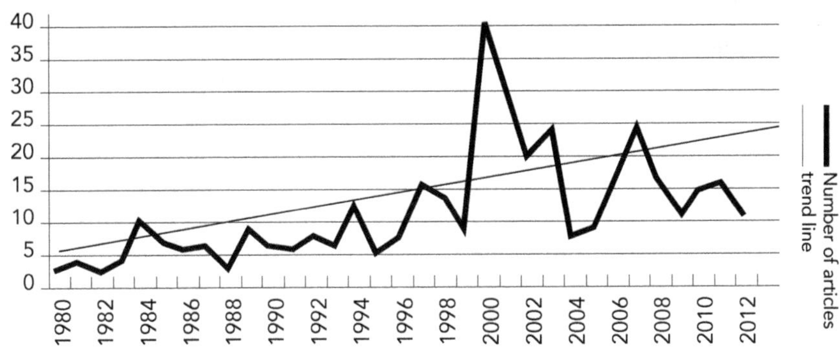

Figure 2. Annual number of articles on Dutch literature in selected English and American newspapers, 1980-2012*

* Corrected for absent data on *The Times* and *The Sunday Times* in 1980-1985 and *The Independent* in 1980-1987.

of increasing attention, but this is not a continuous process. The peak was in 2000; after that year the attention tended to diminish, though with fluctuations from year to year. Something similar can be said about the degree of attention in the French and the German newspapers. A strong increase in the 1990s and the first years of the new century was followed by a decline from about 2005 onwards, though again with fluctuations.[6]

The growth in the export of Dutch literature since the 1980s, as indicated by numbers of book translations, corresponding with an overall growth in foreign media attention for this literature, as indicated by numbers of newspaper articles, has been noted from time to time by journalists and critics in these same newspapers. The quotation from *The Independent* in 2000 cited in the opening paragraph illustrates this. Another, earlier, example is an article in the *New York Times* in 1985 (27 October) under the heading 'The Boom in Dutch Fiction'. It describes how Dutch literature flourishes remarkably within the Netherlands, which is hardly noticed outside the country. Yet 'publishers here say there is an awakening interest abroad in Dutch writing'. The number of translations tends to increase, but 'the process has been slow, in spite of all the literary activity in the Netherlands'.

Much more outspoken about the growing interest in Dutch writing is an article in the *Frankfurter Allgemeine Zeitung* on 19 November 1993, shortly after the successful presentation of Dutch and Flemish literature at the Frankfurt Book Fair that year:

> Only a few years ago, hardly anyone in this country was interested in knowing about modern Dutch literature [...]. Today, publishers

> and book sellers do good business with Dutch texts; today, the same people who had been completely ignorant declare that the Netherlands and Flanders provide Europe's most lively literature.[7]

Such statements are repeated again and again in German newspapers in later years. Thus, when Dutch novelist Leon de Winter received the *Welt-Literaturpreis* 2002 from the daily *Die Welt*, an article appeared in this newspaper about German interest in foreign literature in general and Dutch literature in particular (29 June 2002). It is observed that Germans are reading more translated books than they used to do, with a certain shift from English, American, French and Italian to Scandinavian and Irish writers. 'But above all, the growth of interest in Dutch literature has been really explosive.'[8] The author of the article relates this to 'a renaissance of story-telling'[9], a 'victory march of realism'[10], in which precise and subtle descriptions of individual lives within recognizable social settings take pride of place again. It is in this kind of literature that Dutch authors are outstanding and have exerted a significant impact on the German literature.

This perception of increasing German interest in Dutch literature is also expressed in the frequent characterization of quite a number of contemporary Dutch authors – Cees Nooteboom, Harry Mulisch, Leon de Winter, Maarten 't Hart, Margriet de Moor, Anna Enquist, Arnon Grunberg, Connie Palmen, A.F.Th. van der Heijden, Jessica Durlacher – with such terms as 'success author', 'bestseller author', 'star writer' or even *Weltstar*, 'world star'. This usage started in the 1990s and continued in the first decade of the new century.

The tone in French, English and American newspapers is different. Individual authors, like Cees Nooteboom, Harry Mulisch or Hella Haasse, are sometimes highly praised, but they are not seen as belonging to a strong and influential Dutch current in contemporary literature. If a growing interest in Dutch literature is noted, it is against the backdrop of its historical obscurity. Thus, a review by the English writer Tim Parks of a number of recently translated Dutch novels in the *New York Review of Books* of 27 October 2011 was headed 'The Dutch are coming!', as if something new and unexpected was happening.

Yet all in all, foreign interest in contemporary Dutch literature did grow since the 1980s, as can be inferred from the number of book translations, the number of reviews and the content of some of these reviews. How can we explain this trend? I will suggest here, very briefly, five hypothetical explanations, which are not mutually exclusive but may supplement one another.

(1) First of all, we may regard the trend as a corollary of the vast and multifaceted process of *cultural globalization*, in which cultural products increasingly move across geographical and national boundaries and spread over the globe.[11] The worldwide growth in book translations over the years, in absolute numbers and relative to total book production, is part of this process.[12] This

cannot be the whole explanation, however, since the concept of cultural globalization is too general to account for the specific changes with regard to the reception of Dutch literature. The question is, to what extent similar trends of growing export and foreign interest are found for the literature of other nations or languages, and how to account then for the observed similarities and differences.[13]

(2) According an opposite, historical or narrativistic type of explanation, the trend of increasing interest in Dutch literature can be viewed as the outcome of *chains of events*, which revolve around the discovery and launching of the work of individual authors, and include media and organizational events with a high impact on the audience of potential readers. Part of such a narrative would be the international breakthrough of authors such as Cees Nooteboom and Harry Mulisch in the 1980s and 1990s[14], followed by the successful Frankfurt Book Fair of 1993, which spurred the international attention for Dutch literature in general.

(3) A more sociological or institutional explanation refers to *social networks, organizational structures and policies* that contribute to the international dissemination of literature. Translators, publishers, literary agents, booksellers, literary critics and academic literary specialists all participate in these networks. A particularly important role in the spread of Dutch literature has been played by the government-subsidized Foundation for the Translation and Production of Dutch Literature (NLPVF, founded in 1991 as the successor of the less active Dutch Foundation for Translations), which subsidizes translations, helps to establish relations with foreign publishers, and attempts to stimulate the interest in Dutch literature through information, propaganda and organizing or supporting literary events.[15]

(4) Another, *cultural* type of explanation refers to distinct traits of a national literature combined with changes in literary taste. Some critics and journalists writing about the growing interest in Dutch literature have suggested such an explanation. As the experimental currents of modernism and postmodernism have gone out of fashion, they argued, there is a renewed appreciation for social and psychological realism and good story-telling, and this is precisely the type of literary fiction in which Dutch authors excel.[16] If and to what extent this argument is valid, is difficult to say. It is, in any case, not easily applicable to all Dutch fiction writers who have been internationally successful in the past few decades.

(5) Finally, a fifth explanation focuses on the *domestic book market*, in which social-institutional and cultural factors are intertwined. A flourishing market for domestic literature in terms of both supply (production of new titles) and demand (sales) is an important condition for literary export. The expansion of the domestic book market in the Netherlands during the 1980s and 1990s, combined with a lively literary climate (as foreign journalists often reported[17]), probably contributed to the growing visibility of its literature outside the national borders. There is, however, not a fixed and deterministic

causal relation between the two. The expanding market on the national level enhanced the chances for an increasing international spread and appreciation of Dutch literature, but did not determine it as a predictable development.

Each of these five hypothetical explanations suggests possible lines of further research. Ideally, this research should take account of fluctuations over time, including the tendency of *declining* foreign interest in Dutch literature in recent years, as indicated by numbers of translations and the degree of attention in foreign newspapers.

DIFFERENCES IN RECEPTION: A COMPARISON BETWEEN GERMANY, FRANCE, BRITAIN AND THE UNITED STATES

As some quotations from newspapers already indicated, the interest in Dutch literature since the 1990s is much stronger in Germany – or, more broadly, the German language area – than in France, Britain, the United States or any other country or region outside the Netherlands and Flanders. Many more translations of Dutch fiction and literary nonfiction appear in German than in other languages; the translated books are, in general, better sold in Germany than anywhere else; and these books and their authors receive much more media attention than elsewhere. Newspapers such as the *Frankfurter Allgemeine* regularly report literary events in the Netherlands and presentations by Dutch authors in Germany. It is also in Germany that some Dutch writers, most notably Cees Nooteboom, have become famous public personalities and attained a status that surpasses their reputation in their home country.

This is different in other countries. In France, the interest in Dutch writing is more superficial, even though it increased in the past few decades, and more bound to special events, such as the presentation of Dutch and Flemish literature in the literary manifestation *Salon du Livre* in Paris in 2003 under the name '*Phares du Nord*', 'Torches from the North'.[18] As this name suggests, Dutch literature tends to be viewed as coming from a Northern country faraway. Indeed, this literature is often classified as 'Northern European' together with that of the Scandinavian countries. The Netherlands in this perspective seems to be nearer to Sweden than to France. This attitude does not preclude incidental expressions of admiration for Dutch authors in French journals and newspapers.[19] Such articles did not lead, however, to big sales, nor did they have a clear positive effect on French interest in Dutch literature in general.

Contemporary Dutch literature seems even more distant and unknown in the English-speaking world, particularly in the United States. There is more attention in Britain, where, moreover, journalists and critics sometimes show concern about the general neglect of Dutch, or, more broadly, 'European' (i.e. continental) or 'foreign' (i.e. translated) literature in their country. Thus, a short review of Mulisch's novel *Last Call* [*Hoogste Tijd*] in *The Times* of 15 October 1987 opens with the remark:

> The Dutch [...] buy our books and sometimes [...] even publish our novelists before we do. But do we reciprocate the interest? Are we to be spotted in a queue for the latest Maarten 't Hart? Sadly not; although, as one reads Maarten 't Hart, one can understand why.

A report in *The Observer* of 24 January 1999 on the state of the literature in the Low Countries is more explicit. The journalist observes with surprise and amusement that special organizations in the Netherlands and Flanders put great efforts into promoting and protecting their literature against the overwhelming influence of France, Germany and, today above all, the English-speaking world. After having admitted that he was almost completely ignorant about Dutch literature, the reporter explains:

> To English ears the phrase 'fiction in translation' is bound to [...] dishearten the spirit of the most adventurous fiction-buyer. [...] The awkward fact is that, though we buy new fiction in ever-increasing quantities, we have small appetite for new fiction by writers with funny names. Our own literature provides, we believe, all the satisfaction we need. Just as we hardly question our historical superiority, we do not give its contemporary dominance a second look.

The perceived lack of British interest in foreign literature is explained here by referring to the extent and dominance of the English language and literature. Besides, a second reason is sometimes mentioned: the gap between the English or Anglo-Saxon 'empirical' taste and the typically 'European' literary style, which is defined as philosophical and reflexive. In this classification, Britain is placed outside Europe. Thus, in a review in *The Times* (8 August 2001) of Mulisch's novel *The Procedure*, the author is described as 'a very European writer, not widely read in Britain, celebrated in Europe, particularly in the Netherlands and in Germany, for his intense cerebral novels which take on the big questions – life, death, the human condition.' Nooteboom has been characterized in similar ways. Because these authors are part of a typically European literary tradition, reviewers suggest, they have hardly any chance to become popular in Britain.

If we summarize the observed differences between the four countries in a few catchwords, we may say that the American attitude to Dutch literature is predominantly one of indifference and ignorance outside a small circle of professional specialists; the English attitude a mixture of arrogance and self-criticism; the French attitude well-meaning but superficial; and the German orientation open, interested, often enthusiastic.

In order to explain these differences, I take as a starting-point the notion of the literary world-system or, in other terms, the global literary field. This is part of the more encompassing cultural world-system, which is connected with the economic and the political world-system. The literary world-system consists of nationally or linguistically bounded literary fields, which are interconnected in unequal, asymmetrical relations of power and influence.[20] Some national or linguistic literary fields are dominant. A dominant field is more visible to the dominated one and exerts more influence on it than the other way around; the dominant field has, in other terms, a core or center position in relation to the dominated field. The English and American, the French and the German literary field are all dominant in relation to the Dutch literary field, but in different ways and different degrees. Variations in the reception of Dutch literature between the four nations compared can now be explained by 1) differences in the position of these nations in the literary and, more broadly, the cultural world-system; and 2) differences in the specific relation of these nations with the Netherlands.[21]

(1) As English became the unrivalled dominant, super-central language in the world in the course of the twentieth century, it also became dominant in the global literary field.[22] It dominates the global production of books in all genres and the global market for translations. This means, among other things, that book translations *from* the English are by far the largest category (more than fifty percent) of all translated books worldwide, whereas on the other hand translations *into* English make up only a tiny fraction (less than four percent) of all books published in English.[23] In other words, the English-speaking part of the world is indeed relatively closed to the literature from other regions.

Within this vast, highly differentiated and dominant language area the cultural center shifted from England to the United States, together with shifts in economic and political power. The prevailing attitude to foreign literature in the United States can be interpreted as centrist and universalist, which is typical of a dominant power[24]; the implicit assumption seems to be that American culture has universal significance, and that what is culturally important will find its way to the United States anyway. Apart from some academic circles, there is hardly any public concern about a lack of openness to foreign (i.e. originally non-English) literature, if this is observed at all.[25]

This is different in Britain, as the quotations just given illustrate. Britain's weakening power and its increased dependence on 'Europe' gave rise to heated debates and ambivalent feelings about its complicated relations with the European continent. On the one hand, the widespread feeling that 'Europe' is a threat to British autonomy feeds the inclination to distinguish the English or Anglo-Saxon literature sharply from the European literature. On the other hand, the awareness of the dependence on 'Europe' motivates self-critical remarks about a lack of interest in European (or more in particular, Dutch) literature.

Before the dominance of English, French language and literature were hegemonic for a long time in Europe and the world at large, with Paris as the capital of the World Republic of Letters.[26] This changed after the Second

World War. Despite much resistance, the orientation in France towards Anglo-American culture and literature grew strongly, and the interest in the literature of smaller languages, including Dutch, increased at the same time.[27] Yet Dutch literature has remained peripheral in the French perspective, in which the hegemonic past lingers on.

German literature, in spite of its rich tradition and great prestige since the end of the eighteenth century, never acquired such a dominant position. German self-confidence grew during the nineteenth century, but was severely damaged by the defeats in the two world wars of the twentieth century. It was particularly after the Second World War that German intellectuals became highly critical about their own national cultural heritage and looked for positive alternatives in other societies. This makes it understandable that interest in literature from other nations grew, including that of smaller nations such as the Netherlands.

(2) The second basic condition which might explain the differences in reception among the nations considered is created by their specific social (cultural, economic, political) relations with the Netherlands. In general terms, we can say that the geographical, social and cultural distance between two nations correlates inversely with the intensity of transnational cultural exchange: the larger the distance, the less cultural exchange. Among the four nations compared, the distance with the Netherlands is the largest for the United States, the smallest for Germany, with France and England in between; and the differences in attention to Dutch literature correspond with this variation. I will focus here on the historically changing relations with Germany.

Geographical proximity, strong trade and business relations, frequent cross-border traffic and migration, and the similarities of language – all these interconnected conditions contributed to intense cultural exchange between Germany and the Netherlands, and to a relatively strong German interest in Dutch society and culture, including its literature. Throughout the twentieth century, translations into German comprised by far the largest category of translations of Dutch books in general. Until quite recently, most books translated from Dutch into German were popular fiction written by authors who did not enjoy much literary standing, among them Flemish authors who wrote regional novels about country life. The Dutch language area, including the Southern Netherlands or Flanders, was often regarded as a province of the wider Germanic cultural area, in which it represented less refined, simpler, but also more authentic traits. The popular Flemish regional novels confirmed and gave substance to this image.[28]

For the (Northern) Netherlands, or Holland, yet another image circulated among Germans: that of a country of philistine tradesmen, who were only interested in practical matters and money, and whose spiritual life was just as flat as their landscape. Immanuel Kant wrote already in this vein in 1764, and similar remarks were repeated again and again in the decades that followed.[29] As recently as 1931, Graf Hermann Keyserling contended, in a widely read book about European nations, that in Holland 'a culture of ugliness'[30] prevailed, that even elite groups were 'unspiritual'[31] and that social life in general was characterized by a leitmotiv of 'philistinism, banality and parochialism'.[32] Such qualifications did not contribute to a serious interest among Germans for Dutch literature that counted in the Netherlands itself as important and sophisticated.

Such expressions of German superiority vanished after the war. The destruction perpetrated by the Nazi regime brought many Germans to self-criticism about their national cultural heritage and a search for positive counter models. The Netherlands could serve as such: a small, innocent country, tolerant and egalitarian, with strong democratic institutions, which in contrast to its powerful neighbor had remained immune to totalitarianism and extreme nationalism. This image of the Netherlands has been repeatedly evoked in German newspapers. In contrast to Germany, the Netherlands does not have to cope, in this perception, with the burden of a dark past. It is a more relaxed society in which humor and informal sociability are thriving. Such traits are recognized in contemporary Dutch literary fiction, which is said to distinguish itself from the heavier German literature by irony, lightness, directness and down-to-earth realism.

This image of Dutch society and culture undoubtedly contributed to the strong growth of German interest in Dutch literature from the 1990s onwards. The fact that it did not start earlier might have to do with the submerged continuation of the older image of the Dutch as money-oriented philistines without sophisticated or profound culture. But once this new interest arose, triggered by a few successful writers, it grew quickly, encompassing a widening variety of literary work. In the 1990s Germans discovered the Netherlands as a country of interesting, innovative, inspiring, even great literature, which could serve as an example for their own writers. This 'Dutch wave'[33] had no counterpart in other countries.

PERCEPTIONS OF DUTCHNESS IN DUTCH LITERATURE

This assessment of Dutch literature in Germany illustrates that images of a certain nation and the reception of its literature in other countries are interconnected: on the one hand, national images have an impact on how the literature is received, interpreted and judged; on the other hand, this literature is a source of information about the nation concerned and contributes to the formation of national images. While the romantic nationalistic idea that a national literature reflects and reveals the essence of a nation is generally rejected today, at least in academia, the question remains, what makes a nation's literature specific? Or, to put the more empirical question, to what extent are specific national characteristics *attributed* to the literature from a given nation, and what is the nature of these characteristics?[34] Here the question is, to what extent is literary work by Dutch authors understood as typically 'Dutch', and what meanings are then attributed to Dutchness? In order to answer this question, I will again use the articles in the selected newspapers as my empirical basis.

The first thing to be noted is that the degree to which books by Dutch authors are defined as Dutch in these articles, is only limited. In literary reviews, the book in question is usually classified as Dutch by mentioning that the author is Dutch, that the book is translated from the Dutch (though even this information is sometimes lacking), and that, if applicable, the story is located somewhere in the Netherlands. But in most reviews, this is all.

A substantial number of articles however, about one quarter of the total, do refer to Dutch characteristics. These pertain in the first place to the literature itself. Most overview articles on Dutch literature and some book reviews attribute specific traits to this literature, which give it a distinct character. The most mentioned traits are social and psychological realism, the use of detailed, precise descriptions of everyday-life situations (often with a focus on family relations), and a sober, direct, clear style. Wild fantasies, metaphysical speculation and stylistic experiments have no place is this literary tradition.

These literary traits are often seen as reflections of characteristics of the nation – the Dutch national character or culture: soberness, realism, a practical orientation, traits which in turn are connected with commercialism and the religious tradition of Protestantism and more specifically Calvinism. Particularly the latter term is often used. Novels in which the main characters are orthodox Calvinists (such as those by Maarten 't Hart) are regarded as typically Dutch. In most cases, however, reviewers use the term Calvinism in a looser, less religious, metaphorical sense, as a term that summarizes an ethos of frugality, soberness, discipline and moral strictness which permeates Dutch society as a whole and has put its mark on its literature. Thus, in an essay on Dutch poetry published in *The Independent* on October 4th 2003, the South African novelist J.M. Coetzee writes that 'a national way of life strongly imbued with such Calvinist virtues of propriety, dutifulness and moral vigilance has not been conducive to boldness of thought'.

There is however, quite another image of Dutch society that is often evoked: the image of tolerance. Like Calvinism, the idea of tolerance goes back to the seventeenth century, when dissidents and religious minorities took refuge in the Netherlands, books forbidden elsewhere were printed here, and foreigners observed with surprise that in this country different religious groups could live together peacefully. It revived in the 1960s and 1970s, when the Netherlands became widely known for its sexual liberties, toleration of soft drugs and acceptance of euthanasia. In positive terms, it is associated with freedom, openness, plurality, and informality. Sometimes it is interpreted negatively, as indifference and tolerance-going-too-far, a lack of social control leading to confusion and disorder.

There seems to be a tension, even a contradiction between these two conventional images: Calvinism (strictness, discipline, a strong moral framework) on the one hand and tolerance (permissiveness, informality) on the other. If this is noticed, it is sometimes resolved by making time-space distinctions. Some reviewers observed a radical transformation of post-war Dutch society from a conservative, puritan country with a narrow morality and parochial attitudes ('Calvinism') to an open, progressive, permissive, highly secularized, liberal society ('tolerance'), and remarked that Dutch literature gave expression and contributed to these changes.[35]

A second way to reconcile the two prevalent traditional images of the Dutch national character is to suggest a geographical split – between the cities and the countryside, or between Amsterdam and the rest of the Netherlands. It is particularly in Amsterdam that the perceived Dutch traits of tolerance, individual freedom, libertarianism and licentiousness are situated. Amsterdam has been described as Europe's most tolerant city, where drugs are openly used and all kinds of deviant people can be seen in public places. It is romanticized as a warm city with a relaxed atmosphere of informal, easy-going sociability, where people meet in the numerous pubs on an equal footing. It is also described as wild, vulgar, rebellious, anarchistic, freakish, crazy, and decadent. A telling, if rather extreme illustration can be found in a review in the German newspaper *Tages-Anzeiger* (12 July 2003) of a series of seven novels by A.F.Th. van der Heijden (all translated into German), situated in Amsterdam in the 1980s:

> In more than three thousand pages, A.F.Th. van der Heijden created and recreated from memories and the 'pain of imagination' something for which Amsterdam has become famous and infamous: the pubs, gay clubs, snack bars and 'brown cafés' full of junkies, whores and lost provincials, the canals, gutters and prisons in which drop-outs stumble, fuddled by alcohol and drugs, the houses occupied by squatters and the student rooms, in which dreamers, half-criminal drifters and far-out bohemians tried the sexual revolution and the rebellion against the state.[36]

Besides such images of Amsterdam, it is remarkable *how often* foreign reviewers of Dutch literature refer to Amsterdam, as if the rest of the country does not exist or does not matter. This has to some extent a factual basis, as Dutch literary life is highly concentrated in this city, and a disproportional number of Dutch novels and stories are situated here. Yet, the 'Amsterdam bias' is striking, and probably stronger in the reception of Dutch literature abroad than within the Netherlands itself. An indication of this is that publishers give translated books sometimes a new title with 'Amsterdam' in it, with the intention, one may presume, to make the book more recognizable and attractive for potential readers.[37]

The 'Amsterdam bias' illustrates a general mechanism of image formation: there is a selective perception of, and emphasis on, phenomena that fit in and confirm existing images. This pertains also to conventional ideas about Dutch culture and character such as 'Calvinism' and 'tolerance'. Literary critics, like other people, tend to affirm such ideas as they selectively perceive and interpret information – in this case, the information from literary work – in ways that correspond to the images that they already have and share with others.

Yet this self-reinforcing circularity of perception, communication and image formation does not mean that images are fixed and cannot change. New information that challenges existing ideas may come from literary texts, but a more immediate source of change are media messages about current events. As to the Netherlands, the idea of tolerance has been undermined since the beginnings of the new century by reports about dramatic events and political conflicts that lay bare growing tensions between native Dutch and immigrant minority groups.[38] In foreign newspapers' comments on these issues (which included some articles by Dutch authors[39]) the idea of tolerance was not simply brushed aside but reinterpreted in various, conflicting ways.

Images of a nation are, then, not simply given; they evoke criticism and controversy, are open to reinterpretations, and change over time. Yet the newspaper articles studied indicate a fairly high degree of consensus among the receiving nations about what is typically Dutch. In so far as disagreements were found, they were hardly related to national differences. The main difference along national lines – as has been described in the preceding section – consists of the particularly strong inclination among Germans to attribute positive traits to Dutch society, connected with a self-critical attitude toward their own national history and cultural heritage.

There are signs, however, that this is also changing. With fading memories of the Nazi period and the Second World War, the stabilization and normalization of German democratic institutions and the increasing dominance of Germany in Europe, this self-critical attitude, and the corresponding search for exemplary traits to be found in other societies, is weakening. This might explain why it is particularly in Germany that the recent tendency of declining international interest in Dutch literature can be observed, just as the increase of interest in the 1990s was stronger in this country than anywhere else.[40]

CONCLUDING REMARKS

In this article I have tried to demonstrate empirically the fruitfulness of a sociological approach, in which the production, distribution and reception of literature is seen as being part of, and embedded in, social relations or social networks of different scope. Literary activities on the micro level – writing, publishing, book selling, reviewing – can be situated in nationally or linguistically bounded literary fields, which are interconnected in the global literary field, or literary world-system. On this macro level, some national or linguistic fields have a dominant position in relation to other ones. These interconnected literary fields are in turn dependent on, and part of, encompassing social (cultural, economic, political) networks.[41]

In this perspective, the export of literature through translations is part of broader flows of transnational communication. Translated literature – fiction and nonfiction – is one way in which people acquire knowledge and ideas about other cultures and societies. In these transnational communication flows literary critics and journalists play a mediating role by selectively paying attention to some translated books and some authors, interpreting these books and assessing their significance. Sometimes reviewers interpret a translated book by making connections with supposed characteristics of the national society in which it originated. In this way, they inform readers about other nations' cultural and social life, often confirming well-known national images.

This perspective suggests different lines of further research. It is not necessarily opposed to, or sharply demarcated from, other approaches in the study of literature. It could serve as a framework for more detailed research about the international spread and reception of literature, in particular the spread from a small country such as the Netherlands to larger and more dominant nations and language areas.

NOTES

1 The inclusion of the Flemish author Hugo Claus in this series of names exemplifies a recurrent confusion about 'Dutch literature': whether it covers the whole Dutch language area, including Flanders, or is confined to the nation-state in which Dutch is the common language, the Netherlands. The article in *The Independent* suggests by its heading ('Hail the New Orange Order') and its reference to Rembrandt and the Rijksmuseum that it deals with the literature from the (Northern) Netherlands, but then it is inconsistent to mention Claus as one of the authors representing this literature. This paper focuses on the reception of Dutch literature as defined in national terms, i.e. literature from the Netherlands.

2 'Die Niederlande sind kein Land der grossen Schriftsteller [...] Es klingt unglaublich, aber ein Nachbarvolk von fünfzehn Millionen Menschen – dazu kommen noch fünf Millionen Flamen – hat auf die deutsche Literatur keine nennenswerte Einflüsse ausgeübt.' All English translations are by the author.

3 A more extensive report on this investigation is: N. Wilterdink, 'De receptie van Nederlandse literatuur in het buitenland: aandacht, interpretatie, waardering', Chapter 2 in T. Bevers, B. Colenbrander, J. Heilbron, and N. Wilterdink, *Nederlandse kunst in de wereld: Literatuur, architectuur en beeldende kunst 1980-2013* (Nijmegen: Vantilt, 2015), pp. 56-95, 403-405.

4 'Literary nonfiction' as conceived here includes journalistic reports, travel books, political essays, and scientific and scholarly work written for non-specialists. It excludes religious writings, educational textbooks and all kinds of 'how to' books. The fiction covers both 'highbrow' and 'lowbrow' or popular writings. This operational definition of 'literature' largely corresponds with the demarcations in the dataset of Dutch translated literature compiled by the Dutch Foundation for Literature, which has been used for this research (www.vertalingendatabase.nl).

5 Quoted from J. Heilbron and N. van Es, 'In de wereldrepubliek der letteren', in T. Bevers *et al.*, *Nederlandse kunst in de wereld* (Nijmegen: Vantilt, 2015), p. 39, Graph 5.1. The upper line is based on data from the *Koninklijke Bibliotheek (*Royal Library) in The Hague, which collected

information on all book translations from the Dutch; the lower line is based on data from the *Nederlands Letterenfonds* (Dutch Foundation for Literature), which covers translations of literary books, i.e. fiction, poetry, and literary nonfiction (as specified in footnote 4).

6 Exact numbers in Wilterdink, 'De receptie van Nederlandse literatuur in het buitenland', p. 62, Table 2.2.

7 'Vor ein paar Jahren hätte es hierzulande noch kaum jemanden interessiert die Kontur der modernen niederländischen Literatur kennenzulernen. [...] Heute blüht das Geschäft mit niederländischen Texten; heute verkünden dieselben, die damals nichts mitbekamen, aus den Niederländen und Flandern stamme Europas lebendigste Literatur.'

8 'Geradezu explosionsartig aber wuchs vor allem das Interesse an der holländischen Literatur.'

9 'eine Renaissance des Erzählens'.

10 'Siegeszug des Realismus'.

11 See for an introductory overview of cultural globalization processes in connection to economic and political globalization: D. Held *et al.*, *Global Transformations* (Cambridge: Polity Press, 1999), esp. pp. 327-375. A summary of theories on cultural globalization is D. Crane, 'Culture and Globalization: Theoretical Models and Emerging Trends', in: D. Crane, N. Kawashima, K. Kawasaki (eds.), *Global Culture* (London/New York: Routledge, 2002), pp. 1-25.

12 This growth is indicated by UNESCO statistics on translations since 1979, the Index Translationum (www.unesco.org/xtrans). See also G. Sapiro, 'Globalization and Cultural Diversity in the Book Market: The Case of Literary Translations in the US and in France' in *Poetics* 38 (2010), pp. 419-439. Another aspect of cultural globalization could be the growth of media attention to foreign art and literature. A study of changes in the coverage of various art forms, including literature, from other countries by French, German, Dutch and American newspapers between 1955 and 2005 found a steady increase of this attention in Europe but not in the United States; S. Janssen, G. Kuipers, M. Verboord, 'Cultural Globalization and Arts Journalism: The International Orientation of Arts and Culture Coverage in Dutch, French, German and U.S. Newspapers, 1955 to 2005', in *American Sociological Review* 73 (2008), pp. 719-740.

13 According to UNESCO's Index Translationum the total number of book translations from small languages (i.e. all languages apart from the six largest in terms of translations) actually decreased from the 1980s to the 1990s; Sapiro, 'Globalization and Cultural Diversity in the Book Market', p. 424, Table 1. This suggests that the increase in the export of Dutch literature was indeed different from trends in translations from other small languages.

14 Nooteboom's breakthrough came with winning the Pegasus Prize 1983 for his novel *Rituals* (original 1980, English translation 1983). Mulisch's first international success – both commercial and reputational – was with the translation of his novel *The Assault* (original *De aanslag*, 1982) into French (1984), English (1985), German (1986), and subsequently more than twenty other languages.

15 In 2010, this Foundation became part of the Dutch Foundation for Literature, which also gives financial support to a number of individual literary writers. About the Foundation's policy and its impact: Heilbron and Van Es, 'In de wereldrepubliek der letteren', pp. 43-51.

16 This argument was put forward in the articles in *The Independent*, 15 July 2000, and *Die Welt*, 29 June 2002, quoted above.

17 As in the articles in the *New York Times*, 27 October 1985, and the *Frankfurter Allgemeine Zeitung*, 10 October 1993, quoted above.

18 Extensively reported in *Le Monde*, 21 March 2003.

19 An example is a highly positive review of W.F. Hermans' novel *De donkere kamer van Damokles* (*The Darkroom of Damocles*; original 1958; new French translation 2006) by Milan Kundera, the Czech writer who became a French writer, in *Le Monde* 26 January 2007, where he presents his reading experience as a surprising discovery of a great novelist completely unknown in France.

20 The concept of 'world-system' has been developed by Immanuel Wallerstein, who defines it primarily in terms of inequality in economic power; see e.g. I. Wallerstein, *World-Systems Analysis: An Introduction* (Durham: Duke University Press, 2004). The notion of a cultural world-system, which is connected with, but not reducible to, the economic and the political world-system, has been suggested by A. de Swaan, 'The Sociological Study of the Transnational Society', Amsterdam School for Social Science Research, Papers in Progress No. 46 (Amsterdam: University of Amsterdam, 1995); it has been used for the study of translations by J. Heilbron, 'Towards a Sociology of Translation: Book Translations as a Cultural World-System', in *European Journal of Social Theory* 2 (1999), pp. 429-444. The concept of 'literary field' (as a specification of 'cultural field' or the 'field of cultural production') is from Pierre Bourdieu, *The Rules of Art* (Stanford: Stanford University Press, 1995; original French edition 1992), and *The Field of Cultural Production* (Cambridge: Polity Press, 1993).

21 I do not deal here with the, often considerable, national variations in the reception of individual authors – such as the extraordinary success of Maarten 't Hart in Germany, or the relatively high appreciation of the work of Hella Haasse in France –, which may be related to national cultural differences. See for this more detailed analysis N. Wilterdink, 'De receptie van Nederlandse literatuur in het buitenland' and 'Schrijvers en hun reputaties', in T. Bevers *et al.*, *Nederlandse kunst in de wereld* (2015), pp. 75-80, 102-109, 117-140.

22 A. de Swaan, *Words of the World: The Global Language System* (Cambridge: Polity Press, 2001).

23 J. Heilbron and G. Sapiro, 'Outline for a Sociology of Translation: Current Issues and Future Prospects', in M. Wolf and A. Fukari (eds.), *Constructing a Sociology of Translation* (Amsterdam: John Benjamins, 2007), pp. 95-97. English dominance in this respect only increased since the 1980s; Sapiro, 'Globalization and Cultural Diversity in the Book Market', pp. 420-424.

24 As argued by Norbert Elias in his analysis of the 'sociogenesis' of the concepts of civilization and culture in *The Civilizing Process* (Oxford: Blackwell, 2000; original German edition 1939), pp. 3-43.

25 An exception is the Three Percent initiative of the University of Rochester, launched in 2007, which derives its name from the fact that 'only about 3% of all books published in the United States are works in translation'. As to fiction and poetry, 'the number is actually closer to 0.7%'. 'An even greater shame is that only a fraction of the titles that do make their way into English are covered by the mainstream media.' Three Percent aims to help change that 'by bringing readers information about goings-on in the world of international literature, and by providing reviews and samples of books in translation and books that have yet to be translated'. Quoted from www.rochester.edu/College/translation/threepercent.

26 P. Casanova, *The World Republic of Letters* (Cambridge etc.: Harvard University Press, 2004; original French edition 1999).

27 As is indicated by the strong growth of translations into French since 1980. Sapiro, 'Globalization and Cultural Diversity in the Book Market', pp. 424-425.

28 Heilbron and Van Es, 'In de wereldrepubliek der letteren', pp. 31-35; U. Kloos, *Niederlandbild und deutsche Germanistiek 1800-1933* (Amsterdam: Rodopi, 1992).

29 E. Zahn, *Das unbekannte Holland. Regenten, Rebellen und Reformatoren* (Berlin: Siedler Verlag, 1984), pp. 84-95.

30 'eine Kultur der Hässlichkeit'.

31 'ungeistig'.

32 'Philiströsität, Banalität und Banausentum'. Graf Hermann Keyserling, *Das Spektrum Europas* (Stuttgart/Berlin: Deutsche Verlagsanstalt, 1931, 5th edition), p. 256, 260, 267.

33 'holländische Welle'.

34 This is akin to the central question in 'imagology', a branch of literary studies that, in a critical reaction to the view that literature is the reflection of national cultures or characters, studies how images of nations are expressed in literary texts. This article's object, however, is different in that it does not investigate literary texts directly but interpretations of literary texts by reviewers. Besides, the approach is more sociological in that it regards the production and reception of literature as being part of social relations, and as one of several kinds of ways in which people communicate and develop ideas about social reality, including images of other nations. It does not assume, as imagology does according to one of its proponents, that 'it is in the field of imaginary and poetical literature that national stereotypes are first and most effectively formulated, perpetuated and disseminated' – as if, for example, daily media reports and comments on current events would only play a minor role. Nor is it taken for granted here that 'the literary record demonstrates unambiguously that national characters are a matter of commonplace and hearsay rather than empirical observation or statements of objective fact.' Quoted from J. Leerssen, 'Imagology: History and method', in M. Beller and J. Leerssen (eds.), *Imagology. The Cultural Construction and Literary Representation of National Characters* (Amsterdam/New York: Rodopi, 2007), p. 26. It is an open question to what extent, and how, national images are related to empirical observations and experiences. Cf. N. Wilterdink, 'Images of National Character', in *Society* 32: 1 (1994), pp. 43-51.

35 Thus, in an obituary of writer and sculptor Jan Wolkers in the *Washington Post* (21 October 2007) it is noted that his 'sex-charged books helped to shake off the shackles of postwar conservatism in the Netherlands.' Similar remarks about Wolkers in *The Times*, 24 November 2007, and *The Guardian*, 27 November 2007.

36 'Auf über dreitausend Seiten hat A.F.Th. van der Heijden aus Erinnerungen und dem "Schmerz der Vorstellungskraft" nach- en neu geschaffen, wofür Amsterdam berühmt und berüchtigt wurde: die Kneipen, Schwulenbars, Frittenbuden und "braunen" Cafés, in denen Fixer, Stricher und gestrandete Provinzler verkehren, die Grachten, Rinnsteine und Gefängnisse, die von Alkohol und Drogen benebelte Aussteiger stolpern liessen, die besetzen Häuser und Studentenwohnheime, in denen Träumer, halb kriminelle Herumtreiber und durchgeknallte Bohemiens die sexuelle Revolution und den Aufstand gegen den Staat probten.'

37 Thus, a selection of short stories by the Dutch author Nescio (1882-1961) was published in English under the title *Amsterdam Stories* (2012). A collection of short stories by Simon Carmiggelt became in German *Heiteres aus Amsterdam* (1980), another one was published in Italian as *Il venditore di aringhe e altri racconti di Amsterdam* (1992). Arnon Grunberg's first novel *Blauwe maandagen* (1994; English translation *Blue Mondays*, 1997) received in a Portuguese translation the title *Amsterdã blues* (São Paulo, 2003).

38 A widely discussed book about the dramatic events in the first years of the twenty-first century is *Murder in Amsterdam* (London: Atlantic Books, 2006) by Ian Buruma, the Dutch-British essayist writing in English, with the suggestive subtitle *The Death of Theo van Gogh and the Limits of Tolerance.*

39 Such as Marcel Möring in the *Frankfurter Allgemeine Zeitung* of 15 May 2002, Leon de Winter in a series of columns in *Die Welt* in 2004 under the title *Holländisches Tagebuch* (Dutch Diary), and Abdelkader Benali, author of Moroccan origin, in *The Observer* of 3 October 2010.

40 An upsurge of international and specifically German interest in Dutch literature can be noted in relation to the Frankfurt Book Fair of October 2016, in which the Netherlands together with Flanders was 'guest of honour' (*Ehrengast*). It remains to be seen how this will work out in the coming years.

41 See for an explicit and systematic use of this multi-level field approach in an empirical study of selection mechanisms in the spread of Dutch translated literature to the Anglophone world: N. van Es and J. Heilbron, 'Fiction from the Periphery: How Dutch Writers Enter the Field of English-Language Literature', in *Cultural Sociology* 9 (2015), pp. 296-319.

BIBLIOGRAPHY

Bourdieu, P., *The Rules of Art* (Stanford: Stanford University Press, 1995; original French edition 1992).

Bourdieu, P., *The Field of Cultural Production* (Cambridge: Polity Press, 1993).

Buruma, I., *Murder in Amsterdam* (London: Atlantic Books, 2006).

Casanova, P., *The World Republic of Letters* (Cambridge, MA: Harvard University Press, 2004; original French edition 1999).

Crane, D., 'Culture and Globalization: Theoretical Models and Emerging Trends', in D. Crane, N. Kawashima, K. Kawasaki (eds.), *Global Culture* (London/New York: Routledge, 2002), pp. 1-25.

De Swaan, A., 'The Sociological Study of the Transnational Society', Amsterdam School for Social Science Research, Papers in Progress No. 46 (Amsterdam: University of Amsterdam, 1995).

De Swaan, A., *Words of the World: The Global Language System* (Cambridge: Polity Press, 2001).

Es, N. van and J. Heilbron, 'Fiction from the Periphery: How Dutch Writers Enter the Field of English-Language Literature', in *Cultural Sociology* 9 (2015), pp. 296-319.

Elias, N., *The Civilizing Process* (Oxford: Blackwell, 2000; original German edition 1939).

Heilbron, J., 'Towards a Sociology of Translation: Book Translations as a Cultural World-System, in *European Journal of Social Theory* 2 (1999), pp. 429-444.

Heilbron, J. and N. van Es, 'In de wereldrepubliek der letteren', in T. Bevers, B. Colenbrander, J. Heilbron, N. Wilterdink, *Nederlandse kunst in de wereld: Literatuur, architectuur en beeldende kunst 1980-2013* (Nijmegen: Vantilt, 2015), pp. 20-54.

Heilbron, J. and G. Sapiro, 'Outline for a Sociology of Translation: Current Issues and Future Prospects', in M. Wolf and A. Fukari (eds.), *Constructing a Sociology of Translation* (Amsterdam/Philadelphia: John Benjamins Publishing Company, 2007), pp. 93-107.

Held, D. *et al.*, *Global Transformations* (Cambridge: Polity Press, 1999).

Janssen, S., Kuipers, G. and M. Verboord, 'Cultural Globalization and Arts Journalism: The International Orientation of Arts and Culture Coverage in Dutch, French, German and U.S. Newspapers, 1955 to 2005', in *American Sociological Review* 73 (2008), pp. 719-740.

Keyserling, Graf Hermann, *Das Spektrum Europas* (Stuttgart/Berlin: Deutsche Verlagsanstalt, 1931, 5th edition).

Kloos, U., *Niederlandbild und deutsche Germanistiek 1800-1933* (Amsterdam: Rodopi, 1992).

Leerssen, J., 'Imagology: History and method', in M. Beller and J. Leerssen (eds.), *Imagology: The Cultural Construction and Literary Representation of National Characters* (Amsterdam/New York: Rodopi, 2007), pp. 17-32.

Sapiro, G., 'Globalization and Cultural Diversity in the Book Market: The Case of Literary Translations in the US and in France', in *Poetics* 38 (2010), pp. 419-439.

Wallerstein, I., *World-Systems Analysis: An Introduction* (Durham: Duke University Press, 2004).

Wilterdink, N., 'Images of National Character', in *Society* 32: 1 (1994), pp. 43-51.

Wilterdink, N., 'De receptie van Nederlandse literatuur in het buitenland: Aandacht, interpretatie, waardering', in T. Bevers *et al.*, *Nederlandse kunst in de wereld: Literatuur, architectuur en beeldende kunst 1980-2013* (Nijmegen: Vantilt, 2015), pp. 56-95.

Wilterdink, N., 'Schrijvers en hun reputaties', in T. Bevers *et al.*, *Nederlandse kunst in de wereld: Literatuur, architectuur en beeldende kunst 1980-2013* (Nijmegen: Vantilt, 2015), pp. 96-146.

Zahn, E., *Das unbekannte Holland: Regenten, Rebellen und Reformatoren* (Berlin: Siedler Verlag, 1984).

CHAPTER 4

Cultural Mediators in Cultural History

What Do We Learn from Studying Mediators' Complex Transfer Activities in Interwar Belgium?

Reine Meylaerts (University of Leuven, Belgium),
Maud Gonne (University of Leuven, Belgium),
Tessa Lobbes (Utrecht University, The Netherlands),
Diana Sanz Roig (University of Leuven, Belgium)

Cultural history is full of surprises. Let us take an example from the literary field. Georges Eekhoud (1854-1927) was until now mainly well-known as a francophone Belgian novelist, also successful in Paris, with novels like *Escal-Vigor, Kees Doorik, La Nouvelle Carthage.*[1] Recent research about his role as a cultural mediator[2] shows how his canonized literary production cannot be understood without taking into account his complex and overlapping mediating activities as a translator, self-translator, and bilingual critic, who was translating, self-translating, summarizing, and even plagiarizing parts of his popular serial novels in Dutch and French into his official highbrow francophone literary production. Thus, if we want to come to a nuanced and comprehensive understanding of cultural history, we need to study not only the canonized literary or artistic products of cultural actors but also the range of exchange and transfer activities underlying such products. In other words we need to study cultural transfer. This is not new in itself. What is perhaps new is that cultural transfer can be best studied by taking the people who facilitate the transfer as a starting point.[3] In other words, this contribution is a plea to study cultural mediators as key figures in literary and cultural history. The present article aims to give a deeper conceptual and methodological understanding of the figure of the cultural mediator, defined as a cultural actor active across linguistic, cultural and geographical borders, occupying strategic positions within large networks and acting as a carrier of cultural transfer. Next to the more traditional focus on linguistic and (mostly national) geographical border crossing in which cultural mediators are involved, this definition crucially wants to stress the need for a more developed analytical focus on the *process* of transfer, on the *overlap* of actor roles, and on the *transgression* of cultural fields.

We will start with a state-of-the-art of the study of cultural mediators, including the problems and pitfalls of several approaches, and then we will present a more encompassing model for the study of cultural mediators and for understanding their constitutive role in cultural transfer and cultural history. Illustrations will be based on some specific examples of cultural mediators' complex transfer activities in interwar Belgium, the Belgian case being a paradigmatic example of the importance of mediation for relatively young, multilingual and multicultural states. As pointed out by Leerssen, Belgium should be seen 'as a highly suitable test case for the study of complex transcultural interactions, where audiences are multiple and shifting, and where mediations and "brokering" are more obviously necessary than elsewhere'.[4]

STATE OF THE ART

Literary studies have mainly focused on literary texts, neglecting the material aspects of literary circulation, which can shed light on the specific factors involved in the selection and reception of globally disseminated literatures. In this sense, as James English[5] pointed out, the new book history helped to 'democratize the core circuit of literary sociability, restoring vital nodes in the literary production processes, beyond the exclusive club of authors, texts and readers' and made room in the production and circulation of texts for neglected figures such as editors, publishers or booksellers. Still, authorship remains central to literary studies. On the other hand, despite the growing attention to the function of certain actors or institutions within inter-national literary networks,[6] little research has been done on the *multifaceted* and *interdisciplinary* mediators' pivotal roles in cross-border and inter-artistic networks or on the various roles simultaneously performed by supposedly secondary actors. Research on cultural mediators usually takes the form of case studies on individual actors in their particular monolingual national or local literary contexts, but rarely focuses on their multilingual intra-national or transnational relations and their participation in multiple cultural fields.

Among the disciplines dealing with intercultural interaction, Translation Studies and Cultural Transfer Studies stand out as young but influential fields. In the last decade they witnessed an increasing attention for the role of the social and cultural agents who are involved in the process of intercultural interaction.

In Translation Studies, the (albeit rather general) focus on the translator as a mediator between cultures became popular as early as the 1980s when the so-called cultural turn emphasized the cultural context of translated texts more than the linguistic equivalence between source and target text.[7] However, this focus did not imply any conceptualization in terms of plural and overlapping transfer roles: mediators were reduced to their status as (literary) translators and the latter term remained predominantly used.

The expression '*cultural* mediator' was first introduced in 1981 by Taft, referring to a 'person who facilitates communication, understanding and action between persons or groups who differ with respect to language and culture'.[8] Nowadays, and more specifically in response to increased globalization and immigration, the concept of '*inter*cultural mediator' refers to (sometimes still untrained) people, working in refugee camps, hospitals, police stations etc., who 'translate, interpret and do whatever else is necessary to reduce the linguistic, cultural and institutional barriers in favour of their client'.[9] Unlike the traditional professional translators and interpreters they are not bound to text equivalence and suffer from low status and uncertainty. Although this definition has little connection with literary and cultural transfer, it points towards a certain plurality of roles and situations that – we claim – is needed when studying cultural mediators and their role in complex transfer processes.

One of the most successful subfields in Translation Studies, Descriptive Translation Studies, has long focused mainly on texts and other types of discursive products[10] as a privileged way to analyze cultural transfer and understand cultural history. However, 'by focusing on the study of various and variable norms as the 'very epitome' of a target-oriented approach, Toury's model for Descriptive Translation Studies has privileged collective schemes and structures instead of individual actors. It has lent itself to research into texts and their discursive embedding in a broader socio-cultural and political context'.[11] This approach has definitely given valuable insights, among other things into Belgian literary history.[12] Nonetheless, these outcomes should not make us blind to the pitfalls of such a discursive approach as 'a form of rationalization that undermines the active role of those who are involved in the process. This [...] undermines, hence leaves unexplained, the negotiations, struggles, tensions'[13] that accompany all possible translation processes. These negotiations, struggles and tensions are embodied by the translators in the first place, but also by the publishers, critics, art dealers, organizers of exhibitions etc., who are involved in the intercultural interaction.

For more than two decades, Translation Studies has increasingly witnessed a focus on the literary translator, as a result of a growing interest in (mainly bourdieusian)[14] sociological approaches.[15] Many studies have been devoted to the role of translators in spreading literary forms, genres, ideas etc.,[16] however they don't take into consideration the versatile nature and overlap of agent roles that crucially characterize mediators, as we understand them here. Recent process-oriented approaches in Translation Studies[17] opened new perspectives by focusing on network production and by taking into account the collective (collaborative and conflictual) nature of translating projects.[18] While these approaches insist on the various agencies behind a translating project, they still neglect the objects of transfer.

Therefore, in order to understand cultural transfer processes and their role in cultural history, we need a much more flexible category than the one conceptualized by Literary and Translation Studies. Too strong a focus on the supposed specificity of a cultural mediator as a sole translator is untenable both from an analytical and historical viewpoint. There are two main reasons why it makes little sense to split up agents' activities along scholarly or disciplinary viewpoints. First, several roles may be tied together by the same agents and secondly, the interdependency of these roles may change their mutual properties.[19]

Indeed, several studies have already pointed to the fact that successful translators in general have combined different roles. Marc Gouanvic[20] e.g. showed how Boris Vian managed to introduce American science fiction in France because he attended meetings of science fiction amateurs in France and published critiques of science fiction literature and fragments of his translations in various French periodicals. In her study on the Dutch poet and translator Martha Muusses, Petra Broomans[21] stated that if translators want to mediate successfully, they should combine several functions. She observed that cultural mediators, whom she interestingly also called missionaries, are often simultaneously active as critic, publisher, editor, librarian, author, literary historian or literary scholar. Yet, all these roles remain confined within the field of literature.

Next to Literary and Translation Studies, we mentioned Cultural Transfer Studies as another discipline dealing primarily with intercultural interaction. Cultural Transfer Studies examines literary, musical and artistic exchanges, paying great attention to the relationship between cultural encounters and the construction of cultural identities. Transfer practices are analyzed in close relationship to their historical context and to the different networks through which the objects or ideas are transferred. Under the influence of anthropology, micro-history and *Alltagsgeschichte*, Cultural Transfer Studies focuses less on discursive products and more on the reality and materiality of mediating practices and individuals. These individuals are defined, precisely, as cultural mediators, i.e. the carriers of cultural transfers whose institutional mediating practices are studied, as well as their role in transnational and trans-regional networks (art houses, societies, academies, publishing houses, periodicals, salons etc.) in the transfer of cultural products into another culture.[22] Cultural Transfer Studies moreover stresses the merging of, and the reciprocity between, diverse transfer activities taken up by a cultural mediator: e.g. being a painter, a literary critic, an art dealer, a multilingual writer and a translator. Still, actual studies in cultural transfer mostly focus on exchanges between *two* national cultures,[23] thus reproducing the idea of 'static' national entities and binary exchanges.

In order to go beyond the focus on the function of transfers in the sole receiving culture or on a bipolar framework of two nations, Werner and Zimmermann developed the concept of 'histoire croisée', studying points of intersection where cultures meet and where the various elements involved can be affected (to a different extent) by the exchange.[24] 'Histoire croisée' stresses the reciprocity of transfers on all the cultures, including the source culture, involved in the exchange process.

TOWARDS AN AGENT- AND PROCESS-ORIENTED INTERDISCIPLINARY APPROACH

In view of the preceding discussion, it makes more sense to approach cultural mediators from a plural methodological and disciplinary viewpoint, taking into account their plural activities and roles and the various ways in which these activities and roles interact with, and influence each other. If we want to trace a transnational cultural history that complements the investigation of local and national histories we need to be aware of the fact that paths of cultural history are neither linear nor unidirectional. National histories do not follow fixed monolingual or territorial schemes. Still, the study of cultural mediators, clustering a variety of dialectically interacting roles, and thus transgressing conceptual and disciplinary boundaries, makes us critically aware of what should otherwise be evident. It does not make sense to split up fields nor mediators' activities. Rather than being concerned with finished end products within national borders and within a single field, an analytical focus on cultural *mediators* and the transfer *processes* they embody makes it possible to study cultural transfer and cultural history as they develop and change over time.

> We need histories that describe the meshing and shifting of different spatial references, narratives in which historical agency is emphasized, and interpretations acknowledging that the changing patterns of spatialization are processes fraught with tension.[25]

Mediators are active at the levels of production, circulation, transformation, and reception of cultural products, and therefore they play a crucial role in the process of cultural representations. Their complex, partially overlapping roles, which transgress linguistic, artistic, and spatial boundaries form important cultural practices but are rarely acknowledged as such nor studied at large because they transcend the traditional binary concepts of disciplines like translation studies, transfer studies. The study of cultural mediators and their transfer activities should therefore be:

- interdisciplinary and collective, bringing together methods from translation sociology, descriptive translation studies, cultural transfer studies, cultural history, literary studies... In this respect, calls were recently raised to consider the historical and conceptual synergy between (cultural) transfers and translation:[26] this constitutes a first step toward an integrated approach of cultural transfers in multilingual societies.
- process- and actor-oriented, in order to discover the complex intersections of which cultural products are the surface result;
- start from the assumption that transfer techniques have to be studied in relation to each other[27] and that 'le débat académique opposant transferts, comparaisons et croisements se résout de lui-même dans la recherche empirique'.[28]

Within the research project 'Customs officers or smugglers? – the mediating role of intercultural actors within Belgium and between Belgium and France (1850-1920)', financed by the KU Leuven Research Council, translation scholars, historians and literary scholars have studied cultural mediators[29] in the following interdisciplinary way, combining different levels of analysis, based on insights from Translation Studies, Cultural Transfer Studies and Cultural History:

1. A first level analyses the socio-biography of the mediators in order to reconstruct their social and biographical trajectories[30] and to reconstruct their intercultural habitus.[31] How did they perceive and implement their transfer activities? How did they perceive and implement their inter-artistic and intercultural activities (covering both discursive products [see 3] and networking [see 2])? How did they perceive their role in creating new frames of reference and repertoires, and in the process of cultural nation building?

2. A second level maps the mediators' networks,[32] and focuses on the informal and institutional inter-artistic and intercultural networks in which these actors took part. What was a mediator's role in these networks? How did these networks facilitate or control the mediator's transfer activities and the construction of common repertoires? According to the 'histoire croisée' paradigm, individuals and their networks are indeed often the first manifestations of transfer,[33] as agents enter the public sphere through informal and collectively organized activities. In order to describe the actual, i.e. empirically observable, intercultural and inter-artistic relations between actors and between actors and institutions, actors' interactions are studied inductively, as they develop. According to Claisse,[34] network analysis, in this particular sense, is especially suitable for analyzing peripheral cultural systems, as is the case in the present essay.

3. A third level carries out translational research from a double angle.[35] First, a comparison between the transferred products and their sources should reveal the multiple discursive transfer modes that are used: translation, multilingual writing, self-translation, adaptation, summary, parody, plagiarism, pastiche, etc. This analysis should pay special attention to the way in which source and target texts relate to each other but also how they mutually modify each other as a result of this relationship.[36] Especially in multilingual cultures, transfer activities form *continuous* processes, develop in *plural* directions and have *multiple* effects[37] that cannot be hypothesized by Translation Studies' conceptualization in terms of source and target text. Therefore the focus on *actors* and their transfer *processes* reveals crucial to understand the complex intersections and mediation techniques of which the products are just the surface result.

Second, a comparison of the different discursive transfer modes (translation, adaptation, self-translation, summary, pastiche, parody...) among each other. Translation is just one among many discursive transfer modes taking sense and shape in relation to all other transfer modes mediators may use. Recent studies show in this respect how mediators in nineteenth century Europe combined various transfer practices (translation, self-translation, retranslation, summary, parody) even within one work[38] and how this combination was instrumental for shaping a common culture.

4. A fourth level studies the different non-discursive transfer modes (e.g. painting, music, sculpture) from a Cultural History perspective.[39] This approach allows to pay special attention to the multiform inter-artistic activities of mediators: animateurs d'art, directors of art galleries, music academies, conference organizers..., to the relation between cultural transfer processes and the construction of cultural identities and to the political-cultural historical context in which these mediators design their practices. How did these activities transgress linguistic and spatial borders? How did they contribute to the construction of (inter)national and subnational identities? Again, the focus on the process is crucial to discover the dynamics of the actors' activities.[40]

BELGIAN MEDIATORS IN THE INTERWAR PERIOD

Rather than focusing here on each mediator separately,[41] let us give a comprehensive view of some aspects of the profile and role of mediators during the interwar period in Belgium, combining the insights arising from interdisciplinary studies based on the multilevel analysis presented above. In contrast to many studies on cultural transfers *between* nations, we shall focus here mainly, but not exclusively, on the role of cultural mediators *within* the young, multilingual and multicultural nation of Belgium during the interwar period.

Since its creation in 1830, Belgium experienced difficulties with a full embracement of the romantic ideal of one people, one state and one language while divergent ideas about language and identity were circulating, giving mediators a very important role to play in cultural life. During the interwar period, this constantly problematic status of the Belgian nation resulted in growing tensions between the two language groups (Dutch- and French-speakers). Belgium found itself in an 'existential crisis', partly due to the rapidly changing political and cultural context of the 1920s and 1930s. Victory in World War I fuelled a surge in Belgian patriotism, while at the same time the concept of a national identity was challenged by the emergence of regional identities. The country had to contend with an increasingly stark 'linguistic divide' caused by efforts to emancipate the Flemish language and culture. The linguistic conflicts eventually gave rise to the 1932 legislation establishing two distinct monolingual communities. Dutch became the official language of administration and education in the northern region, Flanders, while French was adopted in the south, Wallonia. Brussels was bilingual. At the same time, the very concept of nationalism was being eroded by the existence of the new League of Nations, the peace movements and other internationally-oriented avant-garde factions.[42]

These partially conflicting developments – internationalism *versus* nationalism and regionalism – placed the existing national cultural identity under further strain. There was considerable discussion about the form of a Belgian cultural identity in general, and about the necessity of cultural transfers between the two language communities in particular.[43] Radical Flemings tended to claim that Flemish literature needed to be written in Dutch and were hostile towards multilingual writing and transfer. Cultural mediators, on the other hand, would, as we shall see, play an important role in advocating a national Belgian cultural identity.

Among the important cultural mediators in Belgium during the interwar years were Roger Avermaete, Gaston Pulings, Paul Vanderborght, Stijn Streuvels and André De Ridder. While they all took an active part in inter-artistic, intercultural, and multilingual networks, we will observe that they were not all acting with the same intensity on the same level, that is to say: on transgressing the same kind of borders.

Mediators' profile and transfer practices: a paradox?

Comparing aspects from interwar mediators' socio-biography, we observe that most mediators operating between French and Dutch in Belgium were born in Flanders and were bilingual Flemings who had Dutch as their mother tongue or were in contact with Dutch (and Flemish dialects) from an early age onwards (De Ridder, Avermaete, Streuvels). The important position of the French language within international literary and cultural life encouraged Flemish mediators to make use of their knowledge of French. Francophone mediators, as Vanderborght (1899-1971) and Pulings (1878-1949), were often monolinguals, only able to speak and write in French. Yet, most fascinatingly, Vanderborght's and Pulings' monolingualism did not hinder them from becoming two of the most important mediators of Flemish culture.[44] Indeed, and perhaps surprisingly so, there seemed to be no direct relationship between being a bilingual (Dutch-French) and being a mediator. The most skilled perfect bilinguals were not necessarily the most active mediators and vice versa. Monolingual mediators managed to perform plural activities and roles across linguistic borders. Bestseller Flemish novelist Felix Timmermans hardly spoke French and was not able to write in French. Still, he could read and understand it enough to sporadically translate from French into Dutch. He was also involved in bilingual networks and used these contacts to take up a role as illustrator of his own and other colleagues' translations into French.

Despite their scant knowledge of Dutch, Pulings and Vanderborght were among the most important mediators during the interwar period, promoters of Flemish authors like Wies Moens, Paul van Ostaijen, Herman Teirlinck, and of institutions such as the Vlaamsche Volkstooneel [Flemish Popular Theatre]. Brussels-born Gaston Pulings was raised and educated entirely in French.[45] He had a passive knowledge of Dutch, in that he could read and understand the language, but was unable to write or speak it to any significant degree[46]. Still, Pulings maintained one of the largest bilingual networks of his time, which enabled him to bring together diverse writers, painters (e.g. Jakob Smits, Georges Minne, Valerius De Saedeleer) and fellow mediators like Roger Avermaete, Paul-Gustave van Hecke and Pierre Flouquet from both language communities.

Perhaps paradoxically at first sight, monolingual mediators created new transfer practices and new frames of reference promoting the idea of a 'real' Belgian (Dutch and French) literature and culture. Francophone Pulings promoted, for example, Flemish expressionist painters (Minne, Ensor, Permeke) in *La Nervie* for a French-speaking Belgian audience, which illustrates that non-literary transfer was sometimes easier than a literary one, as it was not linked to the difficult linguistic relationships between Flemish and Francophones at the time. Most innovative was his promotion of the Vlaamsche Volkstooneel among the Francophones. According to him, theatre settings, costumes and gestures created common frames of reference in which the language differences were irrelevant.[47] Therefore, Francophones should attend performances of the Vlaamsche Volkstooneel even if those were entirely in Dutch.

> If Flemish literature has penetrated so easily the French public, this is owed mainly to its playwrights. In order to follow the writings of novelists, storytellers, poets, a profound knowledge of the language is needed, knowledge which is not needed to evaluate a play, the setting and the performance of the actors helping to understand. Go to see Flemish plays![48]

Instead of translation, non-translation and the physical movement and mingling of francophone spectators with their Flemish countrymen were one of the inventive transfer[49] processes Pulings was advocating. As a monolingual mediator and against a background of increasingly fierce language conflicts in which languages were essentialized and linguistic groups torn apart, this was an unconventional and daring point of view. Additionally, Pulings also promoted translation, albeit in a less conventional form. His true ideal in Belgian theatre was achieved when the Vlaamsche Volkstooneel played works by Michel de Ghelderode, a francophone playwright whose francophone plays were not staged in French but translated into Dutch and performed by that group.

For Pulings, as a promoter of Belgian unity, translation was a neutral operation and language was not considered as a dividing feature of Belgian literature. In contrast to the traditional definition of Belgian literature (Flemish inspiration plus the French language) as promulgated by the majority of French-speakers between the wars, for him Belgian identity could achieve its ideal manifestation equally well in Dutch and in French, as the harmonious union of Germanic and Latin elements, resulting in a specific individuality. As a result, the transfers with which Pulings supported his vision were themselves innovative and original.

For the monolingual Vanderborght, director of the Lanterne Sourde group, which was seen as one of the most important cultural networks of the interwar period, conferences formed the main platform on which he established cultural mediation between the two language groups. Approximately ten conferences were organized in Brussels between 1925 and 1931, some of them on Flemish literature in general, others devoted to one specific author, representative of modern Flemish literature, e.g. van Ostaijen, Moens, Teirlinck, Van de Woestijne. In May 1925, Vanderborght organized a manifestation in honour of the Flemish playwright Herman Teirlinck. On that occasion, speeches were given in French and in Flemish, without translation, as is testified by a contemporary.

This way, both national languages kept their character and their own rights. This procedure, based on the free associations of the two languages and the two cultures in Belgium, seemed completely new at that moment, all the more since it was adopted, without any political intention, by a group in which most writers expressed themselves in French. It would be successful and would often be repeated in other similar meetings of La Lanterne Sourde, which in that respect contributed to bring the Francophone and Flemish Belgian writers closer to each other.[50]

Similarly, after the death of the Flemish poet Karel van de Woestijne, Vanderborght organized a big manifestation in honour of the renowned poet on October 16 1929. The meeting was presided over by two celebrated writers, one Flemish (Cyriel Buysse) and one francophone (Hubert Krains). Speeches were given in French (Vanderborght and Vermeylen) and Flemish (Teirlinck). Jacqueline De Kesel read Van de Woestijne's poems both in the original Flemish version and in French translation. A contemporary critic concluded: 'The work of reconciliation between Francophone Belgian and Flemish writers, freely undertaken by "La Lanterne sourde", will not have been useless.'[51]

Again, bilingual manifestations were perceived as the best way to mediate between Flemish and francophone literatures, and to present them as equal partners in a context of increasing socio-linguistic tensions. Not surprisingly, all these manifestations were extensively and positively covered in the Flemish press.[52]

Unlike more conservative initiatives, mainly promoting translations of regionalist and so-called 'inferior' Flemish prose,[53] Vanderborght's and Pulings' roles as cultural mediators were partly based on non-translation, a transfer mode that presupposed a bilingual audience, the physical transfer of people; that then contributed to putting Flemish and Francophone literatures and cultures on a par. This was certainly perceived as a very innovative way to establish intercultural contacts, to which the passage in *La Nervie* testifies.

Bilingual Antwerp-born Fleming Roger Avermaete started as a francophone novelist right after World War I and French would always remain his main literary language. Nevertheless he frequently self-translated his francophone works into Dutch.[54] As editor-in-chief of the internationalist and pacifist avant-garde periodical *Lumière* (1919-1923), Avermaete translated articles by Flemish colleagues in French. As he later said in an interview:

> Frans van de Wijngaard has never written one single letter in French, but collaborated: we simply translated him. Actually, at that moment we would have published in Chinese with as much pleasure. Because of the language itself I played on a bigger level and could reach an international audience.[55]

Avermaete's (self-)translations were not presented as translations but received the status of original, autonomous versions in which the role of the author instead of the translator was stressed. They thus contributed to the independent, legitimate status of Flemish literature as an integral part of Belgian literature. Avermaete also wrote articles in French to support the Flemish Movement and opened his periodical to Flemish activists like Moens, van den Reeck and Mortier. Just as was the case with Pulings' and Vanderborght's transfer activities, the underlying view was that French and Dutch were interchangeable, language a neutral medium, and translation a neutral operation.

The bilingual Fleming André De Ridder was, even more than Avermaete, a man with a mission. From 1905 onwards, and throughout the interwar period when linguistic conflicts were increasing, he dedicated his literary career to the promotion of Flemish literature and art and he did so both in Flemish and in French, in order to promote consciousness about Flemish culture in francophone circles. Just as Avermaete, he defended an instrumental vision on language, stating that Flemish culture could also be written and expressed in French. According to De Ridder, a culture was not exclusively defined by its language: Flemish authors writing in French were also fully part of Flemish culture. This vision clearly underpinned his own practices of multilingual writing. So, he fundamentally disagreed with more radical Flemings who claimed that Flemish literature could only be written and promoted in Flemish, which resulted in diverse conflicts between De Ridder and Flemish writers.[56]

In times of increasing linguistic conflicts, monolingual francophone mediators were fierce promoters of a bilingual Belgian national unity, trying to create a common cultural national framework, often through new transfer practices. They tried to overcome the general francophone inability to understand Flemish culture by transferring it to the francophone community. In this sense, the operation of neutralizing language differences turned out to be crucial for almost every cultural mediator we have analyzed. As mediators who were bridging two language groups, they apparently felt obliged to promote an instrumental vision on language and language difference in order to overcome linguistic tensions. On the other hand, many of the bilingual Flemish cultural mediators were part of the Flemish movement, promoting the Flemish cause and its culture in French. Again, this obliged them to neutralize language differences. These Flemings wanted to convince the francophone elite of the necessity of a flourishing Flemish culture, often – also after World War I – within the framework of a united bilingual Belgian nation. In this respect, cultural mediators were among the last people who held on firmly to the idea of national unity in Belgium. And of course, and more opportunistically, they also benefited from this bilingual national unity kept alive by their activities – 'it was their job'. From a methodological viewpoint, their innovative transfer activities in particular are also good examples of how translation and non-translation signify together and how translation needs to be studied in relation to other transfer modes.

Overlap of roles and multi-directional transfers

Belgian interwar mediators typically combined several interdependent roles across fields. They were art dealers, publishers, editors, conference and exhibition organizers, writers, translators, self-translators, art and literary critics, and journalists. Although mediators differed among each other according to the type of role, the number of roles and the relative importance of each role in their career, none of these figures can be reduced to one single role.

As an arts and theatre chronicler, Pulings published a few articles in Dutch on Michel de Ghelderode, Fernand Séverin and Herman Teirlinck in *Vandaag*[57] and in *Den Gulden Winckel.*[58] The status of these articles remains unclear. Although we can assume he used a translator, there is no textual or para-textual information making that explicit. He endorsed authorship for his Dutch-language publications, giving him the status of a bilingual critic, fully in accordance with his ideal of Belgian culture consisting of two equal parts, one francophone, one Flemish. As was the case for (self-)translations of other cultural mediators in this period, they were presented as original versions, and the role of the author instead of that of the translator was stressed. They thus contributed to the legitimate status of Flemish literature as an integral part of Belgian literature. Some of Pulings' Dutch-language articles had a French-language counterpart, meaning that he filtered the same messages in Dutch and French and thus created common frames of reference, independent of linguistic choice. Yet, he did not create many concrete discursive transfers, such as translations or multilingual writing. This is partly caused by his own monolingualism but it also has to be explained within the changing political-cultural context of Belgium where the crossing of linguistic borders became more complex because of growing linguistic conflicts.

Besides a self-translator, Avermaete was also a bilingual writer, who published separate works, now in French, then in Dutch,[59] in the most diverse genres: prose, poetry, literary and artistic criticism, theatre, literary, artistic and political essays, scenarios for ballet, polemics... Without there being a strict division, most of his essays were written in Dutch and most of his theatre plays in French. As a chronicler Avermaete wrote about Flemish literature in the Francophone Belgian newspaper *L' Indépendance Belge* (1936-1939), thus again promoting his preferred idea of a Belgian literature.[60] This overlap of interconnected discursive transfer activities and roles was all but evident in a cultural situation of increasing tensions between Flemings and Francophones, but, similar to Pulings, Avermaete wanted it to be supportive of the idea of a Belgian literature consisting of two equivalent, more or less independent parts, a Flemish one and a Francophone one.

As the director of the Lanterne Sourde group, Vanderborght maintained important inter-artistic networks. According to the contemporary writer Pierre Daye, Vanderborght was a prodigious animator who played a role not comparable to any other in the Belgian literature of his time.[61] La Lanterne sourde organized conferences, receptions, feasts and exhibitions and invited the most important Belgian (Flemish and Francophone) and European writers, painters and musicians of its time.[62] He also promoted FABER-Faisceau Amical Belgique et Russie, the Amitiés Belgo-Égyptiennes, the Amitiés Hispano-Belgo-Américaines and the Rupert Brooke Committee.

In order to fully understand the fame of De Ridder as a cultural mediator, one has to connect his roles as a literary agent with his roles as an *animateur d'art*. His expertise in Flemish culture and more specifically in Flemish expressionist art was based on the strategic positions he occupied and on the overlapping roles he assumed. In co-operation with Paul-Gustave van Hecke, De Ridder published the francophone artistic journal *Sélection* in which Flemish expressionist and avant-garde art was promoted. *Sélection* was also an art gallery in Brussels, in which De Ridder organized multiple art exhibitions. Moreover, he also promoted studies about Flemish expressionist painters, using his role as editor of the series *Sélection*. Both in his literary activities and in his activities as an art dealer, he defended the same vision – in French – on the importance of Flemish culture within the framework of Belgian national unity.[63]

In what follows we will give some examples of the *interplay* between *discursive* transfer roles and of the *multidirectional* and sometimes *collective* dimensions of mediatorship. Bestselling Flemish novelist Stijn Streuvels found inspiration for his original writings in his translations, which he called language and style exercises. Streuvels translated Flemish francophone writers like Eekhoud and Melloy from French into Dutch, and Eekhoud and Melloy translated Streuvels from Dutch into French in a genuine process of *traductions croisées*.[64] Stijn Streuvels and Georges Eekhoud also corresponded with each other (Streuvels using Dutch and Eekhoud French) and Streuvels aspired to use Eekhoud's extensive francophone network (in France and Belgium) in order to become better known himself in French. He proposed that Eekhoud should be given the exclusive translation rights of his most famous novel *De Vlaschaard* to Eekhoud (which Eekhoud would refuse) and at the same time he translated Eekhoud's short stories 'Le Coq Rouge' [The red cock] and 'La petite servante' [The little maid] into Dutch.[65] In return, Eekhoud would extensively promote Streuvels' work and translate one of Streuvels' short stories 'Naar Buiten' [*La Journée des marchands de sable,*1910] in the Parisian magazine *Le Mercure de France.*

This combination of authorship and translatorship, going back and forth between the two languages making up Belgian bilingual culture, raises again the question of self-translation. In terms of language capacity, Eekhoud and Melloy were sufficiently bilingual to self-translate instead of using, for instance, Streuvels as their translator. Whereas Melloy would only self-translate some of his children's novels at the end of his career, Eekhoud started much earlier but used the pseudonym of Gabriel d'Estrange for self-translations of his popular serial novels. He never self-translated his prestigious Parisian novels. Self-translation as applied by Avermaete seemed to be rather uncommon. In other words, bilingual mediators only sporadically used self-translation as a transfer mode. Those who did so, often hid it, thus contributing to the status of both Flemish and francophone literatures as independent, integral parts of Belgian literature. In his private correspondence Streuvels explicitly referred to translating and writing as two overlapping practices: while translating Eekhoud, he felt as if it was his own work: 'I have translated your Coq Rouge with great satisfaction: that was a pleasure for me. While translating, I felt as if it was my own work.'[66]

The roles of author and translator overlapped not only in Streuvels' self-perception but also with regard to his public image. More than once, Streuvels was presented as the author on the cover of a volume of which in reality he was only the translator. This was, for instance, the case for his translations into Dutch of Pieter Frederik Marie de Pauw's *Gens de mer et pêche maritime* (1934) and Melloy's *Cinq Contes de Noël.* Since Streuvels was a bestselling novelist in Flanders, this was perhaps a selling argument used by the publishers.

CONCLUSION

This essay has aimed to illustrate the potential of studying mediators as key figures of literary and cultural history. What connects mediators is that they often performed activities 'behind the scenes' which did not result into canonized (literary, artistic) products. Even more, many important mediators are now forgotten and belong to the 'hidden part of the iceberg' themselves. They pulled the strings 'behind' cultural life, organizing exhibitions, journals, plays, translations. They were not famous because of their existing production, but because of their complex transfer roles, of which we have often lost track.

Research on cultural mediators has the potential to offer insights on the (evolving) impact of cultural transfer on (multilingual 'national') cultural life, on the variable constellation of cultural mediatorship (from bilingual to more monolingual mediators) and on the relation between (often more successful) artistic transfers and (rather failing) literary transfers, which can be extrapolated from research on other multilingual contexts. Cultural mediators highlight *ties* and help to overcome the simplified idea of a distinct giving and receiving culture. The emphasis on relationships, interactions, and circulation goes beyond the analysis of actual contact to include the consequences as well: e.g. how *practices* acquire new meanings in the transfer process.[67] This relational approach helps to zoom in and out on groups of agents and their related stakeholders and focuses on interactions between small literary or translation zones in relation to their larger counterparts.

Indeed, the analysis of cultural mediators also aims to break with the idea of innovative centers and imitative peripheries. Transfers and exchanges overcome national entities and occur not just from the center to peripheries, but also in reverse and through other routes: periphery to periphery, intra-national etc. Mediators can only be understood in relation to their involvement in large human networks and their interdisciplinary competences within heterogeneous cultural configurations. A process- and actor-oriented study allows us to discover the complex intersections of which cultural products are the surface result. Cultural mediators perform strategic transfer roles, create new mediating practices and institutions and are therefore the true architects of common repertoires and frames of reference that make up cultural history.

This overview also shows that translation makes sense within a complex set of transfer techniques such as multilingual writing, artistic and institutional mediating roles, and should be understood and analyzed in relation to them. Translation as well as non-translation are equally important research objects for understanding cultural transfer processes within multilingual cultures. It is, moreover, the complex relationship between different forms of transfer that urges us to rethink the nature of the relationships between cultures. Complex forms of transfer emerge within multilingual cultures, from relations of proximity instead of distance, from contact zones instead of isolation,[68] and they tend to reconfigure national cultures.

Research on cultural mediators also offers some theoretical and methodological insights. If we want to arrive at a nuanced and in-depth understanding of intercultural relations and their impact on literary and cultural history, we need to study the whole range of official, semi-official and hidden transfer activities. Moreover, these transfer activities are so complex and so entangled that we run the risk of conceptual and methodological blindness if we stick to the traditional concepts and methods of translation studies, transfer studies and literary studies. We should rather take as our starting point the cultural mediators who embody the overlapping transfer roles and complex transfer processes and study them from an interdisciplinary and collective, process- and actor-oriented viewpoint. Studying cultural mediators would then contribute to problematize the fixed distinctions between key concepts and roles (such as author, translator, self-translator, critic, animateur d'art, conference organizer, publisher...): their diverging definitions and functions are partly based upon artificial disciplinary subdivisions. It would also contribute to problematize the fixed distinctions between cultural fields (literature, translation, art...), and between translation and other (complementary, surrounding, competing…) transfer activities.

NOTES

1 See e.g. C. Berg, P. Halen and Ch. Angelet, *Littératures belges de langue française (1830-2000): Histoire et perspectives* (Bruxelles: Le Cri, 2000).

2 R. Meylaerts and M. Gonne, 'Transferring the city – Transgressing borders: Translation, Bilingual Writing and Selftranslation in Antwerp (1850-1930)', in *Translation Studies* 7: 2 (2014); M. Gonne, *Médiation et recyclage culturel. Le 'hard labour' de Georges Eekhoud entre Anvers, Paris et Bruxelles* (Leuven: Leuven University Press, 2017). M. Gonne, 'Recyclages, croisements et transferts dans l'œuvre de Georges Eekhoud', in *Revue d'Histoire Littéraire de la France* 115: 2 (2015).

3 L. D'hulst *et al.*, 'Towards a Multipolar Model of Cultural Mediators within Multicultural Spaces: Cultural Mediators in Belgium, 1830-1945', in *Revue Belge de Philologie et d'Histoire* 92: 4 (2014).

4 J. Leerssen, 'Networks and Patchworks: Communication, Identities, Mediators', in *Revue Belge de Philologie et d'Histoire* 92: 4 (2014), p. 1395.

5 J. English, 'Everywhere and Nowhere: The Sociology of Literature After "the Sociology of Literature"', in *New Literary History* 41: 2 (2010), p. viii.

6 B.-O. Dozo, *La vie littéraire à la toise: Études quantitatives des professions et des sociabilités des écrivains francophones (1918-1940)* (Bruxelles: Le Cri, 2010); C. Verbruggen, *Schrijverschap tijdens de Belgische Belle Époque: Een sociaal-culturele geschiedenis* (Gent/Nijmegen: Academia Press/Vantilt, 2009).

7 D. Katan, 'Intercultural Mediation', in Y. Gambier and L. Van Doorslaer (eds.), *Handbook of Translation Studies* (Amsterdam/Philadelphia: John Benjamins, 2013), p. 84.

8 R. Taft, 'The Role and Personality of the Mediator', in S. Bochner (ed.), *The Mediating Person: Bridges between Cultures* (Cambridge: Schenkman, 1981), p. 53.

9 Katan, 'Intercultural mediation', p. 90.

10 G. Toury, *Descriptive Translation Studies – and beyond*, revised edition (Amsterdam/Philadelphia: John Benjamins, 2012); I. Even-Zohar, 'Polysystem Theory (Revised)', in *Papers in Culture Research* (2005), http://www.tau.ac. il/~itamarez/works/papers/papers/ps-revised.pdf.

11 R. Meylaerts, 'Translators and (Their) Norms: Towards a Sociological Construction of the Individual', in A. Pym, M. Shlesinger and D. Simeoni (eds.), *Beyond Descriptive Translation Studies: Investigations in Homage to Gideon Toury* (Amsterdam/Philadelphia: John Benjamins, 2008), p. 91.

12 See e.g. E. Brems, 'A Case of "Cultural Castration"? Paul de Man's Translation of *De Soldaat Johan* by Filip de Pillecyn', in *Target* 22: 2 (2010); T. van Kalmthout, O. Réthelyi and R. Sleiderink, *Beatrijs de wereld in: vertalingen en bewerkingen van het Middelnederlandse verhaal* (Ghent: Academia, 2013); L. Van Doorslaer, 'Source-nation- or Source-language-based Censorship? The (Non-)Translation of Serial Stories in Flemish Newspapers (1844-1899)', in M. Wolf *et al.*, (eds.), *The Power of the Pen: Translation and Censorship in Nineteenth-century Europe* (Münster: LIT Verlag, 2010).

13 H. Buzelin, 'Unexpected Allies: How Latour's Network Theory Could Complement Bourdieusian Analyses in Translation Studies', in *The Translator* 11: 2 (2005), p. 206.

14 Although Bourdieu has not devoted a single volume to translation within his impressive list of publications, his concepts of field, habitus, capital and illusio are very relevant to Translation Studies. See, for an overview, M. Inghilleri, *Bourdieu and the Sociology of Translation and Interpreting*, special issue of *The Translator* 11: 2 (2005).

15 See e.g. D. Simeoni, 'The Pivotal Status of the Translator's Habitus', in *Target* 10: 1 (1998); J.-M. Gouanvic, 'A Bourdieusian Theory of Translation, or the Coincidence of Practical Instances: Field, "Habitus", Capital and "Illusio"', in *The Translator* 11: 2 (2005); M. Wolf and A. Fukkari (eds.), *Constructing a Sociology of Translation* (Amsterdam/Philadelphia: John Benjamins, 2007).

16 See e.g. G. Vorderobermeier (ed.), *Remapping Habitus in Translation Studies* (Amsterdam: Rodopi, 2014); C.V. Angelelli, *The Sociological Turn in Translation and Interpreting Studies* (Amsterdam/Philadelphia: John Benjamins, 2012); Y. Chung, 'Translators as Social Agents: Translated Fantasy Books in Taiwan', in *New Voices in Translation Studies* 5 (2009).

17 R. Sela-Sheffy, 'The Suspended Potential of Culture Research in TS', in *Target* 12: 3 (2000); A. Chesterman, 'Questions in the Sociology of Translation', in J. Ferreira Duarte, A. Assis Rosa and T. Seruya, *Translation Studies at the interface of disciplines* (Amsterdam/Philadelphia: John Benjamins, 2006).

18 H. Buzelin and D. Folaron (eds.), *La traduction et les études de réseaux*, special issue of *Meta* 52: 4 (2007).

19 D'hulst *et al.*, 'Towards a Multipolar Model of Cultural Mediators within Multicultural Spaces'.

20 Gouanvic, 'A Bourdieusian theory of translation'.

21 P. Broomans, 'Martha Muusses en de drie M's: Over de studie naar cultuurbemiddeling', in P. Broomans *et al.*, *Object: Nederlandse literatuur in het buitenland. Methode: onbekend. Vormen van onderzoek naar de receptie van literatuur uit het Nederlandse taalgebied* (Groningen: Barkhuis Publishing, 2006).

22 See e.g. M. Espagne and M. Werner, 'La construction d'une référence culturelle allemande en France: Genèse et histoire (1750-1914)', in *Annales* 4 (1987); C. Charle *et al.* (eds.), *Transnational Intellectual Networks: Forms of Academic Knowledge and the Search for Cultural Identities* (Frankfurt am Main: Campus, 1994); W. Cortjaens *et al.* (eds.), *Historism and Cultural Identity in the Rhine-Meuse Region* (Leuven: Leuven University Press, 2008). The last few years Cultural Transfer Studies have also legitimised and institutionalised themselves through seminars, conferences etc. See e.g. TransferS, created by Michel Espagne at the École Normale Supérieure in Paris (http://www.transfers.ens.fr/article195.html) or the forum History.transnational, directed by Espagne and Middell (http://geschichte-transnational.clio-online.net/transnat.asp?pn=about).

See also the idea of 'connected histories', 'shared histories', 'entangled histories', e.g. S. Conrad, 'Entangled Memories: Versions of the Past in Germany and Japan, 1945-2001', in *Journal of Contemporary History* 38: 1 (2003); P.-Y., Saunier, 'Circulations, connexions et espaces transnationaux', in *Genèses* 57: 4 (2004).

23 C. Charle *et al.* (eds.), *Anglo-French Attitudes: Comparisons and Transfers between English and French Intellectuals since the Eighteenth Century* (Manchester: Manchester University Press, 2007); J. Konst *et al.* (eds.), *Niederländisch-Deutsche Literaturbeziehungen 1600-1830* (Berlin: Ruprecht Verlag, 2009).

24 M. Werner and B. Zimmermann, 'Penser l'histoire croisée: Entre empirie et réflexivité', in *Annales. Histoire, Sciences Sociales* 58: 1 (2003).

25 M. Middell and K. Naumann, 'Global History and the Spatial Turn: From the Impact of Area Studies to the Study of Critical Junctures of Globalization', in *Journal of Global History* 5: 1 (2010), p. 161.

26 R. Weissbrod, 'From Translation to Transfer', in *Across Languages and Cultures* 5: 1 (2004); S. Göpferich, 'Translation Studies and Transfer Studies', in Y. Gambier, M. Shlesinger and R. Stolze (eds.), *Doubts and Directions in Translation Studies* (Amsterdam: John Benjamins, 2007); L. D'hulst, '(Re)locating Translation History: From Assumed Translation to Assumed Transfer', in *Translation Studies* 5: 2 (2012).

27 D'hulst, '(Re)locating translation history'.

28 C. Charle, 'Comparaisons et transferts en histoire culturelle de l'Europe: Quelques réflexions à propos de recherches récentes', in *Les cahiers Irice* 5: 1 (2010).

29 Alfred Stevens, Joseph Stevens, Arthur Stevens, André Van Hasselt, Octave Delepierre, Charles Potvin, Georges Eekhoud, Roger Avermaete, Gaston Pulings, Paul Vanderborght, Camille Melloy, Stijn Streuvels, Cyriel Buysse, André De Ridder, Paul-Gustave Van Hecke, Edmond Vandercammen. For examples of studies of women mediators, see e.g. D. De Man, 'Mothers of the Matrix: Intercultural Transfer Activities of Henriette Roland Holst and Marie Elisabeth Belpaire', in *Revue Belge de Philologie et d'Histoire* 92: 4 (2014).

30 Trajectory describes the successive positions of a mediator and his perceptions thereof in the various fields. Trajectory wants to be an 'alternative to the essentializing concept of biography, since the latter presupposes a transcendental and static consciousness that conditions the choices and decisions made by writers' (S.-F. Hanna, 'Hamlet Lives Happily Ever After in Arabic: The Genesis of the Field of Drama Translation in Egypt', in *The Translator* 11: 2 (2005), pp. 157-192).

31 See e.g. R. Meylaerts, 'Habitus and Self-Image of Native Literary Authors-Translators in Diglossic Societies', in Tr*anslation and Interpreting Studies* 5: 1 (2010a).

32 A network is understood here as a complex set(s) of relations between different actors, groups or institutions within a cultural or social field. See D. De Marneffe and B. Denis (eds.), *Les Réseaux littéraires* (Bruxelles: Le Cri, 2006).

33 Espagne and Werner, 'La construction d'une référence culturelle', p. 984.

34 F. Claisse, 'De quelques avatars de la notion de réseau en sociologie', in D. De Marneffe and B. Denis (eds.), *Les réseaux littéraires* (Bruxelles: Le Cri, 2006).

35 See e.g. L. D'hulst, 'Traduction et transfert: Pour une démarche intégrée', in *TTR Traduction, Terminologie, Rédaction* 22 (2010); R. Meylaerts, 'Au-delà des oppositions binaires

national/international, traduit/non traduit: Les relations littéraires hier, aujourd'hui et demain', in *TTR Traduction, Terminologie, Rédaction* 22: 2 (2010).

36 M. Werner, B. Zimmermann, 'Penser l'histoire croisée: Entre empirie et réflexivité', in *Annales. Histoire, Sciences Sociales* 58: 1 (2003), p. 12.

37 Werner and Zimmermann, 'Penser l'histoire croisée', p. 15.

38 J. Leerssen, 'Viral Nationalism: Romantic Intellectuals on the Move in 19th-century Europe', in *Nations and nationalism* 17: 2 (2011); R. Ingelbien and V. Eelen, 'Literaire bemiddelaars in bewogen tijden: Thomas Colley Grattan, zijn bronnen en vertalers in de (ex-)Nederlanden, 1828-1840', in *Tijdschrift voor Nederlandse Taal- en Letterkunde* 128 (2012); Gonne, 'Recyclages, croisements et transferts'.

39 T. Verschaffel, 'Par les yeux parler à l'intelligence: The Visualization of the Past in Nineteenth-century Belgium', in M. Wintle (ed.), *Image into Identity: Constructing and Assigning Identity in a Culture of Modernity* (Amsterdam: Rodopi, 2006).

40 Werner and Zimmermann, 'Penser l'histoire croisée', p. 25.

41 For examples, following the methodology described above, see also T. Lobbes and R. Meylaerts, 'Cultural Mediators and the Circulation of Cultural Identities in Interwar Bilingual Belgium: The Case of Gaston Pulings (1885-1941)', in *Orbis Litterarum* 70: 5 (2015); R. Meylaerts, 'The Multiple Lives of Translators', in *TTR Traduction, Terminologie, Rédaction* 26: 2 (2013).

42 M. Beyen, 'Tragically Modern: Centrifugal Sub-nationalisms in Belgium, 1830-2009', in M. Huysseune (ed.), *Handelingen van het Contactforum 'Contemporary Regionalism': Comparing Flanders and Northern Italy* (Brussel: KVAWK, 2011), pp. 21-28; L. Wils, *Van de Belgische naar de Vlaamse natie: Een geschiedenis van de Vlaamse beweging* (Leuven: Acco, 2009, pp. 163-189).

43 R. Meylaerts, 'La construction d'une identité littéraire dans la Belgique de l'entre-deux-guerres', in *Textyles – Revue des Lettres Belges de Langue Française* 15 (1998).

44 Of course, significant francophone mediators from Wallonia transgressed national borders and promoted international and intercultural networks with, firstly, France and Germany, but also with more distant geographies. We will not analyze their socio-biographies, the networks they managed to establish or their discursive and non-discursive transfer modes, but let us remind ourselves of some of their names: Marcel Remy, Franz Hellens, Robert Goffin, and Camille Goemans. Among Belgian women, Alexandra David-Néel was a Belgian-French writer, opera singer, philosopher and spiritualist, well-known for her trips to Tibet and the dissemination of Eastern religion and philosophy.

45 At that time and until 1930 all universities in Belgium were francophone.

46 See Lobbes and Meylaerts, 'Cultural Mediators and the Circulation of Cultural Identities in Interwar Bilingual Belgium'.

47 This idea that Flemish theatre did not need any translation was already common at the turn of the twentieth century and was also related to the low status of Flemish and of the theatre itself as popular artistic expression.

48 G. Pulings, 'Herman Teirlinck', in *La Scène Catholique* 2 (1929), p. 26: 'Si la littérature flamande a pénétré si facilement ces dernières années parmi le public français, elle le doit principalement à ses auteurs dramatiques. Pour suivre les écrits des romanciers, des conteurs, des poètes, il faut une connaissance approfondie de la langue, connaissance qui n'est pas

nécessaire pour juger une pièce, les décors, le jeu des acteurs aidant à la compréhension. Allez voir des pièces flamandes!'. Translated by T. Lobbes.

49 Note that transfer is used here in a very literal sense.

50 *L'activité de la Lanterne sourde,* special issue of *La Nervie* 39: 2-3 (1932), p. 5: '(L)es deux langues du pays gardant ainsi, l'une et l'autre, leur personnalité et leurs droits propres. Ce procédé, fondé sur la libre association des deux langues et des deux cultures en Belgique, apparaît alors tout nouveau, d'autant plus qu'il a été adopté, en dehors de tout esprit politique, par un groupement où la plupart des écrivains s'expriment en français. Il réussira et sera, maintes fois repris, dans d'autres réunions similaires de "La Lanterne Sourde", qui a contribué ainsi au rapprochement confiant des écrivains belges de langue française et de langue flamande.' Translation by T. Lobbes.

51 *L'activité de la Lanterne sourde*, p. 8: 'L'œuvre de rapprochement entre les écrivains belges de langue française et de langue flamande, librement entreprise par "La Lanterne Sourde", n'aura pas été vaine.' Translated by T. Lobbes.

52 M. Alfano and A. Doms, *La Lanterne sourde 1921-1931: Une aventure culturelle internationale*, (Bruxelles: Racine, 2008), p. 100.

53 R. Meylaerts, *L'aventure flamande de la Revue Belge: langues, littératures et cultures dans l'entre-deux-guerres* (Bruxelles/Bern/Berlin: PIE-Peter Lang, 2004).

54 *Une épouse modèle* (1923) into Dutch, *Een voorbeeldige vrouw* [An exemplary wife] (1924).

55 J. Florquin, *Ten Huize van... Roger Avermaete* (Brugge/Leuven: Orion/Davidsfonds, 1962), p. 19: 'Frans van de Wijngaard heeft nooit een letter in het Frans geschreven, maar werkte mee: wij vertaalden hem eenvoudig. Ten andere op dat ogenblik hadden wij met evenveel plezier Chinees uitgegeven. [...] Door de taal zelf speelde ik op groter vlak en kon een internationaal publiek bereiken.'

56 A. De Ridder, *Les Lettres flamandes d'aujourd'hui* (Antwerpen: De Nederlandsche Boekhandel, 1909), p. 17, A. De Ridder, *La Littérature flamande contemporaine* (1890-1923) (Antwerpen: L. Opdebeek, 1923), p. 7.

57 G. Pulings, 'Michel de Ghelderode', in *Vandaag* 5: 15 April 1928, pp. 104-105; G. Pulings, 'Fernand Severin', in *Vandaag* 9: 15 June 1929, pp. 211-212.

58 G. Pulings, 'Terug in Nederland', in *Den Gulden Winckel* 29 (1930), pp. 57-58.

59 The balance between the two languages was about 25% Dutch to 75% French. Avermaete published twelve Dutch-language works that do not appear in French, and fourteen bilingual works, all belonging to the domain of the arts.

60 Avermaete's intra-Belgian transfer activities also had an international dimension in his chronicles about international art and literature in the Flemish Belgian *Volksgazet* [People's Gazette] (1931-1938). He further promoted Belgian literature and art in francophone and Flemish Belgian, Dutch, French, German, and Brazilian magazines. He actively contributed to the Brazilian modernist magazine *Klaxon* (1922-1923), which often referred to the Belgian periodical *Lumière*.

61 *L'activité de la Lanterne sourde*, p. 14.

62 So e.g. the Belgians George Eekhoud, August Vermeylen and Herman Teirlinck; the French Jules Romains and Blaise Cendrars; the French musician Darius Milhaud, the Italian F.T. Marinetti, the Austrian Stefan Zweig, the Russian Ilya Ehrenburg, and the Spanish and

Latin American writers Miguel de Unamuno, Ventura Gassol, Francisco Castilla Nájera and Alfonso Reyes. See also Sanz Roig & Meylaerts (forthcoming).

63 A. De Ridder and P.-G. Van Hecke, *Sélection: chronique de la vie artistique* (Brussels/Antwerp: Sélection, 1920-1933).

64 R. Meylaerts, 'Stijn Streuvels en Camille Melloy: Schrijven en vertalen in België', in *Zacht Lawijd* 10: 2 (2010); M. Gonne and R. Meylaerts 'Fransch kleed uittrekken en Vlaamsch pak aanpassen: Stijn Streuvels vertaalt uit het Frans', in *Streuvels Jaarboek* 19 (2013).

65 Published respectively in *Groot Nederland* and *De Nieuwe Gids*.

66 S. Streuvels to G. Eekhoud, 8 June 1904, unpublished correspondence, MLA 1638, Archives et Musée de la Littérature. 'Ik heb uw Coq Rouge met zeer veel genoegen vertaald: dat was mij eene vreugde. Doende bezigheid, ik voelde het alsof het werk van mijn eigen was.' Translation by R. Meylaerts.

67 Werner and Zimmermann, 'Beyond Comparison: Histoire Croisée and the Challenge of Reflexivity', in *History and Theory* 45: 1 (2006).

68 See S. Simon, *Translating Montreal: Episodes in the Life of a Divided City* (Montreal: McGill-Queens University Press, 2006).

BIBLIOGRAPHY

L'activité de la Lanterne sourde, special issue of: *La Nervie* 39: 2-3 (1932).

Alfano, M. and A. Doms, *La Lanterne sourde 1921-1931: Une aventure culturelle internationale* (Brussels: Racine, 2008).

Angelelli, C.V., *The Sociological Turn in Translation and Interpreting Studies* (Amsterdam/Philadelphia: John Benjamins Publishing Company, 2012).

Béarelle, S., 'La comtesse Marie-Henriette de Lalaing (1787-1866): Portrait d'une des premières médiatrices culturelles belges', in *Textyles – Revue des Lettres Belges de Langue Française* 45 (2014), pp. 17-28.

Berg, C., P. Halen and Ch. Angelet, *Littératures belges de langue française (1830-2000): Histoire et perspectives* (Brussels: Le Cri, 2000).

Beyen, M., 'Tragically Modern: Centrifugal Sub-nationalisms in Belgium, 1830-2009', in M. Huysseune (ed.), *Handelingen van het Contactforum 'Contemporary Regionalism: Comparing Flanders and Northern Italy* (Brussels: KVAWK, 2011), pp. 17-28.

Brems, E., 'A Case of "Cultural Castration"? Paul de Man's Translation of De Soldaat Johan by Filip de Pillecyn', in *Target* 22: 2 (2010), pp. 212-236.

Broomans, P., 'Martha Muusses en de drie M's: Over de studie naar cultuurbemiddeling', in P. Broomans *et al.*, *Object: Nederlandse literatuur in het buitenland. Methode: onbekend: Vormen van onderzoek naar de receptie van literatuur uit het Nederlandse taalgebied* (Groningen: Barkhuis Publishing, 2006), pp. 56-70.

Buzelin, H., 'Unexpected Allies: How Latour's Network Theory Could Complement Bourdieusian Analyses in Translation Studies', in *The Translator* 11: 2 (2005), pp. 193-218.

Buzelin, H. and D. Folaron (eds.), *La traduction et les études de réseaux*, special issue of: *Meta* 52: 4 (2007).

Charle, C., 'Comparaisons et transferts en histoire culturelle de l'Europe: Quelques réflexions à propos de recherches récentes', in *Les Cahiers Irice* 5: 1 (2010), pp. 51-73.

Charle, C., J. Vincent and J. Winter (eds.), *Anglo-French Attitudes: Comparisons and Transfers between English and French Intellectuals since the Eighteenth Century* (Manchester: Manchester University Press, 2007).

Charle, C., J. Schriewer and P. Peter Wagner (eds.), *Transnational Intellectual Networks: Forms of Academic Knowledge and the Search for Cultural Identities* (Frankfurt am Main: Campus, 1994).

Chesterman, A., 'Questions in the Sociology of Translation', in J. Ferreira Duarte, A. Assis Rosa and T. Seruya, *Translation Studies at the Interface of Disciplines* (Amsterdam/Philadelphia: John Benjamins Publishing Company, 2006), pp. 9-27.

Chung, Y., 'Translators as Social Agents: Translated Fantasy Books in Taiwan', in *New Voices in Translation Studies* 5 (2009).

Claisse, F., 'De quelques avatars de la notion de réseau en sociologie', in D. De Marneffe and B. Denis (eds.), *Les réseaux littéraires* (Brussels: Le Cri, 2006), pp. 21-43.

Conrad, S., 'Entangled Memories: Versions of the Past in Germany and Japan, 1945-2001', in *Journal of Contemporary History* 38: 1 (2003), pp. 85-99.

Cortjaens, W., J. De Maeyer and T. Verschaffel (eds.), *Historism and Cultural Identity in the Rhine-Meuse Region* (Leuven: Leuven University Press, 2008).

D'hulst, L., 'Traduction et transfert: Pour une démarche intégrée', in *TTR Traduction, Terminologie, Rédaction* 22 (2010), pp. 133-150.

D'hulst, L., '(Re)locating Translation History: From Assumed Translation to Assumed Transfer', in *Translation Studies* 5: 2 (2012), pp. 139-155.

D'hulst, L., 'Forms and Functions of Anthologies of Translations into French in the Nineteenth Century', in L. D'hulst *et al.* (eds.), *Translation in Anthologies and Collections* (Amsterdam/Philadelphia: John Benjamins, 2013), pp. 17-34.

D'hulst, L., M. Gonne, T. Lobbes, R. Meylaerts and T. Verschaffel, 'Towards a Multipolar Model of Cultural Mediators within Multicultural Spaces: Cultural Mediators in Belgium, 1830-1945', *Revue Belge de Philologie et d'Histoire* 92: 4 (2014), pp. 1255-1275.

De Man, D., 'Mothers of the Matrix: Intercultural Transfer Activities of Henriette Roland Holst and Marie Elisabeth Belpaire', in *Revue Belge de Philologie et d'Histoire* 92: 4 (2014), pp. 1359-1377.

De Marneffe, D. and B. Denis (eds.), *Les Réseaux Littéraires (*Brussels: Le Cri, 2006).

De Ridder, A., *Les Lettres flamandes d'aujourd'hui* (Antwerpen: De Nederlandsche Boekhandel, 1909).

De Ridder, A., *La Littérature flamande contemporaine (1890-1923)* (Antwerp: L. Opdebeek, 1923).

De Vries, A., *Cultural Mediators: Artists and Writers at the Crossroads of Tradition, Innovation and Reception in the Low Countries and Italy, 1450-1650* (Leuven: Peeters, 2008).

Denis, B. and J.-M. Klinkenberg, *La littérature belge: Précis d'histoire sociale* (Brussels: Labor, 2005).

Dozo, B.-O., *La vie littéraire à la toise: Études quantitatives des professions et des sociabilités des écrivains francophones (1918-1940)* (Brussels: Le Cri, 2010).

English, J., 'Everywhere and Nowhere: The Sociology of Literature After "The Sociology of Literature"', in *New Literary History* 41: 2 (2010), pp. v-xxiii.

Espagne, M. and M. Werner, 'La construction d'une référence culturelle allemande en France: Genèse et histoire (1750-1914)', in *Annales* 4 (1987), pp. 969-992.

Espagne, M. and M. Middell, *Von der Elbe bis an die Seine: Kulturtransfer zwischen Sachsen und Frankreich im 18. und 19. Jahrhundert* (Leipzig: Leipziger Universitätsverlag, 1999).

Even-Zohar, I. 'Polysystem Theory (Revised)', in I. Even-Zohar, *Papers in Culture Research* (2005), http://www.tau.ac. il/~itamarez/works/papers/papers/ps-revised.pdf.

Florquin, J., *Ten Huize van... Roger Avermaete* (Brugge/Leuven: Orion/Davidsfonds, 1962).

Gonne, M. 'Recyclages, croisements et transferts dans l'œuvre de Georges Eekhoud', in *Revue d'Histoire Littéraire de la France* 115: 2 (2015), pp. 391-407.

Gonne, M., *Mediation et recyclage culturel: Le 'hard labour' de Georges Eekhoud entre Anvers, Paris et Bruxelles* (Leuven: Leuven University Press, 2017).

Gonne, M. and R. Meylaerts, 'Fransch kleed uittrekken en vlaamsch pak aanpassen: Stijn Streuvels vertaalt uit het Frans', in *Streuvels Jaarboek* 19 (2013), pp. 95-118.

Gonne, M. and K. Vandemeulebroucke, 'Deux générations de médiateurs: Portraits de Charles Potvin (1818-1902) et de Georges Eekhoud (1854-1927)', in *Textyles – Revue des Lettres Belges de Langue Française* 45 (2014), pp. 29-46.

Göpferich, S., 'Translation Studies and Transfer Studies', in Y. Gambier, M. Shlesinger and R. Stolze (eds.), *Doubts and Directions in Translation Studies* (Amsterdam: John Benjamins, 2007), pp. 27-39.

Gouanvic, J.-M., 'A Bourdieusian Theory of Translation, or the Coincidence of Practical Instances: Field, "Habitus", Capital and "Illusio"', in *The Translator* 11: 2 (2005), pp. 147-166.

Gouanvic, J.-M., *Sociologie de la traduction: La science-fiction américaine dans l'espace culturel français des années 1950* (Arras: Artois Presses Université, 1999).

Hanna, S.-F., 'Hamlet Lives Happily Ever After in Arabic: The Genesis of the Field of Drama Translation in Egypt', *The Translator* 11: 2 (2005), pp. 157-192.

Ingelbien, R. and V. Eelen, 'Literaire bemiddelaars in bewogen tijden: Thomas Colley Grattan, zijn bronnen en vertalers in de (ex-)Nederlanden, 1828-1840', in *Tijdschrift voor Nederlandse Taal- en Letterkunde* 128 (2012), pp. 239-254.

Inghilleri, M., *Bourdieu and the Sociology of Translation and Interpreting*, in (special issue of) *The Translator* 11: 2 (2005).

Katan, D., 'Intercultural mediation', in Y. Gambier and L. Van Doorslaer (eds.), *Handbook of Translation Studies* (Amsterdam/Philadelphia: John Benjamins, 2013), pp. 84-91.

Konst, J., I. Leemans and B. Noak (eds.), *Niederländische-Deutsche Literaturbeziehungen 1600-1830* (Berlin: Ruprecht Verlag, 2009).

Leerssen, J., 'Viral Nationalism: Romantic Intellectuals on the Move in 19th-century Europe', in *Nations and Nationalism* 17: 2 (2011), pp. 257-271.

Leerssen, J., 'Networks and Patchworks: Communication, Identities, Mediators', in *Revue Belge de Philologie et d'Histoire* 92: 4 (2014), pp. 1395-1403.

Lobbes, T. and R. Meylaerts, 'Cultural Mediators and the Circulation of Cultural Identities in Interwar Bilingual Belgium: The Case of Gaston Pulings (1885-1941)', in *Orbis Litterarum* 70: 5 (2015), pp. 405-436.

Meylaerts, R., 'La construction d'une identité littéraire dans la Belgique de l'entre-deux-guerres', in *Textyles – Revue des Lettres Belges de Langue Française* 15 (1998), pp. 17-32.

Meylaerts, R., *L'aventure flamande de la Revue Belge: langues, littératures et cultures dans l'entre-deux-guerres* (Brussels etc.: P.I.E.-Lang, 2004).

Meylaerts, R., 'Translators and (Their) Norms: Towards a Sociological Construction of the Individual', in A. Pym, M. Shlesinger and D. Simeoni (eds.), *Beyond Descriptive Translation Studies: Investigations in Homage to Gideon Toury* (Amsterdam/Philadelphia: John Benjamins, 2008), pp. 91-102.

Meylaerts, R., 'Habitus and Self-Image of Native Literary Authors: Translators in Diglossic Societies', in *Translation and Interpreting Studies* 5: 1 (2010), pp. 1-19.

Meylaerts, R., 'Au-delà des oppositions binaires national/international, traduit/non traduit: Les relations littéraires hier, aujourd'hui et demain', in *TTR Traduction, Terminologie, Rédaction* 22: 2 (2010), pp. 93-117.

Meylaerts, R., 'Stijn Streuvels en Camille Melloy: Schrijven en vertalen in België', in *Zacht Lawijd* 10: 2 (2010), pp. 49-69.

Meylaerts, R., 'The Multiple Lives of Translators', in *TTR Traduction, Terminologie, Rédaction* 26: 2 (2013), pp. 103-128.

Meylaerts, R. and M. Gonne, 'Transferring the City – Transgressing Borders: Translation, Bilingual Writing and Selftranslation in Antwerp (1850-1930)', in *Translation Studies* 7: 2 (2014), pp. 133-151.

Middell, M. and K. Naumann, 'Global History and the Spatial Turn: From the Impact of Area Studies to the Study of Critical Junctures of Globalization', in *Journal of Global History* 5: 1 (2010), pp. 149-170.

Pulings, G., 'Michel de Ghelderode', in *Vandaag*, 15 April 1928, pp. 104-105.

Pulings, G., 'Fernand Severin', in *Vandaag*, 15 June 1929, pp. 211-212.

Pulings, G., 'Herman Teirlinck', in *La Scène Catholique* 2 (1929), pp. 25-27.

Pulings, G., 'Terug in Nederland', in *Den Gulden Winckel* 29 (1930), pp. 57-58.

Pym, A., *Method in Translation History* (Manchester: St. Jerome, 1998).

Sanz Roig, D. and R. Meylaerts (eds.), *Customs Officers or Smugglers? Literary Translation and Cultural Mediators in Peripheral Cultures* (London: Palgrave, forthcoming).

Sapiro, G., 'Réseaux, institution(s) et champ', in D. De Marneffe and B. Denis (eds.), *Les réseaux littéraires* (Brussels: Le Cri, 2006), pp. 44-59.

Saunier, P.-Y., 'Circulations, connexions et espaces transnationaux', in *Genèses* 57: 4 (2004), pp. 110-126.

Sela-Sheffy, R., 'The suspended potential of culture research in TS', in *Target* 12: 3 (2000), pp. 345-355.

Sela-Sheffy, R., 'How to be a (Recognized) Translator: Rethinking Habitus, Norms, and the Field of Translation', in *Target* 17: 1 (2005), p. 1-26.

Sela-Sheffy, R. and M. Shlesinger, *Identity and Status in the Translational Professions* (Amsterdam/Philadelphia: John Benjamins, 2011).

Simeoni, D., 'The Pivotal Status of the Translator's Habitus', in *Target* 10: 1 (1998), pp. 1-39.

Simon, S., *Translating Montreal: Episodes in the Life of a Divided City* (Montreal: McGill-Queens University Press, 2006).

Taft, R., 'The Role and Personality of the Mediator', in S. Bochner (ed.), *The Mediating Person: Bridges between Cultures* (Cambridge: Schenkman, 1981), pp. 53-88.

Toury, G., *Descriptive Translation Studies – and beyond*, revised edition (Amsterdam/Philadelphia: John Benjamins, 2012).

Van Doorslaer, L., 'Source-nation- or Source-language-based Censorship? The (Non-)Translation of Serial Stories in Flemish Newspapers (1844-1899)', in M. Wolf *et al.* (eds.), *The Power of the Pen: Translation and Censorship in Nineteenth-century Europe* (Münster: LIT Verlag, 2010), pp. 55-76.

Van Kalmthout, T., O. Réthelyi and R. Sleiderink, *Beatrijs de wereld in: Vertalingen en bewerkingen van het Middelnederlandse verhaal* (Gent: Academia Press, 2013).

Verbruggen, C., *Schrijverschap tijdens de Belgische belle époque: Een sociaal-culturele geschiedenis* (Gent/Nijmegen: Academia Press/Vantilt, 2009).

Verschaffel, T., 'Par les Yeux Parler à l'Intelligence: The Visualization of the Past in Nineteenth-century Belgium', in M. Wintle (ed.), *Image into Identity: Constructing and Assigning Identity in a Culture of Modernity* (Amsterdam: Rodopi, 2006), pp. 131-143.

Vorderobermeier, G. (ed.), *Remapping Habitus in Translation Studies* (Amsterdam: Rodopi, 2014).

Vorderobermeier, G. and M. Wolf (eds.), *'Meine Sprache grenzt mich ab…': Transkulturalität und kulturelle Übersetzung im Kontext von Migration* (Wien/Berlin: LIT, 2000).

Weissbrod, R., 'From Translation to Transfer', in *Across Languages and Cultures* 5: 1 (2004), pp. 23-41.

Werner, M. and B. Zimmermann, 'Penser l'histoire croisée: Entre empirie et réflexivité', in *Annales: Histoire, Sciences Sociales* 58: 1 (2003), pp. 7-36.

Werner, M. and B. Zimmermann, 'Beyond Comparison: Histoire Croisée and the Challenge of Reflexivity', in *History and Theory* 45: 1 (2006), pp. 30-50.

Wils, L., *Van de Belgische naar de Vlaamse natie: Een geschiedenis van de Vlaamse beweging* (Leuven: Acco, 2009).

Wolf, M. and A. Fukkari (eds.), *Constructing a Sociology of Translation* (Amsterdam/Philadelphia: John Benjamins, 2007).

CHAPTER 5

Is it Only the Original which Unfolds Anew in the Reception?

Herbert Van Uffelen (University of Vienna, Austria)

The relationship between literature and its (literary) context is not static but dynamic. That means that literatures and cultures create identities for each other, in and through the confrontation with other literatures and cultures, as well as in and through the interaction with their own contexts and with those of others. Literatures and cultures are not monolithic; their identities are not given entities. They are constantly in motion and change in their relationships with other literatures and (cultural) contexts.

Literature, once translated and/or transported into its target language area, will in its turn influence the literature in the source language. Translations are not only copies or adaptations of the originals. By using another language, by showing that something can be said in a different way, translations also discover the original text, and even become originals in their own right.

In order to describe this dynamic interaction, we will have to define some notions, and therefore we have to imagine for the moment as if the interaction does not exist. We cannot, on the one hand, discuss translations and at the same time refuse to delineate literatures, and systems of source and target language. How else can we talk about transfer? In order to describe the phenomenon 'reception', we have to determine the boundaries, formulate what the differences and similarities are, mark out the positions of the pickets. We must keep in mind the dynamics which on the one hand generate the differences and the similarities, contrasts and hierarchies and on the other hand constantly questions their validity.

The relationship between original and translation is not a question of one-way traffic. The interaction between literatures goes two ways: from the source language system to that of the target language. That means that there is no absolute standpoint from which differences and similarities could be judged. The hierarchy between the two poles of interaction turns out to be reversible. Centre and periphery can shift their positions. That which from one point of view must be considered a loss, can often be viewed as a gain from another perspective. During the process of reception, the object of reception is both discovered as well as created.

Research into reception therefore has to be more than research into what is, or what is not being transported, was or was not integrated, left over, lost, not in the last instance because we ultimately do not really know what we are discussing, what exactly it is that could be or has to be integrated, or what has to remain or could be lost. Reception is a process, a receiving which is at the same time a creating. Just as Oedipus arrived in Colonos as a stranger amongst strangers, to quote Jacques Derrida, so the encounter between literatures is in the first instance an encounter of two strangers who discover each other at the border.[1]

In the relationship between literatures the important thing is that which is constantly created at the border. In essence therefore, the area of investigation of reception research is an interstice which has to be described rather than marked out. Reception research describes the forces which determine no man's land; the interactions, the osmotic processes in other words, which create the space in which the reception takes place.

The power of a literature, and that is true of literature in translation too, does not reside in the familiar, the recognizable (and its antithesis, the unknown, the non-recognizable). It resides in the dynamic with which that which seemed or seems self-evident continuously turns out to be something unknown. Exactly this comes to the fore in and through the reception, and with that I arrive at the theme of this contribution and at the title I chose for it: Is it only the original which unfolds anew in the reception?

With this title I refer to the following statement by Walter Benjamin from his famous essay *Die Aufgabe des Übersetzers* [*The Task of the Translator*] (1923): 'In [translations] the life of the originals attains its latest, continually renewed, and most complete unfolding.'[2] I am indeed in perfect agreement with Benjamin that in reception the (life of the) original experiences a 'continually renewed unfolding'. For me that goes without saying. At the same time, and that is why the title was formulated as a question, I disagree with Benjamin as well.

Especially problematic, in my view, is the status which Benjamin accords the original and the hierarchy between original and translation which he constructs. Benjamin (sup)poses that the central issue is the 'latest' and 'most complete' unfolding. Moreover, he is of the opinion that the 'content and language'[3] of the original form more a 'unity' than in the translation. In what follows I would now like to offer these thoughts for discussion. Not only because I think that Benjamin's theses have to be modified but also to show that in and through the reception not only the original is constantly renewed and developed.

THE 'INEXPLICABLE ORIGINAL'[4]

In the essay mentioned above Walter Benjamin poses that the essence of a poem is not the message, the information, but that what he calls 'the unfathomable, the mysterious, the "poetic"'.[5] His reasoning about the role of the translator and the purpose of translations is fairly complex but in principle follows two main lines:

1. the 'essential quality' of an original is not the 'information' but that which 'lies beyond communication in a literary work'[6] and
2. the 'translation is a form' which is 'transparent', does not 'cover' the original, does not 'block its light' but allows 'the pure language [...] to shine upon the original'.[7]

I do agree with this train of reasoning, especially in so far it concerns the first thesis.

It is clear that in translating the first object is not, in the first instance, to say 'the same' repeatedly and that the essence of a translation is more than 'mediating the information'. In the case of the second thesis, too, I would like to express agreement with Benjamin's reasoning though I do not think that the translation refers to a 'more exalted language than its own' and that it should be the (first) duty of a translator to 'liberate the [pure] language imprisoned in a work in his re-creation of that work'.[8] On the basis of this thesis Benjamin constructs the hierarchy, mentioned earlier, of original and translation:

> Whereas content and language form a certain unity in the original, like a fruit and its skin, the language of the translation envelops its content like a royal robe with ample folds. For it signifies a more exalted language than its own and thus remains unsuited to its content, overpowering and alien.[9]

In the end he deduces from this that translations would be untranslatable:

> The higher the level of a work, the more it remains translatable even if its meaning is touched upon only fleetingly. This, of course, applies to originals only. Translations, in contrast, prove to be untranslatable not because of any inherent difficulty but because of the looseness with which meaning attaches to them.[10]

Of course there is no point in denying in principle that the fact that every translation is in one way or another 'insuited'. What matters is the appreciation, whether one qualifies positively or negatively that which Benjamin calls the 'disjunction'.[11] There are no perfect translations. But that does not at all mean that translations would be inferior and even less that they would not be suitable as source texts for further translation. The problem does not lie in the disjunction but in the essential hierarchy between the original and the translation which Benjamin constructs.

I do not want to deny here either that the 'kinship of languages', or call it even the 'suprahistorical kinship between languages' plays an (important) role in the relationship between originals and their translations. I think that Benjamin rightly points to the fact that originals and translations refer to the 'totality of their intentions supplementing one another'. As far as this is concerned Benjamin's thoughts move in the right direction. Original and translation 'manifest' indeed something comparable.[12] But where I differ from Benjamin is that I think that it is not the 'pure language' which matters but that that to which original and translation refer is situated outside the language.

This is indirectly confirmed by Benjamin. He too is, as mentioned, of the opinion that what matters both in the original and the translation is that which lies 'beyond all communication',[13] that which cannot be formulated with language, with words. And indeed, is that not the purpose of literature: to try and find fitting words to create space for the experience of that which cannot be said, for that for which there are no words? This space, I feel, is the space to which both original and translation refer. Translation and original are transparencies, which afford us insight in, allow access to, the space of that which cannot be put into words.

I will try to illustrate this briefly with an example from Shakespeares *Richard II*, adapted by the Flemish playwrights Tom Lanoye and Luk Perceval (1997).[14] It concerns the following passage:

> Your cares set up do not pluck my cares down.
> My care is loss of care, by old care done;
> Your care is gain of care, by new care won.
> The cares I give, I have, though given away,
> They 'tend the crown', yet still with me they stay.[15]

In Lanoye's and Perceval's translation this is rendered as follows:

Without nothing I still remain not free of care.	Ik blijf ook zonder niet van zorg verschoond.
My care? Lost care, past care.	Mijn zorg? Verloren zorg, de zorg voorbij.
Your care? Acquired care, much added care.	Uw zorg? Verworven zorg, veel zorg erbij.[16]

It is clear that there is adaptation and abridgement here but in both quotations the object appears to be to create a space for the experience of the word 'care'. Shakespeare does this by creating a riddle; in the Dutch adaptation the space is created with alliterations, assonances and parallelism.[17]

The relationship between original and translation is paradoxical. Though literature is untranslatable, it can be translated because it refers to that which cannot be said, to that for which there are no words, to something, therefore, which cannot be translated but can be made into a new experience in and through the translation. In this Benjamin was absolutely right: the translation is a form which confronts us with the untranslatable core of the original, which throws (new) light on the ineffable which is 'meant' by the original.

Benjamin therefore shows us, rightly so, that every original 'is dying for'[18] a translation, not only because the translation creates the original anew but also because the translation shows that what matters is something else than a hierarchical relationship, that there is something more important than something more or less or better or worse. The translation makes newly visible that to which the original too referred: the space of the ineffable. Or, to use a notion of the Dutch author Albert Verwey from the beginning of the previous century, the translation refers just like the original to the 'inexplicable original'[19]

To illustrate this, I once more refer to Shakespeare's *Richard II*, now with a quotation from the beginning of the first act:

Old John of Gaunt, time-honour'd Lancaster,
Hast thou, according to thy oath and band,
Brought hither Henry Hereford thy bold son,
Here to make good the boisterous late appeal,
Which then our leisure would not let us hear,
Against the Duke of Norfolk, Thomas Mowbray[20]

With 'bold' and 'boisterous' Shakespeare makes it immediately clear that there is much at stake here without however revealing what exactly that is. Lanoye and Perceval do it differently but with a comparable result:

Mijn wijze, grijze oom, mijn Jan van Gent, Wiens trouwe vleugels het aloude nest Van Lancaster beschermen lijk een schat, Vertelt mij: Is de aanklacht van uw zoon – Mijn hevig helm boswuivende kozijn – Gegrond op een bewijsbaar, echt verraad Of eerder op een vage, valse vete?[21]	My wise grey uncle, my John of Ghent, Whose faithful wings protect The ancient nest of Lancaster like a treasure, Tell me: is your son's accusation – My strongly helmcrest waving cousin – Founded on a provable real treasonable act Or rather on a vague, false feud?

Here Lanoye and Perceval formulate explicitly what the topic of discussion is: treason or vague, false feud. But at the same time they also open up a view on something that was consciously kept 'open' in the original. They do this via the notion 'helmcrest waving' [helmboswuivend].[22] According to Reichert this word shows up the bombast and the hubris of the cousin but there is more implied here.[23] The term refers also to brave Hector. Besides, the treason, the love, the revenge and the violence form both the ingredient of the Iliad as of Shakespeare's kings' dramas. That which Shakespeare suggests in the openings scene, is not only taken up again by the translators (driest, wild, overmoedig – hevig helmboswuivend – bold, wild, reckless – helmcrest waving) but placed into in broader context at the same time.

It is the task of the translator (male or female) to create a transparent, new form, which on the one hand does not obscure the original and on the other hand adapts the original in such a way that the unexplained original is experienced anew.

To conclude this theme, I would want to vary this thought with a quotation from an interview with Thomas Rosenboom from the beginning of the eighties:

> My motive is not expression, [...] I hope to touch the impersonal via the personal. That for me is the very best prose [...] With poetry you often have to make an effort to understand it, that demand is made of the reader. In my prose I intend the reverse. The reader does not understand the prose but the prose grasps the reader. I wanted to make a tunnel and therefore I withhold from the reader the possibility to understand the protagonist in a wider perspective.[24]

Benjamin's 'new form' is, for Rosenboom, a tunnel which grasps the reader. What both these forms, that of the original and that of the translation, have in common is the light at the end of the tunnel, the insight that the reader acquires which he or she lets him- or herself be grabbed by the tunnel.

THE OBJECT OF RECEPTION RESEARCH

Why so much attention for the tunnel in the context of reception research? With my expatiations about the terrain, the space to which both original and translations refer, I want to show on the one hand that transfer (in the widest sense of that word) signifies more than transport, that it is not so much the translating or translatability of 'something' but that it is a two way and not a one-way traffic. Translations also create originals. On the other hand, I also want to illustrate that there is more at stake than the defending or the conquering of terrain, more than status and power.

The object of reception research is on the one hand a space in which poles and hierarchies are both constructed as deconstructed and on the other hand a form, a transparency which lends insight into and creates space for the experience of that which cannot be formulated in words.

Indeed, this form, which provides insight, modifies the seemingly everlasting discussion about translatability. It is no accident that in the debate about reproduction and production there is repeated discussion of 'keeping' and 'changing' and not about 'changing' and 'keeping'. When judging we usually look from the perspective of the original to the translation and not vice versa; not only that: existing translations also play a role in this hierarchy. Klaus Reichert who together with the Lanoye-translator Rainer Kersten has translated *Ten Oorlog* [Warwards], into German, writes, in this connection, quite rightly: 'To translate Shakespeare beyond Schlegel [...], is difficult.'[25] The translation of *Ten Oorlog* has to prove itself in the 'tension' between the English original and the 'rich [German] tradition'.[26] Both, not only the original but also Schlegel's translation have to echo, according to Reichert, in the new translation, even if only 'as a distant echo'.[27] What gets lost in practice, is the adaptation made by Lanoye and Perceval. That becomes clear in the very first lines. Richaar Deuzième opens the spectacle in the version by Lanoye and Perceval, as mentioned, with the following words:

Mijn wijze, grijze oom,
    mijn Jan van Gent,
Wiens trouwe vleugels het
    aloude nest
Van Lancaster beschermen
    lijk een schat,[28]
	My wise grey uncle, my John
	    of Ghent,
	Whose faithful wings
	    protect
	The ancient nest of Lancaster
	    like a treasure

It is difficult if not impossible to recognise the original text in this, and Reichert and Kersten therefore had to adhere as closely as possible to the Dutch adaptation. They translated the passage as follows:

> Mein weiser greiser Ohm, Johann von Gent,
> Des Adlerschwingen das erlauchte Nest
> Von Lancaster wie einen Schatz beschirmen[29]

In the search of a suitable translation Reichert and Kersten chose to render 'trouwe vleugels' [faithful wings] as 'Adlerschwingen' [eagle's wings]. They let themselves be guided by the fact that, in Lanoye and Perceval's text, the Duchess of Gloucester compares the old John of Gaunt to an eagle ('your chick is crowing and you, the eagle, are silent?' [uw kuiken kraait en gij, de arend, zwijgt?)][30] When Shakespeare makes his John of Gaunt play with his name, things become a bit problematic:

O how that name befits my composition!
Old Gaunt indeed, and gaunt in being old:
Within me grief hath kept a tedious fast;
And who abstains from meat that is not gaunt?
For sleeping England long time have I watch'd;
Watching breeds leanness, leanness is all gaunt:
The pleasure that some fathers feed upon,
Is my strict fast; I mean, my children's looks;
And therein fasting, hast thou made me gaunt:
Gaunt am I for the grave, gaunt as a grave,
Whose hollow womb inherits nought but bones.[31]

It was not possible to use the eagle again in this passage. In search of a solution Reichert and Kersten evidently looked for advice to Schlegel, but his allusions to bankruptcy and public auction with the words 'gant' and 'verganten' – 'Wohl Gaunt: der Tod wird meinen Leib verganten/ Und alter Gaunt, der längst den Gant erwartet'[32] – turned out to be just as unfit for purpose as Shakespeare's original puns with 'gaunt' ('emaciated', 'horrible', 'thin', 'somber', 'arid' etc.). Since neither Shakespeare nor Schlegel offered a solution, they decided to translate 'gent' after all with 'ganter', meaning 'male goose' ('gander' in English) without asking themselves again why Lanoye and Perceval had opted to compare their Jan van Gent with an eagle. Lanoye and Perceval had probably not even thought of a goose: their Jan van Gent is the *morus bassanus*, the powerful seabird with a wingspan of nearly two metres which, however, lets itself be caught very easily and is therefore popularly also known as 'the sea fool' [zeezot]. This paradoxical reference eludes Reichert and Kersten as do a number of other 'jeux de mots'.[33]

Behind the discussion of 'to keep' and 'to change' lies the conviction that the relationship between original and translation (and between the translations among themselves) is logical-chronological-causal. First there is the original, then there is the translation. The original stands for the original, the translation is a deduction, the original possesses more value, a higher status than the translation etc..... The question of the chicken and the egg should not be asked. The original (the first important translation) must not lose its 'untouchable authority'.[34]

This discussion will last till we decide to depart from one of the absolute starting points. We do not necessarily need to look from the original at the translation, we can instead look from the translation at the original, discover what the translation reveals. And we can also try to look from different perspectives, one after the other, and pay attention particularly to the space in which the object of the reception becomes visible. If we shift the discussion about the relationship between original and translation from a discussion about the status to the description of, on the one hand, the interactions and on the other hand the way in which a transparency is created, then the yes-no-yes-no story is finished. Then what matters is the description of the forces which on the one hand generate polarities and hierarchies, points of view, central points, perspectives, causalities, and chronologies, and on the other hand continually eliminate all of these, then it focuses on the space which makes the object of the reception recognisable as something that – I formulate it now as paradoxically as it is – is the same and yet not the same, and ever-changing. Exactly that fascinates us again and again in the objects of the reception.

In the practice of reception research this interaction on the border is seldom the central issue. Mostly what is important is the dynamic of the transport across the border, and we search to see whether 'something' is translated freely or not, whether 'something' was translated with as its focus the source or the target language, how 'something' has been 'contextualised'.[35] Or the object of the research is the role of the mediators, the visualization around and the ideological implications of the reception of 'something', the role of institutions and the status of transferred cultural objects in comparison with other cultural objects etc.... And justly so: with such questions the dynamic of the circulation of literature can be described very accurately and therefore shifts, changes and developments can be illustrated equally well.

But it is striking that this 'something', the cultural object which is mediated, illustrated, selected, translated, received, contextualised, is in this research more or less considered as a given. Even if the dynamic is investigated, it is in fact more important to consider the dynamic of keeping, of not-moving. Things do change but only in shape, in fact everything remains as it was. So simple, however, it is not. As I posed in the beginning of this contribution: cultural objects are not entities, not monoliths which can be transported any old how.

Transfer means more than the placing elsewhere of a work of art, the chronology of the reception does not only move from beginning to end. Influence also works in reverse. Kafka's works, for instance, have changed in and because their reception. Reception is the result of an interaction, happens in two directions, also in chronological and causal respect.

Notions such as source and goal, source and target language, original and translation can help us in describing the phenomenon of reception, but at the same time it is true that without translation there would be no original, without target language area no source language area and vice versa. Titles such as 'Dutch literature abroad' suggests wrongly that there would be 'something' which could simply be transported to an area which is situated 'outside the territory of Dutch literature'. But how can we determine exactly what Dutch literature is, where Dutch literature begins and ends? What to do, for instance, with texts originally published in the area of the target literature? Dutch literature exists by the virtue of its dynamic relationship with other literatures. If there were no French, German, English or other literature, Dutch literature would be world literature.

Of course, I said it at the start of this article, in order to describe the reversal of the hierarchy between poles, we first have to determine the terminology. Without notions such as source and target language, original and translation, we can't proceed. But if we limit ourselves to differences, and reception is diluted to a story of large and small, weak and strong, centre and periphery, then reception does become a story about power and what is then not clear is that interactions in particular play a role and that the relationship between centre and periphery and the hierarchy between, for instance, large and small, are reversible. Cultural objects and their transformations are intertwined. If a translation brings to light new aspects then the original also changes, perhaps in that case the latter really becomes for the first time an original. The object of the reception resembles the original and yet it is different, it is, to quote Müller-Funk, 'a double which is not a double'.[36]

To demonstrate this interaction better, I propose to split up the area which reception research describes in four parts:

1. the area in the country of origin in which the cultural object appears
2. the area in the target territory of target medium in which a second cultural object becomes visible
3. the area in the transnational, overlapping territory which is formed by the spheres of influence of area 1 and area 2
4. the area of so-called world literature in which many literatures reflect themselves or are reflected

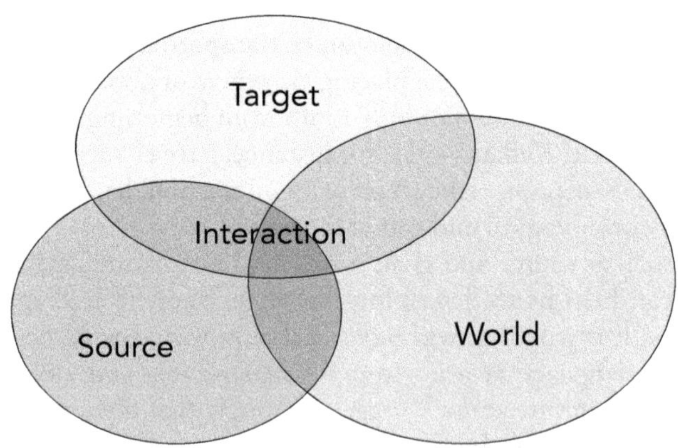

Figure 1. Reception research areas

Unfortunately, it is not possible within the limitations of this article to reflect extensively upon the manner by which the circumference of the various areas could be determined. Cultures are inclined to close themselves off, create homogeneity and I think that therefore in practice the area of the territories of the first and the second area will be much greater than the space in which they overlap, but this does not diminish the importance of the space of the border situated between the first and the second area and in which cultural object 1 and cultural object 2 meet each other. There indeed is the territory where cultural objects become visible as a result of the paradoxical interaction on the one hand and where on the other hand they come under discussion; in which they identify with each other and at the same time exclude each other and where both objects engage in new relationships and interactions with the cultural object of world literature. On the other hand, it becomes clear that there is a form, a transparency which refers, without covering the areas of the individual cultural objects, to an area which is illuminated by all cultural objects.

It is tempting to think in this connection, analogously to Benjamin's 'pure language', or 'pure literature'. With all consequences of that... Immediately questions arise such as; is the relationship between original and translation on the one hand and with world literature on the other hand equally strong, is this relationship not 'broken' etc...? My illustration suggests at first sight also such connections. The area of world literature is, however, also transparent. It is a kind of ozone layer, a kind of smog of the other areas which obscures both our view of the literatures as well as of the space to which all literatures refer.

SPACE ON THE BORDER

Of course, interactions also play a role in the first and the second area. In what follows I would like to focus on that which happens in the third area, there where literatures identify themselves on the one hand and on the other hand present themselves constantly for discussion. Which questions can be asked there? How can we pose questions such as the following in a different manner: what has been translated? by whom? how and to what extent was it received? by whom? how did it get legitimated? which expectations and which social and cultural identity were presented for discussion (that is to say: how did it get contextualized)?

This implies that we should not in the first instance search for fractures, for that which from a historic or comparative point of view is determined or changed but that we also need to discuss the point of departure itself, the 'what'. We have to pay not only adequate attention to the manner in which the point of departure of the reception is identified. We will also have to have more attention for the interaction between source and target area, for the manner in which hierarchies and polarities are determined and discussed, and for the way in which the status of a literature in source and target area is determined as well as undermined.

This is, of course, a very complex enterprise which can probably only be realized in the context of larger research projects and/or with larger research groups. And even then it may not be possible to describe the phenomenon exhaustively but we may have to limit ourselves to certain areas of research. In what follows I will list, by way of illustration, a number of such areas of research with special attention for interactions. The order in which I do this is more or less arbitrary.

A first area of attention is that of the production. The interaction between production and reception is important. To what extent does the production (in a certain language area) determine the reception (in another language area) and vice versa? I think, for example, in this connection of Cees Nooteboom who wrote, it was thought, for the German language area and as a result has never been taken seriously as a Dutch author but seems to have undermined the status of authors such as Hermans and Reve, Mulisch and Claus.[37] Another example is that of Herman Heijermans who published some of his works first in Germany in order not to lose the revenue.[38] Another important factor in this context, in my opinion, is the 'paratextual contextualisation' of texts. It is clear that that is used strategically, just as texts are rewritten strategically in order to be more suitable for a different target group. Can we consider such texts still as the same texts (in a different language) or are they, at least, in part different texts?[39]

And with this I return to the translation. The interaction between original and translation (a free or faithful adaptation…) has already been extensively discussed. Now I would like to pose some additional questions and refer to a special case. What does the translation teach us about the original? Does it cause the original to be opened or closed? In this respect I also reflect on the discussion about the German translation of *Het Verdriet van België* [*The Sorrow of Belgium*], which appeared first with the title *Der Kummer von Flandern* [The Sorrow of Flanders]. Thus far the explanation for this was seen as a result of an increased German-Flanders perspective. But does it not also say something about the Flemish context? And what do we make of the author's statement, that he was not at all unhappy about the German title of his novel because the 'i's' and 'e's' of the original title could not be rendered accurately? What if the author Hugo Claus was first and foremost concerned about the sound?

An area which is difficult to investigate (and rather controversial) but which teaches us much about the paradoxical relationship between originals and their adaptations is that of influence. Influence is not a one-way traffic either. Just as Kafka's work – I mentioned this earlier – changed the work of a whole group of Dutch authors, so this event also influenced his own work. The reception of Kafka's work abroad has altered Kafka's image continually.[40] Influence – and the same is true of reception – is not the result of a single confrontation. Influence and reception are just like writing itself a process of 'becoming', to quote Deleuze.[41] On the other hand: influence is always connected to power. In this context we have to pose questions about the construction and the deconstruction of hierarchies, of oppositions such as 'small and great' and about the role of centre and periphery. Can a small literature be great and which conditions are then imperative? And is the reverse true too? Under which circumstances would a great literature become small? And what does this say, in principle, about the relationship between literatures?

Similar questions can and ought to be asked about the relationship between open and closed originals. To give an example: it is no accident that much is translated in countries such as Sweden and the Netherlands.[42] In small countries 'which have fallen behind in the international competition' examples from abroad have 'a particular attraction'.[43] But does that automatically mean that they are open? Or is this connected to a deceptive move, an attempt to protect the home market? 'What do I care whether I get translated or not', the Dutch author Harry Mulisch is reported as having said, 'I've been world-famous in Amsterdam for a long time'. Is the Netherlands really 'a metropolis of world format'?[44]

In the context of influence and power we also have to ponder the relationship with world literature or the 'world cultural system', to use a notion of Abram de Swaan. It is clear that the process of globalization has not passed by the cultural development. But how should we describe, or rather analyse, its consequences? In the middle of the 'nineties Johan Heilbron has, in this connection, foregrounded 'scope' and 'centrality' as criteria for analysis and he did not only come to the conclusion that larger language groups translate less than smaller groups but also that in the system of world languages there are several centre and several subdivisions and niches and that increasing marginalization does not necessarily result in a 'growing marginalization of peripheral or semi-peripheral language groups'.[45] One of the explanations proffered is the thought that 'international centres' would compete with each other 'in the discovery and transmission of cultural entities from elsewhere'.[46] I do have my doubts about this. I rather suspect that there are determining economic factors. However, that too could be investigated. I do think that, in any case, we have to pose the question whether we can with equal validity talk about a system of world literature as of a system of world languages, for how are we to determine the scope of a literature, and in that context finally its centrality?

Last but not least, a few remarks about the corpus. If the point of departure of research is, for example, a bibliography of Dutch prose in German translation, then the relationship between German and Dutch literature and the influence of Dutch literature in German translation on Dutch literature will naturally almost certainly not be considered. Limiting ourselves to prose will also obscure the relationship of translations with non-fictional texts, with cartoons, prose poems and theatre. And equally obscure, probably, would be the interaction between youth literature or for instance religious literature. The coherence suggested by the choice of a corpus is often a chimera and (mostly) serves to denote a particular area, defend particular positions or legitimate certain identities. If it is true that we are moving increasingly in the direction of a 'global cultural system', that cultures are 'in essence transgressive of borders',[47] then we will also have to modify those corpora which serve as point of departure for our research. And this, I think, signifies: no bibliographies any longer of just one literature in translation. And I leave aside here all that that implies: with or without poetry, drama, non-fiction, child- or youth literature. What we will need in any case are bibliographies of literatures in translations, possibly coupled, on the one hand, with national bibliographies, so that we can indeed arrive at something akin to a transnational bibliography of – simply said – texts from different countries with which links can be made with ever new connections between actors, institutions, publishers, mediators etc. Such a bibliography is not easily realized since precisely in the realm of the bibliography national biases are at work. However: he who closes the borders – and in this connection it is not only Abram de Swaan who makes sensible and clear statements – does no more than 'fight a retreat'.[48]

NOTES

1 See J. Derrida and P. Engelmann (eds.), *Von der Gastfreundschaft* (Vienna: Passagenverlag, 2001).

2 W. Benjamin, 'The Task of the Translator', in M. Bullock and M.W. Jennings (eds.), *Selected Writings Volume 1 – 1913-1926* (Cambridge: The Belknap Press, 2002), p. 255.

3 Benjamin, 'The Task of the Translator', p. 258.

4 'Het onuitgelegd oorspronkelijk'. A. Verwey, as quoted by C. Koster, 'Poëticale rancune: Albert Verwey en de vertaling van Shakespeares sonnetten', in *Neerlandica Extra Muros* 41 (2003), pp. 16-28; see also A. Verwey, 'Iets over vertalen' in *Nieuwe Rotterdamsche Courant*, 11 August 1923, pp. 15-16.

5 Benjamin, 'The Task of the Translator', p. 253.

6 Benjamin, 'The Task of the Translator', p. 253.

7 Benjamin, 'The Task of the Translator', p. 254, p. 260.

8 Benjamin, 'The Task of the Translator', pp. 254-261.

9 Benjamin, 'The Task of the Translator', p. 258.

10 Benjamin, 'The Task of the Translator', p. 262.

11 Benjamin, 'The Task of the Translator', p. 258.

12 Benjamin, 'The Task of the Translator', pp. 256-257.

13 Benjamin, 'The Task of the Translator', p. 261.

14 *Ten Oorlog* (Warwards) is an unparalleled theatre production from 1997, in which Tom Lanoye and Luk Perceval adapted and translated into Dutch eight plays of Shakespeare, resulting in a marathon production of ten hours of theatre. The production was highly acclaimed for the innovative use of language, among other aspects.

15 W. Shakespeare, *Richard II*, in OpenSourceShakespeare (http://www.opensourceshakespeare.org/views/plays/play_view.php?WorkID=richard2, 04-04-2016), pp. 2183-2186.

16 T. Lanoye and L. Perceval, *Ten oorlog* (Amsterdam: Prometheus, 1997), p. 59.

17 See also K. Reichert, *Die unendliche Aufgabe* (Munich/Vienna: Hanser, 2003), p. 207.

18 T. Naaijkens, *De slag om Shelley en andere essays over vertalen* (Nijmegen: Vantilt, 2002), p. 37.

19 'Het onuitgelegd oorspronkelijk'. A. Verwey, as quoted by C. Koster, 'Poëticale rancune', pp. 16-28; see also A. Verwey, 'Iets over vertalen', pp. 15-16.
20 W. Shakespeare, *Richard II*, pp. 3-8.
21 Lanoye and Perceval, *Ten oorlog*, p. 11.
22 Lanoye and Perceval, *Ten oorlog*, p. 11.
23 See also Reichert, *Die unendliche Aufgabe*, p. 204.
24 'Mijn drijfveer is niet expressie, [...] ik hoop door het persoonlijke heen het onpersoonlijke te raken. Dat is voor mij het allerhoogste proza [...] Met poëzie moet je vaak moeite doen om het te begrijpen, die aanspraak wordt op de lezer gemaakt. In mijn proza heb ik het omgekeerde voor. De lezer begrijpt niet het proza, maar het proza begrijpt de lezer. Ik wilde een tunnel maken en daarom onthoud ik de lezer de mogelijkheid om de hoofdpersoon op een bredere manier te begrijpen.' P. Aalbers, 'Thomas Rosenboom: De mensen thuis', in *NRC Handelsblad*, 16 February 1984.
25 'Shakespeare an Schlegel vorbeizuübersetzen, ist schwierig'. Reichert, *Die unendliche Aufgabe*, p. 200.
26 'reiche [...] Tradition'. Reichert, *Die unendliche Aufgabe*, p. 200.
27 'als fernes Echo'. Reichert, *Die unendliche Aufgabe*, p. 200.
29 T. Lanoye and L. Perceval, *Schlachten! nach den Rosenkriegen von William Shakespeare* (Hamburg: Deutsches Schauspielhaus, 1999), p. 9.
28 Lanoye and Perceval, *Ten oorlog*, p. 11.
30 Lanoye and Perceval, *Ten oorlog*, p. 17.
31 Shakespeare, *Richard II*, pp. 757-767.
32 W. Shakespeare, *Dramatische Werke*, translated by A.W. Schlegel and J.J. Eschenburg (Vienna: Pichler, 1810), vol. V, p. 153; see also Reichert, *Die unendliche Aufgabe*, p. 203.
33 Lanoye and Perceval, *Ten oorlog*, p. 34.
34 'ongenaakbare autoriteit'. R. Van den Broeck, *De vertaling als evidentie en paradox* (Antwerpen: Fantom, 1999), p. 36.
35 See also W. Müller-Funk, 'Kontext, Intertextualität und Übersetzung: Thesen und Hypothesen samt einer exemplarischen Analyse: Thomas Bernhards "Gehen", Barbi Marković "Ižlazenje", in H. Van Uffelen *et al.* (eds.), *Literatur im Kontext: Ein gegenseitiges Entbergen* (Vienna: Praesens, 2010), pp. 143-162.
36 'Ein Double, das keines ist'. W. Müller-Funk, 'Benjamin und der Translational Turn: Thesen und Anmerkungen', in P. Hanenberget *et al.* (eds.), *Rahmenwechsel Kulturwissenschaften* (Würzburg: Königshausen & Neumann, 2010), p. 42.
37 See J. Heilbron, 'Nederlandse vertalingen wereldwijd: Kleine landen en culturele mondialisering', in J. Heilbron, W. de Nooy and W. Tichelaar (eds.), *Waarin een klein land: Nederlandse cultuur in internationaal verband* (Amsterdam: Prometheus, 1995), p. 243.
38 S. Eenhuis, 'Die Fische werden schwer bezahlt', in *Jaarboek Letterkundig Museum* 4 (1995), p. 43.
39 D. De Geest and P. Verstraeten, 'Transnationaal, maar toch neerlandistiek?' in *Internationale Neerlandistiek* 48 (2010), p. 80.
40 See also H. Van Uffelen, 'Einfluss anders: Neue Perspektiven auf die Einflussforschung', in H. Van Uffelen and D. De Geest (eds.), *Niederländische Literaturwissenschaft auf neuen Wegen* (Vienna: Praesens Verlag, 2006), pp. 197-213.

41 H. Van Uffelen, 'Het verschil is een vorm van gelijk zijn: Kafka en de Nederlandse literatuur' in K. Van Heuckelom, D. De Bruyn and C. De Strycker (eds.), *Van Eeden tot heden* (Gent: Academia Press, 2013), pp. 135-149.
42 G. Deleuze, 'Die Literatur und das Leben', in G. Deleuze, *Kritik und Klinik* (Frankfurt a.M.: Suhrkamp, 2000), p. 11.
43 See Heilbron, 'Nederlandse vertalingen wereldwijd'.
44 'Voor kleine landen en voor landen die achterop zijn geraakt in de internationale concurrentie [...] hebben buitenlandse voorbeelden dikwijls een bijzondere aantrekkingskracht'. Heilbron, 'Nederlandse vertalingen wereldwijd', p. 209.
45 'een metropool van wereldformaat'. Abram de Swaan as quoted by J. Tollebeek, 'Alle cultuur is overspel', in *Ons Erfdeel* 35 (1992), p. 629.
46 'Toenemende internationalisering of mondialisering betekent niet noodzakelijkerwijs een groeiende marginalisering van perifere of semi-perifere taalgroepen'. Heilbron, 'Nederlandse vertalingen wereldwijd', p. 242.
47 'de internationale centra [wedijveren] met elkaar [...], niet alleen om de afzet van eigen cultuurgoederen, maar ook om de ontdekking en de doorvoer van cultuurgoederen van elders'. Heilbron, 'Nederlandse vertalingen wereldwijd', p. 242.
48 'Zowel de populaire als de hoge cultuur zijn in essentie grensoverschrijdend'. Tollebeek, 'Alle cultuur is overspel', p. 630.
49 'Wie de grenzen wil sluiten, levert een achterhoedegevecht'. Tollebeek, 'Alle cultuur is overspel', p. 630.

BIBLIOGRAPHY

Aalbers, P., 'Thomas Rosenboom: De mensen thuis', in *NRC Handelsblad*, 16 February 1984.

Benjamin, W., 'The Task of the Translator', in M. Bullock and M.W. Jennings (eds.), *Selected Writings Volume 1 – 1913-1926* (Cambridge: The Belknap Press, 2002), pp. 253-263.

De Geest, D. and P. Verstraeten, 'Transnationaal, maar toch neerlandistiek?', in *Internationale Neerlandistiek* 48 (2010), pp. 73-84.

Deleuze, G., 'Die Literatur und das Leben', in G. Deleuze, *Kritik und Klinik* (Frankfurt a.M.: Suhrkamp, 2000), pp. 11-17.

Derrida, J. and P. Engelmann (eds.), *Von der Gastfreundschaft* (Vienna: Passagenverlag, 2001).

Eenhuis, S., 'Die Fische werden schwer bezahlt', in *Jaarboek Letterkundig Museum* 4 (1995), pp. 37-60.

Heilbron, J., 'Nederlandse vertalingen wereldwijd: Kleine landen en culturele mondialisering', in J. Heilbron, W. de Nooy and W. Tichelaar (eds.), *Waarin een klein land: Nederlandse cultuur in internationaal verband* (Amsterdam: Prometheus, 1995), pp. 206-253.

Koster, C., 'Poëticale rancune: Albert Verwey en de vertaling van Shakespeares sonnetten', in *Neerlandica Extra Muros* 41 (2003), pp. 16-28.

Lanoye, T. and L. Perceval, *Ten oorlog* (Amsterdam: Prometheus, 1997).

Lanoye, T. and L. Perceval, *Schlachten! nach den Rosenkriegen von William Shakespeare* (Hamburg: Deutsches Schauspielhaus, 1999).

Müller-Funk, W., 'Benjamin und der Translational Turn: Thesen und Anmerkungen', in P. Hanenberg *et al.* (eds.), *Rahmenwechsel Kulturwissenschaften* (Würzburg: Königshausen & Neumann, 2010), pp. 33-47.

Müller-Funk, W., 'Kontext, Intertextualität und Übersetzung: Thesen und Hypothesen samt einer exemplarischen Analyse: Thomas Bernhards "Gehen", Barbi Marković "Ižlazenje"', in H. Van Uffelen *et al.* (eds.), *Literatur im Kontext: Ein gegenseitiges Entbergen* (Vienna: Praesens, 2010), pp. 143-162.

Naaijkens, T., *De slag om Shelley en andere essays over vertalen* (Nijmegen: Vantilt, 2002).

Reichert, K., *Die unendliche Aufgabe* (Munich/Vienna: Hanser, 2003).

Shakespeare, W., *Dramatische Werke*, translated by A.W. Schlegel and J.J. Eschenburg (Vienna: Pichler, 1810).

Shakespeare, W., *Richard II*, in *OpenSourceShakespeare*, http://www.opensourceshakespeare.org/views/plays/play_view.php?WorkID=richard2, 4 April 2016.

Tollebeek, J., 'Alle cultuur is overspel', in *Ons Erfdeel* 35 (1992), pp. 629-630.

Case Studies

CHAPTER 6

From Medieval Dutch Writer to French Film Character.

The Presence of Hadewijch in France from the Perspective of *Hadewijch*, the movie (2009)

Veerle Fraeters (Ruusbroec Institute, University of Antwerp, Belgium)

Outside of Dutch-speaking countries, contemporary creative responses to Dutch literature are, generally speaking, quite uncommon. Dressed in another language and deprived of the unconditional maternal love of the home culture, translated Dutch literature typically sits in the niche of 'foreign literature' without acquiring an independent, let alone a synergetic and generative, life in the host culture.[1] A notable exception is the middle Dutch author Hadewijch, a thirteenth-century mystic whose oeuvre consists of visions, songs (also called 'stanzaic poems'), mixed poems (also called 'rhymed letters') and prose letters, all of which meditate on one and the same theme: *minne* or mystical love. The oeuvre has come down to us in three fourteenth-century manuscripts that were made in monastic circles in the Duchy of Brabant. Hadewijch's writings did not make it to the printing press and, consequently, she was forgotten until, in 1830, the Leuven professor Franz Joseph Mone discovered two of the aforementioned manuscripts in the Royal (then: Burgundian) Library of Brussels. Puzzled by the odd mixture of religious and courtly themes and language, yet also struck by the obvious literary quality of the texts, philologists were quick to proclaim her passionate poetry on *minne* a gem at the dawn of national literary history. Hadewijch's work continues to hold a secure position in the national literary canon, both in the Netherlands and in Flanders.[2]

Despite intensive research, the historical identity of the author remains unknown. The hybridity of the oeuvre in which the sacred and the profane are fused, together with its radical conception of mystical love, allowed the creation, in the late nineteenth century, of two opposing images of Hadewijch: Catholic intellectuals regarded her as an orthodox nun while liberal scholars heralded her as a free-spirited heretic. During the interwar years, the Jesuit philologist Van Mierlo, the editor of the first critical edition of her oeuvre, created a consensus by placing Hadewijch's oeuvre in the context of the thirteenth-century 'lay religious' or 'beguine' women's movement. In this latter identity, Hadewijch has made her way into recent surveys of Christian mysticism, such as the prestigious multi-volume *The Presence of God. A History of Western Christian Mysticism* by the American theologian Bernard McGinn. Hadewijch is treated quite extensively in the fifth chapter, *Three Great Beguine Mystics* of the third volume 'The Flowering of Mysticism. Men and Women in the New Mysticism, 1200-1350'.[3]

This dual identity as Dutch literary author and medieval female mystic has led to a twofold modern creative reception. Generations of educated people in the Netherlands and Flanders have, at least superficially, been introduced to her mystical poetry at school or during their higher education. Consequently, from ca. 1900 until the present day, her texts have inspired Dutch and Flemish poets, and occasionally also composers, theatre directors and visual artists.[4] Outside the borders of the Dutch-language area, the reception of Hadewijch is based mainly on her identity as a mystic. A good example in case is the English translation of the *Complete Works* of Hadewijch, made by the Benedictine nun Columba Hart and published in 1980 by the American Catholic publishing house Paulist Press in the venerable series *Classics of Western Spirituality*. Her presence in this widespread series has not only generated 'Hadewijch studies' within the Anglo-Saxon academic fields of mystical theology (notably the interest in vernacular theology) and feminist history (pioneered by Carolyn Walker-Bynum), but also enabled some creative responses to her work, such as, e.g., the poem 'Hadewijch of Antwerp Convent Garden, 1233' by the Australian poet James Charlton, published in the volume *So much light* (2007).[5]

Of an entirely different scale than such modest poetic response is the film *Hadewijch*, directed by the French film director Bruno Dumont and released in 2009. As Dumont is an esteemed film director within the field of European art-house cinema, *Hadewijch* was presented at several major film festivals in the winter of 2009 – 2010. It was not as well received as his earlier films, however, and its distribution was relatively limited. Nonetheless, from the perspective of the transnational circulation of Dutch literature, this film presents a unique case of a large-scale creative response to a medieval Dutch author. In this article, I will trace the potentialities of this response and explore this topic from three angles. First, I will present a rough sketch of the reception history of Hadewijch in France: when and by who was she translated and which position does she hold in the French cultural field? This will shed light on the material presence of Hadewijch's works, as well as provide insight into her symbolic value in modern and postmodern French intellectual circles and culture. Second, I will focus on the making of the film. An analysis of interviews given by Dumont when *Hadewijch* was released will inform us about the motives the director explicitly gave for having made a film with this title. Third, I will study the intertextual presence of Hadewijch in the film. An analysis of the script reveals that Dumont integrated literal quotations from Hadewijch. This provides more information on the depth of the influence of Hadewijch's texts on the film. My threefold analysis will allow us to draw conclusions about the presence of this Middle Dutch mystic in postmodern French culture and her agency within it as expressed in the film *Hadewijch.*

HADEWIJCH IN MODERN FRANCE

Pour la Hadewijch en question, c'est comme pour sainte Thérèse – vous n'avez qu'à aller regarder à Rome la statue de Bernin pour comprendre tout de suite qu'elle jouit
(Lacan 1975)

In his article 'Mystique flamande' in de *Revue Encyclopédique* (Paris, 1897), the francophone Ghent writer Maurice Maeterlinck heralded Hadewijch to modern French intellectual audiences as one of the most remarkable and most powerful mystic minds.[6] Despite this strong appreciation by a prominent literary figure and proponent of mysticism, it took until after the Second World War for Hadewijch's work truly to become available to French readers. Although the article on Hadewijch in *Revue d'Ascétique et Mystique* (1926), written in the interwar period by the aforementioned scholar Jozef Van Mierlo, did prompt some translations of individual texts that appeared in a variety of mainly Belgian francophone magazines and anthologies, it was the edition *Hadewijch d'Anvers, Poèmes des béguines*, published in 1954 by Seuil (Paris), that secured Hadewijch's position within French culture.[7]

The translator of the Middle Dutch texts and knowledgeable author of the introduction and the closing essay, was the Carthusian monk Jean-Baptist (born Maximilien) Porion (1899-1987). Born in Wardrecques (Département Pas-de-Calais), Porion, a chemistry graduate, entered the Swiss charterhouse La Valsainte (canton Fribourg) in 1921. Throughout the twentieth century, La Valsainte functioned as an influential centre of Catholic monasticism that attracted intellectuals with an interest in spirituality. Dom Porion in particular, as author of the successful book *Amour et Silence, par un chartreux* (1950, still in print today), caused many French artists and thinkers to visit Valsainte, and some of them came to share his passion for what he called the 'Rheno-Flemish' mystical tradition of Hadewijch, Ruusbroec and Meister Eckhart.[8] His translation of a selection of Hadewijch's *Songs and Mixed Poems* in the aforementioned book (1954), as well as his translation of her Letters (Ad Solem, 1972) and Visions (O.E.I.L., 1987) have never been out of print. Porion's stature lend weight to Hadewijch's importance and stimulated the circulation of Hadewijch in the French cultural field in a multifaceted way. His pioneering work inspired others, predominantly within the Catholic field, to make new translations and include texts by Hadewijch in anthologies of Christian spirituality.[9] For many decades now, Hadewijch has been continually present in French bookshops, not so much on the shelves of translated Dutch literature, but on those of Christian spirituality.

From there, she penetrated a different area, that of psychoanalysis and poststructuralist philosophy. Indeed, influential postwar French thinkers, such as the psychoanalyst Jacques Lacan, the cultural historian Michel de Certeau and postmodern feminists such as Luce Irigaray and Julia Kristeva, have turned to mysticism, and more particularly to female mysticism, to find inspiration for their respective critiques on modern philosophy and culture.[10] Being an exponent of the larger group of 'medieval women mystics', Hadewijch has occasionally been named and quoted. Jacques Lacan referenced her in 1974 in his notorious seminaire XX 'Encore' in which he reflects on Bernini's statue 'Saint Theresia in ecstasy' and on the concept of '*jouissance*', a transgressive erotic fulfillment.[11] Hadewijch is also mentioned in two instances in the seminal monograph *La fable mystique I* (1982) by the Jesuit cultural historian and postmodernist Michel de Certeau.[12] Such references have made Hadewijch known to non-Catholic and even outspokenly atheist audiences with an interest in poststructuralist philosophy.

A comprehensive history of the reception of Hadewijch in modern France remains to be written. However, this brief survey may suffice to evoke the position that the Middle Dutch author held in the French cultural field at the moment when, in the first decade of the twenty-first century, the film director Bruno Dumont embarked on the project which he has alternatively described as 'a reflection on what spirituality can mean today' and 'a film about pure love'.[13] Beside much more famous and widely read medieval and early modern Christian mystics, such as Meister Eckhart, John of Ruusbroec, Therese of Avila and John of the Cross, Hadewijch's material presence was sufficiently strong and her aura sufficiently vibrant in France for her to be a possible source of inspiration. Let us now investigate why she, and no other, became Dumont's main source of inspiration for the protagonist of his film.

THE MAKING OF *HADEWIJCH*

Son ouvrage est très beau, très enflammé
et d'un érotisme étonnant pour une demoiselle chaste
(Dumont 2009)

Bruno Dumont was born in 1957 in Bailleul in French Flanders (Departement du Nord). Having failed the entrance exam of the renowned French film school Idhec (*Institut des hautes etudes cinématographiques)* in Paris, he opted for philosophy studies at Lille, and in 1982 became a teacher of philosophy and cultural history at the lycée in Hazebrouck near the Belgian border. Ten years later, his first short film *Paris* was released, and another five years later his first feature-length film *La vie de Jésus* was presented at the 1997 Cannes Film Festival where it was awarded the Camera d'Or. To date, Dumont has directed seven feature films, all of which combine social realism and avant-garde. Two of his films, *Humanité* (1999) and *Flandres* (2006), have been awarded the Cannes Grand Prix, i.e. the prize bestowed by the jury, and in 2008 he was selected to be a member of the Cannes jury. Dumont employs an unconventional film style characterized by long shots of people and landscapes, and by a minimal use of text and sound.[14] This style is driven by his belief in the supremacy of the visual over the verbal and the conceptual. In his view, image can reveal the embodied aspect of truth, an aspect neglected by Western philosophy because bodily instincts and emotions escape its traditional tools of thought and word. Dumont set his first films in his own region, the economically and socially deprived villages of rural French Flanders that exemplify the antipode of intellectual Paris and thus present the perfect scene for a raw representation of inarticulate characters bound by the instinctive forces of sex and violence.[15]

His fifth film, *Hadewijch* (2009), constituted an arresting rupture with his previous films. It was less well received and was not selected for the Cannes Festival, though it did win the FIPRESCI Prize (Prize of the International Critics for Special Presentation) at the 2009 Toronto Film Festival. Rather than a liminal figure from the forgotten North of France, the main character is an upper class Parisian university student, Céline, who, as a postulant in a Benedictine abbey, adopts the religious name Hadewijch. While Dumont's earlier films present a quasi-aimless sequence of confronting acts, *Hadewijch* presents an elliptical yet recountable narrative, featuring a protagonist who undergoes a transformation. Dumont's method of making films, though, has always remained the same. As a thinker using images as the privileged mode of 'thought', he starts from a specific philosophical question which he then attempts to 'make concrete' by means of a story that is minimally performed by expressive characters and images.[16] *Hadewijch* is the result of Dumont's research into the question 'What can religion mean in society today'?[17] Within the context of this article on the reception of Hadewijch, the specific question of interest to us is: Which factors induced Dumont to boil this broad philosophical question down to a story entitled *Hadewijch*?, or put differently: Why did Dumont use the Middle Dutch mystic Hadewijch, rather than another figure, to address this question? Interviews given in 2009 and 2010 to promote the film's release, shed light upon his motives, at least in so far as he shared them explicitly with the public.[18]

Before pursuing this further, I will present a summary of the plot. The structure of the film is characterized by sudden shifts in setting. The sequence of the various settings reveals a circular pattern: (1) the convent, (2) Paris, which is split into contrasting sites: the sumptuous parental home of Céline in Ile Saint-Louis at the heart of the city, and her Muslim friends' home in the peripheral suburbs, (3) an unidentified war-ravaged city in the Middle East, (4) Paris, (5) the convent. Céline is a young woman, the daughter of a busy politician and a depressed mother. In her youthful search for absolute love, she has become infatuated with Christ and has decided to live a life consecrated to virginity. She is a student of theology and during the summer vacation lives in a convent as a postulant. As she is totally obsessed with her love for the suffering Christ, the abbess rejects her on the basis of excessive asceticism and neglect of the virtue of humility. Feeling no bond with her bourgeois parents, she wanders the streets of Paris and meets Yassim, a young Muslim. He takes her to a site within the city where religion is as vibrantly alive as it is in her own interiority: the Islamic community in the *banlieue*. A friendship develops with Yassim and his brother Nassir, an Islam teacher. We see the three share meals and moments of prayer together, in mutual respect of each other's religion. Nassir talks to Céline about how loving God implies becoming an instrument of His justice. They go to the Middle East where Céline is brutally confronted with the destructiveness of war. Back in Paris, we first see the two standing silently in a metro driving away from the city centre, and then we see a bomb explode near the Place de la Concorde. Céline seeks refuge in the convent. She cries tears of remorse in front of the statue of the Dead Christ Entombed and then goes to the garden pond. When the police arrive, she wades into the pool, as if to drown herself. In the last shot we see the convent's handyman pulling her out of the water in an embrace.

Figure 1. Céline and the convent's handyman in an embrace (with permission of Contact Film, Arnhem)

This handyman is an important secondary character whose story is presented in short sequences that interlace the main story while mirroring it. His journey has a similar circular structure: we see him in the convent, in jail, in his mother's house and back in the convent. He is from a poor background, and intermittently spends time in prison, presumably for committing petty crime. In contrast to Céline's home, which is wealthy but devoid of affection, the handyman has a caring mother who loves him unconditionally. Throughout the movie, the anonymous handyman hardly ever speaks. In contrast to Céline, who is restlessly searching, he is serenity incarnate under all circumstances. His physiognomy and gaze evoke that of traditional representations of Christ. The final shot of the embrace in the pond puzzles film critics. Is it a flashback to the moment before Céline was sent away from the convent? Are we witnessing Céline's near- or after-death experience in which the union with Christ that she had searched for in vain on earth, at last takes place in an altered state of consciousness or in another dimension?[19] Dumont clarified his intention in interviews: Céline at the end of the film is 'reborn to human spirituality'.[20] She was looking for divine love but it is human love that is revealed to her: 'She at last discovers the sweet smell of a man.'[21]

As a declared Marxist and atheist, Dumont sees no value in religion: 'It is a relic of the past.'[22] He does believe, however, that the experience of grace is a basic human feeling that continues to exist in secular society. Therefore, in modern times, Dumont states, spirituality is not religious but human. It resides not in the convent or in virginity, but in the blissful encounter between human beings.[23] Given that in the past, mysticism was the locus where embodied spirituality was explored and expressed, it is only natural that Dumont turned to this tradition to find inspiration for the plot. In interviews, Dumont affirms that he already had a certain fascination for mysticism before he embarked on *Hadewijch*.[24] He shares the mystic philosophers' interest in truth that transcends reason. Also, their resorting to vision to communicate with God, and to imagery to confer the ineffable, resonates with his strategy to turn to film in order to treat philosophical questions. Moreover, Dumont shares with the mystics a fascination with the quest for pure love and its paradoxical bond with violence. We are all fighters, in our nature, born to struggle, Dumont says. And he continues: 'The mystic philosophers say that struggle is necessary for us to evolve.'[25]

It is when talking about his three chosen themes – i.e. embodied spirituality; absolute love and its interconnectedness with violence; intuitive vision as means of accessing truth – that Dumont at times *spontaneously* brings up Hadewijch in interviews. As he was looking for a protagonist who is preoccupied with 'pure love', Hadewijch's texts, and their obsessive focus on *minne*, are eminently suited as a source of inspiration.[26] Furthermore, Dumont mentions that her texts are permeated with courtly metaphors and thus blur the boundary between the divine and the profane, between the spiritual and the physical. Dumont frequently mentions that Hadewijch refers to *jouissance*.[27] Her mystical experience of union with the divine, he says, is phrased as a bodily experience: 'Hadewijch in her writings speaks of direct contact with the body of Christ and the pleasure she takes in his body.'[28] In addition, he stresses that the intertwining of love and violence is a key motif in her work: '"The sweetest thing about love is its violence" is a literal quote from Hadewijch's writings.'[29] Finally, Hadewijch is a visionary, a quality that Dumont has transferred to the characters of Céline and Nassir: 'They are visionaries [...] they can see what to others is invisible and interior.'[30]

In addition to the themes in her work, Dumont was also inspired by the supposed fact that Hadewijch was a beguine.[31] In some of the interviews Dumont explains that the historical beguines had a strained relationship with the Church because of their views on true poverty. Also, they did not retreat into a secluded convent. Rather, they lived a spiritual life while remaining lay persons living in the world. They thus created a hybrid zone in which the profane and the sacred were fused. In this regard, the beguine life represents what Dumont envisions as the paradigm of modern spirituality, and he obviously uses some of the characteristics of the historical beguine movement to furnish his minimal plot and to put flesh on the main character. Céline/Hadewijch being expelled from the convent and consequently having to quest for pure love in the everyday life of the city echoes the beguines opting for a lay religious life in the world. And Céline's fundamental indifference to the affluence and social prestige of her bourgeois parents reverberates with the beguine's turning away from the wealth of the medieval Church and opting for a life of true poverty.

When asked how he learned about Hadewijch in the first place, Dumont merely says that he 'stumbled upon her' when he became interested in mystical philosophy: 'When I was doing research on women mystics for this film, I fell upon Hadewijch, a great mystic and theologian who influenced, among others, John of Ruusbroec.'[32] From this statement it can be deduced that it was by reading about the famous Flemish mystic John of Ruusbroec (d. 1381), that Dumont discovered the less well-known Hadewijch. When asked explicitly, in an interview with the Dutch journalist Peter de Bruijn, whether his own French-Flemish identity makes him feel particularly close to Hadewijch, Dumont granted that this is indeed the case: 'I have a natural affinity with Flanders. Therefore it was natural for me to fall upon Hadewijch the moment I became interested in mysticism.'[33]

As his films are essentially philosophical reflections, Dumont obviously had no intention whatsoever to portray the historical author or to do justice to her writings. On the contrary, he straightforwardly states that he did not mean 'to serve an ancient text that nobody cares for today', but rather 'to search for contemporary spirituality'.[34] He insists that Céline/Hadewijch is to be seen, not as a reference to the historical figure, but as 'a metaphor for our interiority' and 'for the pure love to which we all aspire'.[35] On the other hand, Dumont has affirmed that he was touched by Hadewijch's writings to the degree that they impelled him to choose a young woman in pursuit of pure love as a protagonist.

> Her work is in the spirit of courtly love. It is very beautiful, very passionate and surprisingly erotic for a young woman committed to virginity. Its ardor interested me. So I decided to write a story about a young woman, and I set out to make the script.[36]

The film plot presented above, together with Dumont's peritextual statements, clearly reveals that his image of the medieval beguines in general and of Hadewijch in particular have had a certain influence on the storyline and the contours of the protagonist. However, as the movie is an autonomous piece of art that, apart from its title, contains no explicit references to the historical figure whatsoever, this influence remains elusive. I will now analyze the script from an intertextual perspective. Indeed, Dumont has integrated several unreferenced Hadewijch quotes at significant moments in the narrative. While presenting this intertext, I will also pay attention to the editions and translations used by Dumont, which will deepen our understanding of the material presence of Hadewijch in France addressed above.

HADEWIJCH'S TEXT IN *HADEWIJCH*

Et je vis celui que je cherchais
(Hadewijch, Vision 6)

For the ordinary viewer, the only explicit reference to Hadewijch is the – for a non-Dutch audience enigmatic and hardly pronounceable – film title, which is also the religious name of the main character, Céline.[37] An analysis of the script, however, reveals that four unreferenced Hadewijch quotations are used in the film.[38] Given the fact that Dumont, in line with his cinematographic philosophy, uses word and sound extremely sparingly, these intertextual references are saturated with meaning, all the more so because they are deployed at symbolic places and moments. All three quotations are uttered in traditional religious settings and function as prayer. The opening words of the movie consist of a lengthy quotation from Vision 6, which is read aloud in the convent's refectory while the community of nuns is eating. After the abbess has told her she has to leave the convent, Céline seeks solace at the statue of Christ Entombed and mutters the first stanza of Song 42.

Back in Paris, while aimlessly roaming the city, Céline enters a church and prays before a crucifix using lines from Song 21. The very last words of the movie are spoken, or rather mumbled, by Céline praying before Christ Entombed in the convent, using lines from Song 44. Within the context of this article I cannot provide a thorough analysis of the multilayered meaning these Hadewijch passages bring into the film – I intend to provide it elsewhere. Here, I limit myself to an identification of the quotations and of the editions used by Dumont. After having presented the four literal quotations, I will dwell upon a fifth intertextual reference that is not a quotation *stricto sensu* but rather a visual citation of a passage from Hadewijch's seventh Vision.

For the textual selections from the Songs, Dumont made use of the translation by Rose Vande Plas, *Hadewijch. Poèmes strophiques*, first printed in 1984 by the Catholic publishing house Téqui, Paris. In order to accommodate the devotional reader, Vande Plas opted for a thematic organization and distributed the 45 poems over seven sections illuminating specific moments within the quest for mystical love. This organization allowed Dumont easily to find textual fragments that expressed the motifs with which he wanted to weave his parable on the transition from religious to human spirituality: absolute love, embodied love, the interconnectedness between love and violence. Dumont has selected quotes from three different sections. The first quotation of the Songs used in the film is taken from Section 4 'Le combat pour l'amour' [The combat for Love]. After the abbess tells her that she has to leave the convent, Céline, deeply distressed, rushes to her favorite prayer corner in the convent yard, which is a barred cave representing Christ's grave, with a statue of Christ Entombed. There she mumbles the first stanza of Song 42 in prayer.[39] While most of Hadewijch's songs are set in early spring, thus symbolically evoking the promise of eternal renewal by Love, this song atypically is set in winter and speaks of the lover's despair. The quoted lines quintessentially express Céline's feelings of utter abandonment:

> The sad season has come
> Outdoors, but much more in the heart.
> That you, Beloved, have left us in the lurch,
> Is for us an insuperable grief.
> That good, which you gave in times past,
> Through strange vicissitudes escapes us,
> Together with your rich teaching
> And the knowledge that you are excellent.[40]

The second citation is taken from section 7 'Le paradoxe de l'amour: la souffrance la plus cruelle est la plus haute joie existentielle' [The paradox of love: the cruelest suffering is the highest joy]. Dumont selected the four final lines of the first stanza of Song 21 as the prayer uttered by Céline in a church in Paris. After having listened to a rehearsal by a musical ensemble of Bach's *Gib mir meinen Jesum wieder*, Céline prays in front of the crucifix with the following words:

> I greet you, Love, with undivided love,
> And I am brave and daring.
> I will yet conquer your power,
> Or I will lose myself in the attempt.[41]

These lines indeed express in a succinct way the mystical motifs that Dumont used in his film: in the poem Christ is addressed, not as Christ, but as love; the 'I' is ready to fight unto death, not only *for*, but also *with* love. Given their place within the narrative, the lines can be read as prophetic: soon Céline will join Nassir to the East to become a 'fighter', and at the end of the movie she will be ready to die.

The last quotation from Songs are the final spoken words of the film. Before the moment when she wades into the water, Céline once more visits her favorite praying corner at the convent, the statue of Christ Entombed. There she mutters the following words, which are in fact the last stanza of Song 44:

> Alas, Love, temper your mighty power!
> You have the days, and I the nights.
> Why, when you force me to go out hunting for you,
> Do you flee so far ahead of me?
> You make me pay such a tribute,
> I shudder that ever I was born a human being.[42]

Dumont selected Céline's final words, also the final ones of the script, from section 6 in the edition by Vande Plas on '*Orewoet.* L'Ardeur fougueuse de l'amour' [*Orewoet*, tempestuous ardor of love]. The Middle Dutch term 'orewoet' is an iconic Hadewijch term, which, unlike any other, captures the simultaneity of desire and pain that constitutes the transgressive love that Dumont intends to visualize in his film. In her pursuit for Christ, Céline has embraced everything, including violence. As she has not found him, she is now ready to give up and sacrifice herself. She wades into the pond and we see her disappear under the water's surface. At that point, her abysmal act of self-sacrifice transmogrifies into one of baptismal renewal. The quest for divine love ends in the discovery of human love, symbolized by the blissful embrace of the handyman, her saviour.

The script not only closes with lines from Hadewijch, it also opens with her text. After more than five minutes without speech, the very first words that resound in the movie are a fragment of Vision 6 read out in the refectory.

Figure 2. Lectio at the refectory (with permission of Contact Film, Arnhem)

We see a nun reading from a booklet which, given the format and the textual rendition in the script, can be identified as the translation by Georgette Epiney-Burgard, published in 2000 by Ad Solem in Geneva. As it is a lengthy quotation, I will just provide a paraphrase.[43] The visionary 'I', while in contemplative ecstasy, hears Christ's voice speak with an 'unheard' voice: 'Sich wie ic ben' [See who I am].[44] He then reveals his 'face' in the form of the final judgment at the end of time when every soul is judged and given its predestined seat in heaven or in hell. The 'I' sees that there are different ways in which a soul can, during its earthly life, stay or not stay connected to its allotted seat in eternity: some drift away from their spiritual destiny and reconnect to it later in life; others lose connection and never regain it; others still throughout their lives keep seeking in despair while actually, from a spiritual perspective, they have never lost it; the last category has a conscious connection to their eternal core from birth and stays connected throughout their entire lives. This rather abstract image of distinctive salvific paths then transforms into the more familiar image of Christ in Judgment. More particularly, the 'I' sees the open arms and hands that characterize this iconographic type. In his right hand she sees heaven with all the souls belonging there, in his left hand she sees the sword with which the doomed are slain in hell. At this point, the quotation ends.

I cannot enter into the rich variety of ways in which this text functions as a frame for the narrative of the movie. Suffice it to say that, given its position at the opening of the film, its location in the convent, and its theme of God as Judge, this fragment represents the alpha point of religious spirituality from which Céline's story begins. The final shot of her embrace with the handyman in the pond then functions as the omega point: it brings pre-modern religion to a close and discloses a new era in which human spirituality prevails. Just like the opening sequence of the film, the last sequence at the pond is without speech. For those, however, who are familiar with Hadewijch's oeuvre, the embrace evokes a very specific text, the seventh Vision. Elsewhere I have argued that, within the collected Visions, Vision 7 is an exceptional text in that it is the only one to report, not an ecstatic contemplative experience of God in a meditative state of consciousness, but rather a non-ecstatic, corporeal encounter with Christ who 'appears' to the 'I' in bodily form and, consequently, is experienced by her through her corporeal senses.[45] My preliminary research on modern Hadewijch reception indicates that, after World War II, scholars as well as non-academic readers strongly privileged this one text within Hadewijch's oeuvre that describes a somatic encounter with God.[46] The phrase 'ende [hi] nam me altemale in sine arme ende dwanc me ane hem ende al die lede die ik hadde ghevoelden der siere in al hare ghenoeghen' [[he] took me in his arms, and pressed me to him; and all my members felt his in full felicity] is now undoubtedly the most well-known sentence from Hadewijch.[47] Lacan must have thought of Vision 7 when fleetingly mentioning Hadewijch's name whilst speaking of *jouissance*. For Dumont, this very passage from the seventh Vision must have inspired him to shape the final shot of his film *Hadewijch*.

While the peritextual analysis of interviews given by Dumont revealed that Hadewijch's supposed beguine identity together with the central motifs of her work were of some influence for the creation of the protagonist and the storyline, the intertextual analysis reveals a direct use of Hadewijch's writings at the level of the script. Together, the three literal Hadewijch quotations and the one visual quote selected by Dumont constitute the very crux of the storyline. Dumont indeed did not 'serve a text that nobody cares for today', yet he himself did care for the text to the degree that he allowed it to serve him, not only at the level of inspiration, but also at the level of narration, thus letting Hadewijch's medieval writings have a truly formative impact on his visual reflection on what spirituality means today. In fact, Dumont's parable on the transition from religious to human spirituality is deeply informed by the content as well as the sequence of two of Hadewijch's visions, Vision 6 and 7, which therefore can be seen as the palimpsest of *Hadewijch*, the movie.

CONCLUSION

In conclusion, I list the factors that have facilitated Hadewijch's synergetic agency within the contemporary French cultural sphere as expressed in the creative response to her work by Bruno Dumont. First, Hadewijch is not only a distinguished author belonging to the Dutch and Flemish literary canon, she also is a mystic. This latter identity has stimulated the transnational circulation of her work. Second, the person who translated Hadewijch into French, the Carthusian monk Dom Porion, was an influential figure in the post-war French cultural field. His status secured a continuous material presence of Hadewijch's writing in the form of translations and anthologies published mainly in the Catholic field. This textual presence enabled Hadewijch to share in the symbolic capital that medieval mysticism in general, and the female mystics in particular, came to enjoy, from the seventies onwards, in the field of French post-structuralist philosophy and psychoanalysis, fields that the filmmaker Dumont, being a philosopher by formation, is familiar with, as is attested to by his specific interest in *jouissance*. Last but not least, the two key Hadewijch mediators in post-World War II French culture, translator Porion and filmmaker Dumont, happen originally to be from the North of France, particularly the region of French Flanders.[48] However different their perspectives on the topic may be, the Carthusian monk and the Marxist philosopher share a deep interest in mysticism, and it is this fascination with mysticism in general that must be considered the prime motive for their involvement with mystical authors such as Hadewijch. Yet, as for the extraordinary depth and breadth of their engaged involvement, as translator and filmmaker, particularly with the 'Flemish' mystic Hadewijch, we can safely assume that regional affinity functioned as a forceful vector.

NOTES

1 The terms 'niche' and 'synergia' are borrowed from Zajac's typology of relationships between translated literature and host cultural systems, as presented in H. Van Uffelen, 'Toeval dat na de gebeurtenis noodzaak bleek: Over de onbeschrijflijke onbeschrijfbaarheid van de Nederlandse literatuur in het buitenland', in P. Broomans (ed.), *Object: Nederlandse literatuur in het buitenland, methode: onbekend* (Groningen: Barkhuis, 2006), pp. 15-17.

2 On Hadewijch, see P. Mommaers and E. Dutton, *Hadewijch: Writer – Beguine – Love Mystic* (Leuven: Peeters, 2004); F. van Oostrom, *Stemmen op schrift: Geschiedenis van de Nederlandse literatuur vanaf het begin tot 1300* (Amsterdam: Bert Bakker, 2006), pp. 419-459. Hadewijch in the literary canon in the Netherlands: R. van Stipriaan (ed.), 'De Nederlandse klassieken anno 2002: Een enquête naar de canon onder de leden van de Maatschappij der Nederlandse Letterkunde', in *Digitale Bibliotheek voor de Nederlandse Letteren*, June 2002; in Flanders: E. Vlaminck (ed.), *De canon: De 50+1 mooiste literaire werken uit de Nederlanden* (Antwerpen: KANTL and Uitgeverij Vrijdag, 2015), pp. 20-31.

3 B. McGinn, *The Flowering of Mysticism: Men and Women in the New Mysticism 1200-1350* (New York: Crossroad Publishing, 1989), pp. 200-222.

4 As yet there is no exhaustive inventory. For a preliminary survey of traces of Hadewijch in modern Dutch literature, see H. Groenewegen, 'Een nachtboot vol glinsterende athleten', in *Revolver* 135 (34/2, 2007), pp. 81-114. For some examples of Hadewijch as source of inspiration for modern artists in Belgium and the Netherlands, see: https://www.kb.nl/themas/nederlandse-poezie/dichters-uit-het-verleden/hadewijch-1200-1250/hadewijch-bij-moderne-kunstenaars (accessed 18 January 2016).

5 On the Anglo-Saxon scholarly reception of Hadewijch after 1980, see V. Fraeters, 'Foreword', in Mommaers and Dutton, *Hadewijch*, pp. V-XII. An inventory of international creative responses to Hadewijch does not yet exist.

6 M. Maeterlinck, 'La Mystique Flamande', in *Revue Encyclopédique Larousse* 7 (1897), p. 627: 'Cette femme est parmi les esprits mystiques de cette époque l'un des plus curieux et des plus puissants.'

7 F. Willaert, 'II. Hadewijch', in G.J. Lewis, *Bibliographie zur deutschen Frauenmystik des Mittelalters* (Berlin: Erich Schmidt Verlag, 1989), pp. 358-360, nos. 2911, 2912, 2914, 2921, 2927.

8 On Porion, see N. Nabert (ed.), *Dom Jean-Baptiste Porion: Lettres et écrits spirituels* (Paris: Beauchesne, 2011), 'Introduction'.

9 Although no French publisher has hitherto undertaken a project similar to the English 'Hadewijch, *Complete Works*' (Mahwah: Paulist Press, 1980), all her texts have been translated into French except for Mixed Poem 14. My unpublished list of French translations, including fragments, by Hadewijch shows 33 titles (I thank Daniël Cunin for kindly providing me his unpublished list of French Hadewijch translations). For French translations before 1987, see the French entries in Willaert, 'Hadewijch', pp. 354-368: 2. Textausgaben.

10 The history of the appropriation of certain forms of Christian mysticism by twentieth-century French intellectuals is critically discussed in A. Hollywood, *Sensible Ecstacy: Mysticism, Sexual Difference, and the Demands of History* (Chicago: Chicago University Press, 1999). As to, specifically, French postmodern feminists and medieval women mystics, see the essays by Luce Irigaray and Julia Kristeva in P. Vandenbroeck, *Le jardin clos de l'âme: l'Imaginaire des religieuses dans les Pays-Bas du Sud, depuis le 13e siècle* (Brussels: Société des Expositions Palais des Beaux-Arts de Bruxelles, 1994), pp. 155-178.

11 J. Lacan, *Le Séminaire, Livre XX : Encore 1972-1973* (Paris: Seuil, 1975), p. 97.

12 M. de Certeau, *La fable mystique (XVIe-XVIIe siècle), tome I* (Paris: Gallimard, 1982), p. 29 and 140.

13 M. Guillen, 'Raven in the Rain: A Conversation with Bruno Dumont', in *Notebook. Digital Magazine of International Cinema and Film Culture*, 30 September 2009, https://mubi.com/notebook/posts/raven-in-the-rain-a-conversation-with-bruno-dumont (accessed 22 January 2016); N. Azalbert and S. Delorme, 'Un éveil: Entretien avec Bruno Dumont', in *Cahiers du Cinéma* 650 (2009), p. 41, and L. Danvers, *Entretien avec Bruno Dumont*, in *Hadewijch: Een film van Bruno Dumont* [DVD] (Arnhem: Contact Film, 2009/2010).

14 On Dumont's transcendental or 'Bressonian' visual style, see P. Verstraten, 'Mesmerized by Mysticism: the Transcendental Style of Bruno Dumont's Hadewijch', in *Journal of Dutch Literature* 2 (2011), pp. 27-45.

15 D. Hughes, 'Bruno Dumont's Bodies', in *Senses of Cinema* 19 (2002), http://sensesofcinema.com/2002/feature-articles/dumont_bodies/ (accessed 22 January 2016).

16 M. Naafs, '"Films zijn toverspreuken": Bruno Dumont over Hadewijch', in *De Filmkrant* 320 (2010), http://www.filmkrant.nl/TS_april_2010/12969 (accessed 22 January 2016).

17 Guillen, 'Raven in the Rain'.

18 The corpus consists of seven interviews: six interviews given during the film festivals of San Sebastian, Toronto, New York and Rotterdam and published in French, English and Dutch film magazines and cultural media, and a long interview included as 'extra' on the

DVD of the film released by Contact film. I have focused exclusively on passages relevant to Hadewijch reception. Consequently, the controversy provoked by Dumont's nonjudgmental portrayal of Muslim terrorism in the film, an important topic in interviews as well as in reviews, remains unaddressed in this article.

19 De Bruijn, 'Jezus is haar vent', p. 4; D. Verbeke, 'Een queeste naar de absolute minne: De film "Hadewijch" van Bruno Dumont', in *De Franse Nederlanden* 35 (2010), p. 207.

20 Anon., 'Bruno Dumont, Hadewijch', in *Filmmaker Magazine Blog of Independent Film,* 19 September 2009.

21 'Elle découvre enfin la douce odeur d'un homme.' (English translation VF) Azalbert and Delorme, 'Un éveil', p. 44.

22 Guillen, 'Raven in the Rain'.

23 Dumont on being atheist and believer in 'human spirituality': Danvers, *Entretien avec Bruno Dumont*; Azalbert and Delorme, 'Un éveil', p. 41; *Filmmaker* 2009, 'Bruno Dumont, Hadewijch'; Sartor, 'Bruno Dumont over Hadewijch', p. 19; Guillen, 'Raven in the Rain'.

24 Dumont on his interest in mysticism and the parallels with film: Danvers, *Entretien avec Bruno Dumont*; Guillen, 'Raven in the Rain'; *Filmmaker* 2009, 'Bruno Dumont, Hadewijch'; De Bruijn, 'Jezus is haar vent'; Sartor, 'Bruno Dumont over Hadewijch'; Naafs, 'Films zijn toverspreuken'.

25 Anon., 'Bruno Dumont, Hadewijch'.

26 Azalbert and Delorme, 'Un éveil', p. 41: 'J'avais besoin de quelque chose plus fort qu'une simple histoire d'amour entre deux personnes. [...] je suis tombé sur Hadewijch d'Anvers. Là j'ai trouvé l'amour tel que je l'imaginais.' (I needed something stronger than the simple love story between two people. [...] I stumbled upon Hadewijch of Antwerp and that's where I found the kind of love I was looking for; translation VF)

27 E.g. Azalbert and Delorme, 'Un éveil', p. 42: 'Hadewijch parle de la jouissance.'

28 Guillen,'Raven in the Rain'. See also De Bruijn, 'Jezus is haar vent' and I. Schelstrate, '*Hadewijch* verbijstert Britten', in *De Standaard* 22 October 2009, p. 38.

29 Guillen,'Raven in the Rain'. See also De Bruijn, 'Jezus is haar vent'; Sartor, 'Bruno Dumont over Hadewijch', p. 19.

30 Guillen,'Raven in the Rain'.

31 Dumont elaborates on Hadewijch and the beguine movement in Azalbert and Delorme, 'Un éveil', p. 41 and 45.

32 'Toen ik mystieke dichteressen zocht voor deze film, kwam ik puur toevallig bij Hadewijch uit, omdat ze een grote mystica en theologe was, die onder anderen Jan van Ruusbroec inspireerde.' (English translation VF) Schelstrate, '*Hadewijch* verbijstert Britten'. See also Azalbert and Delorme, 'Un éveil', n. 26.

33 'Ik heb een natuurlijke band met Vlaanderen. Daarom was het voor mij vanzelfsprekend dat ik bij Hadewijch uitkwam, toen ik geïnteresseerd raakte in mystiek.' (English translation VF) De Bruijn, 'Jezus is haar vent'.

34 Azalbert and Delorme, 'Un éveil', p. 41: 'Ça me paraissait beaucoup plus intéressant de trouver la spiritualité aujourd'hui que de servir un texte ancien dont on se fout un peu. Il s'agissait de trouver dans la *jeunesse* une expression de l'amour absolu, qui chacun peut avoir en soi et qu'elle avait en elle.'

35 Sartor, 'Bruno Dumont over Hadewijch', p. 18: 'Hadewijch is de incarnatie van onze innerlijkheid. [...] Zij is een metafoor.'

36 'Son ouvrage à elle est dans l'esprit de l'amour courtois. C'est très beau, très enflammé et d'un érotisme étonnant pour une demoiselle chaste. Il y avait une chaleur qui m'intéressait beaucoup. Donc je suis parti vers le récit d'une jeune femme d'aujourd'hui, et j'ai écrit le scénario.' (English translation VF) Azalbert and Delorme, 'Un éveil', p. 41.

37 The name 'Hadewijch' is articulated in the movie just two times. Before going to the Middle East, Céline walks with Nassir to the convent and says to him: 'Ici je suis né, Hadewijch' (It is here that I am born Hadewijch). At the very end of the movie, when the police arrive at the convent, one of the nuns goes to find her while calling her name 'Hadewijch'.

38 I thank Marjolein Tevel, translator of the Dutch subtitles for the film in the Netherlands, for giving me the text of the French script (mail dd. 10 April 2014). Five years earlier, in November 2009, she had contacted Frank Willaert (University of Antwerp) and myself, requesting our assistance for the translation of a few passages that she presumed to be quotes from Hadewijch. It is on that occasion that the three Hadewijch quotations were identified. Afterwards I provided this information concerning the Hadewijch intertext to Peter Verstraten for his article 'Mesmerized by Mysticism'.

39 The words of this prayer are not spelled out in the script; they are merely referred to as 'chuchotement' (whispering). In the movie they are barely audible. I thank the French film critic Ludovic Maubreuil for forwarding me the few phrases and words that he was able to discern (mail dd. 27 April 16). This allowed me to identify the prayer as the first stanza of Song 42.

40 Vande Plas, *Hadewijch d'Amour*, p. 119. 'Voice venu l'hiver et sa mélancholie; / Mais plus sombre encore Est la tristess de nos coeurs. / Que tu sois, Bien-Aimé, si loin de nous, / Est une douleur qui n'a pas de guérison. / Les bienfaits dont jadis tu nous as comblés, / Par caprice du sort, / Nous sont aujourd'hui refusés/ Ainsi que la richesse de ta parole, / Et la parfaite beauté que tu es en toi-même' (translation Hart, *Hadewijch: The Complete Works*, p. 248).

41 R. Vande Plas (trans.), *Hadewijch d'Amour. Amour est tout: Poèmes strophiques* (Paris: Téqui, 1984), p. 250. Je te salue amour. / Je suis impertinente et fière. / Ta puissance je veux la vaincre. / Au risque de succomber et mourir (translation C. Hart, *Hadewijch: The Complete Works* (Mahwah: Paulist Press, 1980), p. 183).

42 Vande Plas, *Hadewijch d'Amour*, p. 208. Amour, par la puissance sans nom, sois-moi clément. / Tu es la lumière du jour, et mes jours sont des nuits. / Pourquoi? Pourquoi me forces-tu à te poursuivre sans cesse? / Pourquoi m'échappes-tu? De plus en plus loin… / Tu me fais payer, Amour, un prix trop haut… / Malheur… Malheur… Malheur à moi d'être une créature humaine. (translation Hart, *Hadewijch: The Complete Works*, p. 256).

43 The passage is on p. 47 in G. Epiney-Burgard (trans.), *Hadewijch d'Anvers: Les visions* (Geneva: Ad Solem, 2000). English version: C. Hart, *Hadewijch: The Complete Works*, pp. 278-280.

44 F. Willaert (ed.), *Hadewijch: Visioenen* (Amsterdam: Prometheus/Bert Bakker, 1996), p. 74; English translation C. Hart, *Hadewijch: The Complete Works*, p. 278.

45 V. Fraeters, 'The Mystic's *sensorium*: Modes of Perceiving and Knowing God in Hadewijch's Visions', in Rob Faesen (ed.), *Mystical Anthropology in the Low Countries* (Abingdon: Routledge, 2016), p. 29.

46 An overview of instances in Fraeters,'The mystic's *sensorium*', n. 14.
47 Willaert, *Hadewijch: Visioenen*, p. 82; Hart, *Hadewijch: The Complete Works*, p. 281.
48 On Porion and his French Flemish background see W. Corsmit, 'Pater Porion: Een Frans-Vlaamse Liefde Voor Hadewijch', in *Komitee voor Frans-Vlaanderen (KVF)-Mededelingen* 23: 3 (1995). For Dumont and his French Flemish background, see his statements on this topic herein, and Verbeke, 'Een queeste naar de absolute minne'.

BIBLIOGRAPHY

Anon., 'Bruno Dumont, Hadewijch', in *Filmmaker Magazine Blog of Independent Film*, 19 September 2009, http://filmmakermagazine.com/16909-bruno-dumont-hadewijch/.

Azalbert, N. and S. Delorme, 'Un éveil: Entretien avec Bruno Dumont', in *Cahiers du Cinéma* 650, November 2009, pp. 41-45.

Broomans, P. (ed.), *Object: Nederlandse literatuur in het buitenland, methode: onbekend* (Groningen: Barkhuis, 2006).

Charlton, J., *So Much Light* (Lauderdale: Pardolete Press, 2007).

Corsmit, W., 'Pater Porion: Een Frans-Vlaamse liefde voor Hadewijch', in *Komitee voor Frans-Vlaanderen (KVF)-Mededelingen* 23: 3 (1995), pp. 13-15.

Danvers, L., 'Entretien avec Bruno Dumont', in *Hadewijch: Een film van Bruno Dumont* [DVD] (Arnhem: Contact Film, 2009/2010).

De Bruijn, P., '"Jezus is haar vent". Bruno Dumont over zijn film Hadewijch', in *NRC Handelsblad, Cultureel supplement*, 27 January 2010, p. 4.

De Certeau, M., *La fable mystique (XVI*[e]*-XVII*[e] *siècle)*, tome I (Paris: Gallimard, 1982).

Epiney-Burgard, G. (trans.), *Hadewijch d'Anvers, Les visions* (Geneva: Ad Solem, 2000).

Fraeters, V., 'The Mystic's *Sensorium*. Modes of Perceiving and Knowing God in Hadewijch's *Visions*', in Rob Faesen (ed.), *Mystical Anthropology in the Low Countries* (Abingdon: Routledge, 2016), pp. 28-40.

Groenewegen, H., 'Een nachtboot vol glinsterende athleten', in *Revolver* 34: 2 (2007), pp. 81-114.

Guillen, M., 'Raven in the Rain: A Conversation with Bruno Dumont', in *Notebook: Digital Magazine of International Cinema and Film Culture*, 30 September 2009, https://mubi.com/notebook/posts/raven-in-the-rain-a-conversation-with-bruno-dumont.

Hart, C., O.S.B. (trans.), *Hadewijch, The Complete Works*, Preface by Paul Mommaers (Mahwah: Paulist Press, 1980).

Hollywood, A., *Sensible Ecstacy: Mysticism, Sexual Difference, and the Demands of History* (Chicago: Chicago University Press, 1999).

Hughes, D., 'Bruno Dumont's Bodies', in *Senses of Cinema* 19, March 2002, http://sensesofcinema.com/2002/feature-articles/dumont_bodies/.

Lacan, J., *Le Séminaire, Livre XX: Encore 1972-1973*, Texte établi par Jacques-Alain Miller (Paris: Seuil, 1975).

Maeterlinck, M., 'La Mystique Flamande', in *Revue Encyclopédique Larousse* 7 (1897), pp. 626-627.

McGinn, B., *The Flowering of Mysticism: Men and Women in the New Mysticism 1200-1350* (New York: Crossroad Publishing, 1989).

Mommaers, P. and E. Dutton, *Hadewijch: Writer – Beguine – Love Mystic* (Leuven: Peeters, 2004).

Naafs, M., '"Films zijn toverspreuken". Bruno Dumont over Hadewijch', in *De Filmkrant* 320, April 2010, http://www.filmkrant.nl/TS_april_2010/12969.

Nabert, N. (ed.), *Dom Jean-Baptiste Porion, Lettres et écrits spirituels* (Paris: Beauchesne, 2011).

Porion, J.-B. (trans.), *Hadewijch d'Anvers, Poèmes des béguines* (Paris: Seuil, 1954).

Porion, J.-B. (trans.), *Hadewijch, Lettres spirituelles; Beatrice de Nazareth, Sept degrés d'amour* (Genève: Ad Solem, 1972).

Porion, J.-B. (trans.), *Hadewijch, Visions* (Paris: O.E.I.L, 1987).

Sartor, F., 'Bruno Dumont over Hadewijch', in *Filmmagie* 603, March 2010, pp. 16-19.

Schelstrate, I., '*Hadewijch* verbijstert Britten', in *De Standaard*, 22 October 2009, p. 38.

Vande Plas, R. (trans.), *Hadewijch d'Amour. Amour est tout. Poèmes strophiques* (Paris: Téqui, 1984).

Vandenbroeck, P., *Le jardin clos de l'âme: l'Imaginaire des religieuses dans les Pays-Bas du Sud, depuis le 13e siècle* (Brussels: Société des Expositions Palais des Beaux-Arts de Bruxelles, 1994).

Van Oostrom, F., *Stemmen op schrift: Geschiedenis van de Nederlandse literatuur vanaf het begin tot 1300* (Amsterdam: Bert Bakker, 2006).

Van Stipriaan, R. (ed.), 'De Nederlandse klassieken anno 2002. Een enquête naar de canon onder de leden van de Maatschappij der Nederlandse Letterkunde', in *Digitale Bibliotheek voor de Nederlandse Letteren*, June 2002, http://www.dbnl.org/letterkunde/enquete/enquete_dbnlmnl_21062002.php.

Van Uffelen, H., 'Toeval dat na de gebeurtenis noodzaak bleek: Over de onbeschrijflijke onbeschrijfbaarheid van de Nederlandse literatuur in het buitenland', in P. Broomans (ed.), *Object: Nederlandse literatuur in het buitenland, methode: onbekend* (Groningen: Barkhuis, 2006), pp. 9-19.

Verbeke, D., 'Een queeste naar de absolute minne: De film "Hadewijch" van Bruno Dumont', in *De Franse Nederlanden* 35 (2010), pp. 202-209.

Verstraten, P., 'Mesmerized by mysticism: The transcendental style of Bruno Dumont's Hadewijch', in *Journal of Dutch Literature* 2 (2011), pp. 27-45.

Vlaminck, E. (ed.), *De canon: De 50+1 mooiste literaire werken uit de Nederlanden* (Antwerpen: KANTL/Uitgeverij Vrijdag, 2015), http://literairecanon.be/werken/liederen.

Willaert, F. (ed.), *Hadewijch, Visioenen*, vertaald door Imme Dros (Amsterdam: Prometheus / Bert Bakker, 1996).

Willaert, F., 'II. Hadewijch', in G.J. Lewis, *Bibliographie zur deutschen Frauenmystik des Mittelalters*, mit einem Anhang zu *Beatrijs van Nazareth und Hadewijch* von Frank Willaert und Marie-José Govers (Berlin: Erich Schmidt Verlag, 1989), pp. 351-410.

CHAPTER 7

Elckerlijc, Everyman, Jedermann and *Akárki* in Hungary

Max Reinhardt and the Transfer of Medieval Dutch Literature

Orsolya Réthelyi (Eötvös Loránd University, Budapest, Huygens ING, Amsterdam, The Netherlands)

When the figure of 'Everyman' was first summoned to appear before his Maker on the Hungarian stage on 25 April 1912, he was called 'Jedermann'.[1] Impersonated by Eduard von Winterstein, actor of the Deutsches Theater of Berlin, he spoke with the German phrases of Hugo van Hofmannsthal and performed under the direction of Max Reinhardt.[2] A hundred years later any Hungarian spectator wishing to see the morality depicting the drama of the individual's encounter with death, could choose from the performances of at least four texts by outstanding Hungarian contemporary authors, beside the appearance of the still appealing translations of two older texts in Hungarian translation, or any combinations of these in the form of street art performances and puppet theatre. There can be no doubt about the popularity and vigorous literary and artistic presence of the Everyman theme in the Hungarian literary system. One text is conspicuously missing from this rich intertextual network of literature, the Middle Dutch *Elckerlijc*, to which all later texts can be traced back through translation and adaptation. This situation raises a number of theoretical questions within a project dealing with the international circulation of Dutch literature, such as CODL.

In the following pages I would like to make a few points on the international circulation of the canonical Middle Dutch morality, *Den spyeghel der salicheyt van Elckerlijc* (c. 1500), usually referred to as the *Elckerlijc*, by zooming in on the reception history of the Everyman theme from two methodological points of departure, the production side and the reception side. On the one hand I wish to map the origins of Reinhardt's *Jedermann* productions and its relationship with the *Elckerlijc*. On the other hand, I wish to show the reception history of the play produced by Reinhardt in Hungary. As comparative material, especially to illustrate the reception process, I will use another famous Reinhardt production, which – as I have argued in an earlier article – is similar to the *Jedermann*, in that it was also based on a Middle Dutch literary work, the *Beatrijs*.[3] The underlying general research question focuses on the dynamics and patterns of the circulation of literature in an international space, and on the question of who the main players – individuals and institutions – in these processes are. Specifically, I'm looking for answers to three questions. The first is more general in nature and is about particular characteristics of the reception of older texts. In which ways does this show a different pattern compared to what we know about the reception of modern literature? The second concerns the role of the intermediary: when discussing the reception of the *Elckerlijc* can we speak at all about the reception of Dutch literature, in Hungary, where the *Elckerlijc* itself has not yet been translated and published? Should one regard Max Reinhardt as an important figure in the international intermediation and reception of Dutch literature in this period? The third question focuses on the process of cultural transfer and reception: when can one consider the reception of a literary work as successful in a new language and culture?

HUGO VON HOFMANNSTHAL'S *JEDERMANN: DAS SPIEL VOM STERBEN DES REICHEN MANNES*

The focus of this article does not allow a discussion of the early history of the *Elckerlijc/Everyman* in translation and adaptation.[4] For my argument it is important to state that the Middle Dutch *Elckerlijc*, written in the late fifteenth century, was already translated into English in the early sixteenth century and appears in print between ca. 1510 – 1529. That the *Everyman* was derived from the Middle Dutch text and not the other way around was the subject of a long scholarly debate, but is generally accepted as a fact since the second half of the twentieth century. It is uncertain whether the Dutch version was written for the stage or functioned as a form of reading drama, but as far as we know the English *Everyman* was only performed four centuries later. The first performance was directed by William Poel and played by the Elizabethan Stage Society in July 1901 as open-air theatre in the Charterhouse of London. This performance was also attended by Max Reinhardt.[5] The production was characterized by the style of the Pre-Raphaelites, visible for example, in the costumes, which were based on images from Flemish tapestries. The production was a great success.[6] In the season of 1902-03 it travelled to New York with a new director, Ben Greet, using the set design and costumes of Edward Gordon Craig. The production went on tour in the United States, where it became a sensation.[7] Hugo von Hofmannsthal was informed about the play in 1903 in a letter from his friend, Clemens Freiherr zu Franckenstein, who saw the production in London. In addition to his letter, Clemens described the performance in detail on separate sheets. Hofmannsthal started working on his own adaptation of the *Everyman* the same year, but was not yet done with it in 1910, despite the pressure put on him by Max Reinhardt to complete the work. Reinhardt made his dramaturge Arthur Kahane write a letter to Hofmannsthal to urge him on.

> Now Reinhardt is asking you with great emphasis to deal with *Everyman* in all seriousness. The thought of using the idea of a circus for the mystery play is so self-evident, that any moment somebody could forestall us: since anybody is free to use one of the existing translations of *Everyman*, it could easily happen that the matter gets thwarted for a long time by an enterprise like this theatre. However, in the Circus Schumann, in the second half of the season for instance, our shows could have a very strong impact and also offer a wonderful business possibility.[8]

Hofmannsthal then completes his adaptation and the play is performed in 1911 under the title *Jedermann*. I cannot discuss *The Miracle* / *Das Miracle* here in detail, but will limit myself to a comparison of the production of the two plays.

THE *JEDERMANN* AND *DAS MIRAKEL* / *THE MIRACLE*

On 1 December 1911 the play *Jedermann: Das Spiel vom Sterben des reichen Mannes* by the poet Hugo von Hofmannsthal was performed for the first time on stage in front of an audience consisting of approximately 5000 people in the Zirkus Schuman in Berlin. The production was that of Max Reinhardt, then already a widely acknowledged theatre maker; retrospectively he can be called one of the most influential theatrical directors of the period. Three weeks later, on 23 December Reinhardt produced the pantomime *The Miracle* (*Das Mirakel*) based on the script of Karl Gustav Vollmoeller in London.[9] There are several similarities between *Jedermann* and *Das Mirakel* / *The Miracle*. Both productions were directed by Max Reinhardt as mass theatre performances. This was a period when Reinhardt wanted to recreate the Greek collective theatre experience for a modern public, by experimenting first with antique and then medieval theatre.[10] For mass productions, the so-called ' Theatres der Fünftausend ' circus buildings – such as the Zirkus Schuman in Berlin – were used, making real art available to people by offering high quality theatre at discount prices. These mass theatre performances would later get their definitive form in Reinhardt's 'Festspiele'.[11]

Both productions brought the authors unprecedented artistic and financial success. In the twenty-first century, we think of Reinhardt especially in connection with his *Jedermann* direction which was included in the program of the Salzburg Festival in 1920 for the first time. From then on *Jedermann* has almost continuously been staged in Salzburg with unprecedented success, and was financially also very profitable. It is perhaps less known that the other mega-production, *Das Mirakel*, brought even more profit for Reinhardt and his production team. The biographer of Karl Vollmoeller, the author of the script of the pantomime, describes the play as a 'cashcow' for more than twenty years, making the purchase of Schloss Leopoldskron for Reinhardt possible, among other things.[12]

Both productions were widely circulated in West and Central Europe, and this is true for the plays as well as for the different products derived from them, such as films, adaptations, and translations. The growth of such derived products was especially true of the spectacular production of *Das Mirakel*, since this was a pantomime by genre and was therefore not limited by language barriers. This production travelled through Europe with performances opening in Vienna in 1912, in Prague in 1913, in Berlin in 1914. There were also at least two filmed versions. Of one of these the performance was adapted for the film by Michael Carré in collaboration with Max Reinhardt, also under the title *Das Mirakel*. The film was first screened in December 1912, a year after the stage premiere. Travelling throughout Europe the effect can only be compared with that of the most successful and profitable Hollywood blockbusters. According to conservative estimates by Vollmoeller's biographer, the film was seen by twelve to fifteen million people.[13]

Both productions have medieval spiritual themes. A Virgin Mary miracle in the case of *Das Mirakel*, and how a person must give an account of his/her life to God when death is imminent, as in the case of *Jedermann*. Furthermore, both are based on medieval literary works translated/rewritten/adapted in commission for Reinhardt. That, of course, need not surprise us. It is a truism that the elitist *fin-de-siècle* fascination with the middle ages and mysticism was still present in the early twentieth century and was broadened and popularized for a general public.[14] Even more important in this period is the interest in new forms, amongst theatre-makers in Europe, as already mentioned, such as mass theatre, open-air performances and performances outside established theatres, which provided an escape from the stagnant theatre system of the nineteenth century. Apart from these similarities, both pieces can – in one way or another – be traced back to Middle Dutch literary works, which are today considered fundamental works of the Dutch literary canon.

ADAPTATION THEORY AND TRANSFER STUDIES

Reinhardt had the literary works rewritten/adapted/translated in both cases. This was typical for his manner of working; he generally asked writers, with whom he collaborated on a regular basis to translate/adapt the plays he wished to produce. In the same manner, for instance, he commissioned Vollmoeller to adapt Aeschylus' *Oresteia*, and asked Hofmannsthal to do the same for Sophocles' *Oedipus Rex*. This process is quite common for theatrical productions, but is also a useful way to avoid arguments about copyright and financial complications, as we can see in the argumentation of Kahane (cited above). It is generally difficult to draw a distinct line between translations and adaptations, but the fact that these are drama texts, which have a special status in the theory of modern translation and adaptation studies, makes the distinctions even less clear cut than usual.[15]

Jedermann and *Das Mirakel* are evidently adaptations, if we look at the context of their origins. It is, however, difficult to say exactly which works of art we should consider as the source texts of these works. *Jedermann* is the simpler case. We know that the performance of *Everyman* in London was crucial for the creation of *Jedermann* and it is completely clear even at first reading that the Middle English text and the German adaptation resemble each other both textually and in their plot to a significant extent. Hofmannsthal also acknowledged this connection by giving his work the title 'Jedermann', a literal translation of the word 'Everyman'. Because we know that *Everyman* is a relatively close translation of *Elckerlijc*, one can claim that *Jedermann* – with some additional scenes and some intertextual references to other medieval literary works –, is a derivative of the Middle Dutch *Elckerlijc*, through *Everyman*. In the case of *Das Mirakel* the picture is not as clear cut because the Beatrijs-story circulated throughout Europe in many versions.[16] The tracing of source texts is also made difficult by the genre of *Das Mirakel*, which is a pantomime with dance and singing. Therefore, no stable written text, which could be compared to other textual variants, survived.[17] The plot of the story shows evident similarities with *Soeur Béatrice* written by Maurice Maeterlinck, which – in turn – is a free adaptation of the Middle Dutch *Beatrijs*.[18] Volmoeller claimed to have based his work on the medieval Latin exempla of Caesarius of Heisterbach, which also provided the source material for the *Beatrijs*.[19] Despite all these connections it is difficult to argue that *Das Mirakel* is a derivative of the *Beatrijs*, all one could claim is that *Das Mirakel*, as does the *Beatrijs*, belongs to the rich family of sacristan-legends, which became so popular in the first half of the twentieth century.

Despite the recent intensive research focus on adaptation theory, the terminology within this relatively new field of research is still problematic, because there is no consensus about the concepts.[20] According to the definition of Linda Hutcheon in her recent work on the theory of adaptation the product of a process of adaptation is (1) an acknowledged transposition of a recognizable other work, (2) a creative and an interpretive act of appropriation/salvaging and (3) an extended intertextual engagement with the adapted work.[21] For my argumentation the first point is crucial since the other two are derived from this point. However, Hutcheon's adaptation theory defines adaptation as an acknowledged transposition, which obviously does not completely apply to either the *Jedermann* and *Das Mirakel.* Hofmannsthal does refer to his work as a translation/adaptation of the *Everyman*, he also acknowledges this debt in his title. However, he – just like his contemporaries – was convinced that *Everyman* was the original text, and the *Elckerlijc* a Middle Dutch translation.[22] In the case of *Das Mirakel* Vollmoeller and Reinhardt seem to dissociate themselves from the *Beatrijs* or Maeterlinck's *Soeur Béatrice*. Not only did they choose a different title, but the protagonist is also given a name, which differs from the variants of 'Beatrix' most frequently occurring in these legends. Nevertheless, both works were recognized by Dutch speakers as variations of *Beatrijs* and the *Elckerlijc*.[23]

THE RECEPTION OF *JEDERMANN* IN HUNGARY

Max Reinhardt had strong ties with Hungary from his early career onwards. He toured Vienna, Prague and Budapest with his new productions from the turn of the nineteenth century since the cultural elite in these towns spoke German, at least as a second language. In September 1911 he directed the first mass theatre arena-production, *Oedipus Rex*, with Hungarian actors in the Beketow Circus in Budapest.[24] These strong ties are also visible in the Hungarian *Jedermann* reception. In 1912, directly after the premiere of *Jedermann* in Berlin Reinhardt brought his production to Frankfurt-am-Main and Budapest, where the performance of the *Deutsches Theater* was greeted enthusiastically. A year later Reinhardt brought his newest plays to Budapest and *Jedermann* was again – this time played by his famous lead actor Alexander Moissi – included in the programme.[25] From 1920 on, when the play became a regular element of the Salzburger Festspiele we see that it receives much attention in the Hungarian press, also because this event continued to be the meeting place of the social and cultural elite. Reinhardt often engaged Hungarian actors for his play, such as the famous actress Lili Darvas from 1926. In 1926 a well-known poet, Miklós Kállay, made a verse translation of *Jedermann,* which made it possible to perform the play in different places in Hungary, under different directors.[26] Between 1934 and 1938, in the summer months, *Jedermann* was also staged as open-air performance on the Margaret Island of Budapest.

Figure 1. Book cover of von Hofmannsthal's *Akárki: Játék a gazdag ember haláláról* [Akárki. The play about the death of a rich man], translated by Miklós Kállay (1924)

Another form of reception that should be mentioned is the effort made by different groups of people to introduce not only the play, but also its artistic context, the phenomenon of the 'Festspiele' in Hungary. The idea to have *Jedermann* staged in one of the large towns of Hungary, Szeged or Pécs, was soon followed by a public discussion in the Hungarian press, in which strong arguments were presented to produce Hungarian literary or musical productions and Festspiele, modelled on those of Reinhardt.[27] Reinhardt was asked to direct the famous Hungarian play, the *Tragedy of man* by Imre Madách in Szeged, which he did not accept, instead referring to the excellent local talent present in Hungary.[28] At the end Festspiele were started up in both Pécs and Szeged in the early thirties with Hungarian art works and without the Reinhardt's participation. A similar story can be told about the reception of *Das Mirakel* in Hungary, which I will not here elaborate.[29] However, I have not come across any reference in the Hungarian press of the interwar period to the Dutch, or Flemish connections of the plays. The complete lack of any knowledge of this is made more conspicuous by the fact that the intellectual public in Hungary did follow the theatrical developments in the Netherlands and Belgium with interest. This can be seen, for instance, in one of the articles from 1931 in a daily paper, which discusses the theory and practice of theatrical mass-spectacle and includes a detailed description of the theatrical experiments of the esteemed Dutch theatre director, Johan de Meester jr. in 1925.[30]

If one looks at the present status of the two works in Hungary one can discern a significant difference in the long term reception of the two works. *Das Mirakel* has basically disappeared from contemporary literary memory in Hungary. Studies of theatre history make mention of it when discussing Reinhardt's influence on Hungarian theatre. The absence of *Das Mirakel* in the modern literary culture in Hungary should not surprise us. The work also disappeared from the European shared literary system culture. This is probably mainly caused by the fact that Reinhardt abandoned language to be able to reach the collective mass experience he sought, and built his production on strong visual impressions with song and movement. What became the ultimate form of reaching a huge public worldwide and make the production a financial success stood in the way of a deeper reception in the long run, because no stable text manifestation was available to translate and create a record for future generations.

On the other hand, the *Jedermann/Everyman* story became deeply rooted in the Hungarian culture. As I have noted before, a verse translation of the *Jedermann* was published in 1924, under the title 'Akárki', which in Hungarian literally means 'anybody'. Sixty years later, in 1984, the Middle English *Everyman* was also translated in an appealing Hungarian verse translation by Gyula Tellér, specifically for publication in a volume of selected medieval dramatic works. Tellér gave the same title to his translation of *Everyman* as Gyula Kállay to the Hungarian translation of *Jedermann*, producing a second literary work with the title 'Akárki', and creating a precedent – as would become clear later – that was followed by other Hungarian authors. In fact, the editors of the volume decided to use the name 'Akárki' as the title for the whole collection of medieval plays. This illustrates not only the canonical status, which *Everyman* had achieved in world literature by this time, but also shows that the literary theme was at this time well known in Hungary and was popular enough to be used for the cover of a new volume and to persuade the public to buy the book. By the eighties the political climate in Hungary had become much more tolerant, making it possible to publish a book with religious drama texts. In the afterword, however, the writer, dramaturge and literary translator András Benedek still gave a quasi-anti-clerical interpretation of the story. In the same afterword there is already a reference to the Low Countries in relation to *Everyman*, but the chronological priority of *Elckerlijc* is not yet referred to as a fact.[31] The fact that the TEAMS edition of the text of *Everyman*, together with the text of *Elckerlijc* was published on-line in 2007, making it readily available for a wide international audience, brought a turn in the common knowledge about the relationship between the two works. The priority of the *Elckerlijc* is not only acknowledged in the TEAMS edition by the editors, but an English prose translation is provided for the Middle Dutch text, to make a comparison of the two medieval texts easier, and making international recognition of the *Elckerlijc* more widespread.[32]

Figure 2. Book cover of *Akárki: Misztériumjátékok, mirákulumok, moralitások* [Akárki: Mystery plays, miracles and moralities], edited by Szenczi Miklós (1984)

In 1993 the well-known Hungarian drama author and director Péter Kárpáti made a very successful modern adaptation of *Everyman*, and once again under the title *Akárki*. In this adaptation the main role is played by a divorced woman, Emma, living in decent poverty, who is confronted with her – supposed – approaching death and tries to settle the things around her. The play is full of symbolically laden intertextual references to both *Everyman* and *Jedermann*. This play is still frequently performed in Hungary, and is considered a modern classic. The play has also been translated into English (under the title *Everywoman*) and has been performed outside Hungary.[33] Furthermore, the Everyman-material has inspired a number of other recent Hungarian literary works, all of which acknowledge this relationship by referring to it in their title. Some of the best contemporary Hungarian authors have written their own adaptation of the theme, such as László Garaczi (*Jedermann*, first published in 1993), Katalin Thuróczi (*Akárki*, first published in 2001), Szilárd Borbély (*Akár Akárki* [Hung. Perhaps Anyone / Even Everyman], first published in 2010).[34] In his recent dissertation about theatre history, the author and theatre director Miklós Tóth analysed eight modern plays, Hungarian and international, which – according to his interpretation – are all recent adaptations of the *Everyman/Jedermann* theme.[35] Not only the intensive literary production and the academic interest in the theme shows the exceptional popularity of the theme, but also the dramatic practice. All of the plays mentioned here have been frequently performed in the past years in Hungary, but conspicuously also in Hungarian theatres in the neighbouring countries with large Hungarian-speaking minorities. In addition, there are plays which are produced by some kind of combination of these texts, such as the progressive puppet theatre performance for adults, *Akárki Hivatása* [The summoning / The profession of Everyman]' (2012) by the Füge Produkció under the direction of Tamás Kovács which uses a script 'based on an English morality play from the fifteenth century, the *Everyman* by an anonymous author, as well as other adaptations of the text (medieval texts, Hugo von Hoffmanstahl, Philip Roth, Péter Kárpáti).'[36] Another recent example of this phenomenon is the musical street-theatre performance, *Akárki – Moralitásjáték* (2012) performed by the Mesebolt Bábszínház from Szombathely and directed by András Veres, just to mention two examples.[37] It would be worthwhile to dedicate a detailed study to the question why the *Elckerlijc/Everyman/Jedermann* theme should strike such a sensitive cord for Hungarian audiences around the turn of the twentieth century, since its conspicuous popularity for large audiences of different dramatic media is clearly evident.

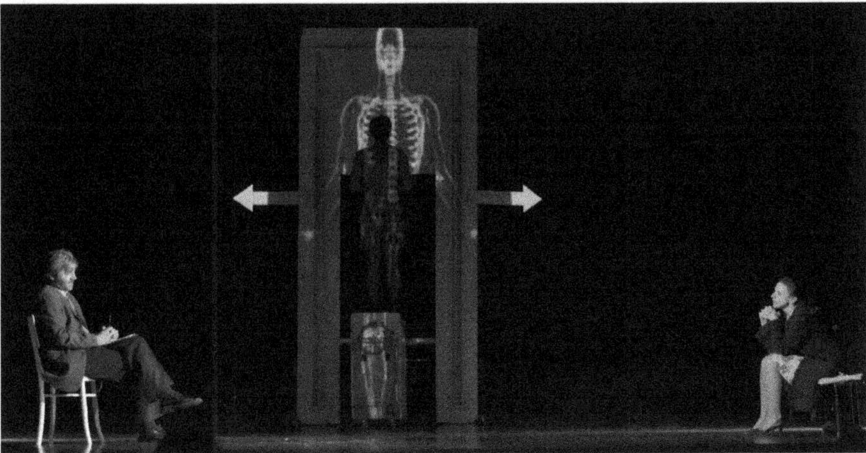

Figure 3. Péter Kárpáti's *Akárki*. Performance at the Thália Színház Theatre (Hungarian theatre in Slovakia of Košice, premiere 2 December 2013), with Judit Márkus in the role of Emma and Szilárd Petrik in the role of the Doctor. Directed by József Czajlik. Photography: Emese Tóth.

It seems to me that part of the successful in-depth reception of the theme in Hungary is reinforced by a translatological process specific to the circulation of literature through translation and adaptation: the question of transferring titles from one language to the other. As we have noted earlier, the word 'Everyman', denoting the title and the main character of the English morality is a fairly precise translation of the word 'Elckerlijc'. Hofmannsthal in turn expresses his indebtedness to *Everyman* by translating the title word precisely into German with the word 'Jedermann'. In Hungary both works were translated with the Hungarian word 'Akárki', in which word the meaning shifts from 'every' to 'any', and is gender neutral, as in 'anybody' or 'anyone'. Furthermore, a number of later adaptations use the same title in exactly the same form (Kárpáti, Thuróczi), or in a slightly altered version (Borbély), or refer back to the German title word (Garaczi). This results in a number of texts clearly stating their relationship to a given historical body of texts, forming a strong intertextual network and system of texts.[38]

The Middle Dutch *Beatrijs* has been published in the excellent verse translation of Zsuzsa Rakovszky, in the *olla vogala / minden madár* series of older Dutch literature in Hungarian translation.[39] Turning to the future, the verse translation of the *Elckerlijc* by the acclaimed poet Anna Szabó T. completed in 2016 will also be published in this series, causing the *Elckerlijc* to come to life in Hungarian. Which title this new translation will bear, is at this moment still undecided. With these two translations a new chapter opens for the Hungarian reception of these masterpieces of the Dutch literary canon.

CONCLUSION

My first question focused on the specific characteristics of the reception of older literature and an appropriate methodology to study these. I cannot do more than begin to formulate cautious attempts to answer this question. Important characteristics of *Elckerlijc/Everyman* and *Beatrijs* is that they both go back to older stories, which appear as themes in many works of literature throughout Europe. This feature makes the reception of these narratives less akin to that of modern literature, and more similar to 'schriftlische folklore', in the well-known terminology of Aleida Assman.[40] She defines stories in this category as being characterised by an openness, variability in form, anonymous authors, furthermore, literature in this category provides greater freedom for changes. One can often find the same characteristics in the case of children's literature, especially fairy-tales or older stories that appear as shared cultural heritage in ever renewed forms.[41] It is striking that Hugo von Hofmannsthal describes exactly these characteristics in his introduction to the first edition of his *Jedermann:*

> They say that German folk-tales do not have an author. They are supposed to have been passed on mouth to mouth, until after a long time,

> when they were in danger of being forgotten or losing their real nature by changes and additions, two men ultimately wrote them down. The story of Everyman's summons to God's judgment seat might also be regarded as such a tale. Throughout the Middle Ages, it was told at many places in many versions; then an Englishman of the fifteenth century told it in a specific way, where he let the various characters appear personified on stage, he put the suitable words in their mouth, and this way, divided the whole story between the figures. He was followed by a Dutch man, then by scholarly Germans, who used Latin or Greek for the same opus. [...] That's why there has been a new attempt at writing down in all humility this timeless and universally valid tale.[42]

Furthermore, I believe that in the case of the reception of *Elckerlijc/Everyman*, as well as that of *Beatrijs* it was crucial that the authors were unknown. Hofmannsthal's emphasis on the complete freedom of the translator/adapter is largely made possible because there were no known authors of the original texts. This means that everybody is free to appropriate the story and use his name as author of the new adaptation. On the title page of *Oedipus Rex*, which was translated/adapted by Hofmannsthal in a similar manner, commissioned by Reinhardt and adapted as mass performance, we encounter the following title: 'Sophokles. *König Ödipus*. Tragödie Übersetzt und für die neuere Bühne eingerichtet von Hugo von Hofmannsthal.'[43] Because the name of the author of this drama from antiquity is known, the adapter is pushed into the role of the translator, which has a very different status and prestige.[44] In the case of anonymous works this is not the case and the adaptation is seen more as the intellectual property of the adaptor.[45] The fact that Hofmannsthal is regarded as an author in the case of *Jedermann* and as a translator in the case of *Oedipus Rex* shows how difficult it is to draw a line between these two categories. This also means that being perceived as belonging in one or the other of these categories often has nothing to do with the process or the product, but rather with arbitrary formal or historical circumstances, for instance whether the name of the author survives to our day, or not.

Can Max Reinhardt then be regarded as a mediator of Middle Dutch literature? It is clear that Reinhardt's productions are not in accordance with Hutcheon's first point. In his case it was less a desire of achieving a 'palimpsestuous intertextual pleasure' – using the term of Linda Hutcheon – in his audience and more a case of the ancient practice of finding suitable old stories, which he transformed by adapting them to a new experimental form, which was attractive for contemporary audiences. For practical and financial reasons, he had a system in which he commissioned authors with whom he collaborated on a regular basis, to translate/adapt/rewrite these stories in German. This was relatively easy to do since both works were anonymous – like most medieval stories – and had, moreover, been known in different forms in the different literatures of Europe. His goal was definitely not philological, or literary-historical, though there is some sign of acknowledgement in the case of *Jedermann*. Even more importantly, Reinhardt and his co-workers probably did not know the texts of the *Elckerlijc* and the *Beatrijs*, and if they did have knowledge of their existence, they thought of them as derivatives of older stories. Therefore, they cannot be regarded as mediators intentionally popularizing Middle Dutch literature in Europe.

Reinhardt is certainly not the single inventor of producing medieval literature for the modern stage. That is clear if we think of the very successful productions of *Soeur Béatrice* by Maeterlinck and the *Everyman* directed by Poel, mentioned before, but also of the revolutionary production of *Elckerlijc* by Eduard Verkade and Willem Royaards in the Netherlands, which is seen by Dutch scholarship as the birth of modern theatre.[46] In many European countries we can see parallel developments in this period, experimenting with the staging of medieval theatre, and deciding which themes and forms are most suitable for this purpose. And yet – looking at the production side – Max Reinhardt was a key actor of his age in making these plays available for a wide public through mass theatrical productions and Festspiele as well as collaborating in adaptations for the film industry. On the reception side of the process, he was also a welcome guest in the large cities of Central-Europe, where a major part of the urban elite used German as their native, or second language, and he became an important cultural mediator of new theatrical themes and forms. In the case of a successful reception these themes and forms were subsequently integrated in the native language and culture, and adapted by and for the locals.

The reception of *Elckerlijc/Everyman/Jedermann* in Hungary then is a near perfect example with which to demonstrate such successful cultural transfer, including the consecutive steps of translation, adaptation and approppriation.[47] Reinhardt brought the form of mass performance to Hungary with his *Oedipus Rex* in 1911, when he directed the play with Hungarian actors in the Beketow Circus in Budapest. A year later, in 1912, he brought *Jedermann* to Budapest, performed in German, played by his own Deutsches Theater from Berlin. In a next step, a Hungarian translation of the *Jedermann* was made which was performed in various indoor and open-air theatres. Around this time the possibilities and advantages of mass theatre performances modelled on the Salzburger Festspiele were widely discussed in the Hungarian press, resulting in the first Festspiel in the Southern Hungarian town of Szeged in 1930. Reinhardt was invited to direct his *Jedermann* in Hungary, but declined, and it was replaced by a Hungarian play, directed by a Hungarian director. After years of an anti-clerical communist regime, *Jedermann* was performed again in Hungary in 1983. One year later the *Everyman* was translated. A few years later Péter Kárpáti made a modern, secularised adaptation of the theme, based on both texts and the theme of confrontation with death. Kárpáti's *Akárki* is still played today and discussed in reviews and scientific discourse. A number of new plays, adaptations and performances sprang up in the twenty-first century in Hungary, all indebted in some way to *Elckerlijc/Everyman/Jedermann*, and acknowledging this relation. What do we see if we list these events chronologically? Within a century the *Everyman*-story and theme became an integral part of Hungarian literary culture, with a wide variety of literary texts, performances and interpretations. Within this network, the knowledge that the Middle Dutch *Elckerlijc* is the original source text has also become accepted, even if the text itself is not readily available.

The reception process in Hungary is an example of a successful reception in which all the steps of in-depth reception and cultural transfer can be found. Reinhardt's *Jedermann* production was the first and decisive step of this process, which resonated for years, and set in motion the integration and acculturation of the theme in Hungarian literary culture. The fact that *Elckerlijc* itself does not yet play a role in this reception network in the form of a Hungarian translation is just a question of the temporal perspective from which we view the chronology of the reception process at the end of 2015, the time of writing this article. Whether a newly translated work of literature is integrated into the local repertoire has much to do with recognition from the public, and whether a new text can be anchored to the network of previously existing texts in the target language. Therefore, one can safely advance the prognosis that the chronological line of reception can be drawn further to when the Hungarian translation of *Elckerlijc* will finally be published. Looking at it from that perspective, Reinhardt – who played a decisive role in the origins of this complex network – can be called an unintended, albeit very effective mediator of the *Elckerlijc*, and thus of Middle Dutch literature.

NOTES

1 The research project OTKA nr. 11786 of the Hungarian Scientific Research Fund (OTKA) has provided support for the writing of this article.

2 G. Staud, 'Max Reinhardt in Ungarn' and 'Zeittafel der Reinhardt Gastspiel und Gastinszenierungen', in E. Leisler and G. Prossnitz (eds.), *Max Reinhardt in Europa* (Salzburg: Otto Müller, 1973), pp. 7-31 and 312-319.

3 O. Réthelyi, 'Beatrijzen op de planken: Nederlandstalige toneelbewerkingen van het Beatrijs-verhaal in de eerste helft van de twintigste eeuw' in T. van Kalmthout, O. Réthelyi and R. Sleiderink (eds.), *Beatrijs de wereld in* (Gent: Academia, 2013), pp. 263-295.

4 J. Bloemendal, 'Transfer and Integration of Latin and Vernacular Drama in the Early Modern Period: The Case of Everyman, Elckerlijc, Homulus and Hecastus', in *Arcadia* 44 (2009), pp. 274-288.

5 M. Stevens, 'The reshaping of *Everyman*: Hofmannsthal at Salzburg', in *Germanic Review* 48 (1973), p. 118.

6 See also C. Davidson, M.W. Walsh and T.J. Broos, 'Introduction to Everyman', in C. Davidson, M.W. Walsh, and T.J. Broos (eds.), *Everyman and Its Dutch Original, Elckerlijc*

(TEAMS, Middle English. Texts Series) (Michigan, Kalamazoo: Medieval Institute Publications, 2007), p. 1.

7 E.G. Schreiber, 'Everyman in America', in *Comparative Drama* 9, 2 (1975), pp. 99-115. See also M. Vanhelleputte, 'Herkunft und Originalität von Hofmannsthals "Jedermann"', in E. Leisler and G. Prossnitz (eds.), *Hugo von Hofmannsthals Jedermann: Das Spiel vom Sterben des reichen Mannes und Max Reinhardts Inszenierungen: Texte, Dokumente, Bilder* (Frankfurt am Main: S. Fischer, 1973), p. 89.

8 'Nun bittet Reinhardt Sie sehr, sich doch auf das Ernstliche mit *Everyman* zu beschäftigen. Der Gedanke, die Circus-idee gerade auf das Mysterium auszunützen, liegt so nahe, dass uns jeden Tag irgend jemand zuvorkommen kann: da es jedermann freisteht sich einer der vorhandenen Übersetzungen von *Everyman* zu bedienen, kann es sehr leicht passieren, dass die Sache durch irgend ein Unternehmen etwa wie dieses Ausstellungstheater für lange Zeit hinaus verschandelt wird. Andererseits könnte unsere Aufführungen im Circus Schumann etwa in der zweiten Hälfte der Saison von stärkster Wirkung und auch den schönsten geschäftlichen Chancen sein.' Leisler and Prossnitz (eds.), *Hugo von Hofmannsthals Jedermann*, p. 176.

9 H. Kindermann, *Theatergeschichte Europas. VIII. Band: Naturalismus und Impressionismus. I. Teil: Deutschland/Österreich/Schweiz* (Salzburg: Otto Müller, 1968), p. 463.

10 J.L. Styan, *Modern Drama in Theory and Practice 3: Expressionism and Epic Theatre* (Cambridge: Cambridge University Press, 1983), pp. 70-71.

11 Kindermann, *Theatergeschichte Europas*, pp. 366-373.

12 F.D. Tunnat, *Karl Vollmoeller – Dichter und Kulturmanager: Eine Biographie* (Hamburg: Tredition, 2008), pp. 288-289.

13 Tunnat, *Karl Vollmoeller*, pp. 288-289.

14 J. Bel, 'Middeleeuwen en mystiek in het fin-de-*siècle*', in *Literatuur* 7 (1990), pp. 276-278.

15 M. Carlson, 'Theatrical Performance: Illustration, Translation, Fulfillment, or Supplement?', in *Theatre Journal*, March 1985, pp. 5-11.

16 Van Kalmthout, Réthelyi and Sleiderink (eds.), *Beatrijs de wereld in*, pp. 11-12.

17 Different text variants were made for the different productions, but these were continuously rewritten and adjusted to the context of the performance.

18 Styan, *Modern Drama*, p. 70.; Réthelyi, 'Beatrijzen op de planken'; M. Maeterlinck, *Théatre III. Aglavaine et Sélysette (1896); Ariane et Barbe-Bleue (1901); Soeur Béatrice. Miracle en trois actes (1901)* (Bruxelles: P. Lacomblez, 1901).

19 Tunnat, *Karl Vollmoeller*, p. 284.

20 J. Milton, 'Translation Studies and Adaptation Studies', in A. Pym and A. Perekrestenko (eds.), *Translation Research Projects 2* (Tarragona: Intercultural Studies Group, 2009), p. 51.

21 L. Hutcheon, *A Theory of Adaptation* (New York/London: Routledge, 2006), p. 8.

22 Vanhelleputte, 'Herkunft und Originalität', p. 81.

23 Réthelyi, 'Beatrijzen op de planken', p. 270.

24 Staud, 'Max Reinhardt in Ungarn', p. 23 and p. 316.

25 Staud, 'Max Reinhardt in Ungarn', p. 25.

26 H. von Hofmannsthal, *Akárki: Játék a gazdag ember haláláról* [Akárki: The play about the death of a rich man], translated by Miklós Kállay (Budapest: Genius, 1924). J. Kálmán,

'Nemcsak a Salzburgi Ünnepi Játékokon, a Fővárosi Operettszínházban is sikert aratott a *Jedermann*, a "Gazdag ember" élete és halála.' [The *Jedermann*, or The life and death of the "Rich man" was a great success, not only in Salzburg, but also in the Operette Theatre of Budapest] *Színházi élet*, 11 October 1926, reprinted in *Post Festum*: *Szabadtéri játékok a két világháború között Salzburgban, Szegeden és Pécsett* [Post Festum: Open-air-theatre in Salzburg, Szeged and Pécs between the two world wars], edited by A. Kerekes, M. Kindl and J. Szabó (Budapest: Gondolat, 2009), p. 437.

27 A. Kerekes, M. Kindl and J. Szabó, 'Előszó [Introduction]', in *Post Festum* (Budapest: Gondolat, 2009), pp. 18-19.

28 J. Paál, 'Reinhardt professzor a szegedi ünnepi játékokról [Professor Reinhardt on the subject of the open-air festival of Szeged]', in *Délmagyarország*, 15 August 1931. Reprinted in *Post Festum*, p. 106.

29 I have written on the subject in another article. See O. Réthelyi, 'Beatrijs a nagyvilágban. A Beatrijs és a holland irodalmi kánon [Beatrijs in the wide world: The *Beatrijs* and the Dutch literary canon]', in Zs. Rakovszky, A. Daróczi and O. Réthelyi, *Beatrijs: Egy apáca története* [Beatrijs: The story of a nun] (Budapest: L'Harmattan, 2012), pp. 95-109.

30 F. Hont, 'Szabadtéri színjáték [Open-air performances]', in *Délmagyarország*, 14 June 1931, reprinted in *Post Festum*, p. 106.

31 A. Benedek, 'Misztérium, mirákulum, moralitás – és a mai színjáték [Mystey, miracle and morality – and the theatre of our days]', in Szenczi Miklós (ed.), *Akárki: Misztérium-játékok, mirákulumok, moralitások* (Budapest: Európa, 1984), pp. 540-541.

32 Davidson, Walsh and Broos, 'Introduction to Everyman', p. 1.

33 P. Kárpáti, 'Akárki: Moralitásjáték', in *Színház drámamelléklet* 3 (1993); P. Kárpáti, 'Every-woman', in *Hungarian Plays: New Drama from Hungary* (London: Nick Hern Books, 1996); P. Kárpáti, 'Akárki: Moralitásjáték', in P. Kárpáti, *Világvevő: Öt színdarab* (Pécs: Jelenkor, 1999).

34 L. Garaczi. 'Jedermann', in *Bálnák tánca* [The dance of whales] (Budapest: Pesti Szalon, 1994); K. Thuróczy, 'Akárki', in *Csütörtökünnep* [Thursday feast] (Budapest: Neoprológus Bt, 2000); Sz. Borbély, 'Akár Akárki', in *Szemünk előtt vonulnak el* [They proceed before our eyes] (Budapest: Palatinus, 2011).

35 M. Tóth, *'Akárki' a kortárs európai drámairodalomban* [*'Akárki/Everyman'* in contemporary European drama]. PhD dissertation submitted to the Theatre Academy of Budapest, 2013. I only listed those recent Hungarian works of literature which acknowledge their indebtedness to *Everyman* or *Jedermann* in their title. The Tóth's criteria are somewhat different and he also adds to the titles mentioned above the morality *Finito* by István Tasnádi, published in 2005.

36 As this is described in the introductory text of the play: 'Az előadás szövegkönyvének alapja egy XV. századi angol moralitás, egy ismeretlen szerző *Everyman* című írása, illetve a szöveg további feldolgozásai (középkori szövegemlékek, Hugo von Hoffmanstahl, Philip Roth, Kárpáti Péter). Az *Akárki hivatása* az Akárki-történet modern adaptációja.' [The script of the performance is based on an English morality play from the fifteenth century, the *Everyman* by an anonymous author, as well as other adaptations of the text (medieval texts, Hugo von Hoffmanstahl, Philip Roth, Péter Kárpáti). The *Akárki hivatása* is a modern adaptation of the Akárki/Everyman story] (my translation O.R.). N.N. 'Akárki hivatása – Bábos moralitás és platformjáték'. *Szinhaz.hu Magyar Színházi Portál*, 2012. March 5. URL:

http://szinhaz.hu/budapest/44791-akarki-hivatasa-babos-moralitas-es-platformjatek. Last consulted on 14 January 2016.

37 'A középkor végére egész Európában elterjedő moralitásjátékok a keresztény kultúra egészen különleges pillanatának lenyomatai. [...] A haláltól való félelem és a halállal szembenéző Akárki magányossága már túlmutat a középkori, keresztény halálfelfogáson. Maga a cím is roppant erős és kifejező jelzés: akárki-valaki közülünk. A főszereplő utolsó útján különböző allegorikus figurákkal találkozik. Ezeket a stációkat egy időn kívüli vidámpark megelevenedő attrakciói képviselik. Akárki ebben a záróra előtti wurstliban bolyong, és marad végül egyedül a tömegben [The morality play, which had spread over all of Europe, provides us with records of a very special moment of the Christian culture. [...] The fear of death and the loneliness of the protagonist, Akárki, who looks death in the face, goes beyond the medieval, Christian idea of death. The title in itself is a very strong and significant sign: anybody-somebody from among us. The protagonist meets a number of allegorical figures on his/her last journey. These junctures are represented by the coming to life of the attractions of a timeless amusement-park. Akárki wanders around in this fun-fair just before closing time, and eventually finds himself alone within the crowd]' N.N, 'Akárki – Moralitásjáték' (2012) Website of the Mesebolt Bábszínház. URL: http://meseboltbabszinhaz.hu/repertoar/akarki-moralitas-jatek-felnotteknek-szolo-utcaszinhazi-eloadas, (accessed 14 January 2016).

38 G. Allen, *Intertextuality* (London: Routledge, 2000).

39 Rakovszky, Daróczi and Réthelyi, *Beatrijs*.

40 A. Assmann, 'Schriftliche Folklore: Zur Entstehung und Funktion eines Überlieferungstyps', in J. Assmann, A. Assmann and Ch. Hardmeier (eds.), *Schrift und Gedächtnis: Beiträge zur Archäologie der Literarische Kommunikation* (München: Wilhelm Fink, 1983), pp.175-193.

41 For a discussion on how these aspects influence the translation of fairy tales see J. Van Coillie, 'Nibble, Nibble Like a Mouse: Who is Nibbling at the Source Text's House? Retranslating Fairy Tales: Untangling the Web of Causation', in V. Douglas and F. Cabaret, *Retranslating Children's Literature* (Brussels: Peter Lang, 2014), pp. 39-52.

42 'Die deutschen Hausmärchen, pflegt man zu sagen, haben keinen Verfasser. Sie wurden von Mund zu Mund weitergegeben, bis am Ende langer Zeiten, als Gefahr war, sie könnten vergessen werden oder durch Abenderungen und Zutaten ihr wahres Gesicht verlieren, zwei Männer sie endgültig aufschrieben. Als ein solches Märchen mag man auch die Geschichte von Jedermanns Ladung vor Gottes Richterstuhl ansehen. Man hat sie das Mittelalter hindurch an vielen Orten in vielen Fassungen erzählt; dann erzählte sie ein Engländer des fünfzehnten Jahrhunderts in der Weise, dass er die einzelnen Gestalten lebendig auf eine Bühne treten ließ, jeder die ihr gemäßen Reden in den Mund legte und so die ganze Erzählung unter die gestalte aufteilte. Diesem folgte ein Niederländer, dann gelehrte Deutsche, die sich der Lateinischen oder der griechischen Sprache zu dem gleichen Werk bedienten. [...]. Darum wurde neuerlich versucht, dieses allen Zeiten gehörige und allgemeingültige Marchen abermals in Bescheidenheit aufzuzeichnen.' H. von Hofmannsthal, 'Introduction' in Leisler and Prossnitz (eds.), *Jedermann*, p. 103.

43 Sophokles, *König Ödipus: Tragödie,* übersetzt und für die neuere Bühne eingerichtet von Hugo von Hofmannsthal. (Berlin: S. Fischer Verlag, 1911).

44 S. Bassnett, *Translation Studies* (New York/London: Psychology Press, 2002), p. 45.
45 The same process can be seen in the case of Maeterlinck's *Soeur Béatrice*.
46 R.L. Erenstein, 'Zomerspelen in Laren onder leiding van Royaards en Verkade, in R.L. Erenstein (ed.), *Een theatergeschiedenis der Nederlanden* (Amsterdam: Amsterdam University Press, 1996), pp. 552-559.
47 See also in the framework of the well-known classification of Roman Jakobson, expanded by Itamar Even-Zohar. R. Jakobson, 'On Linguistic Aspects of Translation', in L. Venuti (ed.), *Translation Studies Reader*, (New York: Routledge, 2004, 2nd edition), pp. 113-119; I. Even-Zohar, 'Culture Repertoire and Transfer', in Susan Petrilli (ed.), *Translation Translation* (Amsterdam-New York: Rodopi, 2003), pp. 425-431.

BIBLIOGRAPHY

Allen, G., *Intertextuality* (London: Routledge, 2000).

Assmann, A., 'Schriftliche Folklore: Zur Entstehung und Funktion eines Überlieferungstyps', in J. Assmann, A. Assmann and Christof Hardmeier (eds.), *Schrift und Gedächtnis: Beiträge zur Archäologie der Literarische Kommunikation* (München: Wilhelm Fink, 1983), pp.175-193.

Bassnett, S., *Translation Studies* (New York/London: Psychology Press, 2002).

Bel, J., 'Middeleeuwen en mystiek in het fin-de-siècle', in *Literatuur* 7 (1990), pp. 276-284.

Benedek, A., 'Misztérium, mirákulum, moralitás – és a mai színjáték [Mystery, miracle and morality – and the theatre of our days]', in Szenczi Miklós (ed.), *Akárki. Misztériumjátékok, mirákulumok, moralitások* (Budapest: Európa, 1984), pp. 511-541.

Bloemendal, J., 'Transfer and Integration of Latin and Vernacular Drama in the Early Modern Period: The Case of Everyman, Elckerlijc, Homulus and Hecastus', in *Arcadia* 44 (2009), pp. 274-288.

Borbély, Sz., 'Akár Akárki', in *Szemünk előtt vonulnak el* [They proceed before our eyes] (Budapest: Palatinus, 2011).

Carlson, M., 'Theatrical performance: Illustration, Translation, Fulfilment, or Supplement?', in *Theatre Journal*, March 1985, pp. 5-11.

Davidson, C., M.W. Walsh and T.J. Broos, 'Introduction to Everyman', in C. Davidson, M.W. Walsh and T.J. Broos (eds.), *Everyman and Its Dutch Original, Elckerlijc* (Michigan Kalamazoo: Medieval Institute Publications, 2007), p. 1-14.

Erenstein, R.L., 'Zomerspelen in Laren onder leiding van Royaards en Verkade', in R.L. Erenstein (ed.), *Een theatergeschiedenis der Nederlanden* (Amsterdam: Amsterdam University Press, 1996), pp. 552-559.

Erenstein, R.L., 'De receptie van middeleeuws toneel in de twintigste eeuw', in H. van Dijk *et al.* (eds.), *Spel en spektakel* (Amsterdam: Prometheus, 2001), pp. 282-304.

Even-Zohar, I., 'Culture Repertoire and Transfer', in S. Petrilli (ed.), *Translation Translation* (Amsterdam/New York: Rodopi, 2003), pp. 425-431.

Garaczi, L., 'Jedermann', in *Bálnák tánca* [The dance of whales] (Budapest: Pesti Szalon 1994), pp. 91-129.

Göpferich, S., 'Transfer and Transfer Studies', in Y. Gambier and L. Van Doorslaer (eds.), *Handbook of Translation Studies*, vol. 1 (Amsterdam/Philadelphia: John Benjamins Publishing, 2010), pp. 374-377.

Guiette, R., *La légende de la sacristine: Etude de littérature comparée* (Paris: Slatkine, 1927).

Hont, F., 'Szabadtéri színjáték [Open-air performances]', in *Délmagyarország*, 14 June 1931. Reprinted in A. Kerekes, M. Kindl and J. Szabó (eds.), *Post Festum: Szabadtéri játékok a két világháború között Salzburgban, Szegeden és Pécsett* [Post Festum: Open-air-theatre in Salzburg, Szeged and Pécs between the two World Wars] (Budapest: Gondolat, 2009), p. 106.

Hutcheon, L., *A Theory of Adaptation* (New York/London: Routledge, 2006).

Jakobson, R., 'On Linguistic Aspects of Translation', in L. Venuti (ed.), *Translation Studies Reader*, 2nd edition (New York: Routledge, 2004), pp. 113-119.

Kálmán, J., 'Nemcsak a Salzburgi Ünnepi Játékokon, a Fővárosi Operettszínházban is sikert aratott a *Jedermann*, a "Gazdag ember" élete és halála.' [The *Jedermann*, or The life and death of the 'Rich man' had great success, not only in Salzburg, but also in the Operette Theatre of Budapest] in *Színházi élet*, 11 October 1926, reprinted in A. Kerekes, M. Kindl and J. Szabó (eds.), *Post Festum: Szabadtéri játékok a két világháború között Salzburgban, Szegeden és Pécsett* [Post Festum: Open-air-theatre in Salzburg, Szeged and Pécs between the two World Wars] (Budapest: Gondolat, 2009), p. 437.

Kárpáti, P., 'Akárki: Moralitásjáték [Akárki: Morality]', in *Színház drámamelléklet* 3 (1993).

Kárpáti, P., 'Everywoman', in *Hungarian Plays. New Drama from Hungary* (London: Nick Hern Books, 1996).

Kárpáti, P., 'Akárki: Moralitásjáték [Akárki: Morality]', in P. Kárpáti, *Világvevő: Öt színdarab* [World receiver: Five plays] (Pécs: Jelenkor, 1999).

Kerekes, A., M. Kindl and J. Szabó, 'Előszó [Introduction]', in *Post Festum: Szabadtéri játékok a két világháború között Salzburgban, Szegeden és Pécsett* [Post Festum: Open-air-theatre in Salzburg, Szeged and Pécs between the two World Wars] (Budapest: Gondolat, 2009), pp. 13-49.

Kindermann, H., *Theatergeschichte Europas. VIII. Band: Naturalismus und Impressionismus. I. Teil: Deutschland/*Österreich/Schweiz (Salzburg: Otto Müller, 1968).

Leisler, E. and G. Prossnitz (eds), *Hugo von Hofmannsthals' Jedermann. Das Spiel vom Sterben des reichen Mannes' und Max Reinhardts Inszenierungen: Texte, Dokumente, Bilder* (Frankfurt: S. Fischer, 1973).

Maeterlinck, M., *Théatre III: Aglavaine et* Sélysette (1896); Ariane et Barbe-Bleue (1901); Soeur Béatrice. *Miracle en trois actes (1901)* (Bruxelles: P. Lacomblez, 1901).

Miklós, S. (ed.), 'Akárki' (translated by Gyula Tellér), in Szenczi Miklós (ed.), *Akárki: Misztériumjátékok, mirákulumok, moralitások* [Akárki: Mystery plays, miracles and moralities] (Budapest: Európa, 1984).

Milton, J., 'Translation Studies and Adaptation Studies', in A. Pym and A. Perekrestenko (eds.), *Translation Research Projects 2* (Tarragona: Intercultural Studies Group, 2009), pp. 51-58.

N.N., 'Akárki hivatása – Bábos moralitás és platformjáték [The summoning of Everyman – Morality and platform drama with puppets]', in *Szinhaz.hu Magyar Színházi Portál*, 2012 March 5, http://szinhaz.hu/budapest/44791-akarki-hivatasa-babos-moralitas-es-platform-jatek.

N.N., 'Akárki – Moralitásjáték [Akárki – Morality play]', (2012) Website of the Mesebolt Bábszínház, http://meseboltbabszinhaz.hu/repertoar/akarki-moralitasjatek-felnotteknek-szolo-utcaszinhazi-eloadas, last consulted on 14 January 2016.

Paál, J., 'Reinhardt professzor a szegedi ünnepi játékokról [Professor Reinhardt on the subject of the open-air festival of Szeged]', in *Délmagyarország*, 15 August 1931. Reprinted in A. Kerekes, M. Kindl and J. Szabó (eds.), *Post Festum: Szabadtéri játékok a két világháború között Salzburgban, Szegeden és Pécsett* [Post Festum: Open-air-theatre in Salzburg, Szeged and Pécs between the two World Wars] (Budapest: Gondolat, 2009), p. 106.

Rakovszky, Zs., A. Daróczi and O. Réthelyi, *Beatrijs: Egy apáca története* [Beatrijs: The story of a nun] (Budapest: L'Harmattan, 2012).

Réthelyi, O., 'Beatrijs a nagyvilágban: A Beatrijs és a holland irodalmi kánon [Beatrijs in the wide world: The *Beatrijs* and the Dutch literary canon]', in Zs. Rakovszky, A. Daróczi and O. Réthelyi, *Beatrijs: Egy apáca története* [Beatrijs: The story of a nun] (Budapest: L'Harmattan, 2012), pp. 95-109.

Réthelyi, O., 'Beatrijzen op de planken: Nederlandstalige toneelbewerkingen van het Beatrijs-verhaal in de eerste helft van de twintigste eeuw [Beatrices on the stage: Dutch language adaptations of the medieval Beatrijs-story in the first half of the twentieth century]', in T. van Kalmthout, O. Réthelyi and R. Sleiderink (eds.), *Beatrijs de wereld in* (Gent: Academia, 2013), pp. 263-295.

Schreiber, E.G., 'Everyman in America', in *Comparative Drama* 9: 2 (1975), pp. 99-115.

Sophokles, *König Ödipus: Tragödie, übersetzt und für die neuere Bühne eingerichtet von Hugo von Hofmannsthal* (Berlin: S. Fischer Verlag, 1911).

Staud, G., 'Max Reinhardt in Ungarn' and 'Zeittafel der Reinhardt Gastspiel und Gastinszenierungen', in E. Leisler and G. Prossnit (eds.), *Max Reinhardt in Europa* (Salzburg: S. Fischer, 1973), pp. 7-31 and pp. 312-319.

Stevens, M., 'The Reshaping of *Everyman:* Hofmannsthal at Salzburg', in *Germanic Review* 48 (1973), pp. 117-131.

Styan, J.L., *Modern Drama in Theory and Practice 3: Expressionism and Epic Theatre* (Cambridge: Cambridge University Press, 1983).

Tasnádi I., 'Finito', in *Fédra fitnesz: Verses drámák* [Phaedra fitness: Plays in verse] (Budapest: Palatinus, 2010).

Thuróczy, K., 'Akárki', in *Csütörtökünnep* (Budapest: Neoprológus Bt., 2000).

Tóth, M., *'Akárki' a kortárs európai drámairodalomban* ['*Akárki*/*Everyman*' in contemporary European drama] (PhD dissertation submitted to the Theatre Academy of Budapest, 2013).

Tunnat, F.D., *Karl Vollmoeller – Dichter und Kulturmanager: Eine Biographie* (Hamburg: Tredition, 2008).

Van Coillie, J., 'Nibble, Nibble Like a Mouse. Who is Nibbling at the Source Text's House? Retranslating Fairy Tales: Untangling the Web of Causation', in V. Douglas and F. Cabaret (eds.), *Retranslating Children's Literature* (Wien: Peter Lang, 2014), p. 39-52.

Van Elslander, A. (ed.), *Den spyeghel der salicheyt van Elckerlijc* (Antwerpen: De Nederlandsche Boekhandel, 1985).

Van Kalmthout, T., O. Réthelyi and R. Sleiderink (eds.), *Beatrijs de wereld in* (Gent: Academia Press, 2013).

Van Kalmthout, T., O. Réthelyi and R. Sleiderink (eds.), 'Beatrijs de wereld in. Inleiding', in T. van Kalmthout, O. Réthelyi and R. Sleiderink (eds.), *Beatrijs de wereld in* (Gent: Academia, 2013), pp. 5-18.

Vanhelleputte, M., 'Herkunft und Originalität von Hofmannsthals "Jedermann"', in E. Leisler and G. Prossnitz (eds.), *Hugo von Hofmannsthals Jedermann: Das Spiel vom Sterben des reichen Mannes und Max Reinhardts Inszenierungen* (Frankfurt am Main: S. Fischer, 1973), pp. 81-98.

Von Hofmannsthal, H., *Akárki. Játék a gazdag ember haláláról* [Akárki. The play about the death of a rich man], translated by Miklós Kállay (Budapest: Genius, 1924).

CHAPTER 8

The Splendour of Vondel's *Lucifer*

Canonicity and Cultural Memory

Chiara Beltrami Gottmer (University of Amsterdam, The Netherlands),
Marijke Meijer Drees (University of Groningen, The Netherlands),
Marco Prandoni (University of Bologna, Italy),
Rita Schlusemann (Free University of Berlin, Germany)*

For the stage director Hans Croiset, Joost van den Vondel's *Lucifer* is a lifelong companion. In 2010, Croiset wrote the novel *Lucifer onder de Linden* [Lucifer under the linden].[1] The book deals with a fictional case of the reception of Vondel's play (1654) in Nazi Germany. In 1935, a Jewish Dutch actor, Moritz Ackerman, finds himself involved in the direction of the play in Berlin, in German translation. In this novel Croiset reflects on translation, performance, performance in translation and (trans)cultural memory, and the book was a great source of inspiration for our research team on Vondel's *Lucifer*.

Lucifer proved to have a remarkable, though contentious, persistence in Dutch cultural memory and the text has travelled widely via translations in different contexts, across the borders of the Dutch cultural space, and through different media. Albert Vogel senior recited it for varied audiences in Dutch as well as in translation. It reached thoroughly different audiences in Java (1916), Paris (1927), London (1988), Milan (1999). Music adaptations were performed in Germany (1851) and the USA (1914). In 2006 H.E.R.R. published the CD *Lucifer*, in which the English translation functions as a sort of libretto for what might be called a neo-folk opera. Most performers, like the composer Michiel Spapé, are Dutch, but located in different countries: *Lucifer* can still appeal to contemporary, globalised subcultures. In some extreme cases, these may have far-right political leanings.

Lucifer's translation, adaptation and transformation dynamics are thus not just confined to university departments of Dutch Studies. This international

* Marco Prandoni wrote sections 1, 2 and 6; Rita Schlusemann section 3; Marijke Meijer Drees section 4; Chiara Beltrami Gottmer section 5.

success story is quite exceptional in Dutch literature and in the theatre of the Golden Age, which seldom functioned outside the Dutch-speaking area.[2] In this paper we want to address Lucifer's continuing appeal: its awkward, controversial canonical status in the Low Countries, its circulation across time, space and cultural barriers and its transcultural memory potential. We will particularly concentrate on *Lucifer*'s canonicity and reception dynamics between the nineteenth and the twentieth century: in the confessionalised Dutch cultural memory; in Germany, a neighbouring country with close relations with the Dutch cultural space and which has a certain cross-national intercourse with it; in South Africa and the Dutch Indies, two contexts which were geographically remote but closely related to the Dutch one. We are doing this within the theoretical frameworks of cultural memory, cultural transfer and Translation Studies.

The case of Germany is very interesting, since the play was translated several times, integrally or partially, in the nineteenth century, at a time when the German and Dutch national literary spaces were also shaped by means of canonical literary works and authors from the past who seemed to embody national (and sometimes confessional) identities. How did *Lucifer* function and who were the translators? How did the national and the confessional element interact in both the Netherlands and Germany? Did memory cross confessional as well as national boundaries?

The cases of South Africa and the Dutch Indies will help us understand whether the play was mobilised, in translation and/or in performance, to propagate Dutchness and the Dutch cultural heritage in contexts where communities existed (such as the colonial elite in the Indies and the Boers in South Africa) which might be expected to be interested in such a mnemonic challenge. And did the play also evoke other cultural memories than the Dutch one, displaying thus a transcultural memorial potential?

A CONTROVERSIAL CANONICITY

First of all, Lucifer's controversial status concerns its theatricality. This dimension of Vondel's text has long been set aside, denied, and forgotten. Vondel shaped a stage plot which already circulated in many literary and extra-literary discursive practices on which he could draw. In late medieval drama, the subject-matter, usually interwoven with the fall of Adam and Eve, was staged in mystery plays. The last scene in Vondel's play, Adam and Eve's fall, which disturbed so many classicist readers of Vondel, bears traces of the celestial cycle, typical of late medieval performance culture.[3]

The Dutch Renaissance theatre was situated between literature and stage, within that dynamic tension. However, *Lucifer* lost its function as a play-text as a consequence of the censorship in 1654, when the city magistrate decided to forbid the staging of the play after only two performances because it was felt to be blasphemous. For two and a half centuries it was confined to the domain of literature, only available as a reading text.[4] Later, in the eighteenth century, nobody thought of staging it again: the play did not at all conform to classicist aesthetics. Moreover, owing to the complex multi-confessional structure of the Republic, religious topics were off-limits, and especially so if the author was a Catholic, as was Vondel when he wrote *Lucifer*.

We might wonder why *Lucifer* did not return to the stage in the nineteenth century, at a time when literature and theatre enjoyed immense cultural power and were important memory genres.[5] After the independence of the new Kingdom of The Netherlands, theatre repertoires experienced a nationalist turn. Vondel was singled out as a champion of the Golden Age, an era to which the new rulers looked for legitimization. Vondel's validation by cultural, social and political institutions is clear from his presence in school curricula, the annotated editions of his works (for instance by the romantic critic and novel-writer Van Lennep, who organised private performances of the play), statues, museums and public celebrations. However, Vondel's conversion to Catholicism made his national annexation somewhat awkward and selective.[6] For public re-use, he first had to be deconfessionalised. From the second half of the century onwards, Dutch Catholics began profiling themselves, in search of recognition and historical foundations for their identity politics. Now Vondel became instrumental in a mnemonic challenge, as a vehicle of self-definition. He was annexed by those who wanted to equip themselves with a historical Catholic identity, claiming a genealogy in the Golden Age. As a consequence, during the decennia of the social fragmentation of Dutch society, Vondel occupied a highly ambivalent position: at the same time national icon-monument and confession-specific Catholic author. Several memory communities[7] existed side-by-side and partially overlapped with each other, partially were in competition with each other. *Lucifer* belonged to a shared core canon, but with different accents and a specific emphasis on confessional elements inside the Catholic pillar, which tried to re-enact it as means of enculturation. It enjoyed a great success among Catholic scholars who emphasised Vondel's use of patristic and scholastic sources. In the edition of Vondel's complete works published in the 1930s, the commentary by father Molkenboer displayed great theological erudition. Catholics had apparently won the mnemonic struggle or rather, found their way to a national podium.[8]

Despite this (pillarised) success, *Lucifer* did not reach the stage until the twentieth century. The play was deemed unstageable, with its location in heaven and its offputting long narrative passages. Translation Studies have shown that drama is always culture-bound, and that expectations about theatre and performance change constantly.[9] In the nineteenth century most people shared the view that universals of performability existed, but in fact they just shared a romantic and realistic paradigm of theatre. It was only because of the efforts of the director Willem Royaards that *Lucifer* made its comeback on stage in 1910.[10] He heralded a new concept of theatre, inspired by international innovators like Craig and Appia. It was a triumph. For Royaards and many other later directors, in the Netherlands and abroad, the setting in heaven was an imaginative and practical challenge. A striking example of this was provided in Paris in 1927 by the 'Vlaams Volkstoneel', which combined an interesting mixture of Catholic revival and avant-gardism, directed by Johan de Meester jr. Picasso and his friends had to cope with the Dutch text, reduced to sheer 'sound' for the non-Dutch speaking audience, as in the best surrealistic tradition. To get around this problem, other staging devices were used, by which meaning was encoded.[11] *Lucifer* functioned very well as performance, despite the opaqueness of the spoken text. Royaards and De Meester worked together with leading artists to realise 'complete' works of art: a symbolist idea of theatre, which could draw inspiration from *Lucifer*'s 'medieval' theatricality.[12] From then on it became possible to revive the stage dimension of the play-text.

The newly established tradition was, however, only stable for a short period. At the end of the Sixties, Vondel was one of the first victims of the cultural revolution: he once again became an icon, but this time of a fossilised tradition. In the following decade, Vondel's work experienced a severe loss of status and many critics heralded its death in Dutch contemporary culture. Hans Croiset would prove they were wrong and created a bridge between *Lucifer* (and Vondel's work in general) and his own time in 1979, together with Guus Rekers, and again later, in 2001.[13] Cultural remembrance became prominent, and the play functioned again as a mediator of re-enacted memory. Vondel's *Lucifer* proved to possess that combination of monumentality and malleability which, according to Ann Rigney, explains the long-term cultural life and the afterlives of what is called a classic.[14]

In his novel *Lucifer onder de Linden*, Hans Croiset interweaves fiction and autobiographical elements in many ways. The play which Moritz directs in Nazi Germany is a *figura*, an anticipation of Croiset's own *Lucifer* direction in 1979: angels are Chaplin-like, clumsy clowns. What seems ridiculous at first sight acquires a political depth later, as the angels realise that they have been misled by God's mendacious propaganda. This profoundly political staging of the play, which gained the appreciation of audiences in the Netherlands and Flanders, actualises elements which are potentially present in the performance text itself. Critics have addressed the highly puzzling nature of the play, which perhaps lies at the heart of its continuing appeal, and is a central element of its ambivalence. Croiset's interpretation is thus capable of actualisation, as are others'. It suffices to read recent Vondel-studies[15] to realise that completely different interpretations of this polyvalent play are possible.

After discussing *Lucifer*'s controversial canonicity in the Dutch literary and theatrical space, we want to understand, by means of several case-studies, how this work circulated outside the Dutch borders, in the first place in neighbouring Germany, and whether it negotiated a transconfessional memory at a time of heightened nationalisms.

TRANSNATIONAL AND TRANSRELIGIOUS MEMORY: VONDEL'S *LUCIFER* IN GERMANY IN THE NINETEENTH CENTURY

The memory of an author such as Vondel has something of a hybrid character. Of course, he is *the* major Dutch poet and wrote in Dutch, but his works were often translated, from the mid-1850s onwards, into German. He is also remembered as a poet in Germany because he was born in Cologne.

Figure 1. Joost van den Vondel sculptured by Paul de Swaaf, Cologne, Town Hall, 1991. © Raimond Spekking / CC BY-SA 4.0 (via Wikimedia Commons)

Therefore we have to ask: should we regard Vondel's oeuvre predominantly from a Dutch perspective (and focus on the transfer from Dutch into other languages), or would it be better to stress his transnational dimension, and therefore consider him as a transnational author, especially from about 1850 onwards, after the first German translations of his *Lucifer* were published? The basic assumption for research on cultural transfer is that culture is 'genuinely intercultural',[16] as it analyses the non-national aspects of a culture, and in fact principally denies the concept of 'the national'. Cultural transfer research not only deals with transfer, but also with the processes of cultural exchange. The concept of 'cultural exchange' 'emphasises the bi-directional and multi-directional nature of cultural transfer',[17] and therefore must be viewed as being border-free, which implies predominantly thinking beyond or outside national categories. European cultures are always to be seen as intercultural, which runs counter to common notions such as national or continental (self-)identifications. As a consequence, the notion of cultural transfer has to be complemented by the 'transnational turn', which, in effect means that the translation is regarded as a 'social and cultural praxis'.[18] In a comparable way, memories can circulate transnationally, as was recently argued by De Cesari and Rigney.[19] They chart the rich production of memory across and beyond national borders and analyse questions of circulation and the scales of memory.

Even though there is some research about the translations of Vondel's literary works into German, the focus remains mostly national, with most of the publications stressing the national importance of these transfers. For example, Van Gemert states that – especially in the second half of the nineteenth century – Germany showed an interest in Vondel for the following reasons: because of the new concepts of national literature and world literature, and because German literary history as a national philology underwent a process of self-discovery, and therefore showed interest in neighbouring 'national' literatures as well.[20] Those literatures which counted as classical literatures were supposed to be interesting. Furthermore, literature of the early modern period was generally promoted. For example, in 1876, Wilhelm Braune initiated a series which edited sixteenth- and seventeenth-century German literature.[21] As Vondel was regarded as a major poet of the Dutch Golden Age, his works were translated.

Owing to the popularity of German translations of Vondel's *Lucifer* from the 1850s onwards and especially after 1868, the activities in Germany can be characterised as an indicator of the transnational quality of this tragedy.[22] The fact that there were four different German translations of *Lucifer* within two years underscores the fact that Germans recognised the quality of Vondel's work, and, at the same time, this contributed to the enhanced status of this literary work in the 'home country'. Therefore, these translations had a general positive effect on the prestige of *Lucifer* and of the author Vondel, and its importance not only for national, but rather for *trans*national memory. Through the German translations presented here as an example, Vondel's *Lucifer* made its entrance onto the stage of European literatures, and made a further step forward in the realm of world dramatic literature. The translations enabled a change in the Dutch Vondel-perspective, away from an exaggerated sense of idiocentrism and demarcation of boundaries, and towards a broader international view.

In the first extensive publication about Vondel's *Lucifer* in Germany, Glaser (1857) emphasised that religious and political aspects had become intertwined in an excellent manner, and praised the tragedy as the 'highest masterpiece', comparing it with Milton's *Paradise Lost*. Vondel had succeeded in narrating the fight between the 'appalled legions' and divine power in an intoxicating way.[23]

In the Netherlands, Jozef Alberdingk Thijm (1820-1889), a poet who was committed to the emancipation of the Catholics, can be seen as the major figure in the Catholic presentation of Vondel in the second half of the nineteenth century. But Thijm was also influential with regard to the opening of the famous Wallraf-Richartz Museum in Cologne in 1861. In his correspondence with August Reichensperger (1808-1895), we can detect an important exchange of opinions. A friend of Reichensperger's, the painter

Eduard Steinle (1810-1886), was asked to make frescoes for the new museum depicting the cultural history of the Rhine region on the walls around the stairs. In 1860, Reichensperger asked Thijm to support him in his proposal that Vondel also should be part of the frescoes: 'With your help we could influence Steinle to offer the space to Vondel [instead of Rubens]', and 'surely, there must be a good portrait of Vondel?'[24]

The fresco itself has not been preserved; however, we do have a watercolour painting that can be dated to the years 1861-1864 – having served as an early draft of the fresco – with the title *The New Renaissance*.

Figure 2. Eduard Steinle, draft for the stairwell fresco *The New Renaissance* in the Wallraf-Richartz-Museum, 1861-1864 (Source: Rheinisches Bildarchiv, rba_d033527)

Vondel is depicted on the left. Obviously, Reichensberger was successful in promoting his ideas. Ten other people who were regarded as major representatives of the new renaissance, and who were supposed to enhance the prestige of the museum as a place of cultural memory were included: among these were Johann Wolfgang von Goethe, but also Peter Paul Rubens, who was born in Cologne, but lived in Antwerp, Mechelen, Mantua, Spain, and London.

Next to Vondel, we see Anna Maria van Schurman (also Schürmann), (1607-1678), whose father came from Antwerp, her mother from the Eifel, and who herself lived in Cologne, Utrecht, Amsterdam and Altona near Hamburg, which belonged to Denmark at that time.[25] Of course, the fresco was intended to portray Cologne's famous figures, but if we were to draw a map of their addresses, nearly all European countries would be included. The people contributed to the transnational memory in a personal way. Next to the other prominent artists and scholars on the walls of the staircase, Vondel is depicted as a protagonist of transnational memory, representing the new Renaissance in a distinct de-bordered way.

At the same time, Alberdingk Thijm himself not only designed the pedestal of the famous Vondel monument in Amsterdam, but he was also a member of the commission who planned this memorial and the celebration of its unveiling. Its presentation to the city of Amsterdam in 1867 was seen as a national event – even the minister of domestic affairs gave a speech. The monument, which presents Vondel as a national hero, claimed a general national identification and can be regarded as an official interdenominational mythization.[26]

The participation of women during the festivities, which lasted three days and could only be attended by invitation, was an exceptional occurrence – and in fact only one German woman took part: Lina Schneider. Born in Weimar in 1831, she moved to Rotterdam in 1862, and in 1869, received a degree in Dutch studies and physics. She not only greatly admired Vondel, but also translated his poems and recited her German translations in cities throughout the Netherlands: in Amsterdam, Leiden, Dordrecht, Rotterdam and The Hague, but also in Germany. We can distinguish these activities as further proof of the genuine transcultural celebration of the poet in both Germany and the Netherlands at the same time. We will have the opportunity to examine her contribution in depth later on in this paper.

The first German translation of *Lucifer* is an *overture* composed by Jan Albert van Eyken (1851). In the late 1860s, three integral German translations of Vondel's *Lucifer* were published, followed by another five partial translations.[27] Especially in their paratexts, the first three – by Quadt, Grimmelt (both in 1868) and De Wilde (1869) – accentuate the inherent transnational characteristics of the play.

Quadt portrays Vondel as a genuine European dramatist, presenting the poet laureate as an important cultural icon in such cities as Cologne, Antwerp, Rome, and Rotterdam. Vondel is presented as one of the greatest luminaries of Catholic literature, and is mentioned in the same breath as Corneille, Racine, Molière and Milton. Vondel's visual and outspoken cultural memory is not limited to one or two nations, but surpasses and transcends boundaries. Quadt calls Vondel one of the 'greatest experts of Catholic literature in general [...] the best poet of fables of the country, its most comic satirist, its most solid didactic, its most spirited lyrical author, its greatest dramatist, and even its most skilful prose author'.[28] As such, Quadt links Vondel's outstanding transnational literary qualities with his Catholic background.

According to Grimmelt, *Lucifer* – because of its depiction of the fight between good and evil – is a timeless subject. Grimmelt specifies two purposes for his translation: to pay attention to the merits of the greatest Dutch poet, and to provide provide something especially contemporary to the reader;[29] the drama 'narrates the beginning and the first end of the fight between truth and lie, between light and darkness, which from then on was fought in all centuries, and especially in our time'.[30] By incorporating a drawing of the Vondel monument in Amsterdam, Vondel's outstanding importance for transnational memory is further underscored.

De Wilde also explicitly explains his motivation for the translation of Vondel's *Lucifer*. As the poet has been nearly forgotten in Germany, and as none can deny the poet's place in world literature, after De Wilde's own translation of the *Gysbrecht* and of *De Gebroeders* [The Brothers], he intends to add a translation of Vondel's masterpiece, *Lucifer*. He finds it hard to understand how the masterpiece remained unnoticed in Germany. De Wilde, too, presents Vondel as the predecessor of Milton's *Paradise Lost,* and is unsure whether Milton knew the text. In order to stress the importance of *Lucifer*, De Wilde also mentions the commotion after the first performances in Amsterdam: the play had to disappear from the stage after only two performances, and the first edition comprising 1,000 copies was sold within eight days. In his preface, we can detect a distinct plea for *Lucifer* as an example of canonical world literature, a text indispensable for transnational memory.

Lina Schneider played an active role when the Vondel monument in Amsterdam was opened in 1867, but her transnational role is not limited to this event. In July 1870, Alberdingk Thijm received a letter signed by a certain Wilhelm Berg. Thijm was asked to send a photograph of the beloved Vondel. Thijm must have sent the photograph very soon, as only three weeks later, on 5 August 1870, he received a letter in which the writer expressed thanks. This letter was signed by Lina Schneider, now not using the pseudonym Wilhelm Berg, which she had used for some translations, too.[31] Schneider not only expressed her admiration for the author Vondel, but she even addressed Vondel directly: 'Sleep, Vondel, sleep … But, old friend, let the foreign woman admire you and worship you, she does not have the same faith as you …', and a little later, 'Vondel, my Protestant heart beats for your Catholic soul, do you understand?'

In October 1876 Schneider was granted her petition to fix a commemorative plaque at Vondel's birth-place in Cologne, to her great delight. In February 1879 she also attended the Vondel-festivities in Amsterdam and recited a poem she had written herself: 'It is not the question, which faith Vondel had, but he takes the credit in his grave'. In her letter of the 3rd of February 1879, she mentioned that on the 8th of February 1879 she would recite *Lucifer* in Cologne and that Samuel de Lange would play the 'Ouvertüre zu Lucifer', which had already been performed in Prague in 1862.[32]

To sum up, we can identify several activities in the nineteenth century, resulting in nine German *Lucifer*-translations, with the year 1868 as the year of the breakthrough. Lina Schneider in particular promoted Vondel's *Lucifer* and other works of her beloved author in Germany and the Netherlands. Lina Schneider herself can be considered a greatly relevant transnational and transreligious actor in the literary and cultural field, who was a considerable contributor to Vondel's transnational and transreligious memory.

Now we will turn to cultural contexts which for centuries were deeply interconnected with the Dutch one: those of South Africa and of the Dutch Indies. Does *Lucifer* function there as vehicle of transcultural memory and, if this was the case, with which ideological implications? Is it hybridised with other cultural memories apart from the Dutch one, or just enacted as monument of Dutchness?

LUCIFER IN SOUTH AFRICA: LINGUISTIC AFFINITY AND THE MEMORY OF FAMILY KINSHIP

Two editions of Vondel's *Lucifer* have been published in South Africa.[33] The oldest dates from 1925. It is a volume in the series 'Afrikaanse Vondel-uitgawe' (African Vondel publications), a joint initiative of the publishing firms De Bussy in Pretoria and the Hollands-Afrikaanse Uitgeversmaatschappij (the Dutch African Publishing Company), formerly Jacques Dusseau & Co, in Cape Town.[34] The other *Lucifer*-edition, from 1968, is a volume in the series 'Vondel vir Suid-Afrika' published by Van Schaik in Pretoria.[35] The publishers had historical ties with the book trade in the Netherlands.[36] The main editors were full professors at the University of Pretoria.[37] They presented *Lucifer* in Vondel's seventeenth-century Dutch, albeit with an introduction in Afrikaans and also with annotations in Afrikaans which were based on older Dutch editions.[38] Both *Lucifer*-editions were used for educational purposes in university departments 'Afrikaans en Nederlands' (African and Dutch).

These practices point to the complicated past that South Africa shares with the Netherlands. Two aspects of this shared past will be highlighted: firstly, the linguistic affinity between Afrikaans and Dutch; secondly, the memory of the so-called *stamverwantschap* or family kinship.[39]

When Afrikaans and Dutch speakers meet, they can usually understand each other's language, at least to some degree. The similarities can be explained by the fact that both languages have emerged from early modern Dutch, though they developed in different directions. In South Africa this older Dutch was mixed, for instance, with the native language of the Khoi-Khoin and the languages that French, English, German and Asian immigrants brought along.[40]

From 1925 onwards Afrikaans and English became the two official languages in the Union of South Africa (the predecessor of the present Republic of SA) and according to the Union Act 'Afrikaans' included 'Dutch'.[41] In the context of the extending socio-economic influence and political power of white nationalists, the so-called 'Afrikaners', Afrikaans was cultivated and its development into a language of its own was actively fostered. This process became intensified from 1948 on, when the National Party government preferred to communicate in Afrikaans, and it became the lingua franca in cities, on farms and, from 1974 onwards, it also had to be used in black schools as the medium of instruction. The Constitution of 1983 mentioned only Afrikaans and English.[42] Since 1994, when Apartheid was officially abolished, Afrikaans has been one of the country's 11 official languages. It is the first language of more than 6 million South Africans, of whom the vast majority is coloured. For these South-Africans Afrikaans originally was, and still is, their mother tongue and first language, although they have been politically excluded and socially marginalised during Apartheid.

So much for this briefly sketched history of linguistic affinity between Afrikaans and Dutch. The context makes it more or less understandable why Vondel's seventeenth-century Dutch was maintained by both *Lucifer*-editions. We will now turn to the memory of family kinship.

The memory of a Dutch-South African *stamverwantschap* [family kinship] has its basis in the heroic reputation of the Dutchman Jan van Riebeeck (who landed on the Cape in April 1652) as the founder of South Africa.[43] This memory was informed by the assumption that the South African 'Boers' or 'Afrikaners' were descendants of the Dutch colonists who had settled in the Cape Province in the footsteps of Van Riebeeck. The Boers considered themselves as the 'verre neven' [distant cousins] of the Dutch.

During the last decades of the nineteenth century, the memory of family kinship produced massive support in the Netherlands for the Boer during their freedom wars against British domination (known as the first Anglo-Boer War (1880-81) and the second Anglo-Boer War (1899-1902)). Opinion leaders in the pillarised Netherlands of those days were searching for public expressions of a unifying cultural nationalism that was rooted in Dutch history, notably the heroicised past of the Golden Age. But historical ties with the Dutch colonial past, for instance those with South Africa, also offered opportunities to strengthen cultural nationalism and concord.[44] The Anglo-Boer Wars worked as a catalyst for Dutch identification with the Afrikaner 'kinsmen' of the Zuid-Afrikaanse Republiek [South African Republic].[45] The idea that the Boers had historical ties with the Dutch formed the basis of emotional involvement with the war against the British and of compassion with the women and children who died in British concentration camps. Dutch poets made highly emotive contributions. For instance, Herman Schaepman (priest, poet and fervent admirer of Vondel) wrote the poem *Voor de Boeren* [For the Boers] which starts with the sentence:

> A cry of despair reaches us from Africa; it is littered there with palaces of death, full of cruelty; now that one does not report false victories from the battlefield, woman and child have to pay the price to cruel violence.[46]

In the twentieth century, South-African Afrikaners continued to seek the support of their Dutch kinsmen, in order to stimulate the elevation of their own African language and culture. Literary scholars promoted a common cultural ideal that was known as 'Diets' and that united the literatures of the Netherlands and Flanders with South Africa's Afrikaans literature on the same level. One of its advocates was professor Kritzinger, the author of *Die Opstands-motief by Vondel* from 1930, which was the first scholarly monograph in Afrikaans about Vondel (including a chapter on *Lucifer*). When Kritzinger accepted the chair in 'Afrikaanse en Nederlandse letterkunde' at the University of Pretoria, he referred in his inaugural lecture to 'Diets' literature and connected it metaphorically with the memory of family kinship:

> When I consider the field of Diets literature, taken in its broadest sense (and in that I include Dutch, Flemish and Afrikaans literature), I prefer to see it as a unit. One should view it as a large tree that has grown in this particular way. Middle Dutch and part of the literature of the later period until approximately 1652, when Jan van Riebeeck landed at the southern tip of our country, form the trunk. [...] It is the literature of a large segment of our forefathers [...], and therefore it also belongs to us. All the work of the seventeenth-century writers, such as Hooft, Bredero, and to a large extent Vondel, to mention but a few names from the first generation from the so-called Golden Age is ours, because their work was already in existence when Jan van Riebeeck [...] laid the foundations for the future South Africa [...]. From this moment onward the trunk sprouted a Dutch-Afrikaans branch. From this branch the real Afrikaans branch [...] developed [...]. At times the Dutch and Flemish branches stopped developing, only to continue growing strongly again. For us it is important to know that they also produced wonderful fruit. At our university we will not neglect any part of this extended Dutch literature.[47]

During the Second World War the memory of *stamverwantschap* became somewhat tainted in Dutch public opinion. The former sense of kinship turned into aversion owing to pro-German feelings which were propagated by nationalist Afrikaners as a result of their anti-British attitude.[48] But at the level of politics the memory of kinship was kept alive. The Dutch government stimulated Dutch people to emigrate to South-Africa by making them aware of their kinship with the Afrikaners.[49] Moreover, the government stayed loyal for many years to the National Party which dominated South Africa's politics since 1948 and legislated Apartheid (1948-1990). As such the memory of kinship formed a strong basis for Dutch-South African relationship until well into the twentieth century.

The shared Dutch-South African past, with linguistic affinity and the memory of kinship as its pillars, stimulated Afrikaans-speaking literary scholars and writers to consider Dutch literature as a natural source for African literature. At the university departments 'Afrikaans en Nederlands' Dutch literature, modern and historical as well, was taught as a part of the African literary system and of African literary history. From the 1920's to the 1990's South African editions of canonic Dutch literature were produced, such as Vondel's tragedy *Lucifer*.

But what about the current post-Apartheid era? Is *Lucifer* still read and studied in today's University Departments of Afrikaans and Nederlands? This question was put to several South-African colleagues at the university departments of Afrikaans and Dutch of Bloemfontein, Johannesburg, Stellenbosch, Potchefstroom, Port Elizabeth, Pretoria (both universities) and Western Cape. The response makes clear that historical Dutch literature occupies only a very modest place in today's teaching curricula or, in a few cases, is not taught any longer. Vondel's poetry is usually represented by some of his well-known personal poems, such as *Uitvaert van mijn dochterken* [Funeral of my little daughter]. One of the professors wrote: 'During my own years of study (the late sixties) it [*Lucifer*] was a compulsory item on the reading list. Nowadays I would never dare to confront my students with a drama of Vondel'.[50]

LUCIFER IN THE INDIES

During the Dutch colonial period in what is now known as Indonesia, many people, from all over Europe, sought their fortune in the colonial army and on the plantations scattered all over the island chain. These European settlers formed the heart of the white population in the colony, while the Dutch-speaking elite imported part of its own culture and made it blossom in the Indies. Theatre was one aspect of this. The Netherlands always were the great example to follow, both on a cultural and a traditional level. The elite in the colony tried therefore to import what was canonical in the motherland and stubbornly held onto it. This is how the *Gysbrecht van Amstel* was nurtured and staged in the Indies. Theatre served as a means to perpetuate the cultural memory of long lost polders amidst the waving palms of the equator.

Theatre in the Indies[51] was a performing art and it had many forms, among which the shadow puppets better known as 'Wayan Kulit'. A typical Indonesian shadow theatre, it still comes in more than one form: the 'Wayan Kulit' and the 'Wayan Wong', characteristic of the royal courts of Central Java. 'Wayan Wong' was frequently staged with actors, who would mime the actions, instead of puppets. 'Wayan' is always supported by music, especially in royal courts. 'Gamelan' orchestras were very common in the traditional indigenous performing arts, and they were often accompanied by mime and dance.

'Komedie Stambul' theatre is the hybrid form that sprouted in the Indies thanks to its creator, August Mahieu, in 1891. Mahieu was an Indo, that is part Indonesian and part European. He mixed the theatre forms of both his heritages in what became known as Stamboel: Wayan, Gamelan and mime together with European theatre. Mostly staged in Malay, the most common *lingua franca* in Asia at that time, Stamboel was not accessible to everyone, as not everyone spoke Malay, but it was connected to the cultural background of the audience, and it was a form of entertainment accessible even to the illiterate, thanks to the music and mime; horses and acrobats were sometimes added to the show. 'Komedie Stamboel' died with Mahieu in 1903, the remains have a presence in many other art forms and a few aspects of 'Stamboel' evolved and became the foundation for modern Indonesian television, for example.

Newspapers are the only source of information, because of a lack of studies. In our research we came across many reports about the *Lucifer*, with some interesting approaches. We know for a fact that the Dutch elite did have amateur acting groups as well as musical ensembles, and the indigenous elite might have had such groups as well. In fact, Vondel was hardly ever staged in the island chain, neither by the elite nor by the locals. Apparently, there was a lack of interest in a complete staging of the plays, both on Java and Sumatra. People seemed to be little concerned with the more sophisticated aspects of the culture belonging to the Dutch canon.

Dutch people often felt isolated in the Indies, cut off from all civilization, and this was most keenly felt by women, who sought to bring some refinement to the colony. In an attempt to fight back the sense of loss they felt, they tried to include Vondel in official ceremonies. On those occasions, the choruses would be recited, especially by academics. A great playwright such as Vondel was the perfect means of forging a solid tradition based on the heroes of the motherland, in order to strengthen the cultural identity and patriotism of the people born and raised in the colony. Establishing such traditions would certainly give a stronger sense of identity and common origins, just as much as Sinterklaas. The issue of the *Soerabaisch Handelsblad* of 15 November 1937 announces such a ceremony, Vondel's birthday. People were invited to join the celebration of the great poet, through a huge cultural festival, in the presence of the East-Java governor, who would give a speech and would be followed by prominent members of the artists groups of the area. Parts of the

Lucifer and *Gysbrecht van Amstel* would be staged. We also found references to recitals of the choruses from the *Lucifer* by professional actors. Albert Vogel sr. for example toured the colony in 1906, while his son, Albert Vogel jr., did the same in 1946. On these long tours actors could visit many parts of the Dutch Indies. Such events reinforced the national historical culture, plugging into the nascent tradition of honouring the great figures of the past.

The *Java-Post* of 19 May 1916 announced that a pupil at the Muntilan school rewrote the *Lucifer* in Javanese, using Javanese metrics and compressing the whole plot in a hundred strophes, thus transposing it into the style of traditional Javanese poetry, used not only in theatrical performances but in every cultural activity in Javanese courts. The name of Raden Mas Poerwo Lelono comes to mind as he described his journeys through Java, *Reizen van Raden Mas Arjo Poerwo Lelono*.[52] He too used traditional verse when describing the natural elements he encountered on his travels. The *Lucifer* poem was later printed in the magazine *Djawi-Sraja*, as reported in the article in the Java-Post, even if the author of the poem kept his true identity hidden. The Dutch journalist praised the translation, saying that it kept the original musicality of the play, despite the lack of identical metrical conventions, owing to the importance of the rhythm and the sweet flowing sounds. For the staging, gamelan music was added, in the tradition of Javanese theatre associated with 'Wayan Wong'. The Muntilan school obviously had an important function in bridging Javanese and Western culture.

We can reach the conclusion that no real effort was spent on staging all of Vondel's work in the colony, not even the *Gysbrecht*, although it was often referred to. Vondel's work was represented only by his choruses and used primarily for celebration purposes. It might be argued that a chorus declaimed as an entity in itself must be seen as a form of performance. Clearly, the elite in the colony was interested in different aspects of art than the elite in the mothercountry. The discrepancy between the two groups made a difference in the representation of the arts in the Netherlands and in the Dutch Indies. One aspect of this was the absence of Lucifer from the colonial stage except in its most spectacular form, the Javanese adaptation at Muntilan, in this respect the most interesting school of the colony.

CONCLUSION

Despite Vondel's controversial status, a source of disagreement in terms of its canonical value and *Lucifer*'s ban from the stage in the Netherlands for two and a half centuries, the play proved to be a survivor, although solely as a reading text. It did twice make its come-back on stage: in 1910 with Willem Royaards and in 1979 with Hans Croiset. Performances in London and Milan would follow. *Lucifer* is a remarkable case of a Dutch play functioning outside the Dutch borders, in translation as a reading text and on the stage.

In this it differs greatly from Vondel's *Gysbreght van Aemstel*, which remained uninterruptedly on the stage in the Netherlands but was little known outside the Dutch-speaking area, probably because of its character as a very specific Dutch (Amsterdam) history play. *Lucifer*'s success can be ascribed to its universal subject-matter and to his disquieting and therefore fascinating main character, as in the case of Milton's *Paradise Lost*. The poly-interpretability of the tragedy and its daring dramatic structure – appealing to twentieth-century stage directors – have certainly played a role in it.

The case of Germany in the second half of the nineteenth century illustrates the attempt by German intellectuals, thanks to important transcultural agents like Lina Schneider who put them in touch with prominent Dutch Catholic intellectuals, to promote *Lucifer* to *Weltliteratur*, and its author to the status of classic in a shared transcultural memory, as a representative of a supranational and supraconfessional German-Dutch Renaissance. At different times, even earlier in Germany than in the Netherlands, the play and its author were employed in highly institutionalised forms of remembrance, which opened up a transnational memory space.

In a completely different context, in South Africa, the university departments of literature considered Vondel an icon of shared Dutch-Afrikaans kinship for a considerable period. Here Vondel was used as a vehicle of self-definition. *Lucifer* was part of the school and university curricula and its editions presented the original text without translation: this can be considered a statement in order to underline the mutual intelligibility of the two languages and the kinship of the two literary traditions and cultural memories, which was fostered by prominent intellectuals in the Netherlands as well, in the first half of the twentieth century. Nowadays little attention seems to be paid to classic Dutch literature and theatre in post-Apartheid South Africa.

The success of *Lucifer*, and of Vondel in general, in the Dutch Indies was limited to celebrations by which the colonial elite tried to ritualise its own culture and legitimate itself, and to the declamations by Dutch actors touring the colonies. However, from what we can gather from accounts of those days, in 1916 an anonymous student from the Muntilan school was able to realise a daring adaptation of the text in a completely new poetic form. In the performance the codifications of Dutch Renaissance drama were blended with Javanese performance practices and the Dutch cultural memory was hybridised with other cultural memories.

APPENDIX

German translations of Vondel's *Lucifer* in the nineteenth century:

- *Ouverture, Entre-acte und Chöre zum Trauerspiel Lucifer für Solo, Chor und Orchester.* Componirt von J.A. van Eyken, Elberfeld 1851.
- *Joost van den Vondel's Lucifer. Ein Trauerspiel.* Übersetzt von Max Werner Quadt, Aachen 1868.
- *Joost van den Vondel's Lucifer. Ein Trauerspiel in 5 Acten.* Aus dem Holländischen übersetzt von Ferdinand Grimmelt, Münster 1868.
- *Lucifer. Trauerspiel von Joost van den Vondel aus dem Jahr 1654.* Übertragen von G.H. de Wilde, Leipzig 1869.
- *Mein treuer Belial.* Übersetzt von Luise von Ploennies, in *Bildersaal der Weltliteratur*, vol. 2, Stuttgart 1869, pp. 607-609, vv. 1-201.
- *Ehrsucht.* Übersetzt von F. Grimmelt und Andreas Jansen, in *Gedichte von Joost van den Vondel*, Münster 1873, p. 50 (act 3, vv. 1320-1330).
- Werner Otto, in: *Die Grenzboten. Zeitschrift für Politik, Literatur und Kunst* 35 (1876), p. 6, vv. 281-336.
- Alexander Baumgartner, Freiburg 1882, pp. 220-232, vv. 281-347; vv. 569-586; vv. 1256-1273; vv. 1463-1568; vv. 2144-2183.
- *Geschichte der niederländischen Literatur.* Mit Benutzung der hinterlassenen Arbeit von Ferdinand von Hellwald verfasst und durch Proben veranschaulicht von L. Schneider. Leipzig 1887, pp. 365-366.

NOTES

1 H. Croiset, *Lucifer onder de Linden* (Amsterdam: Cossee, 2010).

2 G. van Gemert, 'Between Disregard and Political Mobilization', in J. Bloemendal and F.-W. Korsten (eds.), *Joost van den Vondel (1587-1679): Dutch Playwright in the Golden Age* (Leiden/Boston: Brill, 2012), pp. 171-198.

3 J. van den Vondel, *Lucifer*, ed. Lieven Rens (Den Haag: Martinus Nijhoff, 1979), p. 9.

4 In the edition of Vondel's complete works in 1720 (*Alle de treurspelen*, Amsterdam: J. van Oosterwyk, 1720), *Lucifer* was printed first.

5 A. Erll, *Memory in Culture* (Basingstoke: Palgrave Macmillan, 2011), p. 229.

6 M.-Th. Leuker, '"Vondel op wijwater" of de legitimiteit van de non-conformiteit', in *De Negentiende Eeuw* 30 (2006), pp. 65-78.

7 Erll, *Memory in Culture*, p. 122.

8 R. Schenkeveld-van der Dussen, 'Vondel's Works for the Stage Read and Studied Over the Centuries', in J. Bloemendal and F.-W. Korsten (eds.), *Joost van den Vondel*, pp. 7-22 (16).

9 S. Bassnett, 'Translating for the Theatre: The Case Against Performability', in *TTR* 4 (1991), pp. 99-111.

10 M.B. Smits-Veldt, 'Vondel Dramas: Their Afterlives in Performance', in J. Bloemendal and F.-W. Korsten (eds.), *Joost van den Vondel*, pp. 157-70 (166).

11 G. Opsomer, 'Mei-juni 1927: Het Vlaamsche Volkstooneel (VVT)', in R.L. Erenstein (ed.), *Een theatergeschiedenis der Nederlanden* (Amsterdam: Amsterdam University Press, 1996), pp. 626-631.

12 R. Erenstein, 'De receptie van middeleeuws toneel in de twintigste eeuw', in H. van Dijk *et al.* (eds.), *Spel en spektakel* (Amsterdam: Prometheus, 2001), pp. 282-304.

13 P. de Kock, '15 december 1979: Het Publiekstheater speelt een opmerkelijke *Lucifer* van Joost van den Vondel', in R.L. Erenstein (ed.), *Een theatergeschiedenis der Nederlanden*, pp. 806-813.

14 A. Rigney, 'The Dynamics of Remembrance: Texts Between Monumentality and Morphing', in A. Erll and A. Nünning (eds.), *Cultural Memory Studies. An International and Interdisciplinary Handbook*, (Berlin-New York: De Gruyter, 2008), pp. 345-353 (349).

15 F.-W. Korsten, *Sovereignty as Inviolability: Joost van den Vondel's Theatrical Explorations in the Dutch Republic* (Hilversum: Verloren, 2009); J.F. van Dijkhuizen and H. Helmers, 'Religion and Politics – Lucifer and Milton's Paradise Lost (1674)', in Bloemendal and Korsten (eds.), *Joost van den Vondel*, pp. 377-405.

16 See for the following W. Schmale, *Cultural Transfer*, in http://ieg-ego.eu/en/threads/theories-and-methods/cultural-transfer, 2012 [accessed 10 May 2015], p. 9; L. Musner, 'Kultur als Transfer: Ein regulationstheoretischer Zugang am Beispiel der Architektur', in H. Mitterbauer and K. Scherke (eds.), *Entgrenzte Räume: Kulturelle Transfers um 1900 und in der Gegenwart* (Wien: Passagen, 2005), pp. 173-194.

17 Schmale, *Cultural Transfer*, p. 33.

18 D. Bachmann-Medik, *Cultural Turns: Neuorientierungen in den Kulturwissenschaften* (Reinbek: Rowohlt, 2006), esp. pp. 238-283.

19 C. De Cesari and A. Rigney (eds.), *Transnational Memory: Circulation, Articulation, Scales* (Berlin: De Gruyter, 2014).

20 G. van Gemert, 'Germanje groet u als haar groten zoon: Zu Vondels Renommee im deutschen Sprachraum', in J. Enklaar and H. Ester (eds.), *Wechseltausch: Übersetzen als Kulturvermittlung: Deutschland und die Niederlande* (Amsterdam-Atlanta: Rodopi, 1995), pp. 64-92 (68).

21 The title of the series was: *Neudrucke deutscher Litteraturwerke des XVI. und XVII. Jahrhunderts.*

22 For research on Vondel in Germany in the nineteenth century, characterised as 'between philology and mediation of culture', see J. Konst, 'Tussen Philologie en Kulturvermittlung: Vondelbeschouwing in Duitsland tijdens de tweede helft van de negentiende eeuw', in M. Hüning, J. Konst and T. Holzhey (eds.), *Neerlandistiek in Europa: Bijdragen tot de geschiedenis van de universitaire Neerlandistiek buiten Nederland en Vlaanderen* (Münster: Waxmann Verlag, 2010), pp. 101-129.

23 A. Glaser, 'Joost van den Vondel und sein Lucifer', in *Archiv für das Studium der Neueren Sprachen und Literaturen* 22 (1857), pp. 119-130.

24 'Mit Ihrer Hülfe wird nun wohl Steinle dahin zu bringen seijn, daß er den Platz an Vondel überträgt' and 'man hat doch auch wohl ein gutes Portrait von Vondel?' (translated by RS).

25 M. Spang, *Wenn sie ein Mann wäre: Leben und Werk der Anna Maria von Schürmann* (Darmstadt: Wissenschaftliche Buchgesellschaft, 2009).

26 M.-Th. Leuker, *Künstler als Helden und Heilige* (Münster: Waxmann Verlag, 2001), pp. 158-160.

27 See the appendix for the full titles.

28 'größten Choryphäen der katholischen Literatur überhaupt [...] des Landes bester Fabeldichter, sein witzigster Satyriker, sein gediegenster Didaktiker, sein schwungvoller Lyriker, sein größter Dramatiker, ja sogar sein gewandtester Prosaiker' (p. 11).

29 'etwas Zeitgemäßes' (translated by RS, p. III).

30 'schildert also den Anfang und ersten Ausgang eines Kampfes zwischen Wahrheit und Lüge, zwischen Licht und Finsterniß, der seitdem durch alle Jahrhunderte geführt wurde und besonders in unserer Zeit' (translated by RS, pp. III-IV).

31 The original letters are accessible online, published by the archive of Thijm of the Katholiek Documentatiecentrum at the University of Nijmegen (www.ru.nl/kdc-english).

32 The performance was organised by "Cäcilienverein", see *Niederrheinische Musik-Zeitung* 10 (19 April 1862), p. 128.

33 There is no evidence for performances of *Lucifer* in South Africa.

34 Reprinted in 1932 and 1942.

35 Reprinted in 1989.

36 N.S. Coetzee (ed.), *'n Halfeeuw van letterkunde uit Suid-Afrika: 'n Bloemlesing opgestel ter herdenking van die vyftigjarige bestaan van die firmas H.A.U.M. v/h Jacques Dusseau en J.H. de Bussy 1894-1944* (Kaapstad-Pretoria: H.A.U.M.-J.H. de Bussy, 1944), pp. i-vv. M. Coetzee, 'Papers of J.L. van Schaik Publishers', Unisa Library Manuscripts Collection, 2001, updated 2012, p. 1: http://uir.unisa.ac.za/handle/10500/5239.

37 T.H. le Roux was a full professor in Pretoria, as well as A.P. Grové; S. Strydom, the series editor of 'Vondel vir Suid-Afrika' worked at the same university as a lecturer. Jacobus Johannes Groeneweg, a vicar's son of Dutch origin, was a teacher. See http://www.let.leidenuniv.nl/Dutch/ModerneLetterkunde/Groeneweg1.html.

38 Respectively the edition Cramer/Molkenboer from the series 'Zwolsche herdrukken' (first printed in 1917, the fifth edition dates from 1922) and the so-called 'W.B.uitgave' with Vondel's complete works.

39 This contextual approach implies that there will be hardly any attention paid to the contents of the two editions.

40 See Ch. van Rensburg, *So kry ons Afrikaans* (Pretoria: LAPA Uitgewers, 2012), and W.A.M. Carstens and N. Bosman (eds.), *Kontemporêre Afrikaanse taalkunde* (Pretoria: Van Schaik Uitgewers, 2014).

41 http://en.wikisource.org/wiki/Official_Languages_of_the_Union_Act,_1925. South Africa's Constitution of 1961 states (article 119): '"Afrikaans" includes Dutch': http://en.wikisource.org/wiki/Republic_of_South_Africa_Constitution_Act,_1961.

42 The sentence 'Afrikaans includes Dutch' had been removed. See the Constitution of 1983, article X, 89: http://en.wikisource.org/wiki/Republic_of_South_Africa_Constitution_Act,_1983.

43 See W.-P. van Ledden, *Jan van Riebeeck tussen wal en schip: Een onderzoek naar de beeldvorming over Jan van Riebeeck in Nederland en Zuid-Afrika omstreeks 1900, 1950 en 2000* (Hilversum: Verloren, 2005).

44 See M. Bossenbroek, *Holland op zijn breedst: Indië en Zuid-Afrika in de Nederlandse cultuur omstreeks 1900* (Amsterdam: Bert Bakker, 1996).

45 Van Ledden, *Jan van Riebeeck*, pp. 32-33.

46 http://www.geheugenvannederland.nl/?/nl/items/KBMI01:42663: 'Een jammerkreet komt tot ons reizen / Uit Afrika, / Het wemeldt daar van doodspaleizen / Vol ongena; / Nu men geen valsche zegepralen / Van 't slagveld meldt, / Moet vrouw en kind den tol betalen / Aan 't wreed geweld'. Contemporary readers will have recognised Vondel's satirical poem entitled 'Monsters onzer eeuwe' [Monsters of our century], in which the 'monstrous' British were mentioned as a *totum pro parte* for the Parliament under Cromwell.

47 M.S.B. Kritzinger, *Afrikaanse en Nederlandse letterkunde as studievak aan die Universiteit van Pretoria: Rede by die aanvaarding van die Professoraat in die Afrikaanse en Nederlandse Letterkunde aan die Universiteit van Pretoria, gehou op 29 April 1936* (Pretoria: Universiteit van Pretoria, 1936), p. 4: 'Wanneer ek die gebied van die Dietse Letterkunde oorsien (en daaronder reken ek die Nederlandse, Vlaamse en Afrikaanse) dan beskou ek dit die graagste as 'n eenheid [et cetera]'.

48 E. Jansen, 'De culturele relatie Nederland-Zuid-Afrika: vroeger en nu', in *Ons Erfdeel* 41 (1998), pp. 677-683.

49 B. Henkes, 'Een warm welkom voor blanke nieuwkomers? Nederlandse emigratie en Zuid-Afrikaanse natievorming (1902-1960)', in *Tijdschrift voor Sociale en Economische Geschiedenis* 10 (2013), pp. 2-39.

50 Private communication Wium van Zyl, 4 november 2014.

51 See M.I. Cohen, *The Komedie Stamboel: Popular Theater in Colonial Indonesia, 1891-1903* (Athens: Ohio University Press, 2006), pp. 19-22.

52 Best available source in Dutch of the journey by Poerwo Lelono is the translation by J.E. Bosnak and F.X. Koot, *Op reis met een Javaanse edelman: Een levendig portret van Koloniaal Java in de negentiende eeuw (1860-1875)* (Zutphen: Walburg Pers, 2013).

BIBLIOGRAPHY

Bachmann-Medik, D., *Cultural Turns: Neuorientierungen in den Kulturwissenschaften* (Reinbek: Rowohlt, 2006), pp. 238-283.

Bassnett, S., 'Translating for the Theatre: The Case Against Performability', in *TTR* 4 (1991), pp. 99-111.

Bosnak, J.E. and F.X. Koot, *Op reis met een Javaanse edelman: Een levendig portret van Koloniaal Java in de negentiende eeuw (1860-1875)* (Zutphen: Walburg Pers, 2013).

Bossenbroek, M., *Holland op zijn breedst: Indië en Zuid-Afrika in de Nederlandse cultuur omstreeks 1900* (Amsterdam: Bert Bakker, 1996).

Carstens, W.A.M. and N. Bosman (eds.), *Kontemporêre Afrikaanse taalkunde* (Pretoria: Van Schaik Uitgewers, 2014).

Coetzee, N.S. (ed.), *'n Halfeeuw van letterkunde uit Suid-Afrika: 'n Bloemlesing opgestel ter herdenking van die vyftigjarige bestaan van die firmas H.A.U.M. v/h Jacques Dusseau en J.H. de Bussy 1894-1944* (Kaapstad/Pretoria: H.A.U.M. and J.H. de Bussy, 1944).

Cohen, M.I., *The Komedie Stamboel: Popular Theater in Colonial Indonesia, 1891-1903*, (Athens: Ohio University Press, 2006).

Croiset, H., *Lucifer onder de Linden* (Amsterdam: Cossee, 2010).

De Cesari C. and A. Rigney (eds.), *Transnational Memory: Circulation, Articulation, Scales* (Berlin: De Gruyter, 2014).

De Kock, P., '15 december 1979: Het Publiekstheater speelt een opmerkelijke *Lucifer* van Joost van den Vondel: Traditie en vernieuwing bij de repertoiregezelschappen in Amsterdam', in R.L. Erenstein (ed.), *Een theatergeschiedenis der Nederlanden: Tien eeuwen drama en theater in Nederland en Vlaanderen* (Amsterdam: Amsterdam University Press, 1996), pp. 806-813.

Dijkhuizen, J.F. van and H. Helmers, 'Religion and Politics – Lucifer and Milton's *Paradise Lost* (1674)', in J. Bloemendal and F.-W. Korsten (eds.), *Joost van den Vondel (1587-1679): Dutch Playwright in the Golden Age* (Leiden/Boston: Brill, 2012), pp. 377-405.

Erenstein, R., 'De receptie van middeleeuws toneel in de twintigste eeuw', in H. van Dijk *et al.* (eds.), *Spel en spektakel* (Amsterdam: Prometheus, 2001), pp. 282-304.

Erll, A., *Memory in Culture* (Basingstoke: Palgrave Macmillan, 2011).

Gemert, G. van, 'Germanje groet u als haar groten zoon: Zu Vondels Renommee im deutschen Sprachraum', in J. Enklaar and H. Ester (eds.), *Wechseltausch: Übersetzen als Kulturvermittlung: Deutschland und die Niederlande* (Amsterdam/Atlanta: Rodopi, 1995), pp. 64-92.

Gemert, G. van, 'Between Disregard and Political Mobilization: Vondel as a Playwright in Contemporary European Context: England, France and the German Lands', in J. Bloemendal and F.-W. Korsten (eds.), *Joost van den Vondel (1587-1679), Dutch Playwright in the Golden Age* (Leiden/Boston: Brill, 2012), pp. 171-198.

Glaser, A., 'Joost van den Vondel und sein Lucifer', in *Archiv für das Studium der Neueren Sprachen und Literaturen* 22 (1857), pp. 119-130.

Grové, A.P. (ed.), *Joost van den Vondel. Lucifer: Treurspel* (Pretoria: Van Schaik, 1968, reprinted in 1989).

Henkes, B., 'Een warm welkom voor blanke nieuwkomers? Nederlandse emigratie en Zuid-Afrikaanse natievorming (1902-1960)', in *Tijdschrift voor Sociale en Economische Geschiedenis* 10 (2013), pp. 2-39.

Jansen, E., 'De culturele relatie Nederland-Zuid-Afrika vroeger en nu', in *Ons Erfdeel* 41 (1998), pp. 677-683.

Konst, J., 'Tussen Philologie en Kulturvermittlung: Vondelbeschouwing in Duitsland tijdens de tweede helft van de negentiende eeuw', in M. Hüning, J. Konst and T. Holzhey (eds.), *Neerlandistiek in Europa: Bijdragen tot de geschiedenis van de universitaire Neerlandistiek buiten Nederland en Vlaanderen* (Münster: Waxmann Verlag, 2010), pp. 101-129.

Korsten, F.-W., *Sovereignty as Inviolability: Joost van den Vondel's Theatrical Explorations in the Dutch Republic* (Hilversum: Verloren, 2009).

Kritzinger, M.S.B., Afrikaanse en Nederlandse letterkunde as studievak aan die Universiteit van Pretoria: Rede by die aanvaarding van die Professoraat in die Afrikaanse en Nederlandse Letterkunde aan die Universiteit van Pretoria, gehou op 29 April 1936 (Pretoria: Universiteit van Pretoria, 1936).

Ledden, W.-P. van, *Jan van Riebeeck tussen wal en schip: Een onderzoek naar de beeldvorming over Jan van Riebeeck in Nederland en Zuid-Afrika omstreeks 1900, 1950 en 2000* (Hilversum: Verloren, 2005).

Le Roux, Th.H. and J.J. Groeneweg (eds.), *Joost van den Vondel: Lucifer* (Pretoria/Kaapstad: De Bussy and H.A.U.M., 1925, reprinted in 1932 and 1942).

Leuker, M.-Th., *Künstler als Helden und Heilige* (Münster: Waxmann Verlag, 2001).

Leuker, M.-Th., '"Vondel op wijwater" of de legitimiteit van de non-conformiteit', in *De Negentiende Eeuw* 30 (2006), pp. 65-78.

Musner, L., 'Kultur als Transfer: Ein regulationstheoretischer Zugang am Beispiel der Architektur', in H. Mitterbauer and K. Scherke (eds.), *Entgrenzte Räume: Kulturelle Transfers um 1900 und in der Gegenwart* (Wien: Passagen, 2005), pp. 173-194.

Opsomer, G., 'Mei-juni 1927: Het Vlaamsche Volkstooneel (VVT) en de opvoeringen van *Lucifer* en *Tijl* in Parijs: Internationale faam en mythevorming rond het VVT', in R.L. Erenstein (ed.), *Een theatergeschiedenis der Nederlanden* (Amsterdam: Amsterdam University Press, 1996), pp. 626-631.

Rens, L. (ed.), *Joost van den Vondel: Lucifer* (Den Haag: Martinus Nijhoff, 1979).

Rensburg, Ch. van, *So kry ons Afrikaans* (Pretoria: LAPA Uitgewers, 2012).

Rigney, A., 'The Dynamics of Remembrance: Texts Between Monumentality and Morphing', in A. Erll and A. Nünning (eds.), *Cultural Memory Studies: An International and Interdisciplinary Handbook* (Berlin/New York: De Gruyter, 2008), pp. 345-353.

Schmale, W., *Cultural Transfer*, http://ieg-ego.eu/en/threads/theories-and-methods/cultural-transfer, 2012, (accessed 10 May 2015).

Schenkeveld-van der Dussen, R., 'Vondel's Works for the Stage Read and Studied Over the Centuries', in J. Bloemendal and F.-W. Korsten (eds.), *Joost van den Vondel (1587-1679), Dutch Playwright in the Golden Age* (Leiden/Boston: Brill, 2012), pp. 7-22.

Smits-Veldt, M.B., 'Vondel Dramas: Their Afterlives in Performance', in J. Bloemendal and F.-W. Korsten (eds.), *Joost van den Vondel (1587-1679), Dutch Playwright in the Golden Age* (Leiden/Boston: Brill, 2012), pp. 157-170.

Spang, M., *Wenn sie ein Mann wäre: Leben und Werk der Anna Maria von Schürmann* (Darmstadt: Wissenschaftliche Buchgesellschaft, 2009).

Vondel, J van den, *Alle de treurspelen* (Amsterdam: J. van Oosterwyk, 1720).

CHAPTER 9

Vondel's *Lucifer*

Translating the Text, Translating the Culture

Natalia Stachura (Adam Mickiewicz University, Poznan, Poland)

Vondel's drama *Lucifer* was translated into Polish quite recently, in 2002. It is the first Polish translation of this author so far.[1] Despite the effort of the translator, Piotr Oczko, to bring the text as close as possible to the modern reader, the translation has only been a moderate success on the Polish book market. Oczko not only translated and commented on Vondel's drama in a foreword and footnotes, but also published two scholarly, eminently accessible books about it. *In Holland Dearest… Essays on the Seventeenth-Century Dutch Drama and Culture* (2009) is a very informative publication about the main figures and events in Dutch Culture of the Golden Age, whereas *The Myth of Lucifer: The Literary Representations of the Fallen Angel from the Antiquity to the Seventeenth Century* (2005) is a monograph, based on Oczko's doctoral dissertation.

The focus of my reflection is the vital problem of presenting a text from a remote literary époque and foreign culture to the modern reader. In *Lucifer*'s case the problem seems even bigger, as apparently no text similar to Vondel's masterpiece exists in Polish baroque literature. A closer examination of Polish baroque culture displays its isolation from the common European heritage and a different approach to a literary work. This historical approach is necessary to understand and explain the reasons why both Vondel's play and Oczko's publications were read in Poland as factual books rather than literature. On the other hand, by looking at Polish culture as a post-dependent one, I will argue that the misplaced reading of *Lucifer* and its paratext[2] may prove refreshing and inspiring for the established, canonical reading of the Dutch masterpiece. The non-fictional approach to the text offers both the drama and its diabolic hero a kind of 'afterlife'.[3] In the following sections I will look at the process of cultural translation from a historical perspective, trying to understand why the text was misunderstood. I will also briefly mention the generic differences between Dutch and Polish literature and point out the potential of such misreading for the further interpretations of Vondel's drama.

WALTER BENJAMIN, THE BAROQUE AND THE CULTURE TURN IN TRANSLATION STUDIES

Walter Benjamin's discussion of 'the task of the translator' seems particularly applicable to cultural translation and baroque literature. His concept of the 'afterlife' of a literary masterpiece in other culture(s), made possible by translation, predated many recent reflections on the nature and function of translation. The translated work lives again, develops, as a living organism, quite independently of the original, and in translation 'the original's life achieves its constantly renewed, latest and most comprehensive unfolding',[4] 'understood in the vegetative sense of the unfolding of the "leaves" or of a "seed", as an expressive relation' between the translation and the original work of art. In fact, 'translation is part of the essential life of the historical entity. Its historicity does not merely consist in its original historical place but in its effects, in its being part of history that continues'.[5]

Translation is a medium that empowers the work of art to cross the borders of time, language and culture. 'That original and translation have a vital connection implies that they do not have to resemble each other – descendants do not have to resemble those who have generated them – and that the conventional criteria of translation, freedom and fidelity, are problematic',[6] and thus translation is genetically related to the original work of art, but leads an independent life in another cultural and historical dimension. Still, Benjamin's thought goes further than accepting an independent status of the translation and acknowledging its role as a mediator between cultures and times. His concept of 'afterlife' implies the necessity of the death of the original.

> For Benjamin, the work of art lives on, but it lives on differently, it survives, it has its afterlife and that is a life after life. [...] This distinction implies a recognition of a caesura between life and afterlife, namely a recognition of death: Afterlife is the life after death. Remarkably, but consistently, this is never stated explicitly in Benjamin's text, in which we would not find any reference to 'death' or 'dying' [...] not her indirect reference in Benjamin, namely his relation of the afterlife of works of art to their fame, den 'Ruhm', an idea which is essentially linked to death in the literary tradition at least since Horace: Fame is what the poet achieves after death, it is poetic immortality.[7]

Among the many concepts that can be readily associated with Benjamin's essay and Weidner's commentary on it, I would like to mention the concept of 'the death of the author'[8] and of 'the birth of the reader'[9] and their possible similarity to Benjamin's idea of the afterlife. Mary Snell-Hornby argues that '(t)he frame "death" is now not necessarily understood as preliminary to the Resurrection, but all too often implies annihilation', while the 'birth' of the reader 'particularly for purposes of translation, need not "destroy" an author (or his/her work), but rather creates the potential for a further existence'.[10] Snell-Hornby's reflection on Rosemary Arrojo's concept of translation confirms an ongoing existence of the original text, transformed and adapted to the needs of the target culture. It also shows similarities with Benjamin's idea of organic growth, of the unfolding of the original within and through translation.

Other important common ground between the German philosopher and the postmodern and postcolonial concepts of Arrojo, arising from the aesthetic 'Anthropophagy Movement' in Brazil of the 1920s, is Arrojo's concept of palimpsest and Benjamin's idea of interlinear translation. Arrojo's palimpsest 'can be seen as a text which in every cultural community and in every epoch can be erased to make place for another "rewrite" (or interpretation, reading or translation) of the "same" text'.[11] The original, although erased and replaced with the translation, adapted to the needs of its anticipated readers, is still present within the translation and shines through the lines of its modernized version. Benjamin's concept of the interlinear translation[12] recalls the special status of the original text, which should be immanently present in the translation.

> The interlinear translation indeed expresses that original and translation belong together; it is by no means a final abrogation of difference, but rather highlights and marks it.[13]

The complicated and multi-faceted relationship between the original and translated text was expressed by Benjamin in religious terms, evoking the 'afterlife', or 'the persistence of religious meaning in a modern, seemingly disenchanted world'.[14] Postcolonial intellectuals opted for metaphors of cannibalism,[15] hybridity,[16] or palimpsest.[17] What connects all the above expressions is the conviction that translation has a specific status, being at the same time an independent being, deeply rooted in the target culture and understandable for its contemporary reader, and a vehicle through which the original text, often from a remote time and space, lives in new circumstances.

The special place occupied by Translation Studies within the wide range of postcolonial studies seems understandable in the context of literatures 'writing back' at former colonial empires.[18] In this essay, I will try to apply some of the concepts developed within postcolonial and translation studies, to highlight the specific location of Polish baroque and of Polish postmodern culture. The geographical and mental positioning of Poland, partially due to the complicated history of the country, is not an easy task, which is illustrated by the ongoing debate about post-colonial or post-dependence studies of Polish culture.[19] Most studies discuss the double status of seventeenth-century Poland (or more properly the Polish-Lithuanian Commonwealth) as both a colonizer of smaller nations (from the fifteenth to the eighteenth century), and a country colonized by mightier neighbours (1795-1918, 1939-1989). It is generally agreed that this double status has complex implications for Polish culture today, ranging from business practices to educational codes of conduct in schools.[20]

While looking at the reception of the translation of Vondel's *Lucifer* and accompanying publications, especially Oczko's study of the 'cultural biography' of Lucifer, I will argue that the peculiar, misplaced way of reading Vondel in Poland may be, paradoxically, refreshing for international Vondel and baroque studies. The Polish reading, which reintroduces the 'religious meaning' into the 'seemingly disenchanted world' exemplifies Bruno Latour's thesis on the hybrid nature of modernity, suggesting that modern patterns of thinking combine high-tech and magic, and are constantly enchanting the visible and invisible world.[21] Hybridity, a certain 'monstrosity' or 'aberration' of rational thinking, seems thus to be a part of the postmodern condition, especially in the context of post-colonial or post-dependent cultures.[22]

The Polish (mis)reading of *Lucifer* and its paratexts provokes a rethinking of the idea of translation. Translation, defined in organic terms already by Benjamin, as a form of 'afterlife', is often 'associated with transfusion and transplanting between human bodies' Michael Hanne writes further:

> The translation of a culturally significant text might also be described as a kind of organ transplant, that requires the translator to undertake delicate microsurgery to connect the work up to the cultural blood vessels and nerves which will keep it alive in this different body. If not, the transplanted organ will certainly suffer rejection.[23]

The question that needs to be raised in the case of *Lucifer*'s translation into Polish is in how far such a transplantation was possible, considering the specificity of the Polish baroque.

Another metaphor, of blood transfusion, can, as Hanne highlights, be of a dubious nature: it might be a rescue to the target culture and nourishment to the translator, but at the same time '[a] more cynical version of this metaphor would treat the translator as [...] a blood-sucking parasite on the body of the source text or culture'.[24] The life-saving, nourishing aspect of translation can be tracked back to Benjamin, Barthes and Derrida,[25] but also to De Campos and the concept of anthropophagy. De Campos calls translation,

> [A] 'parallel canto', a dialogue not only with the original's voice, but with other textual voices [...]. Translation as transtextualization or transcreation demythicizes the ideology of fidelity. If translation transtextualizes, it is no longer a one-way flow, and de Campos concludes his text with two anthropophagic metaphors [of 'blood transfusion' and

> 'transluciferation'] [...]. Translation that unsettles the single reference, the logocentric tyranny of the original, translation that has the devilish dimension of usurpation [...], translation that disturbs linear flows and power hierarchies – demonic dimensions that coexist with the *a priori* gesture of tribute to the other inherent in translating and the giving of one's own vitality to the other. Transcreation – the poetics that disrupts the primacy of the one model – a rupture and a recourse to the one and the other. Translation can be servitude, translation can also be freedom.[26]

Although Oczko's translation of *Lucifer* keeps close to the original, and the translator has used a neutral and contemporary register of Polish, accessible for a possibly wide strata of readers, the subversive, 'satanic' potential of Vondel's literary creation proved to be quite vital and vivifying for the cultural debate in Poland. The play and Oczko's comments, the text and its paratext, opened a way for a literal reading of *Lucifer* as a factual biography, a non-fictional text. This way of reading, which is apparently popular in Poland, questions the very core of modernity, and reinforces Latour's concept of the hybrid nature of the post-modern mind. Still, the readers' interest was inspired rather by Oczko's paratext than by the actual translation. To understand why, I will in the following section examine the specificity of Polish baroque literature, the processes of canonisation, reception and rediscovery in the twentieth century. I will also highlight the disproportion between Vondel's interest in Poland and Poland's lack of interest in Vondel, which was not changed by the translation of *Lucifer*.

VONDEL AND THE POLISH BAROQUE

Despite the fact that Joost van den Vondel wrote about Poland, the Polish royal couple, and the Polish aristocracy in numerous occasional poems and in his drama *Gysbreght van Aemstel*, it seems that his writings were not known to Polish readers until 2002. Although not much research on this disparity has been done so far, is seems convincing that the cultural influence between the two literatures can be only considered within the frame of *latinitas*.[27] The shared European heritage, accessible through the medium of Latin, enabled numerous Polish noblemen to study in the Low Countries. The Latin poetry of Daniel Heinsius, as well as Hugo de Groot's treatises, were admired, read and discussed in Poland. Jan Andrzej Morsztyn, an acclaimed Polish poet and politician, translated Latin poems from Hugo de Groot's *Erotopaegnia Catulliana* into Polish, and wrote a poem about the courage of de Groot's wife.[28] In the Netherlands, P.C. Hooft, in one of his letters, compared the Polish Latin poet Maciej Kazimierz Sarbiewski (whose latinised name was Matthias Casimir Sarbievius) to Horace.[29]

This vivid cultural exchange factually ceased to exist after the rise of literatures in national languages. The language barrier caused a long-lasting isolation between Dutch and Polish literature. While Vondel became an important source of inspiration for German authors, and his works could have been possibly read by English writers (which led to the infamous controversy around Milton's *Paradise Lost*), Polish culture of the 17th century was deeply indebted to Southern countries: most of the poets read and translated not only from Latin, but also from Italian, French and Spanish. Van Nieukerken's studies confirm clearly that Vondel encountered some of Poland's most prominent noblemen in Paris in 1645, where he also witnessed the symbolical wedding of Marie Louise Gonzaga to the glove of Władysław IV Vasa, the elected Polish king of Swedish origin. It is also likely that Vondel, while in Paris, exchanged political views with Polish envoys. Another such encounter probably took place during Vondel's travel to Denmark in 1655, and resulted in a panegyric poem devoted to the Polish envoy in Copenhagen, Tobiasz Morsztyn.[30] The poem also mentions Tobiasz' brother, the aforementioned famous poet, nobleman and politician Jan Andrzej Morsztyn, but Van Nieukerken excludes definitely the possibility of personal encounter or any form of exchange or inspiration between the two poets.

Vondel's occasional poems devoted to Polish themes show a vivid interest in international politics and economy. The concept of Poland as *antemuros christianitatis*, an outpost defending (Catholic) Europe against the Turks, Tatars, Cossacks, Russians and Swedes, and Poland as Europe's nurturer (huge transports of Ukrainian grain were shipped through the port in Gdańsk/Danzig to Amsterdam and distributed throughout Western Europe) was, most probably, indebted to the Polish diplomat Krzysztof Opaliński, whom Vondel met in Paris. The Polish *raison d'État* fitted very well in Vondel's idea of Europe, united under the sceptre of a Catholic emperor, freed from the threat of Turkish invasion, leading a God-fearing, peaceful and cornucopian existence. In the times of conflict, the king of Poland, leading numerous wars with neighbouring countries including the Osman Empire, replaced in Vondel's vision his former Scandinavian favourite, the Danish queen Christina, known for her pacifist convictions.

This favourable vision of Poland, represented in many poems,[31] took a religious-mythical dimension in one of Vondel's most successful dramas, *Gysbreght van Aemstel.* In the last stanzas the eponymous hero, a leader of refugees, forced to leave Amsterdam, has a vision of Archangel Raphael, who orders him to go to the alluvial delta of Vistula River in Poland, and erect there a city called New Holland.[32] The episode is relevant not only as one of few literary sources documenting the actual Dutch migration to Poland, but also as a pastoral picture of the rich, fertile and blessed country, embracing refugees and giving them a chance for a new beginning.

It is quite astonishing that Vondel's vision of Poland's moral, military and economic mission in Europe, so compatible with the image created by Polish poets and writers, remains actually unknown in Poland. Vondel's poems were never translated into Polish, nor was his apologetic drama *Gysbreght van Aemstel.*

This is even more surprising as Vondel's picture of Poland fits well into the Polish imaginary self-perception as a heroic but peace-loving nation, chosen by God to protect (and in later époques to suffer for) other, less eminent nations. The Polish baroque predilection for pastoral narratives was criticised heavily by Polish Romantic poets, who instead introduced the image of the Christ- or Prometheus-like nation, suffering for mankind and for its own political freedom. Still, Polish patriotic literature in the nineteenth century established a certain canon of baroque texts, which served as a basis for historic novels, displaying the greatness of the Polish-Lithuanian Commonwealth in the seventeenth century. This canon was based mostly on memoirs of small landed gentry, focusing on military actions and daily life, hunting, farming, conflict with neighbours and local politics. It celebrated the political anarchy of landed gentry, and their raising class influence on the course of internal and external politics of the country. Some place was reserved for moral lessons, but religion was treated rather ornamentally. Meantime, Polish court drama and poetry, as well as Polish religious metaphysical poetry of the seventeenth century, remained largely unknown until the 1960s, when the baroque was 'rediscovered' by Polish scholars and presented to the wider public.

Metaphysical fears, which were characteristic for European baroque, were rarely represented in Polish religious poetry, compared by some scholars to its English counterpart, the school of Metaphysical Poets.[33] If at all, the anxieties were generally expressed through conventional imagery rooted in Catholic orthodoxy, and derived from writings by Theresa d'Avilla and St. John of the Cross, or, in case of Polish Calvinist poets, such as Daniel Naborowski, did not go too far from approved theological thought. From this perspective a text comparable to Vondel's *Lucifer* or Milton's *Paradise Lost* has never been produced by a Polish baroque poet, and it would probably have been immediately rejected by the public, accustomed to clear moral metaphors and examples, and not to theological disputes about the implications of acts of free will.

The spirit of rebellion and Faustian longing for absolute knowledge, inherent in Romantic literature, but already represented in Western European baroque, seem quite marginal in Polish literature. The predilection for the pastoral can explain some aspects of the specificity of Polish literature, as well as the general rootedness of the culture in the agrarian model of life. The baroque, being, according to Jose Antonio Maravall, a basically urban culture, born from social unrest, the rise of industrialisation, and the modern absolutist state, was fascinated with the artificial and the mechanical, felt exposed to the caprices of the blind Fortune, and doubted about the inherent goodness of human nature.[34] Such qualities were virtually absent from Polish baroque literature and culture in general.

This was because Polish-Lithuanian Commonwealth never went through most of the processes that occurred in most Western European countries in the seventeenth century. Instead of solidifying, the central power practically ceased to exist; the irregular army consisting of the gentry and their dependants tried to protect the territory, not to expand it; the urbanisation and industrialisation were marginal processes within the Polish borders.[35] Even if the counter-reformation won the religious battle without sending 'heretics' to stakes, it meant a gradual erosion of important intellectual centres, which had been led by various Protestant denominations. In several of waves of migration, talented and resourceful Polish non-Catholics emigrated to more tolerant countries. In the seventeenth century, the Poland that emerged from the Renaissance, a multi-national state exercising religious tolerance, supporting economic growth and open to Westernisation,[36] was gradually devolving into a stagnant backwater, closed in its geographical and mental borders, a nation detached from contemporary world, and mentally encapsulated in its glorious past. Although Poland was formally independent until 1795, after the seventeenth century the territory of Poland was degrading into a colony of the modern European powers, and was eventually divided and annexed in 1795 by three powerful neighbours: Austria, Prussia and Russia. The short period of Polish independence between the two world wars in the twentieth century did not compensate for the period of economic, political and intellectual underdevelopment.[37]

This may seem a simplified look at Polish history and Polish literature, but it describes a course of events which seems inevitable in view of the positioning of Polish culture within the common European heritage during and after the seventeenth century. Another important factor of the 'otherness' of Polish baroque culture was its orientalization, which progressed throughout the seventeenth century. The much-feared Osman Empire became a source of inspiration for everyday culture of Polish gentry (which was the political and military class in Polish society). At the same time, the fabulous ideology of Sarmatism, based on the myth that Polish gentry descended from ancient Sarmatians, a nation inhabiting today's area of Iran and speaking Scythian[38], became a pillar of Polish identity. Polish culture became thus voluntarily encapsulated within a myth, explaining the country's uniqueness. The structure of Polish imagined identity was strengthened by the fact that the country was not independent for nearly 200 years. Sarmatism, which was initially the ideology of landed gentry, gradually became a staple of Polish national identity for all social classes.

Paradoxically, a similar founding myth, deriving the Dutch from the ancient Germanic tribe of Batavi, was present in the Dutch culture from the Eighty Years War. It helped to display the bravery of Dutch republicans, fighting against the Spanish Habsburgs in the sixteenth and seventeenth century, and of Dutch revolutionaries, spreading ideas of the French Revolution in the eighteenth century. In the meanwhile, the Batavian myth legitimized colonisation in East and West Indies. Still, the Dutch Republic, unlike the Polish-Lithuanian Commonwealth, due to its geopolitical situation, was unable to encapsulate itself within a myth of remote past, and despite its unique status of a merchant oligarchy, the country's development followed in the seventeenth and eighteenth centuries the common, Western European routes of urbanisation, industrialisation and territorial expansion. The crisis of central power in the eighteenth century led to a short period of occupation by France, and in the new order established at Vienna Congress there was no place for a mighty Dutch state, but the country was continuously present on the map of Europe, and played a vital role in the newly established balance of power in the nineteenth century. This longish, yet necessarily simplified look at Polish history appears indispensable for understanding the crucial differences not only between Polish and European baroque literature and mentality, but also the essentially different approach to literature, its task and place in social life in contemporary Poland.

THE TRANSLATION OF *LUCIFER* AND ITS IMPLICATIONS

The publication of Vondel's Lucifer in 2002 was the result of one man's passion. Piotr Oczko, working on his PhD project about cultural history of the eponymous hero, decided not only to translate Vondel's drama into Polish, but also to try to bring the baroque text as close as possible to the postmodern reader. For this purpose he refrained from using archaic stylisation, and decided that only the final passages in each act should rhyme. The language appears quite neutral to a modern Polish reader; it does not resemble neither bombastic formulations of Polish baroque literature, nor Vondel's seventeenth century Dutch. Sometimes, in my opinion, it even becomes too close to modern Polish and consequently, the angelic dialogues about hierarchy and obedience tend to resemble discussions between contemporary employees of a big, hierarchic corporation. Also, Oczko's decision to reduce the rhyming sections to the minimum, seems a fortunate one: the choral songs at the end of each act strongly suggest that the very talented translator is not necessarily a master of the poetic register of Polish.

The translator also provided a detailed discussion of *Lucifer*'s possible genesis and sources of inspiration, including Du Bartas' *Les Semaines* as a common source for Vondel and Milton. The controversy around similarities between *Paradise Lost* and *Lucifer*, which preceded Milton's epic, is highlighted in the foreword. Together with the clear discussion of differences between baroque and romantic visions of Lucifer's fall, the foreword provides information that is very relevant for the Polish reader. Paradoxically, although Oczko states clearly that Vondel's classical taste supports comparisons with Racine and Dryden rather than with Shakespeare,[39] he begins the foreword with presenting Vondel as the 'Dutch Shakespeare',[40] and this comparison returns in book advertisements by the publisher and in short summaries circulating in the internet.

Lucifer, introducing the topics of disobedience, jealousy, fear of disorder and displaying the ontological roots of evil, focuses on most relevant motives of seventeenth century literature, which are, to a large extent, missing in the Polish baroque. Although Vondel's play may seem quite remote to the readers, the tragic hero of the drama awakened a relatively strong interest among the Polish public. It was, however, not the original Dutch masterpiece that moved the readers so deeply, but Oczko's publication about the character Lucifer, which focused on Vondel's drama, but eventually transgressed it. In *The Myth of Lucifer: The Literary Representations of the Fallen Angel from the Antiquity to the Seventeenth Century* he tried to reconstruct the narratives about the fallen angel and their impact on Vondel. This book was intensively and ardently misread, as a theological work, by various and numerous groups of Polish readers. Fragments of Oczko's book were published, without the author's consent, in Catholic internet portals. He was also asked by a Jesuit magazine to contribute an article about Lucifer's demonic presence throughout the ages, despite the author's clear self-description as a non-religious person.

From Oczko's correspondence with Martyna Pędzisz, PhD candidate at AMU Poznań, it transpires clearly that the translator involuntarily became not only a theological authority on Lucifer, but also a rescuer of high school students, who often prepare exam presentations about the figure of the devil in European culture, and who are desperate for accessible secondary literature. Martyna Pędzisz conducted a survey among those students, and it turns out that despite their careful reading of Oczko's book on the history of Lucifer, most students refrained from reading Vondel, or even Milton, and preferred to focus on the standard 'diabolic' works by Bulgakov and Dostoyevsky. Oczko also mentioned receiving some enthusiastic emails from readers who described themselves as Satanists, and who thanked him for what they perceived as a biography of their 'hero'.

These misadventures, stemming from undesired popularity of Oczko's book about Lucifer, and rather moderate interest in his excellent collection of essays about Dutch culture, *In Holland Dearest... Essays on the Seventeenth-Century Dutch Drama and Culture*, and in his translation of Vondel, are indicative of an interesting tendency: Polish readers seem not to be interested in the literary classic, and focus on its subject instead, not distinguishing clearly between literary creation and the spiritual reality which remains beyond the grasp of literature. This astonishing, hybrid reading of Vondel's and Oczko's *Lucifers* depicts the fragile and illusionary character of rationality and modernity in Poland. At the same time, this reading brings literature back to its sources, to the enquiry not about aesthetical but about ethical and spiritual values. In this context, the Polish reading of Vondel and its paratext is anthropophagic; it devours the classic drama, frees its content from theoretical and poetic burden, and shapes its own network of meanings, neglecting the historical and cultural context of the original text. This 'barbaric' Polish reading can, paradoxically, serve as a 'life-saving transfusion' of fresh insight into the very core of literature, bearing at the same time a testimony of Vondel's genius. Even if the play does not sound convincing to the contemporary Polish reader, the main conflict of *Lucifer* is still speaking to Polish hearts and minds.

CONCLUSION

The Polish case of misreading *Lucifer*, despite its specificity and uniqueness, can be seen as a general tendency in reception of Dutch literature. As Ria Vanderauwera wrote thirty years ago:

> The road translated books have to travel is the same as for any other book at the target pole: publication, distribution, exposure in the media – the 'gatekeepers between books-in-themselves and books-for-others' (Hall 1979:48). Compared with originals, however, translations are already a step ahead as 'books-for-others'. They are made and commissioned to fulfil a particular purpose: that of 'making known a foreign literature to an audience which has no access to it otherwise'.[41]

Despite this and the fact that translations, especially of classic works, receive structural help from cultural institutions (in case of *Lucifer* the Dutch Foundation for Literature and the Prins Bernhard Cultuurfonds), they usually do not sell well on a foreign market, not only because of 'the simple discrepancy between source and target literatures, in different ideas about what literature is or should be',[42] but also, as in Vondel's case, because of the huge time lag between the original publication (and staging) and the publication in Poland.

Although Vanderauwera's research in reception of Dutch literature focused on English-speaking countries between 1961 and 1980, some of her observations reflect the status of translations of Dutch-language literature in Poland in the recent years: 'the tough publishing and distribution situation [...] favours (potential) bestsellers, preferably in the nonfiction area, at the expense of more "literary" work'.[43] Non-fiction literature and children- and young adults' literature top the list of translated titles, published yearly by the Dutch Embassy in Poland, while translation of Dutch and Flemish fictional prose and poetry play a rather marginal role. A reason for this may be surely 'poetics: source and target literature hold slightly different opinions about literature, prose fiction, and the novel in particular'.[44] To change this, Vanderauwera suggested in 1980s a twofold solution:

> The easy one is to play to the gallery by translating and promoting works that fit assumed demand and taste at the target pole, thus neutralizing aesthetic as well as commercial objections. The more difficult and hazardous one, and one that will require some patience, is to try and project a certain image of Dutch fiction.[45]

In Poland, at the beginning of the twenty-first century, the first solution is being applied quite successfully, while the second one, especially in the context of classic literature, seems rather unpromising. Still, as demonstrated by the confused and lively Polish reaction to Vondel's and Oczko's *Lucifer*, the results of publishing of a classical masterwork might be quite astonishing. In a way, the approach of the Polish general reader to Vondel's hero, and the tendency to read the drama and its paratext as non-fiction literature, questions, in a sense, fixed Western European opinions about literature, its social impact and aesthetical value. In the preface to the English translation of Benjamin's *The Origin of German Tragic Drama*, discovering, among other things, the similarities between the baroque and expressionism, George Steiner commented: 'a study of the baroque is no mere antiquarian, archival hobby: it mirrors, it anticipates and helps grasp the dark present'.[46] One can only hope that Vondel's *Lucifer* in its Polish version, circulating for more than a decade, will be rediscovered in the 'dark present', creatively absorbed by the Polish culture, and 'translated' into a language addressing anxieties and conflicts of the rapidly changing society.

NOTES

1 I am deeply indebted to Martyna Pędzisz, PhD candidate from the Department of Dutch and South African Studies, for contacting the translator, Piotr Oczko, researching on knowledge of Oczko's book among her fellow students and presenting the initial version of this paper at the Vondel conference in Bologna in November 2014. Without her substantial help the research would not have been completed.

2 G. Genette, *Palimpsests: Literature in the Second Degree* (Lincoln/London: University of Nebraska Press, 1997 [1982]).

3 W. Benjamin, 'The Task of the translator', in M. Bullock and M.W. Jennings (eds.), *Selected Writings, Volume 1, 1913-1926* (Cambridge/London: The Belknap Press of Harvard UP, 2002 [1923]), pp. 253-263.

4 Benjamin, 'The Task of the translator', p. 255.

5 D. Weidner, 'Life after Life: A Figure of Thought in Walter Benjamin', paper given at the Conference *Afterlife: Writing and Image in Walter Benjamin and Aby Warburg*, Universidad Federal de Minais Gerais, Belo Horizonte, Brasil, 2012, p. 7.

6 Weidner, 'Life after Life', p. 7.

7 Weidner, 'Life after Life', pp. 9-10.

8 R. Barthes, 'The Death of the Author', in *Aspen* 5 and 6 (1967), item 3.

9 R. Arrojo, 'The "Death" of the Author and the Limits of the Translator's Visibility', in M. Snell-Hornby, Z. Jettmarová and K. Kaindl (eds.), *Translation as Intercultural Communication: Selected Papers from the EST Congress, Prague 1995* (Prague: John Benjamins, 1997), pp. 21-32.

10 M. Snell-Hornby, *The Turns of Translation Studies: New Paradigms or Shifting Viewpoints?* (Amsterdam/Philadelphia: John Benjamins Publishing Company, 2006), p. 63.

11 Pages 23-24, quoted in Snell-Hornby, *The Turns of Translation Studies*, p. 61.

12 Benjamin, 'The Task of the translator', pp. 262-263.

13 Weidner, 'Life after Life', p. 11.

14 Weidner, 'Life after Life', p. 12.

15 O. de Andrade, 'The Cannibalist Manifesto', in *Latin American Literary Review* 19: 38 (July-Dec. 1991), pp. 38-47.

16 H. Bhabha, *The Location of Culture* (London: Routledge, 1994).

17 R. Arrojo, *Oficina de tradução: A teoria na prática* (São Paulo: Editora Ática, 1986).

18 B. Ashcroft, G. Griffiths and H. Tiffin, *The Empire Writes Back: Theory and Practice in Post-Colonial Literatures* (London/New York: Routledge, 2002 [1989]).

19 See for example: E. Thompson, *Imperial Knowledge: Russian Literature and Colonialism* (Westport/London: Greenwood, 2000); C. Cavanagh, 'Postcolonial Poland', in *Common Knowledge*, 10 (2004), pp. 82-92; A. Fiut, 'In the Shadow of Empires: Post-colonialism in Central and Eastern Europe – Why Not?', in J. Korek (ed.), *Sovietology to Popstcoloniality: Poland and Ukraine from a Postcolonial Perspective* (Huddinge Södertörns Högskola, 2007), pp. 33-40; T. Nycz, 'Polish Post-Colonial and/or Post-Dependence Studies', in *Teksty Drugie* 25 (2014), pp. 5-11.

20 J. Sowa, 'Fantomowe ciało króla: Peryferyjne zmagania z nowoczesną formą' (Kraków: Universitas, 2011).

21 B. Latour, *We have never been modern* (Cambridge: Harvard UP, 1993 [1991]).

22 Bhabha, *The Location of Culture*.

23 M. Hanne, 'Metaphors for the Translator', in S. Bassnett and P. Bush (eds.), *The Translator as Writer* (Continuum: London/New York, 2006), p. 214.

24 Hanne, 'Metaphors for the Translator', p. 214.

25 E. Gentzler, *Contemporary Translation Theories* (Clevedon etc.: Multilingual Matters Ltd., 2001), p. 196.

26 Else Ribeiro Pires Vieira, 'Liberating Calibans: Readings of *Antropofagia* and Haroldo de Campos' poetics of transcreation', in S. Bassnett and H. Trivedi (eds.), *Post-colonial Translation: Theory and Practice* (London/New York: Routledge, 2002 [1999]), p. 110; all quotations from De Campos after Vieira.

27 A. van Nieukerken, '*Adam in Ballingschap* – dichten om terug te keren naar je vaderland', in *Biuletyn* 19 (1998), pp. 5-10; 'Polonica w dwóch wierszach Vondela', in *Pamiętnik Literacki* 84: 2 (1993), pp. 119-125; A. van Nieukerken, 'Vondels "Parnas aen de Belt" en de gebroeders Morsztyn', in *Acta Comenii Societatis Neerlandicorum Europae Centralis et Orientalis* (2002), pp. 127-144.

28 A. Borowski, *Iter Polono-Belgo-Ollandicum: Cultural and Literary Relationships Between the Commonwealth of Poland and the Netherlands in the 16th and the 17th Centuries* (Kraków: Księgarnia Akademicka, 2007), p. 181.

29 Borowski, *Iter Polono-Belgicus*, p. 149.

30 Joost van den Vondel, 'Aen zijne Excellentie, den doorluchtigen Heer, Tobias Morstin, Trucksesz te Krakou, Resident van den Koning en de Kroon Polen by Koning Frederick den derden', in J.F.M. Sterck *et al.* (eds.), *De werken van Vondel: Achtste deel 1656-1660* (Amsterdam: Maatschappij voor Goede en Goedkoope Lectuur, 1935 [1657]), pp. 622-624.

31 Joost van den Vondel, 'Bestand Tusschen Polen en Sweden aen Dantzick', in J.F.M. Sterck *et al.* (eds.), *De werken van Vondel: Derde deel 1627-1640* (Amsterdam: Maatschappij voor Goede en Goedkoope Lectuur, 1929 [1635]), pp. 428-430; 'By-schriften op d'Afbeeldinge van de Koninglijcke Bruit van Polen: Te Parijs geschildert, als een Nymf in bosschaedje, en gouden laken, met diamanten en paerlen geboort', in J.F.M. Sterck *et al.* (eds.), *De werken van Vondel: Vijfde deel 1645-1656* (Amsterdam: Maatschappij voor Goede en Goedkoope Lectuur, 1931 [1645]), pp. 148-149; 'Op de Neerlaegh Der Turcksche Vlote: Aen Venetie', in J.F.M. Sterck *et al.* (eds.), *De werken van Vondel: Vijfde deel 1645-1656* (Amsterdam: Maatschappij voor Goede en Goedkoope Lectuur, 1931 [1649]), pp. 473-475; 'Triomf over Funen', in J.F.M. Sterck *et al.* (eds.), *De werken van Vondel: Achtste deel 1656-1660* (Amsterdam: Maatschappij voor Goede en Goedkoope Lectuur, 1935 [1659]), pp. 764-765; 'Zeemagazyn Gebouwt Op Kattenburgh t'Amsterdam: Aen De weledele en mogende Heeren Zeeraeden ter Amiraliteit in de gemelde stadt', in J.F.M. Sterck *et al.* (eds.), *De werken van Vondel: Achtste deel 1656-1660* (Amsterdam: Maatschappij voor Goede en Goedkoope Lectuur, 1935 [1658]), pp. 653-665.

32 Joost van den Vondel, *Gysbreght van Aemstel.* Met inleidingen en aantekeningen door Mieke B. Smits-Veldt (Amsterdam: AUP, 1994 [1637]), stanzas 1855b-1864.

33 D. Künstler-Langner, 'Światłość i mrok w polskiej i angielskiej poezji metafizycznej XVII w.', in A. Nowicka-Jeżowa (ed.), *Barok polski wobec Europy: Kierunki dialogu* (Warszawa: ANTA, 2003), pp. 273-288; *Anioł w poezji baroku: Dzieje postaci w kulturze dawnej Europy* (Toruń: Wydawnictwo Naukowe UMK., 2007).

34 J.A. Maravall, *Culture of the Baroque: Analysis of a Historical Structure* (Manchester: Manchester UP, 1986 [1975]).

35 S. Nowak-Stalmann, *Epika historyczna Samuela ze Skrzypiny Twardowskiego* (Izabelin: Świat Literacki, 2004), pp. 8-10.

36 J. Tazbir, *W pogoni za Europą.* (Warszawa: Sic!, 1998).

37 Sowa, *Fantomowe ciało króla*, p. 211.

38 P.M. Barford, *The Early Slavs* (Ithaca: Cornell UP, 2001).

39 P. Oczko, 'Wstęp', in Joost van den Vondel, *Lucyfer* (Kraków: Universitas, 2002), p. 48.

40 Oczko, 'Wstęp', p. 5.

41 R. Vanderauwera, 'The Response to Translated Literature: A Sad Example', in T. Hermans (ed.), *The Manipulation of Literature: Studies in Literature Translation* (London-New York: Routledge, 2014 [1985]), p. 198.

42 Vanderauwera, 'The Response to Translated Literature', p.206

43 Vanderauwera, 'The Response to Translated Literature', p. 207.

44 Vanderauwera, 'The Response to Translated Literature', p. 208.

45 Vanderauwera, 'The Response to Translated Literature', p. 209.

46 G. Steiner, 'Introduction' in W. Benjamin, *The Origin of German Tragic Drama* (London-New York: Verso, 2003 [1977], p. 16).

BIBLIOGRAPHY

Arrojo, R., 'The "Death" of the Author and the Limits of the Translator's Visibility', in M. Snell-Hornby, Z. Jettmarová and K. Kaindl (eds.), *Translation as Intercultural Communication: Selected Papers from the EST Congress, Prague 1995* (Prague: John Benjamins, 1997), pp. 21-32.

Ashcroft, B., G. Griffiths and H. Tiffin, *The Empire Writes Back: Theory and Practice in Post-Colonial Literatures* (London/New York: Routledge, 2002 [1989]).

Barford, P.M., *The Early Slavs* (Ithaca: Cornell UP, 2001).

Barthes, R., 'The Death of the Author', in *Aspen* 5/6, item 3, 1967, http://www.ubu.com/aspen/aspen5and6/threeEssays.html#barthes (accessed 10 January 2016).

Bassnett, S. and A. Levefebre (eds.), *Translation, History and Culture* (London: Pinter Publishers, 1990).

Benjamin, W., 'The Task of the Translator', in M. Bullock and M.W. Jennings (eds.), *Selected Writings,* Volume 1, 1913-1926 (Cambridge/London: The Belknap Press of Harvard UP, 2002 [1923]), pp. 253-263.

Benjamin, W., *The Origin of German Tragic Drama* (London/New York: Verso, 2003 [1928]).

Bhaba, H., *The Location of Culture* (London: Routledge, 1994).

Borowski, A., *Iter Polono-Belgo-Ollandicum: Cultural and Literary Relationships Between the Commonwealth of Poland and the Netherlands in the 16th and the 17th Centuries* (Kraków: Księgarnia Akademicka, 2007).

Cavanagh, C., 'Postcolonial Poland', in *Common Knowledge* 10: 1 (2004), pp. 82-92.

De Andrade, O., 'The Cannibalist Manifesto' (1991 [1928]), in *Latin American Literary Review* 19: 38 (1991), pp. 38-47.

Fiut, A., 'In the Shadow of Empires: Post-colonialism in Central and Eastern Europe: Why Not?', in J. Korek (ed.), *Sovietology to Postcoloniality: Poland and Ukraine from a Postcolonial Perspective* (Huddinge Södertörns Högskola, 2007), pp. 33-40.

Genette, G., *Palimpsests: Literature in the Second Degree* (Lincoln/London: University of Nebraska Press, 1997 [1982]).

Gentzler, E., *Contemporary Translation Theories* (Clevedon etc.: Multilingual Matters Ltd., 2001).

Hanne, M., 'Metaphors for the Translator', in S. Bassnett and P. Bush (eds.), *The Translator as Writer* (London/New York: Continuum, 2006), pp. 208-224.

Hernas, Cz., *Barok* (Warszawa: PWN, 1998).

Künstler-Langner, D, 'Światłość i mrok w polskiej i angielskiej poezji metafizycznej XVII w.', in A. Nowicka-Jeżowa (ed.), *Barok polski wobec Europy: Kierunki dialogu* (Warszawa: ANTA, 2003), pp. 273-288.

Künstler-Langner, D., *Anioł w poezji baroku: Dzieje postaci w kulturze dawnej Europy* (Toruń: Wydawnictwo Naukowe UMK, 2007).

Latour, B., *We have never been modern* (Cambridge: Harvard UP, 1993 [1991]).

Maravall, J.A., *Culture of the Baroque: Analysis of a Historical Structure* (Manchester: Manchester UP, 1986 [1975]).

Nieukerken, A. van, '*Adam in Ballingschap* – dichten om terug te keren naar je vaderland', in *Biuletyn* 19 (1998), pp. 5-10.

Nieukerken, A. van, 'Vondels "Parnas aen de Belt" en de gebroeders Morsztyn', in *Acta Comenii Societatis Neerlandicorum Europae Centralis et Orientalis* 6 (2002), pp. 127-144.

Nowak-Stalmann, S., *Epika historyczna Samuela ze Skrzypiny Twardowskiego* (Izabelin: Świat Literacki, 2004).

Nycz, T., 'Polish Post-Colonial and/or Post-Dependence Studies', in *Teksty Drugie* 25 (2014), pp. 5-11.

Oczko, P., 'Wstęp', in J. van den Vondel, *Lucyfer* (Kraków: Universitas, 2002).

Oczko, P., *Mit Lucyfera: Literackie dzieje Upadłego Anioła od starożytności po wiek XVII* [The Myth of Lucifer: The Literary Representations of the Fallen Angel from Antiquity to the Seventeenth Century] (Kraków: TPPK, 2005).

Oczko, P., *W najdroższej Holandyjej... Szkice o siedemnastowiecznym dramacie i kulturze niderlandzkiej* [In Holland Dearest... Essays on the Seventeenth-Century Dutch Drama and Culture] (Kraków: Księgarnia Akademicka, 2009).

Okoń, J., 'Teatr', in A. Skoczek (ed.), *Historia literatury polskiej w dziesięciu tomach,* t. III (Bochnia etc.: Wydawnictwo SMS i Prowincjonalna Oficyna Wydawnicza, 2003), pp. 313-328.

Snell-Hornby, M., *The Turns of Translation Studies: New Paradigms or Shifting Viewpoints?* (Amsterdam/Philadelphia: John Benjamins Publishing Company, 2006).

Sowa, J., *Fantomowe ciało króla: Peryferyjne zmagania z nowoczesną formą* (Kraków: Universitas, 2011).

Steiner, G., 'Introduction', in W. Benjamin, *The Origin of German Tragic Drama* (London/New York: Verso, 2003 [1977]), pp. 7-24.

Tazbir, J., *W pogoni za Europą* (Warszawa: Sic!, 1998).

Thompson, E., *Imperial Knowledge: Russian Literature and Colonialism* (Westport/London: Greenwood, 2000).

Van den Vondel, J., 'Aen zijne Excellentie, den doorluchtigen Heer, Tobias Morstin, Trucksesz te Krakou, Resident van den Koning en de Kroon Polen by Koning Frederick den derden', in J.F.M. Sterck *et al.* (eds.), *De werken van Vondel: Achtste deel 1656-1660,* (Amsterdam: Maatschappij voor Goede en Goedkoope Lectuur, 1935 [1657]), pp. 622-624, http://www.dbnl.org/tekst/vond001dewe08_01/vond001dewe08_01_0199.php (accessed 10 December 2015).

Van den Vondel, J., 'Bestand Tusschen Polen en Sweden aen Dantzick', in J.F.M. Sterck *et al.* (eds.), *De werken van Vondel: Derde deel 1627-1640* (Amsterdam: Maatschappij voor Goede en Goedkoope Lectuur, 1929 [1635]), pp. 428-430, http://www.dbnl.org/tekst/vond001dewe03_01/vond001dewe03_01_0097.php (accessed 12 December 2015).

Van den Vondel, J., 'By-schriften op d'Afbeeldinge van de Koninglijcke Bruit van Polen: Te Parijs geschildert, als een Nymf in bosschaedje, en gouden laken, met diamanten en paerlen geboort', in J.F.M. Sterck *et al.* (eds.), *De werken van Vondel: Vijfde deel 1645-1656* (Amsterdam: Maatschappij voor Goede en Goedkoope Lectuur, 1931 [1645]), pp. 148-149, http://www.dbnl.org/tekst/vond001dewe05_01/vond001dewe05_01_0013.php (accessed 24 November 2015).

Van den Vondel, J., *Gysbreght van Aemstel.* Met inleidingen en aantekeningen door Mieke B. Smits-Veldt (Amsterdam: AUP, 1994 [1637]), http://www.dbnl.org/tekst/vond001gysb01_01/ (accessed 18 December 2015).

Van den Vondel, J., 'Op de Neerlaegh Der Turcksche Vlote: Aen Venetie', in J.F.M. Sterck *et al.* (eds.), *De werken van Vondel: Vijfde deel 1645-1656* (Amsterdam: Maatschappij voor Goede en Goedkoope Lectuur, 1931 [1649]), pp. 473-475, http://www.dbnl.org/tekst/vond001dewe05_01/vond001dewe05_01_0079.php (accessed 8 December 2015).

Van den Vondel, J., 'Triomf over Funen', in J.F.M. Sterck *et al.* (eds.), *De werken van Vondel: Achtste deel 1656-1660* (Amsterdam: Maatschappij voor Goede en Goedkoope Lectuur, 1935 [1659]), pp. 764-765, http://www.dbnl.org/tekst/vond001dewe08_01/vond001dewe08_01_0248.php (accessed 8 December 2015).

Van den Vondel, J., 'Zeemagazyn Gebouwt Op Kattenburgh t'Amsterdam: Aen De weledele en mogende Heeren Zeeraeden ter Amiraliteit in de gemelde stadt', in J.F.M. Sterck *et al.* (eds.), *De werken van Vondel: Achtste deel 1656-1660* (Amsterdam: De Maatschappij voor goede en goedkoope lectuur, 1935 [1658]), pp. 653-665, http://www.dbnl.org/tekst/vond001dewe08_01/vond001dewe08_01_0212.php (accessed 4 December 2015).

Vanderauwera, R., 'The Response to Translated Literature: A Sad Example', in Th. Hermans (ed.), *The Manipulation of Literature: Studies in Literature Translation* (London/New York: Routledge, 2014 [1985]), pp. 198-214.

Vieira, E.R.P., 'Liberating Calibans: Readings of *Antropofagia* and Haroldo de Campos' poetics of transcreation', in S. Bassnett and H. Trivedi (eds.), *Post-colonial Translation: Theory and Practice* (London/New York: Routledge, 2002 [1999]), pp. 95-113.

Weidner, D., 'Life after Life: A Figure of Thought in Walter Benjamin', paper presented at the Conference *Afterlife: Writing and Image in Walter Benjamin and Aby Warburg*, Universidad Federal de Minais Gerais, Belo Horizonte, Brasil, October 2012, http://www.zfl-berlin.org/tl_files/zfl/downloads/personen/weidner/life_after_life.pdf (accessed 10 December 2015).

CHAPTER 10

What Do we Learn from the Characters of the Novel *Sara Burgerhart*?

On the Transfer of Culture and Ideology in the Image of Fictional Characters at the End of the Eighteenth Century[1]

Jan Urbaniak (University of Wroclaw, Poland)

The epistolary novel *Historie van mejuffrouw Sara Burgerhart* by the duo of authors Elisabeth Wolff (1741-1804) and Agatha Deken (1738-1804) was published in the final two decades of the eighteenth century (1782), which was an important, even ground-breaking period in the history of the Northern Netherlands. The Netherlands had by that time already been the scene of the so-called bourgeois 'patriots' revolution (1780-1787). The ruling House of Orange was losing its prestige and the ideology of the Enlightenment with its slogans of equality, liberty and brotherhood, was once more revealed to be a mere dream, while rational literature, offering unspectacular, balanced and dogmatic content was slowly (and reluctantly) giving place to weak, emotional and unreal sentimentalism.[2] Why can this period be perceived as a breakthrough? In 1782, the process, which was completed in 1795, had already started and it resulted in the establishment of a new state – the Batavian Republic. It was established with a significant contribution from the bourgeoisie, it involved dependance on France and was only democratic in appearance. At least that is what the supporters of the House of Orange thought.[3]

Thus, the breakthrough occurred in the social and political sphere. Subsequently, as a result, Dutch literature of the last two decades of the eighteenth century was visibly engaged in the national cause. In the case of *Sara Burgerhart* this is visible in the presentation of the distinctiveness of the Dutch nation compared to, and in its confrontation with, foreign (basically French) culture, religion or customs.[4] However, this uniqueness was not an established feature, rather a goal designed by the authors for their characters. Striving for the ideal, which was clearly defined by the authors, would become the main message of the work, and in the construction of the characters, in their communication and attitude toward their own nation, one can see a range of elements, which – according to Wolff and Deken – reflect their 'Dutchness'.

The paper explores *Sara Burgerhart* as a text engaged in the national cause and presenting a confrontation of the positive (i.e. Dutch) personal model and its negative 'Gallicised' counterpart. Using the example of several of the novel's characters, I will try to answer two questions: firstly, which aspects of these typically Dutch cultural and ideological factors were especially stressed by the authors with respect to the characters; and secondly how these aspects are presented to the reader. In other words, what is the message that the selected characters of *Sara Burgerhart* tried to convey? Similar questions will be asked of characters portrayed negatively in order to show the contrast between them and the positive characters.

'DUTCHNESS' OR IMPOSSIBILITY OF TRANSLATION

As mentioned above, the propaganda function of the novel and the authors' involvement in the national cause resulted in highlighting the distinctiveness of Dutch language, customs and traditions, religious attitudes and propensity towards hard work, within a Europe-wide context. The authors had the intention of creating a work that was somewhat hermetic and difficult to translate. After its publication in 1782, *Sara Burgerhart* was translated only three times, once into French (1787), and twice into German (1789, 1796).[5] One could say that potential translators respected the will of Elisabeth Wolff herself, who did not care for popularity abroad. On the contrary – *Sara Burgerhart* was designed as a monument to the unique 'Dutchness' of local importance. It was noted by J.B. Meerkerk, author of the novel's 1930 edition:

> (Elisabeth Wolff) regarded her work as impossible to translate, something that could be understood exclusively by the Dutch. And she was right, as Busken Huet himself confirmed by writing: 'to appreciate this kind of literature, one has to be a member of this nation'.[6]

This hermetic character of the novel, which affects the potential translations of the text, is evident also – or even mainly – in the shaping of the characters. Wolff and Deken wanted the positive characters to strive to a certain personal ideal, reflecting the unique character of the Dutch society.[7] This was the authors' will. Universal features: righteousness, social commitment, responsibility were perceived by Wolff and Deken as typical national features, unique in comparison with the moral void, over-exaltation and egotism of the negative characters.[8] The latter served as a symbol of human fallibility, weakness and flaws. This negative imagery had educational value equally important as that of the positive characters. Readers could learn from their mistakes and could start intuitively to search for opposite features in himself or herself. As criticism of the negative characters grew more obvious, the more unique positive examples became.[9]

ON THE NOBLE SIDE – THE SOCIAL METAMORPHOSIS OF HENDRIK EDELING

Some characters in the novel are equivocal and maybe these are the most interesting ones. It is difficult to determine the authors' attitude toward them, as if the assessment was left to the reader.[10] This would be the case of Hendrik Edeling, who was in love with the main character and then became her loved one. He went through a long transformation: a hysterical, unstable suitor changed into a responsible, caring husband and father towards the end of the book. He becomes a moral and social role model, as is suggested by his name, which means 'nobleman'.[11] Here, the authors use the antique rhetorical figure, *nomen est omen*, thus describing the character's main features. The use of rhetoric was designed to classify both the positive and negative characters of the novel, which was a way to manipulate the readers and their opinion: from the very beginning, the authors create a clear division between the world of the just, traditional values of the Dutch nation and the world of foreign demoralisation, devoid of principles and meaning. A reader can easily guess whose value hierarchy should be supported and the characters' names serve as a clue.

Some of them involve the specificity of the Dutch language, difficult to translate, though deciphering the eponymous heroine's name is an easy task: Sara Burgerhart is a bourgeois [*burger*] who turns out to be good-hearted [*hart*], but a translator will find Cornelia Slimpslamp a much harder nut to crack – Wolff and Deken present this character negatively as a bigot with quite radical views.[12] The authors describe her milieu of origin as *de fijnen*, which refers to a conservative group in the Calvinist Reformed Church.[13] Cornelia's negative image is shaped by the presentation of the character herself and only partly from the meaning of her name, which may not be easy to translate exactly but nevertheless onomatopoeically, conveys an impression of flabbiness, lack of strength, with its slithery consonants.

Meanwhile, Edeling means 'noble person', influencing the perception of this character significantly. The reader will search for a confirmation of this nobleness, although at the beginning the character is not obviously positive. It should be also noted that Hendrik is not the only character with this patronymic in the novel. There are also Cornelis and Jan Edeling, Hendrik's brother and father respectively. However, while the former is somewhat careless and nonchalant, the latter, in contrast, is stubborn and never changes his views.[14] Therefore, only in the case of Hendrik does the designation 'noble' gain its full and correct meaning.

He matches nobility with a sincere feeling; however at the beginning of the novel Wolff and Deken do not seem to appreciate this fact. His exceedingly emotional attitude to Sara is illustrated by emotions which prevent him from taking any action and which resemble sentimental characters presented by the Dutch author Rhijnvis Feith (1753-1824) who wrote at the same time as Wolff and Deken. In these respects Hendrik comes across as alienated, somewhat phlegmatic, socially useless. Hendrik himself realises his apathy. He confesses in a letter (no. 30) to his brother: 'my phlegmatic nature finds it difficult to submit to any emotions'.[15] Further in the correspondence, he shares his most intimate experiences with his brother, sketching his own feelings, which – paradoxically – take away his will to live:

> I've been in a bad mood since yesterday, anxious, upset, as if I was sick, I'm good for nothing; I'll write a few words in the Registers only to close the books abruptly and forget the numbers; [...] I take my dressing gown off, I dress, but don't go out; my thoughts are a thousand miles from the place where I sit; then, six channels from our home; at moments my face is red with blood, then I am pale as a sheet. What can it be other than endless love?[16]

This description is an implicit criticism of a sentimental, emotional attitude. The authors let the readers themselves assess Hendrik, trying – despite the novel's paraenetic character – not to impose their own views. Both authors promoted socially engaged and rational literature with a strong moral message, and from the beginning they found the sentimentalism of Goethe or Feith's style a dangerous attitude which could demoralise young people.[17] This is why Hendrik could not remain as he was in the above description.

In the case of Hendrik Edeling (as well as other characters in the novel), a metamorphosis is visible which reflects the work's educational message.[18] Wolff and Deken hoped for a positive change in their readers and presented their characters as a model. Letter by letter, Hendrik becomes more and more confident, he takes responsibility for his own choices, he actively strives to gain the reciprocal feelings of his beloved Sara. In a letter (no. 60) to Sara's guardian (Sara is an orphan), Abraham Blankaart, he shows his intentions in a very determined way:

> You will be hardly surprised if I say that I am so overwhelmed by her [Sara's] charm that I simply cannot imagine anything greater than continuing this acquaintance and I will take the opportunity to attempt to obtain her consent.[19]

The phlegmatic admirer who could not cope with the force of his own feelings is replaced by a down-to-earth person who can think rationally and who is convinced that he will be successful in his pursuit of love. This attitude matches

Wolff and Deken's world view with social values determined by constructive actions, reflections of independence and somewhat individualised autonomy – taking into account all the limitations that related to eighteenth-century etiquette. It is true that Hendrik follows the rules of his time, he is not a rebel against the generally accepted customs: he tries to reach Sara cautiously, trying not to seem impudent, he also notifies Blankaart, the girl's uncle, in advance of his plans, showing respect for the conventions. However, a comparison of Hendrik's portrayal in this and in the previous quotation, shows a clear difference: the cautious courting becomes a bold manifestation of an determined young man.

In Hendrik's transformation, there is a clear ideological message: only an active attitude will achieve important matters; people should take their own life in their own hands and not give in to incidents and exaggerated emotionality. This is why Hendrik is eventually successful, becoming a model to be followed by the novel's young readers. Of course, before this happens, there will be some moments of doubt, when the fearful and passive tone known from the first letters (no. 118,126) can be heard again. However, this only makes Hendrik a more realistic character and his transformation becomes clearer and plausible. It shows that a rationalised feeling is included as a category of the Enlightenment's values. The feeling does not lose force this way; on the contrary, it gains new social usefulness in marriage, which makes an Enlightenment man simply better, more valuable and useful for society. In Hendrik's letter (no. 165) to widow Spilgoed, who used to be Sara's landlady and brought her up, he compares a feeling to a will to learn – a starting point of all social changes, and without which a man of the Enlightenment is never complete. The reader is left in no doubt that this is an Enlightenment novel: 'When I married her, it seemed to me that a human heart cannot love more. Oh! A desire to feel and the desire to know are the same: neither knows any limit'.[20] Therefore, in Hendrik Edeling's case, a happy marriage marks the end of a difficult process of adaptation to Dutch society, based on Enlightenment values: reason, respect for traditions, culture, knowledge and individualism; this is a proof of his maturity and a measure of his social status. This is one of the elements of Edeling's nobility, which makes him a role model for Dutch youth at the end of the eigteenth-century and – as the authors intend – shows the exceptional character of his attitude. While Europe is overwhelmed by the fashionable 'Werterian' attitude from Germany, Hendrik can control his feelings and use them for his own and other people's benefit.

FROM A YOUNG REBEL TO A MODEL CITIZEN – SARA BURGERHART

Another positive character, who – just like Edeling – undergoes a metamorphosis, is the title character. In this context, Sara and Hendrik eventually make a perfect couple, a perfect example of a family and feelings. In the epilogue of the book, the authors proudly say: '[...] for ten years, our friend Sara has been in a happy marriage with her noble spouse and she is a mother of five wonderful children whom she meticulously brings up.[21]

However, before Sara becomes an exemplary wife and mother, she will strike readers with her inappropriate behaviour, vehemence and youthful rebellion. It is not irrelevant that Sara is an orphan. Without the natural formative models, she is influenced by somewhat accidental people, e.g. aunt Suzanna Hofland, whose religious fanaticism, despotic nature, lack of knowledge or skills for bringing up a child and incontrollable temper – features which are bluntly contrary to Enlightenment values. At some point, Sara rebels against her guardian: a clear sign of her opposition to this world of false values. Although she goes against eighteenth-century conventions, which required children to submit entirely to the values defined by adults, her rebellion is sensible.[22] Thus, Sara reveals bigotry, hypocrisy and conservatism of *de fynen*, the milieu of traditional Calvinists to which Suzanna Hofland belongs.

At one of the boring receptions at her aunt's house, where a certain brother Benjamin, a physically repulsing figure ('drunkard and loafer like no other'),[23] is one of the guests, Sara can not stand it anymore, and demonstrates flagrantly bad behaviour: she eats pancakes prepared for the guests, angrily throws a napkin on the table, runs to her room and locks it. In a letter (no. 10) to her friend, Aletta Brunier, she describes the reception:

> I put on the dessert. 'Sara, dear, where did you *lose* the little pancakes?' 'I *lost* them in my own belly, Aunt'. The thrown away napkin landed, unluckily, right on the Brother's palm tree-coloured wig, and I hide from the storm in my room. You know I can run fast, I did then. At the last moment, I turned the key.[24]

This is the image of Sara at the beginning of the novel – her abominable behaviour is a starting point of a sort of 're-orientation', and signals the moral improvement of the heroine. In this context, she resembles characters of seventeenth-century Dutch comedies that experienced almost a mystical purification: they changed from fools to supporters of education, from despots into liberal believers in the bourgeois revolution and from misers into generous philanthropists.[25] Similarly Sara, a rebellious young lady, experiences the force of the Enlightenment's education and morality and eventually becomes a model of the right social attitude.

The story of Sara Burgerhart is an example of a social, philosophical and educational metamorphosis used by Wolff and Deken to present the mechanisms of the effects of the right upbringing, to define a set of authorities for the young generation, to indicate models of good behaviour and reprove social faults. In this context, the clever rhetoric of the novel reaches its perfection. The immature main character chaotically searches for her own system of values, and the authors lead her from one failure to another, submitting her to an ordeal and confronting her with a range of variable characters. Once, it is a flirt nicknamed 'R.', then, a careless and lazy Lotje Rien du Tout, who 'sleeps until noon [...] and drinks [...] English ale', or else an idler, Jacob Brunier, who cares only about appearances.[26]

'GALLOPHILIA' AS A COUNTERBALANCE TO NATIONAL VALUES

Jacob and Lotje will be the exact opposites of Hendrik and Sara. The authors describe them as 'triflers' [*lichtmissen*].[27] Their function in the text is important: in a confrontation with such figures as Jacob Brunier or Lotje Rien du Tout, Sara experiences a moral purification. As Jacob Brunier becomes more impudent in his courting of Sara, as Lotje becomes funnier in her childish behaviour, the heroine comes to realise the importance of positive values – the sincere love from Hendrik Edeling, the practical wisdom of her friend Anna Willis or her caring uncle Blankaart. The novel eventually has a classical happy ending.

The novel provides devastating criticism of these negative characters and, similarly to the case of Hendrik Edeling, the criticism is not explicit. However, it will soon be obvious that the negative characters of *Sara Burgerhart* do not suit the system of values defined by the authors. Once again, the first indication in the assessment of a character is 'the meaningful name' (*nomen est omen*). In the case of Jacob Brunier the French-sounding name automatically excludes this character from the world dominated by typically Dutch traditionalism, respect for conventions, reason and moderation. As the antithesis of 'national-gallophilic' clearly defined by Wolff and Deken, Brunier will be the personification of a dangerous plague created in the late eighteenth century by a thoughtless love of all things French cherished by a part of Dutch society.

A reaction to 'gallophilia', in short, is one of the elements of the national strategy aimed at lifting the Netherlands from political chaos, economic regression and cultural decadence.[28] From the 1720s onwards the Netherlands had been losing its strong position gained in the Golden Age. It was visible in economic indicators: long-distance marine and Baltic trade was shrinking, people fled cities, which were growing poorer; it was increasingly difficult to control social unrest.[29] Dutch literature chiefly offered works that were barely original and publishing was largely dominated by foreign books (mostly French).[30]

This situation evoked a national debate supposed to condemn the wrong attitudes, to show who was responsible for the country's bad condition and to find the means needed to lift the Netherlands from this abject state. The debate is remembered as a moral re-orientation of Dutch society [*morele herbewapening*].[31] It focused mainly on criticising 'gallophilia' in different areas. The reaction to 'gallophilia' also took the form of an offensive against the natural religion imported from France – Spinozaism promoted in the milieu of French Huguenots, as well as deism and atheism based on rational reasoning.[32] In social terms, criticism of 'gallophilia' involved condemnation of French customs adopted by the aristocracy and so-called 'regents' – representatives of state authorities of rich bourgeois origin.[33] Politically, the reaction to 'gallophilia' resulted in criticism of political and state concepts and promoted a model of a state with an important role of the Calvinist faith as a measure of cultural and religious tradition; there are also references to the somewhat mythologised Eighty-Years War (1568-1648) of independence of the Netherlands against Spain. These concepts relied on a nation-state, still strong (referring to the hegemony of the Golden Age), devout, and governed stringently by the dynasty of Orange.[34] In terms of literature, criticism focused on the flooding of the Dutch publishing market by French literature, as well as on condemnation of the negative habits of literary characters that did not match Dutch values.

FRENCH DANDY – JACOB BRUNIER

Wolff and Deken joined the fight against 'gallophilia' perfectly with their novel. They condemned the mental alienation of a Dutch nation, as evident in Jacob Brunier. Brunier amalgamates features criticised by supporters of the 'moral re-orientation': vanity, aristocratic manners, amorality, lack of respect for traditions. His lifestyle, based on elusive values, superficial relations with other people, lack of social engagement, become an allegory of the despised French salon culture. Brunier not only opposes traditional Dutch values (Calvinist moderation and patriotism), but he is also the exact opposite of an eighteenth-century male personality.[35] Brunier's 'masculinity' is questioned socially and culturally, portrayed as a lonely egoist, unemployed and unconnected to society. He evinces typically 'feminine' customs and interests and uses those to seduce Sara (!). In one of the letters (no. 31), full of French words, Brunier describes his 'fascinating' plan for a day:

> [...] today I overslept, my friend Edeling came to me at the same time as my barber. After an hour, my hair was done, now I am sitting in my *Soubise* and writing to you. Then, I'll put on the little silk pants and that will take another half an hour, I hate to see them crease. Then, I'll dress up *comme il faut*, so that I can be seen by your keen eyes, *ma chere*. After the meeting, I'll be sorting the grains of *coumarou* for my dear little Friends.[36]

This seems typical of Jacob's days, filled with 'luxury' and 'fashion', two elements associated by the authors with 'gallophilia'. Brunier becomes a personification of this phenomenon. Sara's rejection of Jacob is symbolical for the unequivocal, although indirect commentary of the authors on 'gallophilia': a French dandy gets his well-deserved punishment:

Your extravagance knows no limits! I don't know what is better: to get angry at you as I never used to or just laugh till my sides ache. I have never read such an impertinent combination of foolishness and stupid vision of doubtful merits.[37]

AGAINST THE ENLIGHTENMENT'S CATEGORY OF REASON – LOTJE RIEN DU TOUT

Another 'gallophilic' character is similarly negative – Lotje (Charlotte) Rien du Tout, a naïve, childish lass, whose character is indicated by her French name, meaning 'nothing at all'.[38] Lotje's role is unimportant and at the social periphery; the authors assign her to a place matching her childish behaviour: she teaches Sara and Hendrik Edelings' children to make doll clothes,[39] she has no larger responsibilities. Neither is she an intelligent person: she resists being educated and her knowledge of her mother tongue is not very good. In one of Lotje's letters (no. 69) the authors note that they too correct the text so that '[...] it can be read at all'.[40] Besides, Lotje is forgetful, but most of all she is emotionally unstable. She does not fit in Enlightenment philosophy, which perceived stoics, reasonable, moderate, as better than Epicurean passions.[41] Lotje is moody and lacks moral standing, just like Jacob Brunier, she is, deliberately, left undeveloped. This character's image is well reflected in Sara's letter (no. 26) to her friend Anna Willis. Sara is outspoken about Lotje:

> (Lotje) has no character [...]. Sometimes, she sleeps until eleven o'clock and before that she sits up all night, just sits up, doing nothing. Sometimes she drinks a glass of water, and then an English ale. I see her in a nightgown, and just a moment later she runs out fully dressed. At times, she is agreeability itself; at others – she seems offended if asked to hand a kitchen tissue. Today, she'll give money to a beggar, and tomorrow she'll scream: 'the lazy man should go to work'.[42]

CONCLUSIONS

I focused on the portrayal of the characters and I evaluate their effect on the ideological and cultural message of the novel, in particular on the manner in which the message is communicated to the reader.

An important rhetorical tool used by Wolff and Deken involves emphasizing the contrast between national and foreign, French elements and values. Lotje and Jacob, associated with the extravagance of the French salon, are shown in stark contrast with the positive Dutch characters and this contributes to achieve the authors' goal. It is a triumph of a clearly defined system of values that leaves little space for different attitudes. This is the system that comprises the 'Dutchness', which makes the novel so hermetic. It is based on sincerity, honest living, moderation and striving for knowledge, dominating values that gain the readers' attention. The presentation of the opposite values creates a warning for the reader, and a reference point in the portrayal of positive characters, and proof of the novel's reliability. According to the principles of diligent rationalism and probability in describing reality, as did the British novelist Samuel Richardson (1689-1761), admired by Wolff and Deken.[43] Otherness has to be marked, personified in elegant dandies like Jacob Brunier, or even in the unstable, somewhat sentimental Hendrik Edeling, who eventually develops into a positive character.

The contrast of national versus foreign in the novel plays a central role in the authors' struggle against the plague of 'gallophilia'. It is not accidental that the negative characters have French names and that their behaviour resembles that of the French aristocracy rather than of the Dutch bourgeoisie.

Another linguistic trope is based on 'meaningful names' (*nomen est omen*). The authors organise the novel's world and divide it by moral criteria: the good and noble on one hand and the false and trivial on the other. Not all characters are unequivocal. Some, like Hendrik Edeling need time to prove their social and moral value. To do so, these characters undergo a sort of 're-orientation'. This rhetorical tool is used by Wolff and Deken quite frequently, and certainly in the portrayal of the protagonist: from an immature rebel she grows into a model housewife and mother.

Which features are the most frequent in the context of positive characters, and indicate the uniqueness of Dutch society compared with other European nations? Which traits are criticised by the authors?

As the novel is engaged in the national cause, *Sara Burgerhart* was designed to promote patriotic attitudes, rationalism in all actions and moderation in life. Therefore, personal idealism should involve responsibility for the country and its citizens, reflected in respect for traditions, and care for the national culture and language. This is how Wolff and Deken defined patriotism. Copying cultural models from abroad (manifested by using French wording in letters etc.) is seen as opposed to this ideal.

Reason as a leading value (in the name of rationalism) can be observed in the characters' attitude to knowledge, and their conviction that they can shape their fate effectively – with wise, well-considered choices, and not submitting to emotions, as sentimentalists did – always brings positive results, as Hendrik Edeling found out.

And finally Calvinist self-control (somehow related to rationalism), described earlier by the Dutch humanist Justus Lipsius (1547-1606) as *Constantia*, or moderation, the ability to contain one's emotions and observe permanent life-determining principles, completed the system of values presented in the novel and demonstrated its ideology.[44] Being outside this system immediately signified an anti-state, anti-Dutch manifestation.

NOTES

1 This text can be read as a complementary part of my research presented in an earlier publication (2015) in *Werkwinkel* 10: 2, pp. 89-101, entitled 'De roman als wapen tegen Frankrijk: *Sara Burgerhart* van Wolff en Deken en de strijd tegen de 'gallofilia'' where I also discuss *Sara Burgerhart.* In that earlier case I concentrate only on examples of socially harmful influence of the characters criticised by the authors. They function as an example of 'gallophilia', a phenomenon that I present in my text just from a negative perspective. In this text the perspective is very much broadened. It draws attention not only to the flaws of the novel's characters but, most importantly, it confronts them with positive examples which allows to emphasize the most important aim of the novel, namely morally elevating instruction.

2 About 'patriots' revolution see A. van den Berg, *De papieren oorlog tussen patrioten en prinsgezinden: 'Het Geldersche Zwyn'* (Nijmegen: Nijmeegs Museum 'Commanderie van Sint-Jan', 1987); S. Klein, *Patriots republikanisme: Politieke cultuur in Nederland, 1766-1787* (Amsterdam: University Press, 1995); N. van Sas, *De metamorfose van Nederland: Van oude orde naar moderniteit 1750-1900* (Amsterdam: Amsterdam University Press, 2004); J. Rosendaal, *De Nederlandse Revolutie: Vrijheid, volk en vaderland, 1783-1799* (Nijmegen: Vantilt, 2005); about a weakened impact of the ideology of Enlightenment see A. Hanou, 'Verlichte vrijheid: Iets over een denkbeeld in imaginaire reizen' in E. Haitsma Mulier and W. Velema (eds.), *Vrijheid: Een geschiedenis van de vijftiende tot de twintigste eeuw* (Amsterdam: Amsterdam University Press, 1999), pp. 187-212 (211); J. Kloek and W. Mijnhardt, *1800: Blauwdrukken voor een samenleving* (Den Haag: Sdu, 2001), pp. 103-139; about a clash between a dogmatic content of the rational literature and the sentimentalism see G. Knuvelder, *Handboek tot de geschiedenis der Nederlandse letterkunde*, vol. II (Den Bosch: Malmberg, 1971), p. 443.

3 About the Batavian Republic see: T. Jorissen, 'De Fransche Tijd', in *Historische Bladen* 1 (1890), pp. 392-4; J. Oddens, *Pioniers in schaduwbeeld* (Nijmegen: Vantilt, 2012); M. Rutjes, *Door gelijkheid gegrepen: Democratie, burgerschap en staat in Nederland 1795-1801* (Nijmegen: Vantilt, 2012); F. Grijzenhout, N. van Sas and W. Velema, *Het Bataafsche experiment: Politiek en cultuur rond 1800* (Nijmegen: Vantilt, 2013).

4 P. Buijnsters, *Nederlandse literatuur van de achttiende eeuw* (Utrecht: HES, 1984), p. 70; I. Leemans and G.-J. Johannes, *Worm en donder: Geschiedenis van de Nederlandse literatuur 1700-1800* (Amsterdam: Bert Bakker, 2013), p. 38.

5 H.A. Höweler, 'De Franse vertaling van *Sara Burgerhart*: Voorlopige mededelingen', in *Documentatieblad Werkgroep Achttiende Eeuw* 2 (1970), pp. 18-26; H.A. Höweler, 'De Franse vertaling van *Sara Burgerhart*: Verbetering en aanvulling van de voorlopige mededelingen', in *Documentatieblad Werkgroep Achttiende Eeuw* 3 (1971), pp. 23-24; J. Bundschuh-van Duinkerken, 'Johann Gottwerth Müller als vertaler van de werken van Wolff en Deken', in *Internationale Neerlandistiek* 46 (2008), p. 23.

6 '(Elisabeth Wolff) meende dat haar boek eigenlijk niet te vertalen was en alleen verstaanbaar voor Hollanders. En ze had daarin volkomen gelijk, ook naar het oordeel van Busken Huet, die o.a. schreef: – "om die kunst te waardeeren moet men van de natie zijn."' (All translations in this chapter by JU.) E. Wolff, and A. Deken, *Historie van mejuffrouw Sara Burgerhart* (Amsterdam: Meulenhoff, 1930), p. 2.

7 E. Wolff and A. Deken, *Historie van mejuffrouw Sara Burgerhart* (Den Haag: Isaac van Cleef, 1782), pp. III-XI; N.N., '[Review of] Wolff-Bekker en A. Deken, *Historie van Mejuffrouw Sara Burgerhart*, 2 vols., 's Gravenhage: I. van Cleef, 1782', in *Vaderlandsche Letteroefeningen* 5 (1783), pp. 225-226 (225).

8 L. van Gemert, '"Onwederstanelyken drang": Het vrouwelijk schrijverschap in achttiende-eeuws Nederland', in *De Achttiende Eeuw* 27 (1995), pp. 127-140; J. Kloek, 'Wel Sara, niet Willem en Cornelia', in P. Altena *et al.* (eds.), *Onbreekbare burgerharten: De historie van Betje Wolff en Aagje Deken* (Nijmegen: Vantilt, 2004), p. 113.

9 P. Buijnsters, 'Karakteruitbeelding in de roman Sara Burgerhart', in *De Nieuwe Taalgids* 64 (1971), pp. 193-202.

10 Leemans and Johannes, *Worm en donder*, p. 527.

11 K. van Dalen-Oskam, *De stijl van R.* (Amsterdam: Vossiuspers UvA, 2013), p. 7.

12 Wolff and Deken, *Historie van mejuffrouw Sara Burgerhart* (1782 edition), pp. 25-28.

13 About 'de fijnen' see: F. van Lieburg, *Levens van Vromen: Gereformeerd piëtisme in de achttiende eeuw* (Kampen: De Groot Goudriaan, 1991).

14 Buijnsters, 'Karakteruitbeelding in de roman Sara Burgerhart', p. 196.

15 Wolff and Deken, *Historie van mejuffrouw Sara Burgerhart* (1782 edition), p. 111.

16 'Ik ben, zedert gisteren, ongemaklyk, onrustig, maalagtig, ziek; voer niets uit; schryf nu een paar regels in 't Grootboek, en sla het weer toe; trek een rekening op, en kan de getallen niet onthouden [...]. Ik trek myn Japon uit, kleede my, en blyf in huis: nu ben ik duizend mylen van de plaats daar ik zit; dan geen zes gragten van ons huis; nu vliegt my 't bloed in 't aangezigt, dan zie ik zo bleek als de muur. Wat kan dit alles zyn, zo ik niet dodelyk verlieft ben?' Wolff and Deken, *Historie van mejuffrouw Sara Burgerhart*, (1782 edition), pp. 111-112.

17 About the reception of Goethe's novel and the reaction on the 'Sturm und Drang' movement in the Netherlands see J. Kloek, *Over Werther geschreven... Nederlandse reacties op Goethes Werther 1775-1800: Proeve van historisch receptie-onderzoek* (Utrecht: HES, 1985); P. Altena, 'Die holländischen Himmelsstürmer: Sturm und Drang in der niderländischen Literatur 1770-1800', in B. Plachta, and W. Woesler (eds.), *Sturm und Drang: Geistiger Aufbruch 1770-1790 im Spiegel der Literatur* (Tübingen: Niemeyer, 1997).

18 W. van den Berg, '1 oktober 1782: Wolff en Deken publiceren hun eerste briefroman – Epistolair onderricht: Sara Burgerhart als briefroman', in M.A. Schenkeveld-Van der Dussen (ed.), *Nederlandse Literatuur, een geschiedenis* (Groningen: Noordhoff, 1993), pp. 355-360.

19 'Het kan u niet zeer vreemt voorkomen, als ik u eenvoudig zeg, dat hare [Sara's] bevalligheden my dermate getroffen hebben, dat my niets aangenamers zyn kan, dan myne verkeering met haar voort te zetten, en dus de gelegenheid te krygen van te onderstaan, of zy my met hare goedkeuring zal veréeren.' Wolff and Deken, *Historie van mejuffrouw Sara Burgerhart* (1782 edition), p. 268.

20 'Toen ik haar trouwde, geloofde ik, dat het onmooglyk was voor een menschlyk hart, tedderder te beminnen. Och! 't is met de liefde als met de zucht tot kennis; zy heeft geene grenzen'. Wolff and Deken, *Historie van mejuffrouw Sara Burgerhart* (1782 edition), p. 767.

21 '[...] dat onze Vriendin Burgerhart, zedert, tien jaren, zeer gelukkig leeft met haren braven Man, en reeds Moeder is van vyf aartige Kinderen, die zy voorbeeldig opvoedt'. Wolff and Deken, *Historie van mejuffrouw Sara Burgerhart* (1782 edition), p. I ('Nareden').

22 H. van Lierop-Debrauwer and N. Bastiaansen-Harks, *Over grenzen: De adolescentenroman in het literatuuronderwijs* (Delft: Eburon, 2005), p. 39.

23 'een luije zuipzak van een Kerel'. Wolff and Deken, *Historie van mejuffrouw Sara Burgerhart* (1782 edition), p. 35.

24 'Ik deed zo; zette het Dessertje op. 'Waar *bennen* de Flensjes, Saartje?' 'Die *bennen* in myn maag, Tante.' Snap myn servet neêr gegooit, (by ongeluk tegen Broeders palmhoute pruik) en het onweer op myne kamer ontweken. Gy weet, ik ben tamelyk vlug, dat my toen te pas kwam. Knap de deur op slot.' Wolff and Deken, *Historie van mejuffrouw Sara Burgerhart* (1782 edition), pp. 36-37.

25 K. Porteman and M.B. Smits-Veldt, *Een nieuw vaderland voor de muzen: Geschiedenis van de Nederlandse literatuur 1560-1700* (Amsterdam: Bert Bakker, 2009), pp. 696-697.

26 'slaapt nu eens tot elf uuren [...] en drinkt [...] Engelsch Bier'. Wolff and Deken, *Historie van mejuffrouw Sara Burgerhart* (1782 edition), p. 102; Buijnsters, 'Karakteruitbeelding in de roman Sara Burgerhart', p. 196.

27 Wolff and Deken, *Historie van mejuffrouw Sara Burgerhart* (1782 edition), p. 300.

28 See P. Buijnsters, 'Het heilsperspectief van de Verlichting: Een reflectie bij het 25-jarig bestaan van de Werkgroep 18ᵉ Eeuw', in *Documentatieblad Werkgroep Achttiende Eeuw* (26) 1 (1994) p. 127; A. Hanou, *Nederlandse literatuur van de Verlichting 1670-1830* (Nijmegen: Vantilt, 2002); W. Frijhoff, *Meertaligheid in de gouden eeuw: Een verkenning* (Amsterdam: KNAW Press, 2010), pp. 7-8.

29 See J. Israel, *The Dutch Republic: Its Rise, Greatness and Fall 1477-1806* (Oxford: Oxford University Press, 1995), p. 1129; I. Nijenhuis, 'De ontwikkeling van het politiek-economische vrijheidsbegrip in de Republiek', in E. Haitsma Mulier and W. Velema (eds.), *Vrijheid: Een geschiedenis van de vijftiende tot de twintigste eeuw* (Amsterdam: Amsterdam University Press, 1999), p. 238; A.Th. van Deursen, *De last van veel geluk: De geschiedenis van Nederland, 1555-1702* (Amsterdam: Bert Bakker, 2004), pp. 335-337.

30 Leemans and Johannes, *Worm en donder*, p. 88.

31 About the moral re-orientation of the Dutch society see Buijnsters, *Nederlandse literatuur van de achttiende eeuw*, p. 71; van Sas, *De metamorfose van Nederland*, p. 73.

32 J. Bots, *Tussen Descartes en Darwin: Geloof en natuurwetenschap in de achttiende eeuw in Nederland* (Assen: Van Gorcum, 1972); K. de Pater, 'Fysicotheologie in de achttiende eeuw: Van Boyle tot Paley', in *Bijbel en Wetenschap* 25 (2000), pp. 13-16 and 46-49.

33 H. Rowen, 'The Dutch Republic and the Idea of Freedom', in D. Wootton (ed.), *Republicanism, Liberty and Commercial Society* (Stanford: Stanford University Press, 1994), p. 318.

34 G.O. van de Klashorst, 'De "ware vrijheid", 1650-1672', in E. Haitsma Mulier and W. Velema (eds.), *Vrijheid. Een geschiedenis van de vijftiende tot de twintigste eeuw* (Amsterdam: Amsterdam University Press, 1999), p. 168.

35 J. Outshoorn, *Een irriterend onderwerp: Verschuivende conceptualiseringen van het sekseverschil* (Nijmegen: SUN, 1989), p. 16.

36 '[...] ik heb my verslapen, en myn vriend Edeling kwam met myn Coëffeur te gelyk in. Binnen 't uur was ik gekapt; en nu zit ik, in myn *Soubise*, deezen te schryven. Dan moet ik nog een paar nieuwe zyden koussen aantrekken, daar loopt ook een half uur mêe door, want ik mag niet zien dat er de minste kreuk in zit. Dan moet ik my nog kleden, *comme il faut*, om onder het keurig oog van

u, ma chere, te verschynen. Dan moet ik voor myne Dames Favorites nog eenige *Tonco-Boontjes* sorteeren.' Wolff and Deken, *Historie van mejuffrouw Sara Burgerhart* (1782 edition), p. 119.

37 'Hoe dood vreemt zyt gy omtrent u zelf! Ik moet of boos op u worden, en dat bevalt my niet; of ik moet u hartlyk uitlachen. Nooit zeker las men zo eene ongevallige mengeling van zotteklap, en dwaze inbeelding, op zeer twyffelachtige verdiensten, dan dat schriftje bevat.' Wolff and Deken, *Historie van mejuffrouw Sara Burgerhart* (1782 edition), p. 227.

38 Buijnsters, 'Karakteruitbeelding in de roman Sara Burgerhart', p. 200.

39 Wolff and Deken, *Historie van mejuffrouw Sara Burgerhart* (1782 edition), p. VII ('Nareden').

40 '[...] op dat men die zoude kunnen lezen'. Wolff and Deken, *Historie van mejuffrouw Sara Burgerhart* (1782 edition), p. 308.

41 A. Levi, *French Moralists: The Theory of the Passions, 1585 to 1649* (Oxford: Clarendon Press, 1964), pp. 11-13.

42 '(Lotje) heeft geen karakter [...]. Ze slaapt nu eens tot elf uuren, dan zit zy den nagt over, ofschoon zy niets doet, of te doen heeft. Nu drinkt zy een glas water, dan weer Engelsch Bier. Zo is zy in haar beddejakje, en binnen een oogenblik vliegt zy gekleed de deur uit. Nu is zy de gedienstigheid zelf; dan is het haar fatsoen te na een theedoekje aan te reiken. Vandaag geeft zy een gulden aan een arm mensch; morgen, "mag de luije Bedelaar werken".' Wolff and Deken, *Historie van mejuffrouw Sara Burgerhart* (1782 edition), p. 102.

43 A. Swinnen, *Het slot ontvlucht: De 'vrouwelijke' Bildungsroman in de Nederlandse literatuur* (Amsterdam: Amsterdam University Press, 2006), pp. 43-45.

44 About Lipsius' *Constantia* see J. Jansen, *Brevitas: Beschouwingen over de beknoptheid van vorm en stijl in de renaissance* (Hilversum: Verloren, 1995), pp. 172-173.

BIBLIOGRAPHY

Altena, P., 'Die holländischen Himmelsstürmer: Sturm und Drang in der niederländischen Literatur 1770-1800', in B. Plachta and W. Woesler (eds.), *Sturm und Drang: Geistiger Aufbruch 1770-1790 im Spiegel der Literatur* (Tübingen: Niemeyer, 1997), pp. 183-198.

Bots, J., *Tussen Descartes en Darwin: Geloof en natuurwetenschap in de achttiende eeuw in Nederland* (Assen: Van Gorcum, 1972).

Buijnsters, P., 'Karakteruitbeelding in de roman Sara Burgerhart', in *De Nieuwe Taalgids* 64 (1971), pp. 193-202.

Buijnsters, P., *Nederlandse literatuur van de achttiende eeuw* (Utrecht: HES, 1984).

Buijnsters, P., 'Het heilsperspectief van de Verlichting: Een reflectie bij het 25-jarig bestaan van de Werkgroep 18e Eeuw', in *Documentatieblad Werkgroep Achttiende Eeuw* 26: 1 (1994), pp. 121-132.

Bundschuh-van Duinkerken, J., 'Johann Gottwerth Müller als vertaler van de werken van Wolff en Deken', in *Internationale Neerlandistiek* 46 (2008), pp. 23-32.

De Pater, K., 'Fysicotheologie in de achttiende eeuw: Van Boyle tot Paley', in *Bijbel en Wetenschap* 25 (2000), pp. 13-16 and 46-49.

Frijhoff, W., *Meertaligheid in de gouden eeuw: Een verkenning* (Amsterdam: KNAW Press, 2010).

Grijzenhout, F., N. van Sas and W. Velema, *Het Bataafsche experiment: Politiek en cultuur rond 1800* (Nijmegen: Vantilt, 2013).

Hanou, A., 'Verlichte vrijheid: Iets over een denkbeeld in imaginaire reizen', in E. Haitsma Mulier and W. Velema (eds.), *Vrijheid: Een geschiedenis van de vijftiende tot de twintigste eeuw* (Amsterdam: Amsterdam University Press, 1999), pp. 187-212.

Hanou, A., *Nederlandse literatuur van de Verlichting (1670-1830)* (Nijmegen: Vantilt, 2002).

Höweler, H.A., 'De Franse vertaling van *Sara Burgerhart*: Voorlopige mededelingen', in *Documentatieblad Werkgroep Achttiende Eeuw* 2 (1970), pp. 18-26.

Höweler, H.A., 'De Franse vertaling van *Sara Burgerhart*: Verbetering en aanvulling van de voorlopige mededelingen', in *Documentatieblad Werkgroep Achttiende Eeuw* 3 (1971), pp. 23-24.

Israel, J., *The Dutch Republic: Its Rise, Greatness and Fall 1477-1806* (Oxford: Oxford University Press, 1995).

Jansen, J., *Brevitas: Beschouwingen over de beknoptheid van vorm en stijl in de renaissance* (Hilversum: Verloren, 1995).

Jorissen, T., 'De Fransche Tijd', in *Historische Bladen* 1 (1890), pp. 347-442.

Klein, S., *Patriots republikanisme: Politieke cultuur in Nederland, 1766-1787* (Amsterdam: Amsterdam University Press, 1995).

Kloek, J., *Over Werther geschreven... Nederlandse reacties op Goethes Werther 1775-1800: Proeve van historisch receptie-onderzoek* (Utrecht: HES, 1985).

Kloek, J., 'Wel Sara, niet Willem en Cornelia', in P. Altena *et al.* (eds.), *Onbreekbare burgerharten. De historie van Betje Wolff en Aagje Deken* (Nijmegen: Vantilt, 2004).

Kloek, J. and W. Mijnhardt, *1800: Blauwdrukken voor een samenleving* (Den Haag: Sdu, 2001).

Knuvelder, G., *Handboek tot de geschiedenis der Nederlandse letterkunde*, vol. II (Den Bosch: Malmberg, 1971).

Leemans, I. and G.-J. Johannes, *Worm en donder: Geschiedenis van de Nederlandse literatuur 1700-1800* (Amsterdam: Bert Bakker, 2013).

Levi, A., *French Moralists: The Theory of the Passions, 1585 to 1649* (Oxford: Clarendon Press, 1964).

N.N., '[Review of] Wolff-Bekker en A. Deken, *Historie van Mejuffrouw Sara Burgerhart*, 2 vols., ‚s Gravenhage: I. van Cleef, 1782', in *Vaderlandsche Letteroefeningen* 5 (1783), pp. 225-226.

Nijenhuis, I., 'De ontwikkeling van het politiek-economische vrijheidsbegrip in de Republiek', in E. Haitsma Mulier and W. Velema (eds.), *Vrijheid: Een geschiedenis van de vijftiende tot de twintigste eeuw* (Amsterdam: Amsterdam University Press, 1999), pp. 233-252.

Oddens, J., *Pioniers in schaduwbeeld* (Nijmegen: Vantilt, 2012).

Outshoorn, J., *Een irriterend onderwerp: Verschuivende conceptualiseringen van het sekseverschil* (Nijmegen: SUN, 1989).

Porteman, K. and M.B. Smits-Veldt, *Een nieuw vaderland voor de muzen: Geschiedenis van de Nederlandse literatuur 1560-1700* (Amsterdam: Bert Bakker, 2009).

Rosendaal, J., *De Nederlandse Revolutie: Vrijheid, volk en vaderland, 1783-1799* (Nijmegen: Vantilt, 2005).

Rowen, H., 'The Dutch Republic and the Idea of Freedom', in D. Wootton (ed.), *Republicanism, Liberty and Commercial Society* (Stanford: Stanford University Press, 1994), pp. 311-340.

Rutjes, M., *Door gelijkheid gegrepen: Democratie, burgerschap en staat in Nederland 1795-1801* (Nijmegen: Vantilt, 2012).

Swinnen, A., *Het slot ontvlucht: De 'vrouwelijke' Bildungsroman in de Nederlandse literatuur* (Amsterdam: Amsterdam University Press, 2006).

Van Dalen-Oskam, K., *De stijl van R.* (Amsterdam: Vossiuspers UvA, 2013).

Van de Klashorst, G.O., 'De "ware vrijheid", 1650-1672', in E. Haitsma Mulier and W. Velema (eds.), *Vrijheid: Een geschiedenis van de vijftiende tot de twintigste eeuw* (Amsterdam: Amsterdam University Press, 1999), pp. 157-186.

Van den Berg, A., *De papieren oorlog tussen patrioten en prinsgezinden: 'Het Geldersche Zwyn'*, (Nijmegen: Nijmeegs Museum 'Commanderie van Sint-Jan', 1987).

Van den Berg, W., '1 oktober 1782: Wolff en Deken publiceren hun eerste briefroman – Epistolair onderricht: Sara Burgerhart als briefroman', in M.A. Schenkeveld-van der Dussen (ed.), *Nederlandse Literatuur, een geschiedenis* (Groningen: Noordhoff, 1993), pp. 355-360.

Van Deursen, A.Th., *De last van veel geluk: De geschiedenis van Nederland, 1555-1702*, (Amsterdam: Bert Bakker, 2004).

Van Gemert, L., '"Onwederstanelyken drang": Het vrouwelijk schrijverschap in achttiende-eeuws Nederland', in *De Achttiende Eeuw* 27 (1995), pp. 127-140.

Van Lieburg, F., *Levens van Vromen: Gereformeerd piëtisme in de achttiende eeuw* (Kampen: De Groot Goudriaan, 1991).

Van Lierop-Debrauwer, H. and N. Bastiaansen-Harks, *Over grenzen: De adolescentenroman in het literatuuronderwijs* (Delft: Eburon, 2005).

Van Sas, N., *De metamorfose van Nederland: Van oude orde naar moderniteit 1750-1900* (Amsterdam: Amsterdam University Press, 2004).

Wolff, E. and A. Deken, *Historie van mejuffrouw Sara Burgerhart* (Den Haag: Isaac van Cleef, 1782).

Wolff, E. and A. Deken, *Historie van mejuffrouw Sara Burgerhart* (Amsterdam: Meulenhoff, 1930).

CHAPTER 11

The Flemish Lion: Oscillating between Past and Present

Ideology in German-Language Adaptations of Conscience's *De Leeuw van Vlaenderen* for Young Readers

Christine Hermann (University of Vienna, Austria)

On 11 July 1302, in a famous battle near Kortrijk, which later became known as the Battle of the Golden Spurs,[1] an infantry army of Flemish town militia defeated the numerically superior cavalry (mounted knights) of the French king, Philip IV, and thus gained – at least temporarily – their freedom from French rule. In 1838, this historical event was romanticized by the Flemish writer Hendrik Conscience in his novel *De Leeuw van Vlaenderen of de Slag der Gulden Sporen* [*The Lion of Flanders or the Battle of the Golden Spurs*]. Conscience's novel contributed to an increased national consciousness in nineteenth-century Flanders, became a symbol for national identity and turned into a Flemish founding myth and national epic *par excellence.*

In the foreword to the first edition (no longer included in the revised version of 1843), which can be read as a political statement, Conscience pleads for equal status for the Flemish (Dutch) language in the young Belgian state, where French predominated as the language of the upper classes in literature and government, while Dutch dialects were spoken as a vernacular and considered vulgar. He frankly states his intentions to inspire national consciousness and patriotism, and at the end of his book exhorts the Flemings in his much-quoted last sentence not to forget the glorious past of their forefathers.

De Leeuw van Vlaenderen became the most widely read Flemish novel of the nineteenth century,[2] was translated into numerous languages and inspired a wide range of adaptations across genres and media for different audience groups: it was made into a film, adapted for the stage, turned into comic strips, and – in several languages and in different periods – adapted for young readers (in German alone, twelve different versions can be found).

Why have there been so many different adaptations for young readers over such an extended period? To what extent do they differ, and which functions do they fulfil in their specific (political, social, cultural, literary) target contexts? In this article, I will try to identify these functions on the basis of the ideological charge of the adaptations, which is reflected in paratexts, in adjustments of the text proper, in covers and in illustrations. I understand 'ideology' in the broader sense as norms and values, as all kinds of political, social and moral attitudes and ideas. The historical, sociocultural and literary context of the adaptations (publisher, series, but also the role and position of children's literature at the time) will be considered as well.

ADAPTATION

Sanne Parlevliet identified five functions for the adaptation of classics for young readers: moral, social, cultural (literary) and aesthetic education, as well as entertainment, thus focusing mainly on didactic intentions; in essence, adaptations introduce children to a literary canon as common cultural heritage and convey certain norms and values, while providing a certain 'fun factor' as well.[3] Stephens and McCallum also highlight the initiation of children into the literary heritage and 'the transmission of a culture's central values and assumptions',[4] identifying three main functions: popularization, canonization, and cultural transmission.[5] By making the classics more accessible to young readers, adaptations are instrumental in their continued canonization. On the other hand, adaptations for young readers have often been accused of simplifying, 'downsizing', flattening and homogenizing the style and content of the original classic.

One might wonder to what extent these adjustments are ideologically induced. After all, adaptations reflect contemporary ideologies and adjust the pretexts to the norms and values of the new context. This is perhaps inevitable because '(a)ll novels embody a set of values, whether intentionally or not'.[6] According to Stephens and McCallum, any retelling discloses 'attitudes and ideologies pertaining to the cultural moment in which that retelling is produced'.[7] By this, they 'manipulate literature to function in a given society in a given way'.[8] Parlevliet, too, rightly points to the 'contemporary character' of adaptations, which can provide 'information about the period in which the texts came into being and the context within which they functioned'.[9]

The discourse on adaptation has, however, long been centred on the concept of 'fidelity' or 'faithfulness' to the 'original' as the main criterion for evaluating an adaptation. In the more recent approaches, this primacy of the fidelity concept has lost ground. Modern Adaptation Studies no longer consider adaptation as a more or less 'faithful' copy of an 'original', but as artistic creations in their own right which, in various ways, are related to one another and to the pretext. Adaptation scholar Linda Hutcheon, for instance, defines adaptation as 'an extended, deliberate, announced revisitation of a particular work of art'.[10] In a similar vein, Stephens and McCallum refer to it as 'retelling'. Others consider adaptation as a 'Neuinszenierung'[11] or as 'refraction'.[12]

Any new adaptation constitutes a contemporary re-interpretation, a new perspective of the source text – a view that is influenced by the historical, political, social and cultural context of its time. This article will investigate how the context manifests itself in the various German versions of *De Leeuw van Vlaenderen*. In the first part, the adaptations will be introduced, their publication context (publishing house, adaptor, series) will be presented and the paratexts examined. The foreword, epilogue and blurb often establish a link with the present; these data can then provide a clue as to the ideology supported in the adaptation. Is it a matter of transmitting a nationalist attitude, of stimulating national feelings in the same active manner as Conscience, or do the adaptations carry a different ideological bias? Did the adaptors aim to propagate and popularize the Flemish literary canon, or to transmit historical knowledge? Or was their purpose simply to tell an exciting adventure story? Which values are transmitted?

In the German-speaking parts of the world, about twenty different versions (translations and adaptations) of *De Leeuw van Vlaenderen* have been published since 1846, twelve among them being explicitly addressed to young readers.[13] These adaptations appeared in different historical periods with different political systems and changing social, literary and pedagogical norms: the German Empire, the First World War, the interwar period, the Second World War, and the post-war period (Table 1).

PARATEXTS AND PUBLICATION CONTEXT

The nineteenth century

The first adaptation by O. Heinrichs[14] (1893) was part of the series *Aschendorffs Prachtausgaben wertvoller Jugendschriften*,[15] published with the intention to arouse patriotism in the German people by the good example of the Flemish: 'so that the patriotism of the German people shall be ignited and revived by the fervent love of the Flemish for their country'.[16] Their love of country was emphatically presented as a shining example to the German youth. An introduction by the translator situates the novel in an historical and historiographic context. The novel thus gets a triple didactic value: it is instructive owing to its historical background, its literary value and its moral function as a patriotic role model for the young.

	year	adaptor/translator	publisher, place[17]
German Empire	1893	O. Heinrichs	Aschendorff (Münster)
	1898	A. Schowalter	Lehmann (München)
	1906	W. Spohr	Schaffstein (Köln)
	1912	A. Schowalter	Dietrich (München)
	1917	K. Reichhardt	Meidingers Jugend-schriften (Berlin)
Interwar period	1921	H. Eiler	Jugend & Volk/ Weichert (Berlin)
National-Socialism	1939	E. Stück	Rütten & Loening (Potsdam)
	1942	n.n.	Hausen (Saarlautern)
Post-war years	1950	C. Mandelartz	Hoch (Düsseldorf)
	1953	A. Zimmermanndl	Jungbrunnen (Wien)
	1962	W. Heichen	Neuer Jugendschriften Verlag (Hannover)
	1971	n.n.	Neues Leben (Berlin)

Table 1: German adaptations for young readers

This beloved 'home country' is here clearly 'Flemish', in contrast to the next adaptation by A. Schowalter.[18] His translation first appeared in 1898 in the series *Julius Lohmeyer's Vaterländische Jugendbücherei für Knaben und Mädchen*, addressing all 'deutschgesinnte' parents and teachers who wished to educate young Germans to be loyal to the German Emperor. The series was published by J.F. Lehmann, who issued, besides medical books, numerous *völkische* books, military publications and political pamphlets of the ultra-nationalist *Alldeutsche Verband.*[19] In accordance with the publisher's line, the pan-Germanist tendency cannot be denied in Schowalter's foreword: he writes there that Conscience had 'kept alive among the Germans in dispersion the sense of community with the history and the people of Alldeutschland'.[20] Schowalter not only views the Flemings as part of the German people but claims that even Conscience shared this view, and he considers the historical events narrated in the novel as 'a memorable piece of German history': 'German is the spirit blowing in it, and German are its heroes'.[21]

At the end of the historic appendix, he complements Conscience's famous invocation of the Flemings ('You, Fleming, who have read this book and the glorious deeds it contains, bethink what Flanders was in the past, what it is in the present and above all what it will be in the future, if you forget the venerable example of your forefathers'[22]), with the words 'if you would let yourself be robbed of the blessed memory of your forefathers and would let their free German spirit die off in your midst!'.[23] And he adds a second address, to the Germans:

> And you Germans, enthused by the great deeds of these kindred heroes, may you learn from this how a people united in patriotism, ready to make all sacrifices, is strong enough to defeat even the strongest enemy of its freedom, and may you preserve the true German nature in the German lands[24]

The Flemish-German kinship is thus stressed and a 'German spirit' is imputed to the Flemish heroes. Furthermore, the reader gets the impression that this second appeal to the Germans was also written by Conscience.[25]

During the world wars

Only five years later, in 1917, a new adaptation by Rudolph Reichhardt[26] saw the light of day. He also writes in his foreword that the Flemings are akin to the Germans, to whom they had 'come closer' thanks to the World War. (At that time, after the German invasion into neutral Belgium, Flanders had been annexed by German troops at the time of publication.) Nevertheless, Reichhardt presumes that the Flemings feel a strong bond with the German character, and he too discerns in the novel a 'German spirit, German love for one's country, German valour'.[27]

During the Second World War, a German version of *De Leeuw* appeared in 1942 (translator not mentioned),[28] a reprint of an earlier version, but with a new preface linking the novel to the National-Socialist ideology. We see Nazi-buzzwords popping up, such as 'Blut und Boden'. The Flemish heroes are introduced as 'Führer', as 'leaders who pull back the entire people into the current of the *völkische* mission'.[29] The Flemish leaders rank among the 'pioneers of that *Weltanschauung* which is currently called to save Europe from decline in an international mixture or an anarchic dissolution'.[30] In this way, the introduction connects the novel with the present of the German reader, firmly rooting the story in Nazi-ideology.

After 1945

In the post-war period, the focus was naturally placed elsewhere. However, the adaptations published in West Germany, Austria and the German Democratic Republic (GDR) differ considerably.

In 1950, the blurb of the new adaptation by Carl Mandelartz[31] promises an exciting adventure story on the Flemish war of liberation, recommended for boys from fourteen onwards. An afterword provides information about Conscience and his works, but without any mention of political topics.

Around the same time, in 1953, a new adaptation was published in Austria as well, namely by A. Zimmermanndl,[32] with a telling subtitle: 'a tale from old times, when tiny Flanders was under foreign occupation'.[33] In the year of publication this must have sounded somewhat familiar to Austrian readers: after the end of World War II, Austria was liberated but occupied by the Allies, and it did not gain its independence before 1955. There was also in Austria a definite need for national consciousness among the young.

Jungbrunnen was a socialist publishing house and made a name in the 1950s for high-quality children's literature. *Der Löwe von Flandern* was recommended for boys from twelve on up. One of the criteria for such a recommendation by the *Buchbklub der Jugend* was the conformity to the then dominant social norms and a pacifist orientation, which is clearly reflected in the last chapter, for the novel ends with emphatic praise of peace and freedom: 'And now finally, after so many years of bloodshed, good peace and beloved freedom for the land of Flanders, eked out by its freedom-loving citizens, was ensured for many, many years [...] the good peace, the beloved freedom.'[34]

Twenty years later, in 1971, once again a new adaptation appeared in yet another German-speaking country, the GDR, in the series *Spannend erzählt* (one of the most popular series for young people in the GDR).[35] One of the censors in the application procedure was Hans-Jürgen Hartmann,[36] who also wrote the epilogue. The printing license was granted because of 'the historically correct account of the events'. Apparently, the epilogue had given a helping hand with this 'historical correctness': in the explanation of the historical background, attention is focused on the opposition of the political systems (French monarchy vs. Flemish autonomy). In addition, Hartmann refers to Marx and Engels for an historical interpretation of the events; the novel is thus thoroughly embedded in communist ideology.

Figure 1. Book cover of Zimmermanndl's edition of *Der Löwe von Flandern* (1953)

The paratexts of these adaptations refer – in different ways – to the present of the reader, resulting in a certain tension between past and present. This contemporary context manifests itself in the paratext, but comes to the fore in the text and illustrations as well. Thus, in contrast to other adaptations, on the cover of Zimmermanndl (1953) we do not see any medieval knights, but contemporary people. In the front there is a young blond man, waving the flag with the Lion; in the back an anonymous mass of people (Fig. 1). The layout might remind us of an election poster and evokes rather the present than the 'old times' mentioned in the subtitle. The present is also featured in the illustrations: the book does not contain any drawings but it features contemporary photographs of the Flemish locations where the story takes place, with captions establishing the link between past and present.

IMAGES OF THE HEROES IN THE TEXT PROPER

That the tenor which has become apparent from the paratexts can be confirmed, albeit to a lesser extent, in the text itself will be demonstrated by the following examples that focus on the image of the (Flemish) hero. What kind of picture is drawn of his nationality, of his position as an outstanding individual, of his militancy on the one hand and his religiousness on the other? To which extent is the ideology reflected in the image of the Flemish heroes?

The main heroes in Conscience's novel are Jan Breydel, the leader of the Guild of Butchers and, to a lesser degree, Pieter Deconinck (the Dean of the Guild of Clothworkers); in addition, we must consider Count Robrecht van Bethune (owing to his bravery he received the sobriquet 'Lion of Flanders'), who – temporarily escaping from his imprisonment in France – turns up as the miraculous 'golden knight' in the decisive battle to strengthen his people and lead them to victory.

The Flemishness of the hero

A telling example is the translation of terms of nationality, which reflects Schowalter's view of the Flemish as a German tribe. In the first chapter Breydel has to serve as guide for a troop of French knights, and when he mocks a stumbling knight, he is threatened with being hung. His reaction in Conscience's novel reads 'Hang a Fleming! [...] Flemish ravens will never eat me'.[37] In Schowalter's adaptation, however, we read 'Hang a German? The ravens of Flanders do not eat Germans'.[38] Breydel's nationality is thus changed: whereas the French knights call him a 'Fleming', he himself designates himself as a 'German'. That the famous Flemish hero regards himself as a German strengthens the idea that the Flemings are actually Germans. A similar example can be found in the passage where the French queen Johanna (Joan I of Navarre) blames Machteld (the count's daughter) for her 'German stubbornness',[39] while Conscience obviously had spoken about her 'Flemish' stubbornness. And there are still several other situations where Schowalter replaces 'Flemish' with 'German'. Schowalter is the only adaptor using this replacement of nationality designations; in all the other versions the Flemings stay 'Flemish'.

This shift is matched by the cover of Schowalter's first edition (1898), which features a young man with hunting horn and sword dressed in a fur skirt with a dead dragon at his feet (Fig. 2). This figure represents Siegfried, the German hero par excellence. This illustration shows up on every cover in the series published by Lehmann. It is significant that none of the eight illustrations in the book depict the famous blazon with the lion of the count of Flanders. A 'national' symbol appears only on the cover – and there it has changed into a symbol for Germanness.[40]

In a similar vein, in Reichhardt (1917) the concept and representation of the 'German' Fleming corresponds to the frontispiece, where Jan Breydel is depicted as a muscular young man with blond hair.

The hero as individual or as part of a group

Whether the hero is presented as an individual standing out among others or absorbed within his peer group gives a clear indication as to whether the contemporary culture tends towards a worshipping of heroes or proclaims social equality. Conscience set the Flemish heroes on a pedestal, and the early translations followed him in this. The adaptation from 1942 worships its heroes as well: in the picture of Deconinck being carried in triumph through the city (after his liberation from prison), the people are hailing him with their arms raised (and he returns the salute with a similar gesture). Bearing in mind the time of publication, the picture reminds us starkly of the propaganda films of the *Third Reich*.

But this kind of depiction was to change, especially after the wars. The trend is most pronounced in the version released in the GDR, in which a certain emphasis on social equality – again entirely consistent with communist theory – is evident. Breydel's praise is narrated in only three lines, but the fact that he immediately takes off his brand-new armour – as he did not wish to be better protected than his followers – is elaborately described. The noble knights are often referred to by their military rank (Connetable de Nesle, Seneschall d'Artois); in this way the acquired military rank is accentuated, rather than hereditary nobility. The illustrations possess the same tenor: apart from Breydel, any individual traits are absent in the characters; in fact, they can hardly be distinguished at all (faces not shown, anonymous groups of people - Fig. 4). These characteristics might also be in line with communist ideology, in which the collective ranks above the individual and all are proclaimed to be equal.

Undesirable behaviour

In adaptations of classics for young readers, it is common practice to abridge the text, to put more emphasis on certain aspects and omit or soften others. This 'softening' concerns all kinds of undesired behaviour and all that does not fit into the favoured ideological pattern. Depending on the respective ideological background, this can apply to acts of violence, erotic allusions, profanity, disrespectful behaviour towards authority, the consumption of alcohol, or any political or religious elements.

In their endeavour to adjust the content for young readers, the different adaptors focus on different aspects. Whereas one minimizes acts of violence by summarizing the battle and any brawls, all the while allowing the Flemings to regale themselves with entire barrels of wine (Zimmermanndl), the other omits the abundant alcohol consumption and replaces the wine with the neutral formulation 'something to drink', before describing the fights in all their bloody details (Mandelartz). Even the religiosity of the heroes is an extremely 'delicate' matter, as will be demonstrated in the following paragraph.

The hero and his faith in God

In Conscience's novel religious references are made frequently, either by the narrator (recounting the vocation of Deconinck with words similar to those used in the biblical narrative of the vocation of Moses), or as part of the plot (prayers – e.g., after their massacre in Bruges, the benediction given to the fighters before the decisive battle, and at the end of the novel when the 'golden knight' leaves, the people believing him to be Saint George in person).

These religious elements are retained in early adaptations, but to a large extent omitted from the versions by Zimmermanndl and the GDR. By way of example, in Zimmermanndl's edition (in contrast to all the other versions), the Flemings are not exhorted to think of God, their children and their anxious wives before the battle, but of 'our free Flanders'. While in the early adaptations (and also in Mandelartz), the religious elements are retained, Zimmermanndl consistently deletes all passages in which the Flemings invoke God. At the end, the golden knight is not believed to 'return to heaven' (as in the other versions), but simply leaves. Suffice to say, the Jungbrunnen publishing house had a socialist orientation. The GDR-version can do without prayer as well: in line with an atheistic ideology, there is neither altar nor blessing before the battle, and the golden knight just disappears between the trees.

The hero as a fighter

Another stumbling block is the violent hero. Attention may be focused on 'fighting' (for freedom) or rather on 'freedom' itself (as a desired or achieved goal), on 'militarism' or on 'pacifism'. In the Mandelartz and Schowalter versions, the primary focus is placed on fighting and the battle dominates the plot. This is also reflected in the illustrations, which depict mainly action scenes. Violence and aggressiveness are also made manifest in the chapter headings; especially in the versions by Schowalter and Hausen, these headings sound both martial and pathetic, even polemical, making extensive use of war terminology, clichés and evaluative statements, they are laden with 'infamous actions', 'abominable traitors' and 'sworn enemies'.

The famous battle cry 'The Lion for Flanders! Whoso is French is false; strike home!'[41] of the Brugse Metten[42] is retained in nearly all the adaptations. Only Zimmermanndl – in his pacifistically oriented adaptation – truncates it to 'The Lion for Flanders', thereby eliminating the reference to the hated target group as well as the invitation to batter them to death. In his instructions before the attack, Deconinck indicates 'whoever cannot pronounce this is not a Fleming…',[43] followed by three dots, instead of the explicit order to strike them dead; Conscience's original reads 'whoever cannot pronounce those words properly has a French tongue, and down with him'.[44] Furthermore, Zimmermanndl justifies the violent acts of the Flemish during the Brugse Metten explicitly as 'vengeance'. He prefers to highlight peace and freedom instead of fighting and at the end of a chapter he frequently adds a comment of the narrator, such as 'Freedom was safeguarded for now'.[45] Constant repetition of the catchword ensures that the young readers will not fail to get the message.

CONTEXT: THE FUNCTIONS OF THE ADAPTATIONS IN THEIR TARGET CONTEXTS

In paratexts, illustrations and selective omission or highlighting of certain aspects, we can thus detect a certain ideological bias in the adaptations, which permits us to draw conclusions concerning their function. To confirm this assumption, we will also have to examine how the adaptations were positioned within their respective target context and to identify the function they serve there. In the following we will thus consider the historical, political and social background (the *zeitgeist*), as well as the position and ultimate task of literature for young readers in the respective periods.

During the German Empire (1871-1918), nationalism was fervent in Germany. The Franco-Prussian War (1870-1871) had ended with a decisive German victory and the creation of a unified German Empire. In literature, historical novels – often focused on German national heroes – and war or adventure stories, primarily appealing to the young male population, dominated the market. Several publishing houses launched their own patriotic series for the young. From the early nineteenth century on, children's literature was expected to educate young Germans in a nationalist sense and to arouse national consciousness and a patriot-

Figure 2. Book cover of Schowalter's edition of *Der Löwe von Vlaandern* (1898)

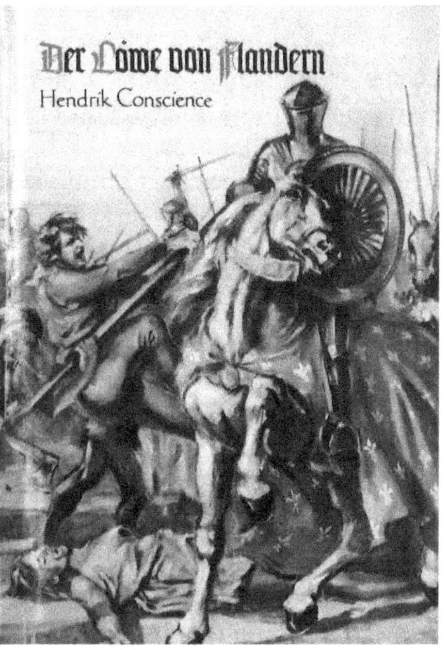

Figure 3. Book cover of Mandelartz's editon of *Der Löwe von Flandern* (1950)

Figure 4. Illustration in *Der Löwe von Flandern* (Series *Spannend erzählt* published by Neues Leben in 1971)

ism that was decidedly anti-French (France was, after all, considered the hereditary enemy of Germany).[46] This was just the right moment for an heroic story of a Germanic people fighting against French oppressors and gaining victory.

Accordingly, both adaptors of that period clearly had didactic objectives. But while Heinrichs presented the Flemish heroes as a model of patriotism to the young Germans, Schowalter went even further: in his view, the Flemings were in fact Germans and indeed, considered themselves part of the German people. Both the heroes of the novel and its author were not *Vlaamsgezind*, but *Duitsgezind*, not Flemish-nationalist, but German-nationalist (pan-Germanist).

Nationalist motivations continued to play a major role in the later adaptations, published during the World Wars: the adaptation from Reichhardt (1917) considers the Flemings to be a Germanic sister nation with a German character, while the foreword of the adaptation from 1942 draws a parallel between the Flemish leaders and a later German 'Führer'.

No such appropriation can be found in the post-war years, although children's literature was then still considered an educational instrument and historic adventure novels continued to be highly appreciated. In one case, the focus was placed on the struggle for freedom in a small, occupied country, as in the Austrian adaptation by Zimmermanndl dating from 1953, a period when 'freedom' was an important catchword in the political discourse in Austria. Following the pacifist orientation in children's literature of the 1950s, Zimmermanndl highlights peace and freedom and minimizes (or justifies) violence, thereby omitting any traces of militant nationalism as much as possible.

In other adaptations, adventure and fighting are the major focus, as in Mandelartz's version from the 1950s, which avoids any political allusion or link with the present and focuses on entertainment. The version published in the GDR (1971), where children's literature was an important means to educate children in the state ideology,[47] situates the novel in the context of the class struggle and the theories of Marx and Engels, thus infusing the story with communist doctrine.

IN CONCLUSION

In the early adaptations, didactical and nationalist objectives are dominant. In the nineteenth and the first half of the twentieth century, the forewords situate the novel in the various contemporary political contexts. A literary or aesthetic function is only suggested in the very early adaptations (released as a series of classics), but even here it is subordinate to nationalist purposes. After 1945 the didactic intentions played a minor role, at least in the West German version. In the 1950s and 1970s, children's literature was still used as an instrument for the social education of young people, but ideological adjustments were made in a more subtle manner (such as the elimination of religious references, or the softening, abridging and justifying of violent acts).

By the use of paratexts, headings, covers and illustrations, selective omissions and accentuations or replacements, the novel was modified in order to fit the then current perception of society – the *Weltanschauung* – and to meet the respective educational demands on literature for young readers. Conscience's nationalist tendency was transposed in very different ways. The novel was instrumentalized for various political and ideological intentions and moulded to suit different needs (patriotic, Flemish-nationalist, German-nationalist, pacifist, Marxist, or just exciting). As a consequence, Conscience's novel was re-nationalized, pacified, reduced to a thrilling adventure story, or transformed into a lesson on Marxism.

Today *De Leeuw* is known mainly – if at all – by its adaptations, sharing the fate of many classics that stay alive owing primarily to their adaptations; only in this way are they able to maintain their place in the collective memory. Adaptations therefore influence the perception of 'the original' as well. They both re-affirm the canonical status of a literary text and keep it 'alive' by rendering it more accessible for a new generation of readers. These 'rewritings' are, however, always influenced by their specific contemporary context. *De Leeuw* has changed, but its myth still remains in the collective memory of each new generation. As Linda Hutcheon states, adaptations give the literary work 'an afterlife it would never have had otherwise'.[48]

NOTES

1 The name owing to the large number of golden spurs that were collected from the fallen French knights.

2 After the Second World War, however, its readership diminished considerably.

3 S. Parlevliet, *Meesterwerken met ezelsoren: Bewerkingen van literaire klassiekers voor kinderen 1850–1950* (Hilversum: Verloren, 2009), pp. 59-87.

4 J. Stephens and R. McCallum, *Retelling Stories, Framing Culture: Traditional Story and Metanarratives in Children's Literature* (New York/London: Garland, 1998), p. 254.

5 Stephens and McCallum, *Retelling Stories*, p. 256.

6 P. Hollindale, 'Ideology and the Children's Book' [1988], in P. Hunt (ed.), *Literature for Children: Contemporary Criticism* (London/New York: Routledge, 1992), p. 20.

7 Stephens and McCallum, *Retelling Stories*, p. ix.

8 A. Lefevere, *Translation, Rewriting, and the Manipulation of Literary Fame* (London/New York: Routledge, 1992), p. vii.

9 Parlevliet, *Meesterwerken met ezelsoren*, p. 382.

10 L. Hutcheon, *A Theory of Adaptation* (New York/London: Routledge, 2006), p. 170.

11 F. Trabert, M. Stuhlfauth-Trabert and J. Waßmer (eds.), *Graphisches Erzählen: Neue Perspektiven auf Literaturcomics* (Bielefeld: transcript, 2015).

12 M. Aragay, 'Introduction: Reflection to Refraction: Adaptation Studies Then and Now', in M. Aragay (ed.), *Books in Motion – Adaptation, Intertextuality, Authorship* (Amsterdam: Rodopi, 2005), p. 26.

13 Cf. the bibliographies by H. Van Uffelen, *Moderne niederländische Literatur im deutschen*

Sprachraum 1830-1990 (Münster: LIT 1993), and P. Arents, 'De Vlaamse schrijvers in vertaling: Proeve van bibliografie. II. Vertalingen in het Duitsch 1800-1939', in *Verslagen en Mededelingen van de Koninklijke Vlaamse Academie voor Taal- en Letterkunde*, 1939.

14 H. Conscience, *Der Löwe von Flandern: Eine geschichtliche Erzählung aus dem 14. Jahrhundert*, für die deutsche Jugend bearbeitet, sowie mit Einleitung und Erläuterungen versehen von Dr. O. Heinrichs (Münster: Aschendorff, 1900 [1893]), hereafter cited as 'Heinrichs'. Besides the *Leeuw*, Heinrichs also translated another novel by Conscience, *De boerenkrijg*, published in the same series.

15 'Deluxe editions of valuable books for young people'. (All translations of German quotations in this chapter are mine, unless otherwise indicated.)

16 'damit der Patriotismus des deutschen Volkes sich an der glühenden Vaterlandsliebe der Flamländer entzünde und belebe' (Heinrichs, n. pag.).

17 Most were published in West Germany, with the version from 1953 having been published in Austria and that of 1971 in the GDR.

18 H. Conscience, *Der Löwe von Vlaandern*, aus dem Niederdeutschen in das Hochdeutsche übertragen und bearbeitet von A. Schowalter (München: Lehmann, 1898), hereafter cited as 'Schowalter'. No other translations by Schowalter are known, but he edited the four-part *Im Kampf um Südafrika* [Fighting for South-Africa], published by Lehmann.

19 Pan-German League, an imperialist movement for supporting German minorities in other countries, whose goal was the political unification of all people speaking German or a Germanic language.

20 'unter den Deutschen in der Zerstreuung das Bewußtsein der Zusammengehörigkeit mit der Geschichte und dem Volke Alldeutschlands wachgehalten' (Schowalter, n. pag.).

21 'ein denkwürdig Stück deutscher Geschichte', [...] '(d)eutsch ist der Geist, der darin weht, und deutsch sind seine Helden' (Schowalter, n. pag.). This reminds us of the epilogue in a later translation by K.L.W. Van der Bleek (Berlin: Borngräber, 1916), written by order of the *Flaminganten-Ausschuss*: 'Denn es sind ja deutsche Kämpfe, deutsche Helden, von denen seine Werke handeln, so wie der Geist und die Art, die aus dem *Löwen von Flandern* zu uns spricht, deutsch ist.'

22 'Gy Vlaming, die dit boek gelezen hebt, overweeg, by de roemryke daden welke hetzelve bevat, wat Vlaenderen eertyds was – wat het nu is – en nog meer wat het worden zal indien gy de heilige voorbeelden uwer Vaderen vergeet!'

23 'wenn du dir das geheiligte Andenken an deine Väter rauben und ihren freien deutschen Geist in deiner Mitte aussterben lässest!'

24 'Und du Deutscher, den die Großtaten dieser stammesverwandten Helden begeistern, lerne daraus, wie ein in der Vaterlandsliebe geeintes und opferfreudiges Volk stark genug ist, auch den mächtigsten Feind seiner Freiheit zu besiegen, und wahre dir deutsche Art im deutschen Lande!' (Schowalter, p. 359)

25 In 1912, Schowalter released a revised edition, published by Georg W. Dietrich Verlag, Munich, who had taken over the series. This edition was considerably shortened and the invocation deleted.

26 H. Conscience, *Der Löwe von Flandern: Eine geschichtliche Erzählung*, für die Jugend bearbeitet von Rudolph Reichhardt (Berlin: Meidinger's Jugendschriften Verlag, [1917]),

hereafter cited as 'Reichhardt'. In the 1920s Reichhardt adapted several adventure novels by Captain Frederick Marryat for German youth, for the same publisher, e.g., *Masterman Ready or The Wreck of the Pacific*; he also adapted *Uncle Tom's Cabin* and *Little Lord Fauntleroy* for young readers.

27 'deutscher Geist, deutsche Vaterlandsliebe, deutscher Heldenmut' (Reichhardt, n. pag.).

28 H. Conscience, *Der Löwe von Flandern* (Saarlautern: Hausen, 1942, 17th edition), hereafter cited as 'Hausen'.

29 'Führer, die [...] das Volksganze [...] in den Strom der völkischen Sendung zurückreißen' (Hausen, p. 4).

30 'Wegbereiter jenes Weltanschauens, das heuer berufen ist, Europa vor dem Versinken in das Dunkel einer internationalen Mischung oder einer anarchischen Auflösung zu bewahren' (Hausen, p. 4).

31 H. Conscience, *Der Löwe von Flandern: Historischer Roman*, bearbeitet von Carl Mandelartz (Düsseldorf: Hoch, 1950), hereafter cited as, 'Mandelartz'.

32 H. Conscience, *Der Löwe von Flandern: Eine Erzählung aus alter Zeit, als das kleine Flandern von Fremden besetzt war*, neu bearbeitet von Anton Zimmermanndl (Wien: Jungbrunnen, 1953), hereafter cited as 'Zimmermanndl'. Not much is known about Zimmermanndl, except that he had translated several novels from French (*Salambo* by Gustave Flaubert in 1937; *1793* by Victor Hugo in 1939).

33 'Eine Erzählung aus alter Zeit, als das kleine Flandern von Fremden besetzt war'.

34 'Nun war endlich, nach so vielen blutigen Jahren, der gute Friede und die so geliebte Freiheit für das Land Flandern, von seinen freiheitsliebenden Bürgern erkämpft, für viele, viele Jahre gesichert [...]... der gute Friede, die geliebte Freiheit' (Zimmermanndl, p. 134).

35 H. Conscience, *Der Löwe von Flandern* (Berlin: Neues Leben, 1971), hereafter cited as 'Neues Leben'.

36 Hartmann had written epilogues for various other translations as well.

37 'Een Vlaming ophangen? [...] De raven van Vlaanderen zullen mij niet eten.' (H. Conscience, *De Leeuw van Vlaanderen*, Brussels: Office de Publicité, [1843] 2nd edition, p. 8; for the English translation: H. Conscience, *The Lion of Flanders* (New York: Collier & Son [1901], p. 25).

38 'Einen Deutschen aufhängen? [...] Die Raben von Vlaandern fressen keinen Deutschen' (Schowalter, p. 5).

39 'Geist deutscher Starrköpfigkeit' (Schowalter, p. 88).

40 The covers of the later editions, however, show other illustrations.

41 'Vlaanderen den leeuw! Wat walsch is, valsch is! Slaet al dood!' (Conscience, 1843, p. 213; for the English translation: Conscience, *The Lion of Flanders*, p. 392).

42 On the morning of 18 May 1302, the rebellious citizens of Bruges murdered every Frenchman they could find, an act known as the *Brugse Metten (Bruges Matins)*; according to legend, all those who could not properly pronounce 'schild en vriend' were slaughtered.

43 'Wer dies nicht aussprechen kann, der ist kein Flame...' (Zimmermanndl, p. 94).

44 'Al wie deze woorden niet kan uitspreken heeft eene fransche tong, men slae hem dood' (Conscience, 1843, p. 212; for the English translation: Conscience, *The Lion of Flanders*, p. 391).

45 'Die Freiheit war fürs erste gerettet' (Zimmermanndl, p. 42).
46 Cf. for the history of German literature for young readers, e.g. H.-H. Ewers, (ed.), *Kinder- und Jugendliteratur: Von der Gründerzeit bis zum Ersten Weltkrieg* (Stuttgart: Reclam, 1994), and K.-U. Pech (ed.), *Kinder- und Jugendliteratur vom Biedermeier bis zum Realismus* (Stuttgart: Reclam, 1985).
47 Cf. on children's literature in the GDR: G. Haas, 'Kinder- und Jugendliteratur in der DDR', in G. Haas (ed.), *Kinder- und Jugendliteratur: Ein Handbuch* (Stuttgart: Reclam, 1984).
48 Hutcheon, *A Theory of Adaptation*, p. 176.

BIBLIOGRAPHY

Aragay, M., 'Introduction: Reflection to Refraction: Adaptation Studies Then and Now', in M. Aragay (ed), *Books in Motion – Adaptation, Intertextuality, Authorship* (Amsterdam: Rodopi, 2005), pp. 11-36.

Arents, P., 'De Vlaamse Schrijvers in vertaling: Proeve van bibliografie. II. Vertalingen in het Duitsch 1800-1939', in *Verslagen en Mededelingen van de Koninklijke Vlaamse Academie voor Taal- en Letterkunde*, 1939, p. 697-807.

Conscience, H., *De Leeuw van Vlaanderen* 2nd ed. (Brussel: Office de Publicité, [1843]).

Conscience, H., *The Lion of Flanders* (New York: P. F. Collier & Son, [1901]).

Conscience, H., *Der Löwe von Flandern: Eine geschichtliche Erzählung aus dem 14. Jahrhundert*, für die deutsche Jugend bearbeitet, sowie mit Einleitung und Erläuterungen versehen von Dr. O. Heinrichs (Münster: Aschendorff, 1900 [1893]).

Conscience, H., *Der Löwe von Vlaandern*, aus dem Niederdeutschen in das Hochdeutsche übertragen und bearbeitet von A. Schowalter (München: Lehmann, 1898).

Conscience, H., *Der Löwe von Flandern: Eine geschichtliche Erzählung*, für die Jugend bearbeitet von Rudolph Reichhardt (Berlin: Meidinger's Jugendschriften Verlag, [1917]).

Conscience, H., *Der Löwe von Flandern* 17th ed. (Saarlautern: Hausen, 1942).

Conscience, H., *Der Löwe von Flandern: Historischer Roman*, bearbeitet von Carl Mandelartz (Düsseldorf: Hoch, 1950).

Conscience, H., *Der Löwe von Flandern: Eine Erzählung aus alter Zeit, als das kleine Flandern von Fremden besetzt war*, neu bearbeitet von Anton Zimmermanndl (Wien: Jungbrunnen, 1953).

Conscience, H., *Der Löwe von Flandern* (Berlin: Neues Leben, 1971).

Ewers, H.-H. (ed.), *Kinder- und Jugendliteratur: Von der Gründerzeit bis zum Ersten Weltkrieg* (Stuttgart: Reclam, 1994).

Haas, G., 'Kinder- und Jugendliteratur in der DDR', in G. Haas (ed.), *Kinder- und Jugendliteratur: Ein Handbuch* (Stuttgart: Reclam, 1984), pp. 22-35.

Hutcheon, L., *A Theory of Adaptation* (New York/London: Routledge, 2006).

Hollindale, P., 'Ideology and the Children's Book' [1988], in P. Hunt (ed.), *Literature for Children: Contemporary Criticism* (London/New York: Routledge, 1992), pp. 19-40.

Lefevere, A., *Translation, Rewriting, and the Manipulation of Literary Fame* (London/New York: Routledge, 1992).

Parlevliet, S., *Meesterwerken met ezelsoren: Bewerkingen van literaire klassiekers voor kinderen 1850–1950* (Hilversum: Verloren, 2009).

Pech, K.-U. (ed.), *Kinder- und Jugendliteratur vom Biedermeier bis zum Realismus* (Stuttgart: Reclam, 1985).

Stephens, J. and R. McCallum, *Retelling Stories, Framing Culture: Traditional Story and Metanarratives in Children's Literature* (New York/London: Garland, 1998).

Trabert, F., M. Stuhlfauth-Trabert and J. Waßmer (eds.), *Graphisches Erzählen: Neue Perspektiven auf Literaturcomics* (Bielefeld: transcript, 2015).

Uffelen, H. Van, *Moderne niederländische Literatur im deutschen Sprachraum 1830-1990* (Münster: LIT, 1993).

CHAPTER 12

The Reception of Louis Couperus' *De Stille Kracht* in the English-Speaking World (1921-2015)

Caroline de Westenholz
(Louis Couperus Museum, The Hague, The Netherlands)

In 1890, the Dutch novelist Frederik van Eeden presented the literary critic and poet Edmund Gosse with a slim volume called *Noodlot,*[1] by a promising young Dutchman, Louis Couperus (1863-1923). Gosse, who had discovered Ibsen for England, had a certain knowledge of Scandinavian and Germanic languages. He liked Couperus' novel and had it translated into English by Clara Bell. In 1891 it appeared as volume seven in Heinemann's International Library, under the title *Footsteps of Fate.*[2]

Couperus' first translated novel enjoyed a great success with the poets and novelists of the Yellow Nineties, although perhaps not for its literary merits only. The story about the slightly dubious relationship between childhood friends Frank and Bertie, ending in murder and a double suicide, appealed to the spirit of the age. Oscar Wilde sent Couperus a congratulatory letter together with a copy of *The Portrait of Dorian Gray,* which Couperus' wife Elisabeth Couperus-Baud subsequently translated into Dutch.[3] John Addington Symonds, sometimes called Soddington Symonds, wrote to Edmund Gosse: 'What a number of Urnings are being portrayed in novels now! *Dorian Gray, Un Rate, Monsieur Venus,* this *Footsteps of Fate.* I stumble on them quite casually and find the same note.'[4] Urnings, of course, was the contemporary euphemism for homosexual.

The next year, Couperus' debut novel, *Eline Vere,*[5] appeared in English in a translation by Jack T. Grein,[6] the founder of the Independent Theatre, which had introduced the playwright George Bernhard Shaw to the English public.

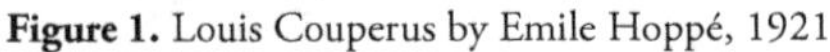

Figure 1. Louis Couperus by Emile Hoppé, 1921

Figure 2. Alexander Teixeira de Mattos (photographer and date unknown)

ALEXANDER TEIXEIRA DE MATTOS

In the early eighteen nineties Louis Couperus was discovered by the translator who would not weary, to the end of his life, in making Couperus known in England and America: Alexander Teixeira de Mattos (1865-1921). 'Tex', as he was known by his friends, was of Dutch and Portuguese-Jewish extraction but had grown up in London. He started his career in the City but in the words of his biographer, Stephen McKenna,[7] he was 'saved for literature' by Jack T. Grein, who made him secretary to the said Independent Theatre. He made his name as a translator of, amongst others, Maeterlinck, Zola, Chateaubriand, De Toqueville, president Kruger of South Africa and Stijn Streuvels.

The first book of Couperus Teixeira de Mattos put his hand to was the theosophically tinted *Extaze. Een boek van geluk* [*Ecstasy*] (1892), followed by *Majesteit* [*Majesty*] (1893), a phantasy about the reluctant heir to an imaginary kingdom.[8] The poets John Gray and Ernest Dowson were involved in these translations too.

In the summer of 1898, Couperus and his wife went to London. They were received in Teixeira's rooms at number 3, Plowdon Buildings, Inner Temple, on the same floor as John Gray and the actor Charles Goodhart. The translator was a friend of Ernest Dowson, Robert Sherard, Willie Wilde (Oscar's brother) and most of the members of the Rhymer's Club, a society of London based poets. Couperus and his wife met some of these fellow writers at a tea in Teixeira de Mattos' rooms. On Sunday June 12 Mr and Mrs Couperus were invited by Edmund Gosse in the latter's house at 29, Delamere Terrace. *The Book of Gosse,* a sort of diary in which the host noted his guests over the years, mentions the couple's names together with those of Arthur Symons, the former editor of the *Savoy,* Robert Ross, who was to be Wilde's literary executor, and the artist William Rothenstein.[9] One would say that by 1900, Louis Couperus had a wonderful entrée into the English world of art and letters.

Yet, in the first decade of the twentieth century only one book of his was translated: the fairy tale *Psyche.*[10] Couperus' publisher L.J. Veen did continue to send books to his personal acquaintance, the English publisher T. Fisher Unwin, including *De stille kracht* [*The Hidden Force*], a tale of black magic and adultery in the former Dutch East Indies when this appeared in 1900. On 24 November of that year Unwin wrote to Veen: 'I beg to thank you for sending me a copy of "De Stille Kracht" by Louis Couperus, but this novel will not do for English readers, and I do not think you will find a publisher for it here.'[11]

The reason that *De stille kracht* 'would not do' for England is not difficult to find. Léonie van Oudijck, the main female character, is a scandalous adulteress who even has an affair with her own stepson. This was not the first time female sexuality featured rather prominently in Couperus' novels. The character Cornélie de Retz van Loo in the preceding book, *Langs lijnen van gelijdelijkheid* [Along the Lines of Similarity, translated as *The Law Inevitable* by Teixeira de Mattos] (1900), is a divorced woman – a subject that was not exactly proper around the turn of the last century. At the end of this novel, Cornélie meets her ravingly attractive, but cruel ex-husband again and again and succumbs to his charms – quite literally. 'I have taken the heroine out of bed, to please Butterworth, just taken her out of bed, without suggesting any alternative resting-place', Teixeira warned the author when he eventually translated this book in 1921.[12] 'Also, Couperus' barely hidden scepticism in *De stille kracht* about the role of the colonialists in the Dutch East Indies jarred with Rudyard Kipling's view of 'the White Man's Burden'.

Couperus' real breakthrough in the Anglo-Saxon world took place off 1914. Teixeira's translation of the four volumes of *De boeken der kleine zielen* (1900) [*The Books of the Small Souls*],[13] a merciless dissection of the decline of an upper class family in The Hague, took the English literary world by storm.

Renowned magazines such as the *Saturday Review,* the *Atheneum* and the *Spectator* devoted glowing reviews to the novels, and so did *The New York Times Review of Books, The Nation, The Bookman, The Dial* and *The Outlook* in the United States. This encouraged Teixeira de Mattos to undertake more translations of Couperus' books. During the war, he translated the psychological novels *Langs lijnen van geleidelijkheid* (1900),[14] *De stille kracht* (1900),[15] *Van oude menschen, de dingen, die voorbij gaan...* [*Old people and the things that pass*] (1906)[16] and the historical novel *Antiek toerisme* [*The Tour. A Story of Ancient Egypt*] (1911).[17] We will continue to discuss the reception of these translations of Couperus' books in the English-speaking world.

THE ENGLISH TRANSLATIONS

The succes of *The Books of the Small Souls* caused Teixeira's other translations to be published. The first one to appear in print was *Old People and the Things that Pass* (1919), a somber account of a crime of passion in the Dutch East Indies in the distant past that haunts four generations of the families involved. This was followed by *The Tour. A Story of Ancient Egypt* (1920), a story about unrequited love in the said country; *The Law Inevitable* (1920 and 1921), and *The Hidden Force* (1921 and 1922), in Britain and in America. In 1921, all these books were discussed in English language newspapers and magazines. Critic A.W.G. Randall wondered whether the author could influence contemporary English literature: 'Today, when Louis Couperus is again beginning to be translated and admired [...] he may yet produce an effect on the development of English fiction.'[18] To a certain extend, he did. The writer Rose Macauley (1881-1958) mentioned him in her novel *Dangerous Ages* (1921). One of the characters in this book falls in love with her aunt's lover. Says she: 'Very surely and truly she loved him, even if after all, he was to be her uncle by marriage, which would make their family life like that in one of Louis Couperus' novels!' The 1922 *Encyclopaedia Brittanica* wrote that *Old People and the Things that Pass* together with *The Books of the Small Souls,* 'showed the austerity and inevitability of Aeschylean tragedy.' Couperus was included into the *Who was who 1916-1928.* In 1927, the Scottish professor of literature James Anderson Russell called Couperus 'a Dutch Henry James and in his classical fancy, a slighter Flaubert.' And about *The Books of the Small Souls* he wrote: 'Louis Couperus did for Holland what Balzac did for France.'[19] Around 1930, fourteen of Couperus' novels, two travel books, one fairy tale and an anthology of short stories were available in English. Unfortunately, Teixeira de Mattos could not enjoy his success for long due to his premature death in December 1921.

COUPERUS IN LONDON 1921

Alexander Teixeira de Mattos certainly did his utmost to promote Couperus internationally. In 1921, he invited the author and his wife to come to London. This visit took place in the summer, when Asquith was planning a come back and Lloyd George was pulling the ropes. The Dutchman found a new admirer in the young society author Stephen McKenna (1888-1967) who, together with Teixeira de Mattos, organized lunches, dinners and celebrations for him. Couperus was invited to a luncheon at the Reform Club where he shared a table with the portrait painter Sir John Lavery, the playwrights Sir Arthur Pinero and Henry Arthur Jones, Earl Russell and then popular writers such as John Drinkwater, Hugh Walpole and Frank Swinnerton. Also, he met George Moore and George Bernard Shaw. His original mentor was now called Sir Edmund Gosse, and had become Librarian to the House of Lords. He had moved to 17, Hanover Terrace, a considerably posher address, he had received an honourary doctorate from Cambridge University and he mixed with the powerful and famous. Unfortunately, the *Book of Gosse* runs to 1920 only, so it was not possible to put an exact date to Couperus' visit to Regent's Park.[20] In his book *Silhouettes* Gosse later described his impression of Couperus on this occasion:

> He was trim and well groomed, with tufts of grey whisker one each side of the pale oval of his face, to which black-rimmed glasses gave a certain owl-like aspect. He held his head a little on one side, with an almost languorous smile, very engaging; and he talked excellent English in a soft, low voice. Nothing about him suggested the conventional idea of a Dutchman.[21]

On 9 June, the day before his fifty-eighth birthday, Couperus lunched 'with the opposition', in other words, with Mr and Mrs Asquith and he dined 'with the government', in the House of Commons. His host there was Cecil Harmsworth, the then minister of Foreign Affairs. This visit was mentioned in a survey of Dutch literature in English translation in *The Independent* of 15 July 2000.[22] It ended as follows:

> When the married homosexual novelist Louis Couperus – Holland's answer to André Gide – visited England before the First World War [sic], he was received both by Prime Minister Asquith and the Opposition Leader. One can hardly see Blair or Hague entertaining a desire to speak to any European novelist.

I hasten to add that it has never been proven that Couperus was homosexual.

THE HIDDEN FORCE

The book that struck English readers most, up to this day, was *De stille kracht.* It was published under the title *The Hidden Force*, even though 'The Silent Force' would have been a better and more literal translation. Because of its subject: colonial life in the former Dutch East Indies, this book was attractive to English critics. As Orlo Williams in *The Times Literary Supplement* stated: 'Station life has been so frequently treated in English fiction that this powerful novel makes a special appeal to us.'[23]

The book appeared first in America (1921). *The New York Times Book Review* called it '…a dark and terrible story, unfolded partly by suggestion, partly in a number of tense scenes, always permeated and influenced by that "hidden force". […] And if the story is dark and terrible, the atmosphere surrounding it is an atmosphere of degeneration and decay.' The publication pointed at the difference between English and Dutch colonial habits:

> The Hollanders [...] have intermarried freely, and the results seem anything but desirable. [...] 'The Hidden Force' is a remarkable and very complicated study of men and women placed in an environment in which they never become acclimatised, either physically or spiritually.[24]

The American edition of *The Bookman* opined: 'Louis Couperus' sensitive style informs the book with a rich melancholy. Our one criticism is that Malay words occur frequently (almost one to the page) without adding particularly to the color.'[25]

In 1922 the book came out in London. Gerald Gould in *The Saturday Review* was very impressed. 'Louis Couperus writes like a master', he maintained: 'Even in translation (the translation is admirable) the writing remains masterly. The plot is grim, wild, apt to the haunting, suffocating atmosphere. [...] The weariness of the heat, the sullenness of the rains, seem like actual experiences. The crawling and quaking of the Black Magic, left severely unequipped with any naturalistic "explaining away", are no less real than the heat and the rain.'[26] The sensuality and complexity of the sexual relationships were credible. The racial prejudices convincing. 'A cruel book, coarse and rather horrible, but full of power, and lit by flashes of compassion.'

Forrest Reid in *The Nation and the Atheneum* compared the book to Joseph Conrad's *Heart of Darkness* (1902), which he considered better because *The Hidden Force* had no real protagonist: 'It is nobody's story in particular'. The adulturous wife of the Dutch governor, Léonie van Oudijck, remained 'commonplace' in his view en 'we never get sufficiently close to Van Oudijck to feel a deep sympathy with either his success or failure.'[27] *The Bookman* summarized the book and concluded: 'A splendid story, wonderfully told.'[28]

The Hidden Force would continue to fascinate the English-speaking world. In 1945 the writer William Plomer[29] reminded the public of Couperus' other novels, the best known was *Old People and the Things that Pass,* but *The Hidden Force* was the most convincing book, in his opinion. Plomer also referred to Conrad: 'Indeed the atmosphere is quite as oppressive as any in Conrad, but it is evoked by a plainer and perhaps more detailed, if not more exact, observation.' Next he pointed at E.M. Forster's *A Passage to India* (1924). Just like Forster, Couperus experienced the difference between East and West more in a poetical than in a political way, Plomer continued. Also, he referred to the difference between the Dutch and the English colonialists:

> We (in *The Hidden Force)* are certainly far from any breezy British convention of colonial life, with its hard-riding, straight-shooting, boyish man, a pipe between his teeth, and his 'little woman' ordering an early tiffin so that they can be in time for the gymkhana... No, the Labuwangi whites are of a different order.[30]

Plomer was surprised that *The Hidden Force* had never been made into a film.

Harold Acton[31] visited the Dutch East Indies in the early 1930s and described the trip in his memoirs. He may have read Plomer's article. In his *Memoirs of an Aesthete* (1948) he mentions the same passage as the critic did. It is the passage in which Van Helderen talks to his wife Eva about the dangers that are lurking in the East. While discussing the Dutch occupation of the Indies and the native rebellion against that Acton states:

> When such gentle people revolt there must be a reason for it. Louis Couperus' novel *The Hidden Force* gave a picture of Java during the last year of the nineteenth and the first year of this century, which was full of prophetic implications. "I'm afraid of the future; there is danger ahead of us!" says one of the Dutch characters. "I think that Java, as our colony, is great; I think that we, in our colony, are great." To which an Eurasian official replies: "Formerly, perhaps, it was so. Nowadays, everything is going wrong, nowadays we are no longer great. You have an artistic nature, you are always looking for artistic perfection in Java...." [32]

This last remark is directed to Eva Eldersma, who is always trying to organise concerts and performances for the Dutch community in Labuwangi. It is interesting that Acton doesn't find it necessary to introduce Couperus to his audience: he simply mentions his name and quotes from the novel.

'A NOCTURNAL BOOK'

In 1985, *The Hidden Force* enjoyed a reprint in the USA. It was revised and edited by E.M. Beekman, professor of Dutch language at the University of Massachusetts. In his excellent introduction he said:

> *The Hidden Force* is a nocturnal book; most of its major scenes take place at night. Announced in the opening sentence, the novel's titular deity is the moon, the lunar symbol of the female force of life. The moon is red, foreboding disaster and the exercise of supernatural power. [...] The solar day is the province of Western authority, and is represented by the resident's ceremonial *pajong* (or sunshade) that is described as 'a furled sun'. But in this novel the female lunar world of intuition, imagination, and magic, triumphs over the male solar world of reason, reflection, and objectivity.[33]

The Australian writer Peter Carey reviewed this book in *Pacific Affairs*:

> English speaking readers the world over will be in his (Beekman's) debt for having opened to them such a rich treasure trove of Dutch-Indies literature, and for having introduced them to authors, who, hitherto, have only been appreciated in a rather narrow circle of Dutch cognoscenti.[34]

Little did he know about Couperus' brief fame in the English-speaking world around 1920.

Ian Buruma discussed the book in *The New York Review of Books.* It is interesting to read what this half English, half Dutch critic wrote about the translation:

> The translation [...] is not great, but Couperus' precious, elaborate, sometimes quite bizarre prose seems less dated in English than in the original Dutch. The reason is not just that the translator was unable to reproduce the luxuriance of Couperus' style, but that the Dutch language itself has changed far more than English has since 1900. [35]

Buruma also mentioned the comparison between East and West 'which Edward Said has identified with colonial apologetics': the East as the passive female principle (the Moon) and the West as the active, rational principle (the Sun). The European fear of sensuality could, according to Buruma, be explained from the puritan northern angst for their own sexuality. The interesting thing, however, the critic notes, is that Couperus does not share this fear: 'And his sympathy for the hybrid, the impure, the ambiguous, gave him (Couperus) a peculiarly modern voice. It is extraordinary that this Dutch dandy, writing in the flowery language of fin-de-siecle decadence, should still sound so fresh.'

In 1992, Quartet Books published this translation in the United Kingdom. Michael Kerrigan reviewed it in *The Scotsman:*

> The tragedy of an honest but uncomprehending official who, in Kipling's phrase, 'tried to hustle the East', Louis Couperus' great novel of Dutch-ruled Java, first published in 1900, is a welcome surprise for English-speaking readers. Couperus' luxuriant prose conjures up all the teeming, unbridled vitality of a tropical Asia resisting the rational order its western conquerors try to impose. Darkest continent of all, however, is Woman, represented here in deceptively nordic form by the official's grey-eyed monster of amoral, voraciously destructive sexuality is none the less an absolutely unforgettable creation.[36]

A CLASSIC PASSAGE TO JAVA

In 2012 an entirely new translation, by Paul Vincent, appeared in London, with Buruma's review as an afterword. The newspaper *The Independent* said of this translation:

> Eerie, lush, psychologically acute, this Dutch masterpiece from 1900 (in a fine new translation by Paul Vincent) is one of the great novels of the colonial era. Couperus was raised in the Dutch East Indies but

> looked on the settlers with the eyes of a detached, mystical (and gay) outsider. He presents the downfall – or salvation? – of colonial officer Van Oudijck with the narrative cunning of a Maugham, the spiritual depth of a Conrad, and the delicate moral compass of a Forster. Their admirers will relish this classic passage to Java.[37]

Although it has to be noted that Couperus was not 'raised' in the Indies, the comparison with Somerset Maugham is new and intriguing.

Andrew Sands wrote a review, which was meant for *The Times Literary Supplement* but never published there. Eventually it appeared, in a Dutch translation, in *Arabesken*, the magazine of the Louis Couperus Genootschap (Society). His view is:

Figure 3. Book cover of Paul Vincent's translation of *De Stille Kracht*

> Couperus' description does not only concern colonial decline, but also something more spiritual. In the next hundred pages [after the first chapter, CdW] black magic is evoked. It is the result of the conflict between Sunario, the mystical Javanese prince, and Van Oudijck, the 'scrupulous' governor. The wind turns, the weather changes, there is the sound of hissing in the trees. The spiritual turns physical, and the consequence is an effective loss of control. Couperus describes this turn of affairs with such fatalism and in such detail that one could think he was an accessory to the sad events in his fictitious Javanese empire.[38]

In the first quarter of the twentieth century, Louis Couperus perhaps was Holland's most translated author. His psychological novels were held in high esteem by critics and readers from the United Kingdom to the United States. After his death, his popularity steadily declined, not in the least because of the late recognition of these very novels in his home country.[39] Slowly, his work is making a come-back on the international stage.

The Hidden Force continues to fascinate the English-speaking world. It is to be hoped that this book, or for that matter any, of Couperus' other great novels, will soon be available in the Penguin Classics Series.

NOTES

1 L. Couperus, *Volledige Werken. 4. Noodlot* (Utrecht/Antwerpen: L.J. Veen, 1990) 1st edition: 1890.

2 L. Couperus, *Footsteps of Fate,* translated by C. Bell (London: William Heinemann, 1891). For a list of all Couperus' translations see R. Breugelmans, *Louis Couperus in den vreemde* (Leiden: Private edition, 2008).

3 O. Wilde, *Het portret van Dorian Gray,* translated by Elisabeth Couperus-Baud (Amsterdam: L.J. Veen, 1893).

4 J. Addington Symonds to E. Gosse, 22 June 1891, Brotherton Library, Dpt. of Special Collections, University of Leeds.

5 L. Couperus, *Volledige Werken. 3. Eline Vere: een Haagsche Roman* (Utrecht/ Antwerpen: L.J. Veen, 1987) 1st edition: 1889.

6 L. Couperus, *Eline Vere,* translated by J. T. Grein (London: Clapman and Hall Ltd., 1892).

7 See S. McKenna, *Tex: A chapter in the life of Alexander Teixeira de Mattos* (London: Thornton Butterworth, 1922).

8 Translated as: *Ecstasy: A Study of Happiness,* translated by A. Teixeira de Mattos and John Gray (London: Henry & Company, 1892); *Majesty,* translated by A. Teixeira de Mattos and Ernest Dowson (London: T. Fisher Unwin, 1894).

9 E. Gosse, *The Book of Gosse,* vol. 1 (1875-1900), facsimile of lost original kept in the Brotherton Library, Dpt. of Special Collections, University of Leeds.

10 L. Couperus, *Psyche,* translated by B.S. Berrington (London: Alston Rivers Ltd, 1908).

11 T. Fisher Unwin to L.J. Veen, 28 November 1900, in H.T.M. van Vliet (ed.), *Louis Couperus. De correspondentie* (Amsterdam: L.J. Veen, 2013) part II, letter nr 393, note 4, p. 125.

12 Teixeira de Mattos to Louis Couperus, 8 September 1921, in H.T.M. van Vliet (ed.), *Louis Couperus. De correspondentie* (Amsterdam: L.J. Veen, 2013) part II, letter nr 1354, p. 924-926. Butterworth was the English publisher.

13 L. Couperus, *Volledige Werken. 19-20. De boeken der kleine zielen* (Amsterdam/Antwerpen: L.J. Veen, 1991) 1st editions: 1901 and 1902.

14 L. Couperus, *Volledige Werken. 16. Langs lijnen van geleidelijkheid* (Utrecht/Antwerpen: L.J. Veen, 1989). 1st edition: 1900.

15 L. Couperus, *Volledige Werken. 49. De stille kracht* (Utrecht/Antwerpen: L.J. Veen, 1998). 1st edition: 1900.

16 L. Couperus, *Volledige Werken. 25. Van oude menschen, de dingen die voorbij gaan...* (Amsterdam/Antwerpen: L.J. Veen 1991) 1st edition: 1906.

17 L. Couperus, *Volledige Werken. 30. Antiek tourisme: roman uit oud Egypte* (Utrecht/Antwerpen: L.J. Veen, 1987) 1st edition: 1911.

18 A.W.G. Randall, 'Literary relations between England and Holland', in *The New World Monthly International Review* 2, 4: 20 (January 1921), pp. 163-168.

19 J. Anderson Russell, 'Couperus in English', in *De Nieuwe Gids* (1927), part I, pp. 522-533, reprinted in J. Anderson Russell, *Romance and realism, trends in Belgo-Dutch prose literature* (Amsterdam: H.G. Paris, 1959), chapter VII.

20 E. Gosse, *The Book of Gosse,* vol. 2 (1900-1920), facsimile of lost original kept in the Brotherton Library, Dpt. of Special Collections, University of Leeds.

21 E. Gosse, 'Louis Couperus: A Tribute and a Memory', in *Silhouettes* (London: Heinemann, 1925), p. 266.
22 J. Evans, 'Hail the new Orange Order', in *The Independent,* 15 July 2000, p. 11.
23 O. Williams, 'New novels: The Hidden Force', in *The Times Literary Supplement,* 21: 1068 (6 July1922), p. 443.
24 L. Maunsell Field, 'Mr Couperus weaves a Javanese mystery', in *The New York Times Book Review,* 8 January 1922, p. 28.
25 'The Hidden Force', in *The Bookman* 54 (January 1922), p. 490.
26 G. Gould, 'New Fiction', in *The Saturday Review* 134: 3482 (22 July 1922), p. 147.
27 F. Reid, 'A group of novels', in *The Nation and the Atheneum,* 4816 (19 August 1922), p. 688.
28 'Contrasts', in *The Bookman* 62: 372 (September 1922), p. 255.
29 William Plomer (1903-1973) grew up in South Africa, which may have been another reason for his interest in colonial Dutch novels. He wrote poetry, novels and a biography of Cecil Rhodes.
30 W. Plomer, 'Louis Couperus', in *New Writing and Daylight* (London: Hogarth Press, 1945). Reprinted in *Electric Delights* (London: Jonathan Cape, 1978).
31 Harold Acton (1904-1994), English author, scholar and connoisseur.
32 H. Acton, *Memoirs of an Aesthete* (London: Hamish Hamilton Ltd. 1984), vol. I, p. 306 (1st edition: 1948).
33 L. Couperus, *The Hidden Force: A Story of Modern Java,* revised, edited and with an introduction by E.M. Beekman (Amherst: The University of Massachusetts Press, 1985; London: Quartet Books, 1992).
34 P. Carey, untitled, in *Pacific Affairs* 59: 1 (1986), pp. 163-164.
35 I. Buruma, 'Revenge in the Indies: The Hidden Force', in *The New York Times Review of Books,* 11 August 1994, pp. 30-32.
36 M. Kerrigan, 'The Hidden Force', in *The Scotsman,* 30 October 1992.
37 B. Tonkin, 'The Hidden Force, by Louis Couperus', in *The Independent,* 3 November 2012.
38 A. Sands, 'Meer dan politiek alleen', in *Arabesken. Tijdschrift van het Louis Couperus Genootschap* 21: 41 (2013), pp. 63-64. (Translation by the author of this article)
39 For the reasons see C. de Westenholz, 'Flying Dutchman: Why Louis Couperus is neglected in his own country', in *The Times Literary Supplement* 4948, 30 January 1998, pp. 15-16 and P. Vincent, 'Forgotten classic: The work of Louis Couperus in English', in *The Low Countries. Arts and society in Flanders and The Netherlands. A Yearbook,* 1998-1999, pp. 103-105.

BIBLIOGRAPHY

Acton, H., *Memoirs of an Aesthete* (London: Hamish Hamilton Ltd, 1984).

Addington Symonds, J., to E. Gosse, 22 June 1891, Brotherton Library, Dpt. of Special Collections, University of Leeds.

Anderson Russell, J., 'Couperus in English', in *De Nieuwe Gids* (1927), part I, pp. 522-533.

Anderson Russell, J., 'Couperus in English', in J.A. Russell, *Romance and realism, trends in Belgo-Dutch prose literature* (Amsterdam: H.J. Paris 1959), ch. VII.

Breugelmans, R., *Louis Couperus in den vreemde* (Leiden: private edition, 2008).

Buruma, I., 'Revenge in the Indies. The Hidden Force', in *The New York Review of Books,* 11 August 1994, pp. 30-32.

Carey, P., untitled, in *Pacific Affairs* 59: 1 (1986), pp. 163-164.

'Contrasts', in *The Bookman* LXII: 372 (September 1922), p. 255.

Couperus, L., *Volledige Werken. 3. Eline Vere: een Haagsche roman* (Utrecht/Antwerpen: L.J. Veen, 1987).

Couperus, L., *Volledige Werken.* 4. *Noodlot* (Utrecht/Antwerpen: L.J. Veen, 1990).

Couperus, L., *Volledige Werken.* 19-20. *De boeken der kleine zielen* (Amsterdam/Antwerpen: L.J. Veen, 1991).

Couperus, L., *Volledige Werken.* 16. *Langs lijnen van geleidelijkheid* (Utrecht/Antwerpen: L.J. Veen, 1989).

Couperus, L., *Volledige Werken.* 49. *De stille kracht* (Utrecht/Antwerpen: L.J. Veen, 1998).

Couperus, L., *Volledige Werken.* 25. *Van oude menschen, de dingen die voorbij gaan...* (Amsterdam/Antwerpen: L.J. Veen 1991).

Couperus, L., *Volledige Werken.* 30. *Antiek tourisme: roman uit oud-Egypte* (Utrecht/Antwerpen: L.J. Veen, 1987).

Couperus, L., *Footsteps of Fate,* translated by C. Bell (London: William Heinemann, 1891).

Couperus, L., *Eline Vere,* translated by J. T. Grein, (London: Clapman and Hall Ltd., 1892).

Couperus, L., *Ecstasy. A Study of Happiness,* translated by A. Teixeira de Mattos and J. Gray (London: Henry & Company, 1892).

Couperus, L., *Majesty,* translated by A. Teixeira de Mattos and E. Dowson (London: T. Fisher Unwin, 1894).

Couperus, L., *Psyche,* translated by B.S. Berrington (London: Alston Rivers Ltd, 1908).

Couperus, L., *The Books of the Small Souls,* including *Small Souls, The Later Life, Twilight of the Souls* and *Dr Adriaan,* translated by A. Teixeira de Mattos (New York/London: Dodd, Mead and Co/William Heinemann, 1914, 1915, 1917 and 1918).

Couperus, L., *Old People and the Things that Pass,* translated by A. Teixeira de Mattos (New York: Dodd, Mead & Co, 1918 and London: Thornton Butterworth Ltd., 1919).

Couperus, L., *The Tour. A story of Ancient Egypt,* translated by A. Teixeira de Mattos (New York: Dodd, Mead & Co, and London: Thornton Butterworth Ltd., 1920).

Couperus, L., *The Inevitable,* translated by A. Teixeira de Mattos (New York: Dodd, Mead & Co, 1920).

Couperus, L., *The Law Inevitable,* translated by A. Teixeira de Mattos (London: Thornton Butterworth Ltd., 1921).

Couperus, L., *The Hidden Force. A Story of Modern Java,* translated by A. Teixeira de Mattos (New York: Dodd, Mead & Co, 1921, and London: Jonathan Cape, 1922).

Couperus, L., *The Hidden Force. A Story of Modern Java,* revised, edited and with an introduction by E.M. Beekman (Amherst: The University of Massachusetts Press, 1985, and London: Quartet Books, 1992).

Couperus, L., *The Hidden Force. A Story of Modern Java,* translated by P. Vincent (London: Pushkin Press, 2012).

'Couperus, L.,' in *Who was who, a companion to who's who containing the biographies of those who died during the period 1916-1928* (London: A. & C. Black, 1967), p. 233.

De Westenholz, C., 'Flying Dutchman: Why Louis Couperus is Neglected in His Own Country', in *The Times Literary Supplement* 4948, 30 January 1998, pp. 15-16.

De Westenholz, C., 'Couperus in English. De verspreiding van het werk van Louis Couperus in het Engelse taalgebied', in *Couperusnummer Vlaanderen* 52: 296 (2003), pp. 169-175.

De Westenholz, C., *Couperus in English. De verspreiding van het werk van Louis Couperus in het Engelse taalgebied. Tekst bij de tentoonstelling in the Louis Couperus Museum (11 April – 13 October 2002)* (The Hague, 2002).

Gosse, E., *The Book of Gosse*, vol. 1 (1875-1900), facsimile of lost original kept in the Brotherton Library, Dpt. of Special Collections, University of Leeds.

Gosse, E., 'Louis Couperus: A Tribute and a Memory', in *Silhouettes* (London: Heinemann, 1925), pp. 259-268.

Gould, G., 'New Fiction', in *The Saturday Review* 134: 3482 (22 July 1922), p. 147.

Evans, J., 'Hail the new Orange Order', in *The Independent*, 15 July 2000, p. 11.

'The Hidden Force', in *The Bookman* 54 (January 1922), p. 490.

Kerrigan, M., 'The Hidden Force', in *The Scotsman*, 30 October 1992.

Macauley, R., *Dangerous Ages* (London: Collins 1921).

Maunsell Field, L., 'Mr Couperus weaves a Javanese mystery', in *The New York Times Book Review*, 8 January 1922, p. 28.

McKenna, S., *Tex. A chapter in the life of Alexander Teixeira de Mattos*, (London: Thornton Butterworth, 1922).

Plomer, W., 'Louis Couperus', in *New Writing and Daylight* (London: Hogarth Press, 1945).

Plomer, W., *Electric Delights* (London: Jonathan Cape, 1978).

Poupard, D. and Person J.E. jr (eds), 'Louis (Marie Anne) Couperus 1863-1923', in *Twentieth Century Literary Criticism* 15 (1985), pp. 41-49.

Randall, A.W.G., 'Literary relations between England and Holland', in *The New World Monthly International Review* 4: 20 (January 1921), pp. 163-168.

Reid, F., 'A group of novels', in *The Nation and the Atheneum* 4816 (19 August 1922), p. 688.

Sands, A., 'Meer dan politiek alleen', in *Arabesken. Tijdschrift van het Louis Couperus Genootschap* 21: 41 (2013), pp. 63-64.

Tonkin, B., 'The Hidden Force, by Louis Couperus', in *The Independent*, 3 November 2012.

Van Vliet, H.T.M. (ed), *Louis Couperus. De correspondentie* (Amsterdam: Atheneum – Polak & Van Gennep, 2013).

Vincent, P., 'Forgotten classic. The work of Louis Couperus in English', in *The Low Countries. Arts and society in Flanders and The Netherlands. A Yearbook* (1998-1999), pp. 103-105.

Wilde, O., *Het portret van Dorian Gray*, translated by Elisabeth Couperus-Baud (Amsterdam: L.J. Veen, 1893).

Williams, O., 'New novels. The Hidden Force', in *The Times Literary Supplement* 21: 1068 (6 July1922), p. 443.

CHAPTER 13

A Communist Compromise

Introducing Willem Elsschot's *Kaas* Soviet Style

Michel De Dobbeleer (Ghent University, Belgium)

This contribution discusses the 1972 Soviet preface to one of Flanders' favourite novels. With the help of its fairly recent reception in the Anglophone world, as a means of comparison, I will scrutinize the way in which the Russian editors tried to deal with the 'un-Soviet' topics of commerce and capitalism which the novel has so famously thematized.

CHEESE'S BELATED ARRIVAL IN THE (ENGLISH-SPEAKING) WORLD, 2002

It would be an exageration to count the Flemish writer Willem Elsschot (pseudonym of Alfons De Ridder, 1882-1960) among authors of world class and fame. Yet, ever since the first English translation of his novel *Kaas* [*Cheese*] (1933) was published – remarkably late[1] – in 2002, Elsschot's star has unmistakably risen in the Anglophone world, and thus, given the 'globality' of English,[2] slowly but surely in the spacious gallery of world literature too.

On behalf of those who are not familiar with *Cheese*, I will first present its story as retold in *A Literary History of the Low Countries* (2009). At the same time, we can infer from this account what the Dutch and Flemish contributors wanted the foreign – certainly not only English or American – reader to learn about *Cheese*. This might be of interest, too, to those who have read the novel.

> *Cheese* (*Kaas*, 1933) is the story of a man who allows himself to be talked into trading in a commodity he knows nothing about, to say nothing of the fact that he lacks any talent for commerce. Laarmans, [...] an ordinary man seduced into entering the world of big business,

> is a frightened rabbit and at the same time a domestic tyrant. Within the four walls of his home, he prides himself on successes he has not yet achieved, and meanwhile he fears the prying eyes of the lady next door. Like a whipped cur, he eventually slinks back with his tail between his legs to the office from which he had with great aplomb taken three months' unpaid sick leave.[3]

In the same year in which this most recent English-language history of Dutch literature appeared, *Cheese* was granted a place on *The Guardian*'s list of '1000 novels everyone must read'. The reviews in the UK and the US (2002-2003) of *Cheese* had indeed been very positive. That they all referred to the novel's commercial theme did not surprise: *Cheese* chiefly deals with the sheer impossibility for protagonist Frans Laarmans of becoming a businessman. In addition, the reviewers referred to the so-called dot-com bubble debacle, around the turn of the century, and thus welcomed the translation as very timely:

> [T]he translation of Willem Elsschot's *Kaas* [...] came onto the market 'devilishly well timed' (*New York Review of Books*, 25 Aug. 2002). For, whether rightly so or not, Frans Laarmans' doomed cheese business *GAFPA*[4] and the bursting of the dot-com bubble which at the time had reached its climax in the Enron debacle, became a popular comparison in almost every newspaper or magazine review in the Anglosphere. 'Laarmans [...] could just as easily be the starry-eyed creator of a doomed dot-com or the duped investor in a corrupt conglomerate' the *New York Review of Books* states [ibid.]. *The Boston Globe* (28 Jan. 2003) presents *Cheese* as a cautionary tale, and *The Daily Telegraph* (16 Feb. 2002) too reads Elsschot's work as a parable: 'Pop a dot and a com on the end of Gafpa, and the message becomes all too clear'. *The Times* (20 Feb. 2002) sarcastically recommends to the *Granta Books* publishers 'to send some copies to the board of Enron'.[5]

SOME WORDS ON (*CHEESE*'S ENGLISH) 'PERITEXT'

At least as relevant to any reception study of a translated work as the reviews are the pages preceding or following the actual literary work, with the help of which it is transmitted to its new reading public. Not for nothing during the last two decades, *paratext*, originally one of the many narrative-related terms coined by Gérard Genette (in his *Seuils*, 1987) has found its way into Translation Studies.[6]

Whereas the quotation above, in Genette's more specific terms, deals with *Cheese*'s *epitext* – i.e., the texts, such as reviews, which are *external* to the work under discussion –, the topicality of the economic events at the time was exploited in *Cheese*'s *peritext* too – i.e., in the text(ual and other element)s *within* the work.[7] Here, two different pieces of peritext[8] refer to Elsschot/De Ridder's actual occupation as an advertising executive. In the six lines 'about the author', on the first page, we read that he was the 'head of a successful advertising agency'. Somewhat further, in Paul Vincent's fine 'Translator's Preface',[9] the author is said to have 'spent most of his working life in advertising' and to have been 'a shrewd and successful businessman'.[10] In this way, Elsschot is given the right authority to evoke what can go wrong when becoming self-employed.

CHEESE'S ARRIVAL IN THE SOVIET UNION, THIRTY YEARS EARLIER

Soviet citizens, for their part, got the chance to make their acquaintance with *Cheese* in 1972, exactly three decades before the English-speaking readers (in their mother tongue). At the height of the Cold War, near the middle of the (Brezhnev) Era of Stagnation (1964-1982), *Syr*, which is Russian for 'cheese', saw the light in an Elsschot collection published by *Progress*,[11] in its 'world-literature series' *Masters of Contemporary Prose* (*Mastera sovremennoj prozy*, 1971-1991). Russian, by the way, was the fifth in the world, but not the first Eastern European language into which *Cheese* had been translated: the 1936 Czech translation was the first ever of an Elsschot novel.[12] By now *Cheese* has appeared in more than twenty-five languages, but only twice in a communist state: in the USSR (1972) and China (2009).

The Russian *Cheese* appeared in a 459-page book with no other 'title' on the cover than the authors' name *Villem Ėlskhot* (in Cyrillic: Виллем Элсхот). Together with *Villa des Roses* (*Villa Roz*, trans. Belokrinitskaia & Shechkova; cf. infra), *Lijmen* [*Soft Soap*] (*Silki*, followed by 'Chast' vtoraia: Noga', i.e., 'Part II: The Leg', trans. Valentin A. Ostrovskii), *Het Tankschip* [*The Tankship*] (*Tanker*, trans. Belokrinitskaia & Elena G. Makarova) and *Het Dwaallicht* [*Will-o'-the-Wisp*] (*Bluzhdaiushchii ogonëk*, trans. Rita Ia. Rait-Kovalëva). *Cheese* was published in what was then, 1972, the most extensive Elsschot collection ever to have appeared in translation. Jan Paul Hinrichs speaks of a 'concise *Collected works*.'[13]

The *Cheese* translation was the work of Sil'viia Semënova Belokrinitskaia, who also translated *The Diary of Anne Frank*, and Liubov' Sergeevna Shechkova. The few scholars who have briefly written about it agree that, given the Soviet circumstances, Belokrinitskaia and Shechkova (just like the other three translators) did a remarkably fine job. All in all, Elsschot's typical, wry style has been treated respectfully, and the text is not too much affected by the merely minor censorial changes.[14] This contribution, however, does *not* deal with the translation of *Cheese* as such, but with its accompanying peritext, more specifically, its Soviet peritext.

Elsschot's *own* quite extensive and heterogeneous peritext – a dedicatory poem, an introductory essay on style, a somewhat ironic list of 'characters' and a clearly ironic list of '(cheese) elements' – was preserved in its entirety in the Russian version, and just as in the Dutch edition, all of it *precedes* the novel.[15]

CHEESE'S SOVIET PERITEXT AND ITS AUTHOR(S)

Villem Ėlskhot would not have appeared in the USSR, had it not been provided with a typical Soviet 'Predislovie' [Foreword],[16] a text type (or if you want, 'subgenre') to which Valerie Pellat's introductory words regarding the paratext in translation (cf. supra) apply very well: [Translation s]cholars are concerned with the cultural implications of paratext, its cultural significance and political, ideological and commercial power'.[17] The rest of this article is in fact devoted to the political and ideological power of the 'Foreword', whether pretended or not. The 'commercial' power (as in Pellatt's quotation) obviously has to be downplayed in the Soviet context, even though the Elsschot theme of 'commerce' is of central importance in the 'Foreword'.

Although we only read the name of 'I. Shkunaeva' under the preface to Elsschot's novels,[18] this dense text – just like the translation of *Cheese* – was the work of more than one person: Inna Dmitrievna Shkunaeva and Elena Mikhailovna Orlova, the latter actually being the *redaktor* [editor] of the collection. The final note of the preface is hers only: 'During the preparation of the edition some changes were made to the text of the foreword by the editorial staff which could not be approved by I.D. Shkunaeva, owing to her death. – *note of the ed.*'[19]

The year before, the eminent expert of Belgian literature, Inna Shkunaeva,[20] had untimely passed away at the age of forty-eight. We will probably never know which 'changes' were made after her death, but in any case: the style of this 'Foreword' is similar to that in *Stories from Belgian writers*, which she edited and prefaced a few years before.[21] A striking difference, however, is the fact that the twelve-page preface to the Elsschot collection contains two quotations from Lenin[22] while her eighteen-page preface to the collection of Belgian stories has none.[23] Therefore, in what follows, I will credit Elena Orlova as a writer of the 'Foreword' as well.

The Lenin quotations are part of the first third of the preface, which, except for the opening two paragraphs, do not deal with Elsschot, but with the socio-historical circumstances in Belgium during the first decades of the twentieth century and the manner in which Flemish writers positioned themselves in the divided Belgian literary landscape. Elsschot's native city, Antwerp, inextricably bound up with most of his prose, serves as the steppingstone between the particular (Elsschot's life and work) and the general (Belgium and its literature):

> Antwerp – like Ghent, Brussels, Liège and other Belgian cities, and the whole of Belgium – was, at the beginning of the 1920s, still full of reminiscences of the heavy disasters of the First World War, when 'a group of predators, with unheard-of bestiality, threw themselves upon Belgium'.[24] The country was plundered and devastated. The common misfortune contributed to the solidarity among its ethnically heterogeneous population: Walloons and Flemings.
>
> But this process was neither simple nor unequivocal.[25]

The picture of Belgian (Flemish) capitalism, bourgeoisie and class struggle then offered[26] *indeed* is, to say the least, equivocal, and it never becomes clear, what exactly Elsschot's connection with this is. Moreover, no distinction seems to have been made between Elsschot the writer and the man behind the writer. We do not learn that Elsschot was a pseudonym of Alfons De Ridder. The characterization of Elsschot (De Ridder), in the early 1920s, as a 'young bourgeois from Antwerp, an anarchist and *flamingant*',[27] and somewhat later on, as a 'deft, enterprising and successful' businessman,[28] may suggest that the author in question was the bad example *par excellence* for the communist reader. Why then he was honoured with an exclusive volume in the *Masters of Contemporary Prose* series?

LONG LIVE CAPITALIST DECLINE!

In her article 'Filtered Through the Iron Curtain', although concentrating on Soviet translations in Latvian, Eva Eglāja-Kristsone offers two instrumental ways in which the regime – not only in Latvia, but in the whole Eastern Bloc – was willing to interpret foreign, in this case Western, literary works:

1) as supporting the communist regime,

2) as exposing capitalist decline in contrast to the Soviet way toward perfection.[29]

Option (1) is obvious, and with the help of (2) many more foreign works could be hauled in as interesting and, even better, edifying and useful. Eglāja-Kristsone, for example, refers to the Soviet characterization of Gore Vidal's *Washington, D.C.* (1967) – from his historical heptalogy *Narratives of Empire* – as a welcome novel about the 'machinations of the USA electoral system'.[30]

Figure 1. Tat'iana Tolstaia's woodcut accompanying *Cheese* in Ėlskhot, *Villem Ėlskhot*, p. 313.

It is crystal-clear that the reasons for granting Elsschot a volume in the Soviet *Masters of Contemporary Prose* series should be looked for in Eglāja-Kristsone's option (2). Within, and thanks to, this option, editors and critics could overcome the possible drawback that a foreign author was or had been a bourgeois, a capitalist and/or a businessman himself. It even lent him all the more authority at those places in the translated work where he denounced the perverted capitalist system. Regardless of Alfons De Ridder's own work as an advertising executive, several of his (Elsschot's) novels could and can certainly be read as an indictment of the capitalist pursuit of money. This neither was nor is at all far-fetched. Given Elsschot's use of irony, however, Shkunaeva and Orlova had to ensure that the Soviet readers would not take his satirical passages seriously. Therefore, the 'Foreword' makes explicit that within Elsschot's oeuvre – summarily called a 'grotesque social comedy'[31] – 'the logical is absurd, and the absurd logical',[32] and that the reigning morality is a 'morality turned upside down'.[33] Hence, probably, the fairly grotesque woodcut, by Tat'iana Tolstaia, accompanying this Soviet version of *Cheese*, and depicting a Laarmans who has visibly gone to seed.

In my view, few Flemish or Dutch readers would imagine Laarmans as such a shabby figure,[34] but it goes without saying that the impact of such a *visual* (or more broadly: 'non-verbal')[35] paratext was more direct than that of any (verbose) preface.

Since he ultimately sees the error of his ways, Frans Laarmans is forgiven for dreaming his absurd capitalist dream in this 'epic of the selling of doomed Edam cheese'.[36] The only *Cheese* quotation inserted in the 'Foreword' ensures that, near the end of the novel (ch 18 of 24), Laarmans' conscience wakes up:

> A father should be consistent. [...] Whether he's a mayor, a bookmaker, a clerk or a craftsman, is not important. He should be a man who steadily fulfils his duty, whatever it is... A husband and father can only resign by doing away with himself.[37]

Shkunaeva and Orlova's following sentence illustrates the Soviet penchant for big words (and erudite comparisons): 'On the surface of the story no centrifugal (like in François Mauriac), but centripetal forces are at work: the forces of indissoluble family ties.'[38]

Does the quoted *Cheese* passage contain the novella's main lesson for the reader? In any case, it reminded him of his duties as a Soviet family member,[39] within this society which arranged everything for its subjects from the cradle to the grave.

THE *CHEESE* CHANNEL? A CONCLUSION ON COMMUNIST CONSECRATION AND COMPROMISE

'When a major literature does translate, it invests source texts with its cultural prestige, performing an act of 'consecration,' especially when those texts originate in a literary minority'.[40] These are Lawrence Venuti's Pascale Casanova-inspired[41] words from a chapter devoted to the immense significance of translations for (the study of) world literature. It may be fruitful, near the end of this article, to apply this observation to the case of our translation into

Russian – certainly the language of a 'literary majority' (in the 1970s) – of a novella, *Cheese*, from a minor – Dutch – literature. It is clear then that Soviet prefaces to translated Western works, designed as they were to guide the readers' mental steps ideologically into the capitalist world, rather *de*secrated than consecrated the source text,[42] at least with hindsight.

Whether these prefaces indeed condemned the activities and ('cheese' and other) dreams of those Western characters as efficiently as the editors (supposedly) wanted them to do is, it goes without saying, another question. This is all the more so when we bear in mind Carolina De Maegd-Soëp's sympathetic picture of the Russian Netherlandists whom she met during her study tour to Moscow at the end of the 1970s.[43] I do not doubt that Shkunaeva and all those other Soviet Russian Netherlandists involved in editing, translating and circulating Elsschot's work were very glad that he wrote and described things and situations which could easily be conceived as belonging to Eglāja-Kristsone's option (2) and thus, I repeat, 'as exposing capitalist decline in contrast to the Soviet way toward perfection.'[44] Of course, the 'system', near the middle of the long Era of Stagnation still required to rhetorically expound this in an elaborate 'Foreword'. Apart from that, the readers were allowed to enjoy these works, in this case fairly well translated, (cf. note 14) as they wished, and they most probably did so in large numbers.[45] Fortunately, no one forced them to read the preface, let alone to believe it (literally).

As we know, communist society was full of such 'compromises'. With regard to prefaces, Irina Michajlova captured this aptly as follows: 'the Soviet citizen of the 1970-80s got used to being continuously sold, in other domains of life too, something needless 'in addition' to something good, and he was perfectly able to identify this 'addition' in literary matters too.'[46] Be that as it may, every Slavist would naturally endorse André Lefevere's oft-quoted pronouncement on the *channel* and *window* metaphors with respect to translations: 'Translation is not just a "window opened on another world,"[47] [...]. Rather, translation is a channel opened, often not without a certain reluctance, through which foreign influences can penetrate the native culture, challenge it, and even contribute to subverting it.'[48]

Unlike several scholars citing these lines, I did not quote them (once again) to suggest that the channel metaphor is the more proper of the two.[49] As for the reception of the English translation of *Cheese*, its paratexts, as we saw, clearly pointed to the surprising 'window capacity' of this (belatedly) translated work. In the paratexts of the Russian *Cheese*, (the risks of) business and capitalism were no less an issue than in the English, but in the Soviet Union, the authorities wanted to press works like *Cheese* indeed into a distorting 'channel'. And certainly, in the twilight of communism, the longer they did this, the more desperate they became. But did they thus also 'contribute to subverting' their Soviet culture?

Let me suffice by answering this question with two other questions and another Lefevere quote: 'why is it necessary to represent a foreign text in one's own culture? Does the very fact of doing that not amount to an admission of the inadequacy of that culture?'[50] If so, it is tempting to conclude then – with regard to *Cheese* – that the Anglophone culture has been longer 'inadequate' than the Russophone. *Thirty years* longer, to be precise.

NOTES

1 Trans. by Paul Vincent; I used the 2003 edition: W. Elsschot, *Cheese* (London: Granta, 2003). I largely owe this introductory treatment of the English reception to Dorien De Man, 'The English Translations of Willem Elsschot's self-declared masterpiece *Kaas* (1933)', *Clina* 2: 2 (2016). In fact, translations of *Cheese* into English had already been made three times before Vincent's, but all of them remained unpublished (De Man, 'The English translation', pp. 42-43). Before *Cheese*, English translations of Elsschot's work had appeared only twice: *Three Novels: Soft Soap / The Leg / Will-o'-the-Wisp* (trans. Alex Brotherton, 1965) and *Villa des Roses* (trans. Vincent, 1992), see Vincent in Elsschot, *Cheese*, p. v).

2 Thought-provokingly critiqued, with respect to world literature, by J. Arac, 'Anglo-Globalism?', in *New Left Review* 16 (2002).

3 J. Goedegebuure, 'Between Two World Wars: 1916-1940', in T. Hermans (ed.), *A Literary History of the Low Countries* (Rochester, NY: Camden House, 2009), p. 561.

4 'GAFPA' is the acronym for Laarmans' ironically (i.e. from the point of view of the author) long-considered company name 'General Antwerp Feeding Products Association', W. Elsschot, *Kaas* (Amsterdam: Athenaeum-Polak & Van Gennep, 2003), pp. 56-58.

5 De Man, 'The English translation', pp. 42-43.

6 Cf. V. Pellatt (ed.), *Text, Extratext, Metatext and Paratext in Translation* (Newcastle upon Tyne: Cambridge Scholars Publishing, 2013).

7 For Genette, *peritext* and *epitext* are both part of the *paratext*: 'pour les amateurs de formules, *paratexte = péritexte + épitexte*' (G. Genette, *Seuils*, (Paris: Seuil, 1987), p. 11), although the broader term is often used with regard to the peritext alone.

8 Elsschot himself provided the actual novel with several kinds of *authorial* peritext (cf. infra).

9 Elsschot, *Cheese*, pp. v-xii.

10 Elsschot, *Cheese*, pp. vi, viii.

11 V. Ėlskhot, *Villem Ėlskhot* (Moskva: Progress, 1972), pp. 312-385.

12 Cf. C.J. Aarts, *Al is hun taal mij zo vreemd: Willem Elsschot in vertaling*, dl. 1 (Antwerpen: Willem Elsschot Genootschap, 2008), pp. 25-39, 82-84; W. Engelbrecht, 'Kázus *Kaas* – recepce děl Elsschota v češtině', in J. Engelbrechtová (ed.), *Willem Elsschot,* Sýr*: mezinárodní recepce novely* Kaas*. Ukázky s prvního českého překladu* (Olomouc: Vydavatelství Univerzity Palackého, 2015), pp. 12-17. Between the Czech and the Russian, the Indonesian (1948), German (1952) and Afrikaans (1969) translations were published. See also the Dutch Foundation for Literature's translation database: https://letterenfonds.secure.force.com/vertalingendatabase.

13 'beknopt *Verzameld werk*'; J.P. Hinrichs, 'Bourgeois Laarmans ontmaskerd', in *De Parelduiker* 9: 5 (2004), p. 70. The mentioned translations of *The Tankship* and *Will-o'-the-Wisp* had already appeared before. The former in *Stories from Belgian writers* (I.D. Shkunaeva, ed., *Rasskazy bel'giiskikh pisatelei*, Moskva: Progress, 1968, pp. 421-457), the latter also in

1972, in the journal *Novii mir* (*New World*), cf. M. De Dobbeleer, '"Epos o prodeji neštěstí přinášejícího eidamského sýru" – Elsschot a *Sýr* v Sovětském svazu a Rusku', in J. Engelbrechtová (ed.), *Willem Elsschot,* Sýr*: mezinárodní recepce novely* Kaas*. Ukázky s prvního českého překladu* (Olomouc: Vydavatelství Univerzity Palackého, 2015), pp. 21-22. Five years after 1972, certainly inspired by the Russian example, precisely the same six works would appear in a Czechoslovak Elsschot collection (in Czech, cf. Engelbrecht, 'Kázus *Kaas*', pp. 17-20).

14 See N. Scheepmaker, 'Drie rijstkakkers = drie donkerhuidigen: Elsschot in het Russisch', in *Het Parool: PS*, 1 maart 1975, and, admittedly, more critically, J. Van Damme, 'Willem Elsschot in het Russisch', in *Dietsche Warande & Belfort* 118: 7 (1973), pp. 541-543. For censorship in post-Stalin USSR, see S. Sherry, 'Better Something Than Nothing: The Editors and Translators of *Inostrannaia literatura* as Censorial Agents', in *Slavonic and East European Review* 91: 4 (2013), who adds 'nuance' (p. 731) to its harshness. As can be inferred from the Russian *Cheese* too, it was 'primarily concerned with the blocking of anti-Soviet and religious messages' (p. 736), and of any (potentially) erotic content, for an example, see De Dobbeleer, '"Epos o prodeji"', p. 24.

15 Ėlskhot, *Villem Ėlskhot*, pp. 315-22. Whether (all of) these peritextual elements should be translated together with the actual novel has generated different (and changing) opinions, cf. G. Faggin, 'Bericht uit Vicenza: Giorgio Faggin over zijn vertaling', in H. Van Belle and K. Rymenants (eds.), *Kaaskwesties: Beschouwingen over Elsschot in vertaling* (Antwerpen: Willem Elsschot Genootschap, 2005), p. 81. In Vincent's English translation, Elsschot's introduction on style *follows* the actual novel (*Cheese*, pp. 127-134). For the 'fuzzy' transition between Elsschot's peritext and text, see K. Rymenants, *Een hoopje vuil in de feestzaal: facetten van het proza van Willem Elsschot* (Antwerpen: Garant, 2009), p. 198.

16 Ėlskhot, *Villem Ėlskhot*, pp. 5-16.

17 Pellatt, *Text, Extratext*, p. 1.

18 Ėlskhot, *Villem Ėlskhot*, p. 16.

19 'При подготовке к изданию в текст предисловия редакцией были внесены некоторые изменения, которые не могли быть согласованы с И. Д. Шкунаевой ввиду ее кончины. – Прим. ред.' (all translations from Russian are my own); Orlova in Ėlskhot, *Villem Ėlskhot*, p. 16.

20 Cf. C. De Maegd-Soëp, 'De Zuidnederlandse literatuur in Rusland: 1', in *Ons Erfdeel* 23: 2 (1980), pp. 173-174); I. Mikhailova, 'Niderlandskaia literatura po-russki: dva veka istorii', in W. Scheltjens (ed.), *Bibliografie van de Nederlandse literatuur in Russische vertaling / Bibliografiia niderlandskoi literatury na russkom iazyke* (Sankt-Peterburg: Aleteiia, 2003), p. 46; J. Van Damme, 'Een (Russisch) boekje opendoen', in *Dietsche Warande & Belfort* 119: 4 (1974), p. 325. In the Soviet Union, far more than in the West, there was a tendency to treat Flemish and Walloon literature together, cf. Leonid Grigor'evich Andreev's *One Hundred Years of Belgian Literature* (*Sto let bel'giiskoi literatury*. Moskva: Izdatel'stvo Moskovskogo universiteta, 1967), in which Elsschot is not yet mentioned. The author is not to be confused with the writer Leonid *Nikolaevich* Andreev, who also wrote about Belgium (cf. R. Detrez, 'De smarten van België: Leonid Andrejev en België tijdens de Eerste Wereldoorlog', in E. Waegemans, ed., *Het land van de Blauwe Vogel: Russen in België*, Antwerpen: Dedalus, 1991).

21 This is the collection *Rasskazy bel'giiskikh pisatelei* (1968), cf. note 13.

22 Regarding the Lenin quotations, Hinrichs ('Bourgeois Laarmans ontmaskerd', p. 70) also hints at Orlova.

23 Shkunaeva (ed.), *Rasskazy bel'giiskikh pisatelei*, pp. 7-24.

24 Here, Shkunaeva and Orlova refer in a footnote to 'В. И. Ленин, Полн. собр. соч., т. 32, стр. 85' ('V.I. Lenin, *Collected Works*, vol. 32, p. 85').

25 'Антверпен – как Гент, Брюссель, Льеж, как другие бельгийские города и вся Бельгия, в начале 20-х годов был еще полон воспоминаний о тяжких бедствиях первой мировой войны, когда "группа хищников с неслыханным зверством обрушилась на Бельгию". Страна была разграблена и унижена. Общая беда способствовала сплочению ее этнически разнородного населения – валлонов и фламандцев.' Но процесс этот не был ни простым, ни однозначным.'; Shkunaeva and Orlova in Ėlskhot, *Villem Ėlskhot*, p. 5.

26 This paves the way for the second Lenin quotation, in which the famous revolutionary ridicules Belgium's so-called heroism by denouncing the pursuit of gain by the country's deceitful bourgeois (see his 'Полн. собр. соч., т. 26, стр. 303', '*Collected Works*, vol. 26, p. 303'; Shkunaeva and Orlova in Ėlskhot, *Villem Ėlskhot*, pp. 5-6).

27 '(М)олодой буржуа из Антверпена, анархист и "фламинган"'. The Russian text reads '"flamingan"' (between inverted commas and spelled according to the French pronunciation), accompanied by the footnote: 'Так называли в Бельгии сторонников националистического "фламандского движения"' ('Thus were called in Belgium the adherents of the nationalist "Flemish Movement"'; Shkunaeva and Orlova in Ėlskhot, *Villem Ėlskhot*, p. 5). For Elsschot as a *flamingant*, still a quite vibrant discussion in Flanders, see esp. Matthijs De Ridder, *Aan Borms. Willem Elsschot, een politiek schrijver: essay* (Antwerpen: Meulenhoff/Manteau, 2007).

28 '(У)мелым, предприимчивым и удачливым'; Shkunaeva and Orlova in Ėlskhot, *Villem Ėlskhot*, p. 5; cf. Vincent's 'peritextual' characterization, quoted above, in Elsschot, *Cheese*, p. viii.

29 E. Eglāja-Kristsone, 'Filtered Through the Iron Curtain: Soviet Methodology for the Canon of World (Foreign) Literature and the Latvian Case', in *Interlitteraria* 17 (2012), p. 345.

30 Eglāja-Kristsone, 'Filtered Through the Iron Curtain', p. 346.

31 'Гротескную социальную комедию'; Shkunaeva and Orlova in Ėlskhot, *Villem Ėlskhot*, p. 16.

32 '(Л)огика абсурдна, а абсурд логичен'; Shkunaeva and Orlova in Ėlskhot, *Villem Ėlskhot*, p. 13. Hinrichs ('Bourgeois Laarmans ontmaskerd', p. 71) already pointed to this telling observation in the 'Foreword'.

33 '(М)ораль навыворот'; Shkunaeva and Orlova in Ėlskhot, *Villem Ėlskhot*, p. 13.

34 I do not completely share Hinrichs' opinion ('Bourgeois Laarmans ontmaskerd', p. 71) that the artist (Tat'iana Vladimirovna Tolstaia, 1929-2005; not to be confused, indeed, with the 1951-born writer Tat'iana *Nikitichna* Tolstaia) has subtly depicted Elsschot's atmosphere. She may also partially have based her woodcuts (one for every Elsschot novel) on the 'Foreword'.

35 Pellatt, *Text, Extratext*, pp. 1-5.

36 Shkunaeva and Orlova in Ėlskhot, *Villem Ėlskhot*, p. 11.

37 'Отец должен быть цельным человеком. [...] Неважно, бургомистр он, букмекер, клерк или ремесленник. Не в этом суть. Он должен быть человеком, который неуклонно

выполняет свой долг, в чем бы он ни состоял... Супруг и отец может уйти, лишь наложив на себя руки'; Shkunaeva and Orlova in Ėlskhot, *Villem Ėlskhot*, p. 11. As for 'ремесленник' ('craftsman'), Paul Vincent's translation, on which I based mine in this quotation (where possible), is more adequate: 'casual labourer' (Elsschot, *Cheese*, p. 109; in Elsschot's Dutch: 'losse werkman', *Kaas*, p. 104).

38 'На поверхность рассказа выступают не центробежные (как у Франсуа Мориака), а центростремительные силы – силы неразрывных семейных обязательств.'; Shkunaeva and Orlova in Ėlskhot, *Villem Ėlskhot*, p. 11. See Zh. Diuklo, '"Marsel'eza" i "Internatsional"', in *Ogonëk* 52: 2269 (1970), for an example of how Mauriac, the French Catholic winner of the 1952 Nobel Prize in Literature, was 'yoked' to the communist cart in those days.

39 R. Schlesinger (ed.), *The Family in the U.S.S.R.: Documents and Readings* (London: Routledge, 2000), pp. 268-269, gives a good assessment of (the rhetoric about) paternal duties in the Soviet Union, while Harris states that, in spite of all Marxist-Leninist theory, '(i)n effect, the ideal Soviet family was to be the bourgeois nuclear family beloved of capitalist states with, instead of a purely domesticated wife, one who took an equal part in 'social production' alongside her household and child-rearing duties' (C. Harris, *Control and Subversion: Gender Relations in Tajikistan*, London: Pluto Press, 2004, p. 37). For that matter, *Cheese* – fans will agree – memorably presents the reader with a (would-be) petty 'bourgeois nuclear family'.

40 L. Venuti, 'World Literature and Translation Studies', in T. D'haen, D. Damrosch and D. Kadir (eds.), *The Routledge Companion to World Literature* (Abingdon: Routledge, 2012), p. 181.

41 '(C)onsecration' is quoted from Casanova's famous *La république mondiale des lettres* (1999; Eng. trans.: P. Casanova, *The World Republic of Letters*, Cambridge, MA: Harvard University Press, 2004, esp. pp. 133-137), in which she puts the prevailing relationships in the World Republic of Letters in an illuminating but 'too French' perspective. In a later article, 'Consécration et accumulation de capital littéraire: la traduction comme échange inégal', in *Actes de la recherche en sciences sociales* 144: 1 (2002), Casanova goes back to this *consécration* concept, though still adhering to her French context. For 'consecration' with the help of prefaces, see Casanova, 'Consécration et accumulation', p. 19; *The World Republic*, p. 115.

42 Irrespective, by the way, of the source text's belonging to a minor literature. I do of course not want to suggest that Venuti has overlooked this communist or other comparable situations. Further on, he acknowledges: 'Because translation always answers to contingencies in the receiving situation, the intercultural hierarchies in which it is implicated turn out to be more complex than the simple binary opposition between major and minor literatures' ('World Literature', p. 181).

43 This hearty picture, offered by this Flemish Slavist (De Maegd-Soëp, 'De Zuidnederlandse literatuur: 1'; 'De Zuidnederlandse literatuur in Rusland: 2', in *Ons Erfdeel* 23: 3, 1980), of this 'circle' of Russian Netherlandists (among whom several Elsschot translators and/or fans) makes me think about the remarkable enthusiasm of the East European Netherlandists whom I met at CODL and other occasions.

44 Eglāja-Kristsone, 'Filtered Through the Iron Curtain', p. 345 (cf. supra). Actually, Elsschot, or rather De Ridder – who more than once has been considered an 'armchair communist'

(cf. De Ridder, *Aan Borms*, pp. 146-173; E. Rinckhout, *Dwaalspoor: op zoek naar de waarheid achter Het Dwaallicht van Willem Elsschot.* Antwerpen: Meulenhoff/Manteau, 2006, pp. 114, 131, 139, and 171: De Ridder as a 'rode romanticus', 'red romantic') –, to a certain degree could even be conceived as belonging to Eglāja-Kristsone's option (1). Needless to say, this might have complicated things considerably, for how could one merely be an *armchair* communist? And thus in this case the Soviets stuck to option (2).

45 Unfortunately, we do not have information on the number of printed copies (Hinrichs, 'Bourgeois Laarmans ontmaskerd', p. 70; nor any Soviet review), but they were sold out in a couple of hours (De Maegd-Soëp, 'De Zuidnederlandse literatuur: 2', p. 325).

46 '(С)оветский человек 70-80-хх гг. пирвык к тому, что и в других сферах жизни ему постоянно продают что-то ненужное "в нагрузку" к чему-то хорошему, и прекрасно умел паспознавать эту литературную "нагрузку"'; Mikhailova, 'Niderlandskaia literatura po-russki', p. 45.

47 It remains unclear (to me) whether these inverted commas (around 'window opened on another world') are actual *quotation* marks. They may paraphrase a sentence from the anonymous translator's preface to the 1611 authorized version of the *Bible* as included further on in Lefevere's edited *Translation/History/Culture: A Sourcebook* (London: Routledge, 1992), p. 72: 'Translation it is that openeth the window, to let in the light'.

48 Lefevere (ed.), *Translation/History/Culture*, p. 2.

49 For good reason, I think, Lefevere says: '*not just* a "window [...]"' (my italics). Unfortunately, in the *Sourcebook*, whose introduction contains his channel metaphor, the Soviet Union remains absent (the 'sources' under question, from Antiquity onwards, just do not reach that far). On two other occasions ('Mother Courage's Cucumbers: Text, System and Refraction in a Theory of Literature', in *Modern Language Studies* 12: 4, 1982; and in the very, if not *too* sympathetic introductions in P. Zlateva, ed., *Translation as Social Action: Russian and Bulgarian Perspectives*, London: Routledge, 1993) Lefevere addresses the communist case, but there he does not use the metaphor. In the former he calls translations refractions representing a 'compromise between two systems' (1982: 7). In my article, though, I also wanted to involve the Soviet readers as *active* 'partners' in a broader, societal compromise.

50 Lefevere (ed.), *Translation/History/Culture*, p. 1.

BIBLIOGRAPHY

Aarts, C.J., *Al is hun taal mij zo vreemd: Willem Elsschot in vertaling dl. 1. Bibliografie van de zelfstandig verschenen vertalingen 1936-2008* (Antwerpen: Willem Elsschot Genootschap, 2008).

Andreev, L.G., *Sto let bel'giiskoi literatury* (Moskva: Izdatel'stvo Moskovskogo universiteta, 1967).

Arac, J., 'Anglo-Globalism?' in *New Left Review* 16 (2002), pp. 35-45.

Casanova, P., 'Consécration et accumulation de capital littéraire: la traduction comme échange inégal', in *Actes de la recherche en sciences sociales* 144: 1 (2002), pp. 7-20.

Casanova, P., *The World Republic of Letters* (trans. M.B. DeBevoise) (Cambridge, MA: Harvard University Press, 2004).

Damme, J. van, 'Willem Elsschot in het Russisch', in *Dietsche Warande & Belfort* 118: 7 (1973), pp. 541-544.

Damme, J. van, 'Een (Russisch) boekje opendoen', in *Dietsche Warande & Belfort* 119: 4 (1974), pp. 318-326.

De Dobbeleer, M., '"Epos o prodeji neštěstí přinášejícího eidamského sýru" – Elsschot a *Sýr* v Sovětském svazu a Rusku' (překl. M. Kluková), in J. Engelbrechtová (ed.), *Willem Elsschot,* Sýr*: mezinárodní recepce novely* Kaas. *Ukázky s prvního českého překladu* (Olomouc: Vydavatelství Univerzity Palackého, 2015), pp. 21-27, 47-50.

De Maegd-Soëp, C., 'De Zuidnederlandse literatuur in Rusland: 1', in *Ons Erfdeel* 23: 2 (1980), pp. 165-177.

De Maegd-Soëp, C., 'De Zuidnederlandse literatuur in Rusland: 2', in *Ons Erfdeel* 23: 3 (1980), pp. 325-337.

De Man, D., 'The English translations of Willem Elsschots self-declared masterpiece *Kaas* (1933)', in *Clina* 2: 2 (2016), pp. 39-54.

De Ridder, M., *Aan Borms: Willem Elsschot, een politiek schrijver. Essay* (Antwerpen: Meulenhoff/Manteau, 2007).

Detrez, R., 'De smarten van België: Leonid Andrejev en België tijdens de Eerste Wereldoorlog', in: E. Waegemans (ed.), *Het land van de Blauwe Vogel: Russen in België* (Antwerpen: Dedalus, 1991), pp. 204-216.

Diuklo, Zh., '"Marsel'eza" i "Internatsional"', in *Ogonëk* 52: 2269 (1970), p. 8.

Eglāja-Kristsone, E., 'Filtered Through the Iron Curtain: Soviet Methodology for the Canon of World (Foreign) Literature and the Latvian Case', in *Interlitteraria* 17 (2012), pp. 341-351.

Ėlskhot, V., *Villem Ėlskhot*, Sost. & predisl. I. Shkunaeva, red. E. Orlova (Moskva: Progress, 1972).

Elsschot, W., *Kaas*, ed. and comm. Constantijn Huygens Instituut der Koninklijke Nederlandse Akademie van Wetenschappen (Amsterdam: Athenaeum-Polak & Van Gennep, 2003).

Elsschot, W., *Cheese*, trans. and pref. P. Vincent (London: Granta, 2003).

Engelbrecht, W., 'Kázus *Kaas* – recepce děl Elsschota v češtině', in J. Engelbrechtová (ed.), *Willem Elsschot, Sýr: mezinárodní recepce novely* Kaas. *Ukázky s prvního českého překladu* (Olomouc: Vydavatelství Univerzity Palackého, 2015), pp. 11-20, 47-51.

Faggin, G., 'Bericht uit Vicenza: Giorgio Faggin over zijn vertaling' (vert. T. de Keyzer), in H. Van Belle and K. Rymenants (eds.), *Kaaskwesties: Beschouwingen over Elsschot in vertaling* (Antwerpen: Willem Elsschot Genootschap, 2005), pp. 81-83.

Genette, G., *Seuils* (Paris: Seuil, 1987).

Goedegebuure, J., 'Between Two World Wars: 1916-1940' (trans. P. Vincent), in T. Hermans (ed.), *A Literary History of the Low Countries* (Rochester, NY: Camden House, 2009), pp. 532-571.

Harris, C., *Control and Subversion: Gender Relations in Tajikistan* (London: Pluto Press, 2004).

Hinrichs, J.P., 'Bourgeois Laarmans ontmaskerd', in *De Parelduiker* 9: 5 (2004), pp. 69-71.

Lefevere, A., 'Mother Courage's Cucumbers: Text, System and Refraction in a Theory of Literature', in *Modern Language Studies* 12: 4 (1982), pp. 3-20.

Lefevere, A. (ed.), *Translation/History/Culture: A Sourcebook* (London: Routledge, 1992).

Mikhailova, I., 'Niderlandskaia literatura po-russki: dva veka istorii', in W. Scheltjens (ed.),

Bibliografie van de Nederlandse literatuur in Russische vertaling / Bibliografiia niderlandskoi literatury na russkom iazyke (Sankt-Peterburg: Aleteiia, 2003), pp. 23-68.

Pellatt, V. (ed.)., *Text, Extratext, Metatext and Paratext in Translation* (Newcastle upon Tyne: Cambridge Scholars Publishing, 2013).

Rinckhout, E., *Dwaalspoor: Op zoek naar de waarheid achter Het Dwaallicht van Willem Elsschot* (Antwerpen: Meulenhoff/Manteau, 2006).

Rymenants, K., *Een hoopje vuil in de feestzaal: facetten van het proza van Willem Elsschot* (Antwerpen: Garant, 2009).

Scheepmaker, N., 'Drie rijstkakkers = drie donkerhuidigen: Elsschot in het Russisch', in *Het Parool: PS*, 1 maart 1975, pp. 10-1.

Schlesinger, R. (ed.), *The Family in the U.S.S.R.: Documents and Readings* [1949] (London: Routledge, 2000).

Sherry, S., 'Better Something Than Nothing: The Editors and Translators of *Inostrannaia literatura* as Censorial Agents', in *Slavonic and East European Review* 91: 4 (2013), pp. 731-758.

Shkunaeva, I.D. (ed.), *Rasskazy bel'giiskikh pisatelei* (Moskva: Progress, 1968).

Venuti, L., 'World Literature and Translation Studies', in T. D'haen, D. Damrosch, and D. Kadir (eds.), *The Routledge Companion to World Literature* (Abingdon: Routledge, 2012), pp. 180-193.

Zlateva, P. (ed.), *Translation as Social Action: Russian and Bulgarian Perspectives* (London: Routledge, 1993).

CHAPTER 14

The Case of *Kaas*

The Reception of Elsschot's Work in the Czech Language[1]

Wilken Engelbrecht (Palacký University, Olomouc, Czech Republic & John Paul II Catholic University of Lublin, Poland)

Dutch, currently with twenty-four million native speakers, is either the smallest of the greater European languages or the largest of the less spoken. Czech with its ten million native speakers is clearly a less spoken language. It is nevertheless one of the languages into which a fairly large number of Dutch literary works has been translated from 1846 up until the present, with 740 titles, out of which 435 came about before 1989. This is not all that much, of course, in comparison with the extensive numbers of Dutch and Flemish works translated into German being 3300 up until 1993.[2] But it does surpass by far even the number of works translated into the larger Slavic languages: Polish (435, of which 277 before 1989) and Russian (some 270, of which only 60 before 1989).[3]

The Czech translation was in several cases actually the first one from Dutch into another language. This is the case with the short novel *Kaas* [*Cheese*], published in 1933 by the Flemish writer Willem Elsschot. Its Czech translation was published in 1936 by the Prague publisher Julius Albert along with the translation *Vrabeček* (literally: The Sparrow) of the novel *Tsjip* (1934). Although Elsschot is considered one of the most important Flemish writers of the period between the World Wars and *Kaas* was his most important work, only two other translations were published before 1945.[4]

This article will examine the main protagonists in the Interbellum period, the translator and the position of the first translation in the Czech environment. Attention will then be turned toward the main figures in the Communist period with a look at the work of Krijtová and the position of her anthology in the Czech environment. But first we should put this in a historical context.

THE CZECH LINGUISTIC AND POLITICAL SITUATION PRIOR TO 1918

In Czech collective memory, the period under Habsburg rule between 1620 (the Battle of White Mountain) and 1918 (the creation of Czechoslovakia) was one involving suppression of national identity including the Czech language and literature. The reality was less black-and-white. The Empress Maria Theresa introduced in her educational reform of 1775 compulsory primary school for all children from the ages of six to twelve in their mother tongue. Because of this, it was necessary to write school books also for Czech language. This was linked with Czech literature which initiated the *národní obrození* [National Revival]. From the middle of the nineteenth century Czech writers began to be interested in translating foreign literature that they considered useful into Czech.

A rather significant part of the Austrian nobility originated in the Kingdom of Bohemia or had vast possessions there, with a number of them actively supporting the Revival. In addition, Bohemia underwent a vigorous industrial revolution from the 1780s onwards, turning the country economically into the strongest part of the Austrian monarchy. The border regions of Bohemia and Austrian Silesia, adjacent to Upper Austria, Bavaria, Saxony and Prussia, were predominantly German-speaking as was the majority of the new trade class in the larger cities. They followed with vivid interest the ideas of burgeoning nationalism in the neighbouring German states. It is, thus, no surprise that German-speaking Bohemians were well represented in the Frankfurt Parliament.[5] The active participation of German-speaking Bohemians in awakening German nationalist movements and their radicalisation during the revolutionary events of 1848 provoked similar feelings in Czech circles. The high-ranking Czech nobility mostly took the side of the Austrian Emperor and those who were Prime Ministers[6] worked not only at accommodating the Slavonic-speaking citizens but also at saving the Empire as such by opposing all-German nationalism and improving the political position of non-German-speaking citizens. The middle-range nobility in Bohemia, often of foreign descent, mostly supported German nationalism.

In contrast with this, Moravia, the eastern part of the Kingdom, remained rural, being basically Czech-speaking with German-speaking majorities only in the larger cities of Brno, Olomouc, Jihlava and Znojmo. Owing to active attempts on the part of the clergy to improve the situation of the Czech-speaking majority, including a strong emphasis on education and cultural edification, the Moravians remained mostly pro-Habsburg and Catholic.[7]

Both the radicalisation of Bohemia and the cultural edification of Moravia brought about a vivid interest in foreign literature. The large numbers of translated foreign literary works, published mostly up until the 1870s in periodicals such as *Česká včela* [The Czech Bee], *Květy* [The Blossom] and *Lumír* [Lumir], meant that Czech scholars began to discuss whether translations should be adjusted for Czech readers by, for example, rendering names in their Czech equivalents or by transferring the story into Czech surroundings, or whether the original setting should be maintained. After the publication (1854) of the article *O překládání klassiků* [On the Translation of the Classics] by Jakub Malý (1811-1885), it became an established custom that highbrow literature should be translated as faithfully as possible, whereas literature devoted to leisure should be adapted to Czech settings.[8]

This had far-reaching consequences for translations from less spoken languages, as there was often not a single translator able to cope with, for example, Dutch. Some 100 Dutch written titles were nevertheless translated prior to 1918. The first translated author was the Flemish pioneer Hendrik Conscience (1811-1883). The first stories by Conscience were translated by leading authors of the National Revival, including the earlier-mentioned Jakub Malý, although the bulk of his work was translated by Catholic priests as 'good Catholic leisure lecture'.[9] As concerns highbrow authors, certain writings by Multatuli (ps. of Eduard Douwes Dekker, 1820-1887), poems from the so-called *Tachtigers* and plays written by Herman Heijermans (1864-1921), were translated, at least formally, directly from Dutch.

Elsschot

The *nom de plume* Willem Elsschot is the pseudonym of the Antwerp businessman Alphons Joseph De Ridder (1882-1960), active mainly as a commercial advertiser. He ranked among the most successful practicioners of the advertising business in Belgium with a monopoly on railway advertisements. Based on his own remarks, however, the work did not please him all that much. He actually criticised his own business in a satirical way in his novels by means of his *alter ego* Laarmans.

Elsschot's love for literature was awakened, during his days as a secondary school student, by his teacher Pol De Mont (1857-1931), one of the most important Flemish poets and critics of the day. Unlike the most popular Flemish writers of his generation such as Ernest Claes (1885-1968), Stijn Streuvels (1871-1969) and Felix Timmermans (1886-1947), Elsschot tried to write an extremely concise and supra-regional form of Dutch, taking most of his material from everyday city life. His life principles were also different from the Flemish mainstream at the beginning of the twentieth century: whereas Flanders was primarily Catholic, Elsschot was a convinced agnostic.

Elsschot began to write before World War I. His first three novels *Villa des Roses* (1913), *Een ontgoocheling* [A Disappointment] (1914) and *De verlossing* [Deliverance] (1916) did not meet with much success. His fourth novel *Lijmen* [*Soft Soap*] (1923) drew the attention of the Dutch critic Jan Greshoff (1888–1971), one of the founders of the important Interbellum periodical *Forum*. He convinced Elsschot to publish his fifth novel *Kaas* [*Cheese*] (1933) in this periodical. This facilitated Elsschot's literary breakthrough.

Elsschot introduced a new type of protagonist into Flemish literature: an insignificant, ordinary man who remained a victim of his own limitations throughout his life. Laarmans first appeared in *Lijmen* and is also the main protagonist in the novels *Kaas* (1933), *Tsjip* (1934) and *Het been* [*The Leg*] (1938).

Laarmans experiences grotesque situations in those novels, e.g. in *Kaas* he becomes a trader in cheese overnight. After his last novel *Het dwaallicht* [*Will-o'-the-Wisp*] (1946), Elsschot began to write a new novel. Owing to a critique of a poem he wrote in 1947, after the execution of the collaborator August Borms (1878-1946), Elsschot suddenly decided to stop writing literature. Borms was not all that active a collaborator during the Nazi occupation of Belgium. His primary act consisted of having been President of a commission for the rehabilitation of Flemish collaborators from World War I. As a result, Elsschot saw his execution as a kind of unjust revenge. Similarly, he had written a poem in 1934 for the Communist Marinus van der Lubbe (1909-1934), the arsonist who allegedly set the *Reichstag* on fire in 1933. In his eyes both Lubbers and Borms were political Laarmans-types.

Elsschot's oeuvre remained restricted to eleven short novels and several collections of verse. His literary greatness was acknowledged by the circle around *Forum* but his international fame only began with the first translations into English in the 1960s. His work was translated in several Communist countries in the 1970s, following the publication of the Russian Elsschot anthology in 1972. A third wave of interest began with the English translation of *Kaas* in 2002.

Elsschot's work was twice translated into Czech. As mentioned above, the first translations of his work were those of *Kaas* and *Tsjip* in 1936 by Lída Faltová. The second coincides with the 'Communist wave' of the 1970s and consisted of translations, published in 1977 by Olga Krijtová (1931-2013), of the same novels which had been published in Russian in 1972: *Villa des Roses, Lijmen/Het been, Het Tankschip* and *Het Dwaallicht.*

The following sections will examine the main protagonists in the Interbellum, the translator and the position of the first translation in the Czech environment. Attention will then be turned toward the main figures in the Communist period with a look at the work of Krijtová and the position of her anthology in the Czech environment.

THE MAIN PROTAGONISTS IN THE INTERBELLUM

With the creation of Czechoslovakia, the literary landscape also changed. Important Catholic publishers now finished their activities, which were taken over by the new publishing house Vyšehrad. Although the important publishing houses Vilímek and Melantrich continued, two newly established publishing houses, Sfinx of the publisher Bohumil Janda (1900-1982), established immediately after the War in 1918, and the cooperative Družstevní práce (Cooperative Labour, DP), established in 1922 were more important for translations of Dutch literature. Both focused strongly on literature. For this purpose, Janda founded *Evropský literární klub* [European Literary Club, ELK] in 1935, functioning as a separate imprint while DP had a system of subscribers which ensured large print runs. Alongside them, a number of smaller, more or less specialised publishers were active on the book market. Owing to the quite stable middle class, the average number of copies was between 2,000 and 5,000; very popular books peaking at 10,000 copies.[10]

The reason for the fairly large number of titles (210 items) translated from Dutch into Czech in the Interbellum, during World War II and immediately afterwards was the existence of several translators able to translate directly from Dutch into Czech: Lída Faltová (1890-1944), Rudolf J. Vonka (1877-1964), Father Antonín Číhal (1881-1940), Father Alois Koudelka (ps. O.S. Vetti, 1861-1942), Arnošt Procházka (1869-1925) and Miloš Slíva (1887-±1944). Several others, mainly philologists in German studies, acquired a passive knowledge of Dutch and were able to translate in a qualitative way: Otto F. Babler (1901-1984), Otokar Fischer (1883-1938), Hugo Kosterka (1867-1956), František V. Krejčí (1867-1941) and the propagator of scouting Miloš Seifert (1887-1941). Lída Faltová was by far the most important of them, contributing with fourty-two titles in fifty-three editions, i.e. around a quarter of the total figure.

Czech translations

The first translation of Elsschot's work was published in 1936 by the Prague publisher Julius Albert (1898-1974). He began his career as a salesclerk at the important Prague publishing house of Josef R. Vilímek and František Topič. Albert started his own firm and focused on contemporary literature in 1923. He began the series *100 – knihy století* [100 – books of the century] in 1934, edited by significant contemporary Czech writers. The Elsschot item appeared as its twentieth volume under the editorship of Jaroslav Seifert (1901-1986), the Czech winner of the Nobel Prize for literature in 1984.[11]

Figure 1 and 2. Dust jacket and cover of *Vrabeček*, the 1936 Czech translation by Lída Faltová of Elsschot's *Kaas* and *Tsjip*.

The dust jacket shows a sparrow, referring to the Czech title of the book, while the cover shows a sparrow being held in a hand, thus referring to the cover of the Dutch original of *Tsjip* showing a baby being held in a hand and surrounded by several swallows. The cover and dust jacket were designed by František Muzíka (1900-1974), one of the most influential figures in the Czech avant garde and a good friend of Jaroslav Seifert. Muzíka designed all the covers of the series *100 – knihy století* but also worked for Melantrich and staged several productions in the Prague National Theatre.[12]

Albert only published a few Dutch titles, the others being *Ježíšek ve Flandřich* (1939), a translation of *Het Kindeken Jezus in Vlaanderen* [The Child Jesus in Flanders] (1917) by the renowned Flemish writer Felix Timmermans and *Krásný rok pana Carola* (1942), a translation of *Het schoone jaar van Carolus* [The Beautiful Year of Carolus] (1920) by the Flemish writer Antoon Thiry (1888–1954), both translated by Rudolf J. Vonka; they appeared in another series by Albert, *Krásné knihy* [Beautiful Books], as nos. 17 and 20.[13]

The book *Vrabeček*, containing both *Kaas* and *Tsjip*, was the only book Lída Faltová translated for Albert. In an interview with the publisher in the literary weekly *Rozhledy po literature a umění* [Prospects of Literature and Art], Julius Albert stated:

> The criteria for The Books of the Century are extremely strict. No book can be published which has appeared elsewhere (e.g. Maurois' *Le cercle de la famille*). There can be no second edition of the book, and above all no book containing an account dating to a period over 100 years ago.[14]

Both *Kaas* and *Tsjip* clearly met these requirements. There is, however, a question as to how a Czech publisher would know about a then rather unknown Flemish author. There were roughly three ways in which books were suggested for translation during the period. A number of Czech publishers had frequent contacts with German and Austrian colleagues. Certain publishers, such as Josef Vilímek, were in contact with French and British colleagues, often through Czech citizens living in these countries. In the case of lesser spoken literatures, such as Dutch, the translators specialising in the literature in question regularly informed their publishers about interesting titles. Finally, writers whose work had already been translated into Czech often mentioned new books themselves.[15] A typical example of a specialised translator was Lída Faltová.

Lída Faltová

Lída Faltová was born 2 October 1890 in the small Moravian village of Žerutky as Ludmila Pospíšilová.[16] She attended the girls' lyceum in Brno from 1904 to 1910 and then worked as an editor for several agricultural reviews. After World War I, she studied Romance studies at the newly established Masaryk University in Brno where she belonged to a circle of students around the symbolist writer, dramaturg and librarian Jiří Mahen (ps. of A. Vančura, 1882-1939). Here, she presumably became acquainted with French-writing Flemish authors such as Maurice Maeterlinck, Emile Verhaeren and Joris-Karl Huysmans, and through them with Dutch-writing authors. When and how Lida Faltová learned Dutch is unknown, perhaps partially via the founder of Brno German studies Antonín Beer (1881-1950) who had an extremely broad concept of German studies.

She married the Social Democrat and publicist Josef Falta (1895-1974) in 1923. When he became secretary of the Czech Senate, the couple moved to Prague where Faltová became one of the main translators and critics of DP, though she also regularly worked for other major publishing houses such as Melantrich, Sfinx and ELK.

The beginning of World War II meant a personal catastrophe for Faltová. Her husband fled to the United States where he was active in emigrant circles and in the Free Czechoslovakia Broadcasting Company. Owing to the Communist putsch of 1948 he never returned to his fatherland. Faltová's son was caught by the Gestapo in 1940 and released after his mother's death. Faltová nevertheless continued translating till just before her death, on 8 December 1944 owing to thyroid gland problems. During her active years 1932–1944 she published sixty literary translations, fourty-two of which from Dutch, making her the main transmitter of Dutch literature in Interbellum Czechoslovakia.

As there were no subsidies from the Netherlands or Belgium in that period for translations from Dutch, or from the Czechoslovak government, it was important that the losses with certain titles were compensated for by the profits made from other books. Bestselling books by authors such as Johan Fabricius, Madelon Székely-Lulofs, Antoon Coolen and A. den Doolaard are consequently found alongside the Faltová translated titles as well as literary works by writers such as Multatuli, Ernest Claes and Stijn Streuvels.

DP had a system of subscriptions, reaching 25,000 in 1939, 40,000 during the war and even 100,000 prior to the nationalization of the publishing house by the Communists in 1948. The lowest print run was some 2,000 copies. If the work was successful (or the author already known by the Czech reading public) the print run could be much bigger.[17] The intended readers were middle class people who made up the backbone of the Czechoslovak Republic. It seems that their taste was in many things similar to that of middle class readers in the Netherlands and Flanders: those published in Czech translation had also sold well in the Low Countries.

Faltová also had her own personal preferences. Jo van Ammers-Küller, who was extremely popular in the Low Countries, Germany, Hungary and Poland was consequently not translated into Czech, owing to her fascist sympathies. At the same time the only translation of the political report *In de loopgraven voor Madrid* [In the Trenches before Madrid] (1937) by the anarchist Jef Last was Faltová's *V zákopech u Madridu* (1937). The fact that the author lost his Dutch citizenship because of being an active combatant of the Spanish Republic was explicitly mentioned in the review in *Panorama*.[18] Faltová's own Social Democrat convictions played a clear role here.

Faltová had a solid knowledge of contemporary Dutch and Flemish literature. One of her strong contacts was the popular writer Johan Fabricius (1899-1981), who visited her in 1934 in Prague.[19] Unfortunately, Faltová's personal archives and that of the Julius Albert publishing house have been lost and the archive of DP is not accessible at this moment.[20] Therefore, we do not know exactly who suggested the novels *Kaas* and *Tsjip* for translation. The correspondence between Faltová and Melantrich makes it clear that she regularly proposed interesting books to Czech publishers. The translation states that the text has been authorised by the author, which means that Faltová would have contacted Elsschot about translation problems. It is complete as it includes the dedication to Gresshoff, the poem at the beginning of *Kaas*, as well as the devices at the beginning of several chapters of *Tsjip*. The translation is precise and executed in beautifully written Czech.

THE MAIN PROTAGONISTS AFTER 1945

After the liberation in May 1945, it seemed that the old times had returned. All the Czech publishing houses either continued or were re-established. Seen from the point of view of translations of Dutch and Flemish literature, the three years of democracy, from 1946 to 1948, were the most successful period in the history of Czech reception of Dutch written literature, producing some thirty five published translations, including a number of new titles.

After the Communist putsch of 25 February 1948, things changed rapidly. All publishing houses were nationalized between 1948 and 1951 and smaller publishers (including Julius Albert) were closed and their possessors and directors banned, sent into forced labour or punished with several years imprisonment. Over the course of the campaign against 'politically unwanted, immoral or superstitious' literature in the years 1950-1952, over 2.5 million books were removed from public libraries throughout the country, including many by Flemish authors. Only three Dutch books were translated between 1951 and 1955.

Things changed once again in the late 1950s. Olga Krijtová (see below) began her translator's career in 1954. In that period, a stable book market had been established. The socialist publisher Melantrich was still functioning and the former avant-garde publisher Odeon, founded in 1925 and closed in 1949, was re-established in 1953 with the tongue-twisting name Státní nakladatelství krásné literature, hudby a umění [State Publishing House for Beautiful Literature, Music and Art. Its pre-war name Odeon was adopted again in 1966]. This became the main publisher for literary works and translations. Other significant publishing houses included Státní nakladatelství dětské knihy [State Publishing House for Children's Literature, founded in 1949], renamed in 1969 as Albatros. Mladá fronta, established as an underground publishing house of the youth resistance movement in 1943, became the main publisher of the Czechoslovak Youth Movement ČSM. Svoboda, founded in 1945 as the publisher of the Communist Party, wanted to bring out political literature; finally in 1953, the former Catholic publisher Vyšehrad was rechristened Lidová demokracie [People's Democracy]. Several of them still exist.

Odeon, Mladá fronta, Melantrich and Albatros were the most important transmitters of translations of Dutch and Flemish literature. Miroslav Drápal (1916-1991) and Ella Kazdová (1909-1982), as well as the Protestant Milada Šimsová (1904-after 2008) began to translate during the 1940s. Of these, Olga Krijtová was by far the most important.

Olga Krijtová

Krijtová was born on 30 March 1931 as Olga Fuchsová in Hradec Králové. After World War II, she studied English and Dutch Philology at Charles University, where she became an assistant professor of the Dutch language at the German Department. In 1956 she married the Dutch refugee Hans Krijt (1927-2011), who had fled to Czechoslovakia when unwilling to fight in the colonial war against the Indonesian insurgents. Her first literary translation was that of the story *De onrustzaaier* [The Troublemaker] by Willem van Maanen (1920-2012) which came out in 1958 in the journal *Světová literatura* [World Literature]. In her capacity as a teacher of Dutch literature at Charles University and as a literary translator she was ideally placed to spread knowledge of Dutch literature.

Over the following half century, Krijtová translated over eighty literary Dutch works in a great variety of genres. The Elsschot collection was her twentieth translation and appeared at a very specific period of her life. After the suppression of the Prague Spring in 1968, Krijtová cancelled her membership in the Communist Party as a protest. A year later, she won the Martinus Nijhoffprijs, the prestigious Dutch award for literary translation. She was, however, punished for her stance with a publishing ban. A number of her translations appeared anonymously, e.g. in the case of *Co dávno odnesl čas* (1974), Krijtová's translation of Couperus' *Van oude menschen de dingen die voorbijgaan* [*Old People and the Things that Pass*] (1906). Other translations such as *Vincent v Haagu* (1975) of the novel *Vincent in Den Haag* [*Vincent in The Hague*] (1963) by the Communist writer Theun de Vries (1907-2005) or *Velký géz* (1978), a translation of *De grote geus* [*The Beggars' Banquet*] (1949) by Johan Fabricius, saw the light under other names, most of these under that of a former student of Krijtova. However, this system was not adhered to consistently. The publishing house Svoboda allegedly did not receive the list of 'forbidden translators' and consequently the Elsschot translation appeared under Krijtová's own name. The unusual lack of a preface or epilogue demonstrates, however, that the situation was not quite normal. Either Krijtová did not wish to draw too much attention to her activities or the publisher knew about the ban but simply ignored it.

During the enforced embargo, Krijtová mainly translated literary work for adults as well as for children. In 1974 and 1975 she published two translations of works by Louis Couperus (1863-1923); in 1980 a trilogy by the Flemish writer Julien Van Remoortere (born 1930) and in 1981 the novel *Zelfportret, Of het galgemaal* [*The Man in the Mirror*] (1955) by Herman Teirlinck (1879-1967). Elsschot's works are typical of her translations in this period. All these works were critical of the respective contemporary social situation in the Netherlands and Flanders, and may be interpreted as a covert criticism of the Czechoslovak system.

After several years, Krijtová's publication ban was lifted or 'forgotten'. It took until 1989, however, before she could continue with her academic career. She defended her habilitation after the Velvet Revolution in 1990 and was associate professor of Dutch language at Charles University until her retirement in 2001. She finally gained Czech recognition for her translation work in 2005 when she won the prize *Cena Josefa Jungmanna* for her rendering of *Následující příběh* of the novel *Het volgende verhaal* [*The Following Story*] (1991) by Cees Nooteboom (born 1933); in 2007 she received the prestigious *Magnesia Litera* prize for her translation *Fámy* (2006) of the long novel *De geruchten* [Rumours] (1996) by the greatest post war Flemish author Hugo Claus (1929–2008). Her last translation of the novel *Mijn soevereine liefde* [My Sovereign Love] (2005) by the Dutch writer Tomas Lieske (ps. of T. van Drunen, born 1943) was published in 2007. Krijtová died on 7 November 2013 in Prague.

Krijtová's Elsschot

Figure 3. Dust jacket of Bludička, the 1977 Czech translation by Krijtová of Elsschot's *Villa des Roses, Kaas, Lijmen/Het been, Het Tankschip,* and *Het dwaallicht*

In 1977 Krijtová made a new translation of six (or seven, if we count *Lijmen* and *Het Been* as two separate items) Elsschot novels. They appeared at Svoboda in the series *jiskry* [Sparks]. This series of 140 volumes spanning the years 1970–1986 was supposed to present foreign social critical, psychological and utopic novels to Czech readers. It was a Czech counterpart of the series Мастера современной прозы [Masters of Contemporary Prose] by the publishing house Progress in Moscow where, indeed, exactly the same selection of Elsschot's work had seen the light in 1972. The print run, 9,750 copies, was a normal one in this series, which was meant exclusively for readers interested in literary texts. During the Communist regime, print runs normally went up to 40,000 copies.

The Czech anthology contains *Villa des Roses*, a translation of Elsschot's debut *Villa des Roses* (1913), *Vějička* [The Egg], a translation of the diptych *Lijmen* (1924) and *Het been* (1938), presented here as a work in two volumes entitled *Díl I: Chytání na lep* [Part I: Catching the Bait] and *Díl II: Noha* [Part II: The Leg]. *Sýr* [*Cheese*], a new translation of *Kaas* (1933), *Tanková loď* [*The Tank Ship*], a translation of *Het tankschip* (1942), and finally *Bludička* [*Will-o'-the-Wisp*], a translation of Elsschot's last novel *Het dwaallicht* (1946). Somewhat earlier, in 1973, a Polish translation *Hochsztapler Laarmans* [Swindler Laarmans] using an English source text, appeared. These three novels had Laarmans as a protagonist; the Polish version followed the English (and Elsschot's own) convention of presenting *Lijmen* and *Het Been* as two separate novels. Owing to the English intermediate *Three Novels: Soft Soap, The Leg, Will-o'-the-Wisp* (1965) the Polish translation presented *Lijmen* and *Het Been* as two separate novels. The Czech translation clearly followed the Russian custom.

Again, for political reasons the usual epilogue was lacking and the reader could only obtain further information through the blurb. The blurb provided some information about the author, presented as a social critical writer in line with the aims of the series. There were brief abstracts of all the novels and the information that two novels had already been published in Czech in 1936.

CONCLUSION

The Czech reception of Elsschot's writings differed significantly from that in other East-Central European languages. His most important novel *Kaas* was, along with *Tsjip*, translated into Czech in a series of 'world authors' in a period when the author was barely known outside a small circle of native speakers with an interest in literature. This may well have been inspired by Lída Faltová's contacts with Johan Fabricius.

The omnibus of the most important novels had been published in Czech in 1977, shortly after the first Polish translation. It was apparent that the Soviet edition of 1972 must have served as a model for the selection and the arrangement were the same. The presentation of Elsschot's work in the series *jiskry* was similar as that in the pre-war series *100 – knihy století.* Elsschot was lauded as an exceptional writer of global importance. It seemed, however, that the current wave of interest in Elsschot's work with many translations into among others Hungarian, Polish and Slovak, did not have an impact on the Czech literary world.

This may partially be a consequence of the specific Czech situation. Large numbers of new publishing houses were established after 1989 and the market became soon saturated. Several long-established houses went bankrupt during the chaotic 1990s (e.g. Odeon, 1994; Svoboda-Libertas, 1998; Melantrich, 1999). Others chose to be more cautious and developed a preference for publishing re-editions of successful titles, such as the Indonesian novels of Madelon Székely-Lulofs. The situation seemed to stabilise at the beginning of this century but it is much more interesting for a publisher to ask for a Dutch or Flemish grant for contemporary work than to commit himself to an edition of older classic texts. From this point of view, Elsschot is, at least temporarily, *passé défini* for Czech literary reception.

NOTES

1 This article has been made possible by grant 7AMB14PL022 *Language–Literature–Culture: Czech, Moravian, Silesian and Polish Connections in the Past and Present* of the Czech Ministry of Education and Science.

2 H. Van Uffelen, *Bibliographie der modernen niederländischen Literatur in deutscher Übersetzung 1830-1990* (Münster: LiT, 1993).

3 Figures according to the database *Translation Database* of the Nederlands Letterenfonds (former Nederlands Literair Vertalers- en Productiefonds), accessible at https://letterenfonds.secure.force.com/vertalingendatabase/search, in combination with my own research in several national databases and libraries.

4 A censored German translation of *Tsjip* in 1936 (*Tschip*) and a Danish translation of *Tsjip* in 1937 (*Adele*).

5 649 members of parliament were originally planned to be elected. The sixty-four places for Czech-speaking regions were not occupied as the Czech refused to participate. Out of the remaining 186 Austrian MP's, 27 were from Bohemia, 24 from Moravia and 9 from Austrian Silesia (making up all together 32 % of all the Austrian delegates and 10 % of the Parliament). All were German-speaking and from predominantly German-speaking regions. For figures see https://de.wikipedia.org/wiki/Liste_der_Mitglieder_der_Frankfurter_Nationalversammlung.

6 Out of the twelve Prime Ministers of the Austrian Empire between 1848 and 1867 and the eleven Prime Ministers of the Austrian-Hungarian Empire between 1867 and 1918, nine were from the Kingdom of Bohemia (Count Kolowrat-Liebsteinsky, Baron von Pillersdorf, Prince Schwarzenberg, Count Mensdorff-Pouilly and Count Belcredi, Count Kálnoky, Baron Lexa von Ärenthal, Count Berchtold and Count Černín).

7 It is thus no coincidence that Prince Schwarzenberg, Prime Minister of the Empire, moved the Austrian Diet to the Moravian city of Kroměříž (Kremsier) in 1848 and that the new Emperor Franz Joseph I ascended the throne in Olomouc in Moravia.

8 Compare W. Engelbrecht, 'A Moravian Picture of Dutch Literature', in Jitka Zehnalová e.a. (eds.), *Tradition and Trends in Trans-Language Communication* (Olomouc: Palacký University, 2013), pp. 215-228 with quoted literature.

9 Engelbrecht, 'A Moravian Picture of Dutch Literature,' pp. 215-228

10 In the case of books published before World War II, the print runs were seldom registered. This changed during the German occupation and in the Communist period owing to censorship and centrally organised paper distribution. Cf. Z. Šimeček and J. Trávníček, *Knihy kupovati… Dějiny knižního trhu v českých zemích* (Praha: Academia, 2015).

11 Data according to A. Zach, 'Julius Albert', in *Slovník českých nakladatelství 1849–1949*. Online version of the encyclopedia (2015).

12 The main work about Muzíka is V. Koubská and V. Tetiva, *František Muzika* (Praha: Gallery, 2012).

13 In fact, a fourth title *Ostrov radostného mládí* (1934) by Hendrik de Leeuw (1891-after 1956) may be counted also among Dutch publications. According to the colofon, the book was translated 'z holandštiny'. The original had been written, however, in English as *Java Jungle Tales* (1933). The Czech title means literally *Island of Joyful Youth*. The work was translated by Božena Paličková who mainly translated for Bohumil Janda from English, German and Italian.

14 J. Šup, 'Hovory s nakladateli. Julius Albert o sobě a o svých knihách', p. 22, my translation.

15 Most of the archives of the publishing houses were confiscated by the Communist regime after the nationalisation of private companies in the years 1949–1951. The preserved archives are mostly stored in the *Památník národního pisemnictví* (Monument of National Literature) in Prague. Unfortunately, the archive of Julius Albert seems not to have survived. I had, however, the possibility to research the correspondence between Lída Faltová and the publishing house Melantrich. My observations are the result of this research.

16 Data according to J. Opelík, 'Lída Faltová,' in V. Forst (ed.), *Lexikon české literatury. Osobnosti, díla, instituce 1 (A-G)* (Praha: Academia, 1985), pp. 680-681.

17 The popular Italian trilogy by Johan Fabricus had for every edition a print run of 7,000 to 8,000 copies.

18 J. Falta, 'V zákopech u Madridu,' *Panorama* 15: 3 (1937), pp. 107-108.

19 Faltová referred to this visit in Faltová 1934. Fabricius also met with the Czech writer Karel Čápek (1890-1938), whom he knew from PEN-congresses.

20 The *Památník národního písmenictví* has built a new archive in Litoměříce. Most of the collections are available for research.

BIBLIOGRAPHY

Elsschot, W., *Vrabeček*, Translation by Lída Faltová of *Kaas* and *Tsjip* (Praha: Julius Albert, 1936).

Elsschot, W., *Bludička*, Translation by Olga Krijtová of *Villa des Roses, Kaas, Lijmen/Het been, Het Tankschip, Het dwaallicht* (Praha: Svoboda, 1977).

Engelbrecht, W., 'Von Conscience bis Fabricius – das Bild der niederländisch-sprachigen Literatur in Tschechischer Übersetzung in der Zwischenkriegszeit', in H. Van Uffelen *et al.* (eds.), *An der Schwelle. 'Eigen' und 'fremd' in der niederländischen Literatur* (Wien: Verlag Praesens, 2010), pp. 181-198.

Engelbrecht, W., 'Een strijder tegen het onrecht. De receptie van Multatuli in Tsjechië en Slowakije' in *Over Multatuli* 33: 66 (2011), pp. 2–41.

Engelbrecht, W., 'A Moravian Picture of Dutch Literature', in J. Zehnalová, O. Molnár and M. Kubánek. (eds.), *Tradition and Trends in Trans-Language Communication: Proceedings of the International Conference Translation and Interpreting Forum Olomouc 2012* (Olomouc: Palacký University, 2013), pp. 215-228.

Engelbrecht, W., 'Literatuur en kunst uit de Lage Landen in *Moderní revue*', in L. Degand *et al.* (eds.), *In het teken van identiteit: Taal en cultuur van de Nederlanden: Huldeboek aangeboden aan Prof. dr. Ludo Beheydt* (Louvain-la-Neuve: UCL Presses Universitaires de Louvain, 2014), pp. 85-92.

Engelbrecht, W., 'AVV – VVK, or Dutch and Flemish Literature from a Czech Catholic View', in J. Walkusz and M. Krupa (eds.), *Universitati serviet. Księga pamiątkowa ku czci Księdza Profesora Stanisława Wilka SDB* (Lublin: Wydawnictwo KUL, 2014), pp. 490-498.

Falta, J., 'V zákopech u Madridu,' *Panorama* 15: 3 (1937), pp. 107-108.

Faltová, L., 'Různé zprávy. Johan Fabricius v Praze', *Panorama* 12: 2 (1934), p. 78-79.

Koubská, V. and V. Tetiva, *František Muzika* (Praha: Gallery, 2012).

Masařík, Z., 'Antonín Beer a široce pojatá germanistika v Brně', in *Brněnská věda a umění meziválečného období (1918–1939) v evropském kontextu. Sborník příspěvků z konference konané v rámci oslav 750. výročí udělení městských práv Brnu ve dnech 22.-25. září 1993* (Brno: Masarykova univerzita, 1993), pp. 76-79.

Opelík, J., 'Lída Faltová', in V. Forst (ed.), *Lexikon české literatury. Osobnosti, díla, instituce 1 (A-G)* (Praha: Academia, 1985), pp. 680-681.

Šámal, P., *Soustružníci lidských duší: lidové knihovny a jejich cenzura na počátku padesátých let 20. století* (Praha: Academia, 2009).

Šimeček, Z. and J. Trávníček, *Knihy kupovati... Dějiny knižního trhu v českých zemích* (Praha: Academia, 2015).

Šup, J., 'Hovory s nakladateli. Julius Albert o sobě a o svých knihách', *Rozhledy po literatuře a umění* 6: 3 (18 January 1937), pp. 20-21.

Van de Reijt, V., *Elsschot – leven en werken van Alfons de Ridder* (Amsterdam: Athenaeum – Polak & Van Gennep, 2011).

Van Uffelen, H., *Bibliographie der modernen niederländischen Literatur in deutscher Übersetzung 1830-1990* (Münster: LiT, 1993).

Zach, A., 'Julius Albert', in *Slovník českých nakladatelství 1849–1949*. Online version of the encyclopedia, 2015, http://www.slovnik-nakladatelstvi.cz/nakladatelstvi/julius-albert.html (accessed 30 December 2015).

Useful websites

http://www.databaze-prekladu.cz/ – a site providing data about translators.

http://www.slovnikceskeliteratury.cz/index.jsp – a site about Czech literature and Czech publishing houses after 1945.

CHAPTER 15

'BaBié, zivoublé!'

Ideology and Cultural Transfer: *De donkere kamer van Damokles*

Peter Kegel (Huygens ING, Amsterdam, The Netherlands),
Marion Prinse (Utrecht University, The Netherlands),
Matthieu Sergier (Université Saint-Louis - Bruxelles, Belgium),
Marc van Zoggel (Huygens ING, Amsterdam, The Netherlands)

Willem Frederik Hermans' 1958 novel *De donkere kamer van Damokles* [*The Dark Room of Damocles*] is widely regarded as one of the major contributions to post-war Dutch literature. In the ranking of popular books among secondary school students, the novel is an annual top-ten contender. 'Nederland Leest' [The Netherlands reads] is an event for the promotion of reading literature which is the Dutch equivalent of the American 'One Book, One City' campaign that originated in Chicago in 2001; in 2012 it centered around *De donkere kamer van Damokles*. In 2013, the 50th edition of the novel was published. Furthermore, Hermans' work appears to have played quite a significant role in a paradigm shift in historiography and subsequently in the public debate concerning the German occupation of the Netherlands (1940-1945). In post-war society, the behavior of the Dutch during the occupation was long considered a case of people having been either good or bad, black or white. Inspired by *De donkere kamer van Damokles* and other Dutch novels set in the Second World War, a different outlook on the events gained momentum: the occupation came to be seen as a period of confusion in which right and wrong were often inextricably tangled up.

Quite to Hermans' own surprise, *De donkere kamer van Damokles* gained both critical acclaim and commercial success. This caught the attention of foreign publishers. A first wave of translations appeared in the early 1960s, with editions in the United Kingdom (1962), France (1962) and the four Scandinavian countries Denmark (1961), Sweden (1962), Norway (1962) and Finland (1963). With a Polish edition (1994) as the sole exception, other translations only appeared after Hermans had passed away in 1995. New translations in French (2006) and English (2007) were substantially more successful than the ones in the 1960s. Furthermore, the novel was published for the first time in German (2001), Greek (2005), Spanish (2009), Czech (2010), Chinese (2011), and Croatian (2015).

In this chapter, we will consider some of the translations mentioned above in the light of the political-historical context of the novel. One may assume that this 'ideological' aspect is in various ways of interest when examining a translation. For instance, the blending of 'good' and 'bad' is in the novel not only illustrated by the chain of events and symbolized by the main character's heterogeneous identity, but also reflected in the role given to the English and German languages and objects. A translator needs to account for the historical embeddedness of the novel and at the same time deal with the presence of a foreign language in the original edition, both in a strictly linguistic sense and with regard to the importance of this 'heterolingualism' for understanding and interpreting the work. Another aspect is the national embeddedness of the political-historical context of the novel. A reviewer needs to familiarize his reading public with this context and at the same time relate it to the situation in the readers' and his own country.

These examples are all aspects of 'cultural transfer' and/or 'cultural transmission', broad and rather vague concepts but here understood in the strict definitions of the Groningen-based Studies on Cultural & Transmission series.[1] Cultural transfer is then defined as 'the one-way activity of translating a literary text', cultural transmission as 'the reciprocal activity of sharing cultural and literary information'. We will discuss the aspects of cultural transfer and transmission outlined in the previous paragraph in two short cases, although in reversed order. First, we will present a frame of reference by briefly discussing the ideological impact of the novel in its country of origin. The first case will then consist of a comparison of the reception of *De donkere kamer van Damokles* in Sweden, Norway and Germany, three countries with greatly differing positions in the Second World War. In the second case, the questions regarding translation will be discussed with reference to the 2006 French translation by Daniel Cunin. We are aware that many more aspects of the cultural transfer and transmission of *De donkere kamer van Damokles* are worth investigating, but for now we will focus on these two, in the end rather separate, issues in order to illustrate the variety of possible approaches.

BLACK, WHITE, GREY: *DE DONKERE KAMER VAN DAMOKLES* AND THE NETHERLANDS

De donkere kamer van Damokles is the story of the adventures and strange behavior of the 'weakling' Henri Osewoudt, or in other words his (as it is called on the dust jacket of the 2007 English translation) 'fateful wanderings through a sadistic universe'. In the course of the utterly chaotic and confusing circumstances of the first days, weeks and months of the Second World War, Osewoudt falls under the spell of his enigmatic look-a-like Dorbeck, at whose request he carries out heroic missions for the Dutch Resistance, not hesitating to commit brutal acts and murder for the good cause. At the end of the war, though, Osewoudt is not being considered a 'hero'. On the contrary, he is accused of treachery and is imprisoned amidst war criminals. Dorbeck, the only person left who would be able to plead for his freedom, seems to have vanished into thin air. When his situation has become desperate, Osewoudt tries to escape, is shot by a guard and bleeds to death.

Among the many reviews that were written directly after the novel was published, only a few touched upon the ideological dimensions of the story. Moreover, reviewers who did so, were predominantly disapproving of the ethical or moral aspect of the book. *Algemeen Handelsblad*-critic Ben Stroman called *De donkere kamer van Damokles* 'one of the most convincing novels that have been written in our country during the last couple of years', but at the same time 'the most perfidious novel':

> Perfidious, first and foremost, because it takes the years of occupation as a standard for life in general. [...] Hermans has situated his story within the context of the Second World War in order to be able to present his ideology. An ideology that is maliciously cynical, maliciously negative. And it is exactly this malice, this willfulness that turns this novel into a disgusting product.

Stroman concludes: 'With this novel, the morality of art has turned into immorality.'[2]

Socialist critic Jef Last, in an essay published in the periodical *De Nieuwe Stem*, gives an even stronger rejection of the novel. According to Last, Hermans writes 'a kind of literature which has as its main task to insinuate, to state that everybody else is in fact nothing but a clumsy fool, or incapable of doing anything at all'. Last fulminates in particular against Hermans' portrait of the Dutch resistance: 'All of us who commemorate our fallen comrades, cannot feel but assaulted by the novels written by mister Hermans, containing only treacherous, spineless, insignificant, incompetent, and at any rate bald resistance workers with body odour and bad breath.' Last situates *De donkere kamer van Damokles* in the category of moral pornography, 'with all apologies the bastards need for their evil. And since the bastards and the stinkers will always be the majority, we foresee a huge number of admiring readers.'[3]

In spite of these negative and rather grim reviews, a great many other critics ignored the ideological aspect of the novel and focused entirely on its literary value. The clever composition of the plot, the frantic pace of the narrative, and the cogent display of the philosophy and poetics of the author dominated the reception, leading many a reviewer to conclude that *De donkere kamer van Damokles* was Hermans' best novel so far. A similar trend can be detected in academic criticism.

Over the years, scholars have written a respectable number of sometimes highly interpretive articles, dissertations and other books on the novel.[4] Popular subjects were the literary *Doppelganger*-motive, the Wittgensteinian linguistic play, and the Modernist claim of the unknowability of reality. The pivotal question was whether the Dorbeck character was real or ultimately a delusion of the mentally unstable Osewoudt. In general, academic literary criticism treated the novel 'as a jigsaw puzzle that with some tricks and maneuvers eventually could be solved'.[5]

The most interesting debates actually took place among historians. In his inaugural lecture of 1983, Hans Blom made a plea for a more analytical historiography of war instead of one concerned with moral issues of right and wrong. It landed on fertile ground in the following decades, culminating in the ground-breaking monograph *Grijs verleden: Nederland en de Tweede Wereldoorlog* [Grey Past: The Netherlands and the Second World War] (2001) by Chris van der Heijden. The author contested the official multivolume *Het Koninkrijk der Nederlanden in de Tweede Wereldoorlog* [The Kingdom of the Netherlands in the Second World War] (1969-1994) by L. de Jong. Contrary to De Jong, Van der Heijden did not highlight the ostensibly transparent choices and heroic or perfidious deeds of individuals. Instead, he focused on 'the mentality of the people at the time'.

Referring to the depiction of the war in novels of authors like Gerard Reve, Harry Mulisch and especially Hermans, Van der Heijden concentrated on 'the doubts, uncertainties, the grey between black and white'. Within this frame, Van der Heijden exposed 'the coincidence, the clumsiness, the littleness' of it all, and stated that in exceptional circumstances everything is always unrealistically magnified: 'Fear is turned into anxiety, nerve into bravery, toughness becomes cruelty. Sceptics turn out to be cowards, boasters in action are wimps, and the wallflower of the group is the only one capable of proper action.' In line with Hermans, Van der Heijden described the situation in the Netherlands above all as chaotic: '*Non luctor et emergo sed fluctuo et fluo*, a laborious splattering and sputtering is typical for the behavior of the large majority of the Dutch people during the first years of the war.'[6]

So although there were some outspoken political dimensions in the reception of the novel within the first 'interpretive community',[7] emphasis was laid mainly on the technical aspects and superb achievement of the novel as a literary work of art. Academic literary criticism did not quite focus on ideological aspects either, but in historiography the depiction of the war and the behavior of individuals in *De donkere kamer van Damokles* and similar war novels played a vital role in the scientific debate.

LEGACY OF THE WAR: RECEPTION IN SWEDEN, NORWAY AND GERMANY

As briefly mentioned in our introduction, several translations of the novel were published in the early 1960s. Initially, a German edition was announced as well, but Hermans was unhappy with the quality of the translation made by Johannes Piron.[8] Instead, *Die Tränen der Akazien* (1968) [*De tranen der acacia's* (1949)], also set against the background of the Second World War, became his first novel published in Germany. Jürgen Hillner was responsible for the translation. It hardly gained any attention, according to Hillner this was because of the post-war circumstances in Germany: in the 1960s, Germans were tired of reading about the war.[9] Although more translations of his works were published in the following years, Hermans remained largely unknown in Germany. This changed when *De donkere kamer van Damokles* was finally translated, by Waltraud Hüsmert. *Die Dunkelkammer des Damokles* (2001) was an instant success: the first print of 15,000 copies sold out within two months' time, making it an official bestseller.[10]

Hillner's statement suggests that the depiction of the Second World War in the novel may very well be a crucial factor here: in the 1960s, Germans were not ready for a 'grey' war novel, forty years later the time was right. We might find some support for this hypothesis by examining the reception of the novel in other countries, with a different history of processing the events of 1940-1945. Swedish and Norwegian critics, for instance, tried to interpret the novel by delving into the specific experience of the Second World War in the Netherlands and connecting this to the situation in their respective home countries. Sweden, Norway and Germany thus provide interesting cases, for every single one of them was involved differently in the war: Sweden remained neutral, Norway was occupied and Germany was the occupier. This resulted into three different 'grand narratives' in the post-war period.

According to the British historian Richard Overy, Swedish neutrality actually was a situation of 'permanent emergency':

> Public opinion was divided over hostility to the Soviet Union and fear of, or dislike of, National Socialism. For the government, the delicate issue remained how far to go in rejecting or compromising German requirements without undermining Swedish independence.[11]

In post-war Sweden there was little interest in the country's difficult position during the war. It was not integrated in the collective memory, because the Swedes could not relate to the classical elements characterizing this war, i.e. deportation, resistance, and Nazi persecution. According to historian Johan Östling, it was only during the 1990s that the socio-political narrative shifted towards a more universal approach of the Second World War.[12] Anyway, this narrative was not available in 1962 when the Swedish translation of *De donkere kamer van Damokles* was published.

The war had a more immediate and substantial impact on the mentality of post-war Norway. As Ole Kristian Grimnes states: 'The German invasion of Norway in 1940 came as a devastating shock to the Norwegians, who had not participated in any war since 1814.'[13] Anti-German feelings only started to disappear gradually in the 1970s. Just a small part of the Norwegians had collaborated with the enemy, the majority of the inhabitants had sympathized with or even been a member of the resistance. The main narrative therefore was 'a resistance-oriented interpretation of the war years'. Norwegian historians 'did not have to face the difficult task of trying to reconcile political collaboration and resistance within the framework of an overall national narrative'.[14]

Germany was left destroyed and divided after the Second World War. There was hardly a German left who had not lost at least one family member, a friend or his home, and most of all there was the mental blow. As Bill Niven notes:

> [F]or a long time, the main victims in the eyes of many West-Germans were the Germans themselves, who had been 'forced' to serve in Hitler's army, bombed by the Allies, treated unjustly in Soviet camps during and after the war.[15]

This self-perception persisted as long as the 1990s, when Germany finally came to grips with its National-Socialist past. The focus shifted towards guilt and responsibility at all levels, 'from the highest, namely Hitler himself, down to that of the "ordinary" German'. Various reasons can be seen as responsible for this change. Niven suggests it was a result of the unification of Germany, which 'brought to an end both the post-Hitler period and a certain way of looking at the Third Reich, one which was itself a product of German division, the Cold War, and conflicting political ideologies'.[16] As Niven and Paver state: 'National Socialism became a legacy as of 8 May 1945, and to this day German memorialization concentrates almost obsessively on this legacy.'[17] With these different afterlives of the Second World War in mind, let us now turn to the reception of Hermans' novel in Sweden, Norway and Germany.

The Swedish translation (1962), by Brita Dahlman, was titled *Mörkrummet*, extracting 'Damokles' from its title. The first literary critic to discuss the book was Folke Isaksson. His was the first of a total of twelve reviews. Three perspectives on the novel can be discerned in the Swedish reception: (1) the Second World War in Holland is of crucial importance for the novel's interpretation; (2) the War is partially important to grasp its message, but not vital; (3) the War merely serves as the background of the novel, the epistemological issues it contains are crucial. The first category is represented by just one review: U. Asplund discusses the German invasion in Holland and emphasizes the degree to which this had an impact on the daily life of Dutch citizens.[18]

The majority of the reviewers begin by giving information about the German occupation of the Netherlands but consider the war setting as merely a means for the author to convey more general, existentialist ideas, also in vogue in Swedish literature at the time. For example, Wallqvist initially remarks that

Mörkrummet shows how small retailers struggled to keep their stores open, but he eventually interprets the novel as a more general discussion about mankind. It thus positions itself amidst war literature 'which is less concerned with the war itself and more with the position of man which is dramatized in war circumstances'.[19] And reviewer 'I.S.' argues that the wartime setting of these novels contributes to the creation of an environment in which individuals become entangled in their own ideas and lost in the labyrinth of their existence.[20]

Figure 1. Book cover of the Norwegian translation by Bjørn Braaten of Hermans' *De donkere kamer van Damokles* (1962)

Figure 2. Book cover of the Swedish translation by Brita Dahlman of Hermans' *De donkere kamer van Damokles* (1962)

In Norway, the novel was titled *Damokles' Mørkerom*, a translation by Bjørn Braaten. The first reviewer who goes beyond the shallow interpretation of the novel as simply a representation of war time is Philip Houm. He praises the structure and composition and discerns a deeper, symbolic meaning.[21] Egil Rasmussen states in a similar way that *De donkere kamer van Damokles* is more than just a war novel, although he does not elaborate on this.[22] Niels Chr. Brøgger argues that the novel should be read as an inquiry into the identity of an individual.[23] However, the majority of the Norwegian critics found it difficult to interpret the work. Haavard Haavardsholm, for example, states that if the novel was intended to have some underlying, symbolic meaning, it must have 'disappeared in the dark'.[24] Willy Dahl is confused as well: 'What the writer eventually wants to convey to the reader is not easy to grasp.' He cautiously presumes the novel attempts to debunk the myth of the heroic resistance.[25]

The emphasis on the Dutch resistance in many Norwegian reviews is an important deviation from the Swedish reception. Frequently discussed are the (lack of) efficiency of the Dutch underground, the ups and downs in the life of a resistance member and the possible motives Osewoudt has for joining this group. 'Home front' is a recurring notion in the Norwegian reception as well. In Norway, this is a wide-ranging concept, originating in the Second World War, and covering the resistance as an organized movement. Yet, the resistance is not the only war element being discussed: both the roles of the Jewish girl Marianne and the young SS member who talks to Osewoudt about the obsoleteness of the humanistic concepts of right and wrong, are repeatedly mentioned. This differs from the Swedish reception, in which the young man is mentioned only once.[26]

The reception of the 2001 German translation demonstrates a different attitude towards the legacy of the Second World War. Some of the reviews merely focus on the recent debates in the Netherlands: 'In the new, well-arranged post-war world, only in appearance is everything divided between good and bad, black and white.' Von Borman states that Hermans discusses a glorious theme of the Dutch post-war period: 'the patriotic resistance against "de Moffen"'.[27] And Jähner complains: 'In Holland, one willingly pushes aside that the National-Socialists were praised until the end, because there everything went smoothly like in no other West European country.'[28]

Cees Nooteboom provided an epilogue for the German edition, in which he claims that *De donkere kamer van Damokles* created a thunderstorm in the Netherlands. Many critics incorporate this claim in their reviews and some of them add that the portrayal of the Dutch resistance in the novel 'as a grotesque, bloodstained joke, caused furious protests'.[29] This is in fact slightly exaggerated, since, as shown above, anger and protest were only present in a small section of the first interpretive community of *De donkere kamer van Damokles.*

Nevertheless, the altered mentality in both the Netherlands and Germany seems to have left its traces in the reception of the novel. German critics realize that neither the Dutch nor the Germans are to be judged as exclusively victims or perpetrators. This also clarifies why critics as Jähner and Henneberg stress that not every Dutchman (or -woman) was part of the resistance, and that in Germany not every person was a Nazi.[30] Although Hermans' philosophy can be considered separately from its origins in the author's experiences in the Second World War, like the Swedish critics had done, the German reviewers deliberately relate it to the German occupation of the Netherlands, although emphasizing other elements than the Norwegian critics tended to do.

Based on these observations, we may cautiously conclude that the difference in impact the Second World War has had in the three countries discussed, equally influenced the reception of *De donkere kamer van Damokles.* Sweden's neutrality during the war was responsible for the fact that it was not until the 1980s that the war became incorporated in the nation's collective memory. The reception of *Mörkrummet* in 1962 reflects this, since in most cases the occupation is not seen as the fundamental theme of the novel; it merely functions as a backdrop for broader epistemological issues. Norwegian reception is almost diametrically opposed to this. Even now, the grand narrative of the Second World War in Norway is still largely a story of black-and-white, presenting the resistance and the collaboration as sheer good and evil. This leaves little room for a 'grey' narrative, as put forward by Hermans and picked up by historians like Van der Heijden. The reception of *Damokles' Mørkerom* mirrors this. By contrast, the grey image of the war that the novel sketches seems to have fitted perfectly in the changing grand narrative in Germany at the beginning of the twenty-first century.

'HETEROLINGUALISM' AND 'OTHERNESS': *LA CHAMBRE NOIRE DE DAMOCLÈS*

As was the case with Johannes Piron's translation of *De donkere kamer van Damokles*, Hermans was also dissatisfied with the first French translation (1962), by Maurice Beerblock. In the 1970s he terminated a contract with Philippe Noble when the translator did not respect deadlines.[31] The 2006 French translation by Daniel Cunin hardly received media attention. Only after Milan Kundera had published an exultant review in *Le Monde* was the novel picked up by press and reading public.[32] In what follows we will use this French translation in order to investigate some of the ideological issues involved in translation as a process of cultural transfer. We will compare so-called 'heterolingual' passages in the original novel with the equivalent fragments in *La chambre noire de Damoclès*. Myriam Suchet defines 'heterolingualism' as follows: '[T]he staging of a more or less foreign language along a continuum of otherness constructed in and by a given discourse (or text).'[33]

The techniques Hermans employs to show the otherness of the different languages in *De donkere kamer van Damokles* are rather traditional. The novel is essentially written in Dutch (or in French as far as the translation is concerned). The other languages are mostly – but not exclusively – spoken by the German and the English characters or written down on packings and signboards. The different languages spoken by the characters in the novel are, in most cases, clearly demarcated. Generally, when a character speaks another language, this is simply mentioned by the narrator of the text, while the text itself is in Dutch, as in the following example:

> Toen zei de officier in zeer gearticuleerd Duits:
> – Neemt u mij niet kwalijk dat ik u aanspreek, zuster! Maar als ik zulke mooie ogen als de uwe zie schreien kan ik niet doorrijden of er niets aan de hand is.[34]

> [Then the officer addressed him in clearly articulated German:
> 'Forgive me for bothering you, Sister! But I simply couldn't just drive on after seeing such lovely eyes filled with tears.'][35]

In French:

> C'est le moment que l'officier choisit pour lui dire en allemand et en séparant bien les syllables:
> - Pardonnez-moi, mademoiselle, si je vous adresse la parole! Mais quand je vois pleurer d'aussi beaux yeux, je ne peux poursuivre mon chemin comme si de rien n'était.[36]

In some cases, however, dialogues in German are rendered in German and not graphically indicated by quotation marks, italics or small caps. Such an *unannounced* way to render the other language disturbs the linear flow of the reading process and interferes with the reader's expectations of a smooth transition to the otherness of the other language. On the other hand, these quotes in German are limited in length and quite easy to comprehend, especially with the help of the context. Even the Dutch characters in the story do not seem to experience difficulties in understanding what is going on. An example:

> De trein ging weer rijden. Hij reed nog geen minuut, of er kwamen twee mannen in leren jassen in de doorloop.
> Polizei! Ausweise bitte.
> - Dat ook nog! zei de vrouw [...].
> - Persohnsbeweise, bitte! zei de voorste man, terwijl hij zijn hand uitstak. [...]
> - Da stimmt was nicht. Kommen sie mal mit.
> Of 'Hé jij' erop gerekend had, stond zij onmiddellijk op en ging mee met de twee mannen in leer, zonder om te kijken.[37]

> [The train set off again. Almost immediately, two men in long leather coats came in from the corridor.
> Polizei! Ausweise bitte.
> 'Not that too!' said the woman. [...]
> 'Identity cards please,' said the man in front, extending his hand.
> 'Da stimmt was nicht. Kommen sie mal mit.'
> Something was wrong. As if expecting this, Hey You rose from her seat and went with the leather-coated duo. She did not look back.][38]

Yet, the 'otherness effect' is somehow reduced in the French translation, which has italics for passages in German and sometimes footnotes with translations in French, or, as in the following example, passages that are translated into

French but with characters pronouncing the words with a thick and exaggerated German accent:

> Le train se remit en route. Moins d'une minute plus tard, deux hommes en manteau de cuir s'engagèrent dans l'allée.
> – *Polizei ! Ausweise bitte.*
> – Manquait plus que ça ! fit la femme [...].
> – BaBié, zivoublé ! dit le premier des deux hommes tout en tendant le bras. [...]
> – *Da stimmt was nicht. Kommen sie mal mit.*[39]

The clear separation between the different languages is accompanied by a lot of 'couleur locale', giving the impression of a well-defined, recognizable and thus authentic reality. The presence of other languages even contributes to the strict demarcation of topographical areas, for example in the form of placards announcing areas where German soldiers are not allowed to go:

> Zij stonden voor een smal winkelraam. Osewoudt lichtte de bril op, knipperde een paar maal met zijn ogen en las op het raam
> INDISCH RESTAURANT PEMATANG SIANTAR
> Een witte kaart was rechts onder in de hoek van het raam achter het glas gezet en daarop stond in gotische letters
>
> **Für Wehrmachtsangehörige verboten**
> **Der Ortskommandant**[40]

> [They were standing in front of a narrow display window. Osewoudt raised the glasses, blinked a few times and read the sign on the pane:
> EAST INDIAN RESTAURANT PEMATANG SIANTAR
> There was a white card behind the glass in the lower right-hand corner, which said, in Gothic script:
> Für wehrmachtsangehörige verboten.
> Der Ortskommandant.][41]

Again, there is a clear separation between Dutch and German. Moreover, the otherness of the latter language is highlighted by the use of a Gothic font. At the same time, however, it is as if the placard also demonstrates a possible 'porosity': in the occupied Netherlands not everything is completely occupied by the other and his or her language. Some areas remain exclusively Dutch, and in this case Dutch Indonesian.

One could also argue that the previous examples demonstrate that the Dutch language allows some porosity with respect to the German language: the novel is written in Dutch, but other languages interfere with it. In fact, the Dutch language is much more occupied (and thus porous) than seems to be the case at first sight. This less obvious form of heterolingualism enables a better understanding of some of the ideological issues in the text, for instance with regard to the presence of proper nouns (brands included) and placards in the novel. Osewoudt does not experience them in their otherness. When the placard 'Für Wehrmachtsangehörige verboten' is mentioned for the first time, the female character Elly asks him for its meaning ('What does it mean?'), to which Osewoudt answers: 'It means,' said Osewoudt, 'that this part of town is unsafe for Germans, which makes it all the safer for us.'[42]

One can even argue that from the moment Osewoudt starts imitating Dorbeck – of whom the narrative never unambiguously discloses whether he is a resistance hero or a henchman of the German occupier –, the narrative marks him as having both an English and a German identity. This contradictory identity is in the first place evoked by his ambivalent deeds and his physical resemblance to Dorbeck, but it is also demonstrated by the brand names of certain products he possesses. For example, he repeatedly shows off his English cigarettes:

> He took a packet of Gold Flake from his pocket and said:
> 'Care for a smoke, Mr Meinarends? A real English cigarette. Do have one, I run a tobacco shop, you see.'[43]

This 'Englishness', which can be regarded an addition to Osewoudt's Dutch identity, has as its counterpart certain German objects, in particular the Leica-camera he possesses. Bearing this in mind, it is revealing that precisely this object is unable to prove his 'English' identity at the very end of the novel, when the roll of film in the Leica does not contain a picture that should have been on the film roll and that would have proved the existence of Dorbeck and subsequently Osewoudt's innocence.

In short, Osewoudt is not completely 'Dutch', he is marked by a certain 'Englishness' and by some 'Germanness' as well. Actually, this is consistent with Osewoudt's lack of genuine patriotism and passion for the good cause:

> My country, he thought, what's that supposed to mean? The blue tram? The yellow tram? The service is the same as before, except for the lights being dimmed after dark. A tobacco shop with empty packaging in the window? Dr Dushkind? North State? Havana cigars? I still have a packet of real English cigarettes on me. If Dorbeck hadn't asked me to develop a film for him I wouldn't have got mixed up in any of this. I'd be at home, safe and sound.[44]

After he is arrested, Osewoudt is transported to England where he is interrogated by English officers. The dialogues are predominantly in Dutch, even when the narrator mentions that they are in fact speaking English. In other words, when we read grammatically and orthographically correct Dutch spoken by the English officers, it is as if the narrator simultaneously translates what is being said. The narrator adds, however, that the English is difficult to understand for Osewoudt. In other situations, for instance when the officer 'really' speaks Dutch, quotations are rendered with an exaggerated English accent, unexpected word choices and with a distorted syntax:

> – De chef is niet vroeg vandaag, zei de jongeman in het Engels, dat is hij trouwens meestal niet.
> Osewoudt kon het met moeite verstaan, maar durfde geen antwoord te geven.
> Toen ging de deur open en een lange man in een bruin tweed pak stapte naar het bureau, waar hij een blauwe map op legde.
> – Ik toevallig ben kolonel Smears, zei hij in het Nederlands, ik ben zeer gelukkig een kleine conversatie met oe te khunnen hebben. Well Percy, how's everything this beautiful morning?
> – Quite well sir, thank you. [...]
> – Well, well, een mooie dag voor de tijd van het jaar. Maar eerst een drop van whisky, juist een drop.[45]

> ['The boss did not arrive early today,' said the young man in English. 'He seldom does.'
> Osewoudt understood with some difficulty what he was saying, but did not trust himself to reply.
> Then the door opened and a tall man in a brown tweed suit entered. He went up to the desk, on which he deposited a blue folder.
> 'I am Colonel Smears, by the way,' he said in heavily accented Dutch. 'I am very glad of this opportunity to have a little conversation with you.'
> Turning to the young man at the typewriter, he switched to English, saying: 'Well Percy, how is everything this beautiful morning?'
> 'Quite well, sir, thank you.' [...]
> 'Well, well, a fine day for the time of year,' he said, reverting to his anglicized form of Dutch. 'But we'll start with a drop of whisky, just a drop.'][46]

Osewoudt's difficulties in understanding the other are less stressed in the French translation. The proper English is italicized and when Smears tries to speak Dutch, these (now French) passages have an accent that is less 'English' than was the case in the original:

> – Le chef n'est pas en avance aujourd'hui, constata le jeune homme en anglais, il ne l'est d'ailleurs pas souvent.

> Avec quelques difficultés, Osewoudt comprit ce que l'autre disait, mais n'osa pas lui répondre.
> La porte s'ouvrit et alors un homme élancé, vêtu d'un costume de tweed brun, s'avança vers le grand bureau sur lequel il posa une chemise bleue.
> – Je suis par chance le colonel Smears, dit-il en hollandais, je suis très content de faire une petite conversation avec vous. *Well, Percy, how's everything this beautiful morning?*
> – *Quite well, sir, thank you.* [...]
> – *Well, well,* belle journée pour la saison. Mais pour commencer, une gouttelette de whisky, juste une gouttelette.[47]

In other words, in the French translation the Dutch is less altered by the other's language than in the original. There is still noticeable heterolingual porosity in this passage, but this time the porosity is no longer a component of Osewoudt's identity. The language porosity is now externalized as a phenomenon situated outside of him. Moreover, this phenomenon is threatening rather than positive, as it forces Osewoudt to reconcile himself with a given but well-delineated identity: a dangerous war criminal. In other words, Osewoudt experiences his identity as positive as long as it is porous and occupied by otherness and/or other languages. This is consistent with Osewoudt's fear that his Jewish girlfriend Marianne might in fact be more in love with Dorbeck than with himself. Osewoudt knows that he is attractive and heroic since he obeys Dorbeck and acts and looks like him.[48]

The heterolingual discourse can contribute to the recognition of otherness. We all are somehow heterolingual subjects, and our singularity, as others perceive it, is partly based on the identity we construct through our languages. The heterolingual discourse functions as a ratification of this distinction-creating process: the heterolingual 'I', through the singular discourse he or she produces, radically constructs himself or herself as 'other' than 'I'. This process of creating a distinctive identity also takes place in Hermans' novel, except that it is exclusively one-sided, exclusively oriented towards the otherness in which the 'I' projects his self-image, until the moment the 'I' has to realize that this otherness – which is supposed to have its 'own', consistent identity – is always already something else than what he thought it was. In the case of Osewoudt, it means that the otherness, unfortunately, has become a kind of black hole that he will never succeed to define, and in which he has lost his way.

As we have seen, the French translation has the tendency to reduce the effects of this heterolingual discourse upon the reader. Accordingly, the ideological issues which the Dutch original discloses are partially lost in the process of cultural transfer, although not fundamentally. This is borne out by Milan Kundera: what he appreciated most in *La chambre noire de Damoclès,* was in the end the 'black poetry' of the novel: the moral ambiguity that always surrounds Osewoudt and his actions. Kundera's review is in fact an exposé of his own literary poetics, and in Hermans he found a writer whom he considered a soulmate. In their view, characters who are morally confused frequently end up as a victim of their own illusions.

CONCLUSIONS

We briefly examined some ideological aspects of cultural transfer and transmission on two different levels, one text-external and one text-internal. In the external case, we looked at the reception of translations of *De donkere kamer van Damokles* in Sweden, Norway and Germany. The references to the political-historical context show that there is a connection between the interpretation and evaluation of the novel and the receiving culture's socio-political situation during and in the wake of the war. In the internal case, we examined the ways in which a translator might cope with the covert ideology within a text, for instance in cases of problematic communication caused by language differences and hierarchies. Certain 'heterolingual' aspects and 'otherness effects' disappeared in the transfer process, some of which were a result of decisions made by the translator.

Similar explorative inquiries into other translations of the novel can contribute to our knowledge of the processes of cultural transfer and transmission of Hermans' *De donkere kamer van Damokles.* From a comparative perspective, research could be extended t o other texts of the same author, and even extrapolated to other forms of adaptation of his works, such as plays and movies. The production of *Beyond Sleep* (2016), an international film adaptation of *Nooit meer slapen*, shows that Hermans is still crossing borders in a variety of ways, creating new opportunities for future research.

NOTES

1 See for example P. Broomans and M. Ronne (eds.), *In the Vanguard of the Cultural Transfer: Cultural Transmitters and Authors in Peripheral Literary Fields* (Groningen: Barkhuis, 2010), and P. Broomans, S. van Voorst and K. Smits (eds.), *Rethinking Cultural Transfer and Transmission: Reflections and New Perspectives* (Groningen: Barkhuis, 2012).

2 B. Stroman, 'Inhalen verboden: wanhoop en sterf: De onvolwaardige held als stuk van overtuiging voor het immoralisme', in *Algemeen Handelsblad*, 21 February 1959. (Unless stated otherwise all quotations from Dutch sources have been translated into English by the authors.)

3 J. Last, 'De defloratie van het verzet', in *De Nieuwe Stem* 14 (1959), pp. 306-310.

4 See for example D. Betlem, 'De geboorte van een dubbelganger', in *Merlyn* 4: 4 (1966), pp. 276-290; D. Betlem, 'Van Jean Paul tot Van der Waals: Nogmaals "De geboorte van een dubbelganger"', in *Raster* 1: 1 (1967), pp. 71-94; J. Weisgerber, 'Proefvlucht in de literaire ruimte (4)', in *Nieuw Vlaams Tijdschrift* 21: 4 (1968), pp. 358-380; R. Delvigne, 'Als twee druppels water?', in *De Revisor* 1: 9-10 (1974), pp. 14-22; G.J.P. Hoek and C.B.M. Wingen,

'De donkere kamer; perspektief en interpretatie van het gebeuren in *De donkere kamer van Damokles* van Willem Frederik Hermans', in *De Nieuwe Taalgids* 67: 2 (1974), pp. 89-118; M. Dupuis, *Eenheid en versplintering van het ik: Een onderzoek naar thema's, motieven en vormen in verband met de problematiek van de enkeling in het verhalend werk van Willem Frederik Hermans* (Hasselt: Heideland-Orbis, 1976); W. Smulders, *De literaire misleiding in De donkere kamer van Damokles* (Utrecht: Hes, 1983); A. Kooyman, '"De donkere kamer van Damokles": een constructie-analyse', in *Forum der letteren* 29: 2 (1988), pp. 116-123; S. Pos, *Dorbeck is alles! Navolging als sleutel tot enkele romans en verhalen van W.F. Hermans* (Amsterdam: Vossiuspers, 2010).

5 W. Otterspeer, *Dorbeck, waar ben je? Een biografisch essay over De donkere kamer van Damokles* (Amsterdam: De Bezige Bij, 2012), p. 86.

6 C. van der Heijden, *Grijs verleden: Nederland en de Tweede Wereldoorlog* (Amsterdam: Contact, 2001), pp. 15-16.

7 See S. Fish, *Is There a Text in This Class? The Authority of Interpretive Communities* (Cambridge: Harvard University Press, 1980), pp. 147-174.

8 H. Eickmans, 'W.F. Hermans in Duitsland', in *Filter* 9: 1 (2002), p. 49.

9 J. Glerum, *Willem Frederik Hermans (1921-1995) / De donkere kamer van Damokles (1958)*, informatiebrochure bij de tentoonstelling 'Willem Frederik Hermans terug in Amsterdam', Openbare Bibliotheek Amsterdam, Fall 2011.

10 Eickmans, 'W.F. Hermans in Duitsland', p. 50.

11 R. Overy, 'Scandinavia in the Second World War', in J. Gillmour and J. Stephenson (eds.), *Hitler's Scandinavian Legacy: The Consequences of the German Invasion for the Scandinavian Countries, Then and Now* (London: Bloomsbury, 2013), pp. 29-30.

12 J. Östling, 'Realism and Idealism: Swedish Narratives of the Second World War: Historiography and Interpretation in the Post-War Era', in Gillmour and Stephenson (eds.), *Hitler's Scandinavian Legacy*, p. 185.

13 O.K. Grimnes, 'Hitler's Norwegian Legacy', in Gillmour and Stephenson (eds.), *Hitler's Scandinavian Legacy*, p. 160.

14 Grimnes, 'Hitler's Norwegian Legacy', p. 168.

15 B. Niven, 'Introduction: The Inclusive Picture', in B. Niven (ed.), *Facing the Nazi Past: United Germany and the Legacy of the Third Reich* (London: Routledge, 2002), p. 3.

16 Niven, 'Introduction: The Inclusive Picture', p. 2.

17 B. Niven and C.E.M. Paver, 'Introduction', in B. Niven and C.E.M. Paver (eds.), *Memorialization in Germany Since 1945* (Basingstoke: Palgrave Macmillan, 2010), p. 5.

18 U. Asplund, 'Krig på fy', in *Göteborgs handels- och sjöfarts Tidning*, 25 September 1962.

19 Ö. Wallqvist, 'Ny holländsk mästare', in *Stockholms Tidningen*, 7 November 1962.

20 I.S., 'Vilse i kriget', in *Jönköpings-Posten*, 15 September 1962.

21 Ph. Houm, 'En bok av usedvanlig slagkraft?' in *Dagbladet*, 20 April 1962.

22 E. Rasmussen, 'Hvem er Dorbeck?' in *Aftenposten*, 4 April 1962.

23 N.C. Brøgger, 'Den gule serie gjenoppstår', in *Nationen*, 10 April 1962.

24 H. Haavardsholm, 'Ny "gul" fra Nederland', in *Arbeiderbladet*, 26 March 1962.

25 W. Dahl, 'Frihetskampen som galehus', in *Bergens Arbeiderblad*, 20 March 1962.

26 F. Isaksson, 'Mannen i mörkrummet', in *Dagens Nyheter*, 18 June 1962.

27 A. von Bormann, 'Der Pfahl im Fleische: Ein großer Niederländer zum Wiederentdecken: Willem Frederik Hermans', in *Die Welt*, 15 December 2001.

28 H. Jähner, 'Die Doppelgänger: Einer der berühmtesten niederländischen Romane erscheint endlich auf Deutch – nach mehr als vierzig Jahren', in *Berliner Zeitung*, 12 January 2002.

29 W. Höbel, 'Henri, der Held', in *Der Spiegel*, 14 January 2002.

30 Jähner, 'Die Doppelgänger'; N. Henneberg, 'Die Tränen des Herrn Osewoudt wiederentdeckt: Ein Agententhriller des holländischen Existenzialisten Willem Frederik Hermans', in *Der Tagesspiegel*, 27 January 2002.

31 See for example A. Fransen, *W.F. Hermans, een Hollander in Parijs* (Amsterdam: De Bezige Bij, 2005) and J.P. van der Sterre, 'De duistere hoeken van de donkere kamer: W.F. Hermans in het Frans, Duits en Engels', in *Filter* 14: 4 (2007), pp. 39-50.

32 M. Kundera, 'La poésie noire et l'ambiguïté: "La chambre noire de Damoclès", une oeuvre capitale, pourtant passée inaperçue, de Willem Frederik Hermans', in *Le Monde*, 26 January 2007.

33 M. Suchet, *L'Imaginaire hétérolingue: Ce que nous apprennent les textes à la croisée des langues* (Paris: Garnier, 2014), p. 19. ('[L]a mise en scène d'une langue plus ou moins étrangère le long d'un continuum d'altérité construit dans et par un discours (ou un texte) donné.')

34 W.F. Hermans, *Volledige Werken, 3. Romans. De donkere kamer van Damokles; Nooit meer slapen*. Jan Gielkens and Peter Kegel (eds.) (Amsterdam: De Bezige Bij, 2010), p. 283.

35 W.F. Hermans, *The Darkroom of Damocles*. Transl. Ina Rilke (London: Harvill Secker, 2007), p. 268.

36 W.F. Hermans, *La chambre noire de Damoclès*. Transl. Daniel Cunin (Paris: Gallimard, 2006), p. 338.

37 Hermans, *Volledige Werken, 3*, p. 165.

38 Hermans, *The Darkroom of Damocles*, p. 156.

39 Hermans, *La chambre noire de Damoclès*, pp. 196-197.

40 Hermans, *Volledige Werken, 3*, p. 80.

41 Hermans, *The Darkroom of Damocles*, p. 73.

42 "Wat betekent dat bord?" / "het betekent [...] dat deze buurt voor Duitsers onveilig is, maar voor ons des te veiliger." Hermans, *Volledige Werken, 3*, p. 68. English translation: Hermans, *The Darkroom of Damocles*, p. 61.

43 "Hij haalde een pakje Gold Flake uit zijn zak en zei: 'Wilt u roken, meneer Meinarends? Een echte Engelse sigaret. Gaat u gerust uw gang, ik heb een sigarenwinkel.'" Hermans, *Volledige Werken, 3*, p. 85. English translation: Hermans, *The Darkroom of Damocles*, p. 78.

44 "Vaderland, wat is dat? dacht hij. De blauwe tram? De gele tram? Ze rijden nu even goed als vroeger, alleen 's avonds met weinig licht. Een sigarenwinkel met ledig expositiemateriaal achter het glas? Dr. Dushkind? North State? Karel Eén? Ik heb echte Engelse sigaretten op zak. Als Dorbeck mij niet gevraagd had een rolfilmpje voor hem te ontwikkelen dan zou ik nergens wat mee te maken hebben. Dan zat ik nu rustig thuis." Hermans, *Volledige Werken, 3*, pp. 89-90. English translation: Hermans, *The Darkroom of Damocles*, pp. 82-83.

45 Hermans, *Volledige Werken, 3*, p. 312.

46 Hermans, *The Darkroom of Damocles*, p. 297.

47 Hermans, *La chambre noire de Damoclès*, pp. 373-374.

48 Hermans, *Volledige Werken, 3*, p. 216.

BIBLIOGRAPHY

Asplund, U., 'Krig på fy', in *Göteborgs handels- och sjöfarts Tidning*, 25 September 1962.

Betlem, D., 'De geboorte van een dubbelganger', in *Merlyn* 4: 4 (1966), pp. 276-290.

Betlem, D., 'Van Jean Paul tot Van der Waals: Nogmaals "De geboorte van een dubbelganger"', in *Raster* 1: 1 (1967), pp. 71-94.

Bormann, A. von., 'Der Pfahl im Fleische. Ein gro⊠er Niederländer zum Wiederentdecken: Willem Frederik Hermans', in *Die Welt*, 15 December 2001.

Brøgger, N.C., 'Den gule serie gjenoppstår', in *Nationen*, 10 April 1962.

Broomans, P. and M. Ronne (eds.), *In the Vanguard of the Cultural Transfer: Cultural Transmitters and Authors in Peripheral Literary Fields* (Groningen: Barkhuis, 2010).

Broomans, P., Voorst, S. van and K. Smits (eds.), *Rethinking Cultural Transfer and Transmission: Reflections and New Perspectives* (Groningen: Barkhuis, 2012).

Dahl, W., 'Frihetskampen som galehus', in *Bergens Arbeiderblad*, 20 March 1962.

Delvigne, R., 'Als twee druppels water?', in *De Revisor* 1: 9-10 (1974), pp. 14-22.

Dupuis, M., *Eenheid en versplintering van het ik: Een onderzoek naar thema's, motieven en vormen in verband met de problematiek van de enkeling in het verhalend werk van Willem Frederik Hermans* (Hasselt: Heideland-Orbis, 1976).

Eickmans, H., 'W.F. Hermans in Duitsland', in *Filter* 9: 1 (2002), pp. 49-52.

Fish, S., *Is There a Text in This Class? The Authority of Interpretive Communities*, (Cambridge: Harvard University Press, 1980).

Fransen, A., *W.F. Hermans, een Hollander in Parijs* (Amsterdam: De Bezige Bij, 2005).

Glerum, J., *Willem Frederik Hermans (1921-1995) / De donkere kamer van Damokles (1958)*, Informatiebrochure bij de tentoonstelling 'Willem Frederik Hermans terug in Amsterdam', Openbare Bibliotheek Amsterdam, Fall 2011.

Grimnes, O.K., 'Hitler's Norwegian Legacy', in J. Gillmour and J. Stephenson (eds.), *Hitler's Scandinavian Legacy: The Consequences of the German Invasion for the Scandinavian Countries, Then and Now* (London: Bloomsbury, 2013), pp. 159-177.

Haavardsholm, H., 'Ny "gul" fra Nederland', in *Arbeiderbladet*, 26 March 1962.

Heijden, C. van der, *Grijs verleden: Nederland en de Tweede Wereldoorlog* (Amsterdam: Contact, 2001).

Henneberg, N., 'Die Tränen des Herrn Osewoudt wiederentdeckt: Ein Agententhriller des holländischen Existenzialisten Willem Frederik Hermans', in *Der Tagesspiegel*, 27 January 2002.

Hermans, W.F., *La chambre noire de Damoclès*, transl. D. Cunin (Paris: Gallimard, 2006).

Hermans, W.F., *Damokles' Mørkerom*, transl. B. Braaten (Oslo: Gyldendal Norsk Forlag, 1962).

Hermans, W.F. *The Darkroom of Damocles*, transl. I. Rilke (London: Harvill Secker, 2007).

Hermans, W.F., *Mörkrummet*, transl. B. Dahlman (Stockholm: P.A. Norstedt & Söners Förlag, 1962).

Hermans, W.F., *Volledige Werken. 3. Romans. De donkere kamer van Damokles; Nooit meer slapen*, Jan Gielkens and Peter Kegel (eds.) (Amsterdam: De Bezige Bij, 2010).

Höbel, W., 'Henri, der Held', in *Der Spiegel*, 14 January 2002.

Hoek, G.J.P. van and C.B.M. Wingen, 'De donkere kamer: perspektief en interpretatie van het gebeuren in *De donkere kamer van Damokles* van Willem Frederik Hermans', in *De Nieuwe Taalgids* 67: 2 (1974), pp. 89-118.

Houm, P., 'En bok av usedvanlig slagkraft?', in *Dagbladet*, 20 April 1962.

Isaksson, F., 'Mannen i mörkrummet', in *Dagens Nyheter*, 18 June 1962.

Jähner, H., 'Die Doppelgänger: Einer der berühmtesten niederländischen Romane erscheint endlich auf Deutsch – nach mehr als vierzig Jahren', in *Berliner Zeitung*, 12 January 2002.

Kooyman, A., '"De donkere kamer van Damokles": een constructie-analyse', in *Forum der letteren* 29: 2 (1988), pp. 116-23.

Kundera, M., 'La poésie noire et l'ambiguïté: "La chambre noire de Damoclès", une oeuvre capitale, pourtant passée inaperçue, de Willem Frederik Hermans', in *Le Monde*, 26 January 2007.

Last, J., 'De defloratie van het verzet', in *De Nieuwe Stem* 14 (1959), pp. 306-310.

Niven, B., 'Introduction: The Inclusive Picture', in B. Niven (ed.), *Facing the Nazi Past. United Germany and the Legacy of the Third Reich* (London: Routledge, 2002), pp. 1-9.

Niven, B. and C.E.M. Paver, 'Introduction', in B. Niven and C.E.M. Paver (eds.), *Memorialization in Germany Since 1945* (Basingstoke: Palgrave Macmillan, 2010), pp. 1-12.

Östling, J., 'Realism and Idealism: Swedish Narratives of the Second World War: Historiography and Interpretation in the Post-War Era', in J. Gillmour and J. Stephenson (eds.), *Hitler's Scandinavian Legacy: The Consequences of the German Invasion for the Scandinavian Countries, Then and Now* (London: Bloomsbury, 2013), pp. 179-197.

Otterspeer, W., *Dorbeck, waar ben je? Een biografisch essay over De donkere kamer van Damokles* (Amsterdam: De Bezige Bij, 2012).

Overy, R., 'Scandinavia in the Second World War', in J. Gillmour and J. Stephenson (eds.), *Hitler's Scandinavian Legacy: The Consequences of the German Invasion for the Scandinavian Countries, Then and Now* (London: Bloomsbury, 2013), pp. 13-37.

Pos, S., *Dorbeck is alles! Navolging als sleutel tot enkele romans en verhalen van W.F. Hermans* (Amsterdam: Vossiuspers, 2010).

Rasmussen, E., 'Hvem er Dorbeck?', in *Aftenposten*, 4 April 1962.

S., I., 'Vilse i kriget', in *Jönköpings-Posten*, 15 September 1962.

Smulders, W., *De literaire misleiding in De donkere kamer van Damokles* (Utrecht: Hes, 1983).

Sterre, J. P. van der, 'De duistere hoeken van de donkere kamer: W.F. Hermans in het Frans, Duits en Engels', in *Filter* 14: 4 (2007), pp. 39-50.

Stroman, B., 'Inhalen verboden: wanhoop en sterf: De onvolwaardige held als stuk van overtuiging voor het immoralisme', in *Algemeen Handelsblad*, 21 February 1959.

Suchet, M., *L'Imaginaire hétérolingue: Ce que nous apprennent les textes à la croisée des langues* (Paris: Garnier, 2014).

Wallqvist, Ö., 'Ny holländsk mästare', in *Stockholms Tidningen*, 7 November 1962.

Weisgerber, J., 'Proefvlucht in de literaire ruimte (4)', in *Nieuw Vlaams Tijdschrift* 21: 4 (1968), pp. 358-380.

CHAPTER 16

'Unexpectedly Moving'[1]?

An Inquiry into the Intermedial and International Trajectory of a Flemish Novel

Elke Brems (University of Leuven, Belgium),
Pieter Boulogne (University of Leuven & Ghent University, Belgium),
Stéphanie Vanasten (University of Louvain-la-Neuve, Belgium)

The novel *De helaasheid der dingen* [*The Misfortunates*] by the Dutch-speaking Belgian (Flemish) writer Dimitri Verhulst has not gone unnoticed since it was first published in 2006. By March 2016 it had already reached its 60th impression and in both Flanders and the Netherlands it has had steady sales for the last ten years. Not only does the novel have robust sales and a sizeable readership, it has also been very well received by literary critics. The combination of popular success and critical acclaim indicates that the book is firmly established as a core text in the Dutch-speaking literary field. The novel has a wide circulation, too, outside the Dutch and Belgian borders. Up until the beginning of 2016 it had been translated into seventeen different languages, which is exceptional for a contemporary Flemish novel.[2] Furthermore, in 2008 the novel was adapted by the director Felix Van Groeningen into a film which in its turn has had widespread distribution, nationally and internationally, with great success. The cultural dissemination of Verhulst's narrative raises the question of the cultural acceptance by a global audience of local-culture-bound works: what make narratives, even from a small language area, more likely to achieve an international circulation, either in book form or in the form of other media?

De helaasheid der dingen (literally 'The Alas-ness of things'[3]) is a partly autobiographical novel; the protagonist is also called Dimitri Verhulst. The young Dimitri grows up in the fictitious Flemish town of Reetveerdegem, surrounded by alcohol, trash and his completely useless and sexist father and uncles. Notwithstanding his underprivileged family background, he manages to escape the life that seemed to await him. The book has a first-person narrator who recalls a few key scenes from his own youth in a tone that mixes irony and nostalgia. The film tells more or less the same story, but adds a narrative frame in which the adult narrator has become a writer: the gap between the young and the adult protagonist is emphasised.

A comparative and interdisciplinary analysis of the broader international circulation of Dimitri Verhulst's successful novel offers an opportunity to gain insight into two contemporaneous phenomena that have received much critical attention in recent years, but which rarely lead to complementary research approaches. The first is the cultural transfer of Dutch-language literature across languages and across geographical and political areas. The second is the 'extension' or 'diversion'[4] of Dutch literature across media, covering intermedial transposition from book to another medium, as in, for example, the adaptation into film of Verhulst's book.[5] In studying the way in which *De helaasheid der dingen* has been taken up in other countries, it has proved to be crucial to take into account both the translational and intermedial manifestations of the novel. In some countries (e.g. Russia) the book or the film made their way in the host culture quite independently of each other; in other countries, such as France, the book was published after the release of the film and the favourable response to it. Conscious of this interaction, the Flemish Literature Fund [*Vlaams Fonds voor de Letteren*], which has funded no fewer than thirteen of the available translations, uses the film to promote the book at international book fairs. The study of the transposition of *De helaasheid der dingen* abroad reveals how book, translations and film-adaptation have become different artistic expressions in a network around one narrative, challenging the traditional two-way distinction between 'original' source text and 'derivative' target work and stressing the dynamic nature of relations between the cultures involved.

The present paper builds on research concerning *De helaasheid der dingen* conducted within the framework of CODL. This collective research studied the critical reception and the spread of the novel, the book-translations, the film adaptation and the audiovisual translations in eight languages and countries (Italy, Portugal, Japan, South Korea, Poland, the Czech Republic, France, Russia). It brought together academics, translators, audiovisual translators and the author himself to discuss a wide range of aspects related to the circulation of this particular novel.[6] Taking as a starting point the synthesis of the results of this focus group, the current contribution discusses the dynamic complexity of exchange between Dutch-language literary works and their multi-semiotic and cross-cultural circulation abroad, by reflecting on the translation of culture-specific elements, including linguistic items (such as idioms, locutions, dialects or intratextual references).

To study the successful international trajectory of a novel in translation, contextual as well as textual factors have to be taken into account. In her introduction to the book *Traduire la littérature et les sciences humaines. Conditions et obstacles* Sapiro reminds us that apart from the text itself, the cultural and economic context are important factors in whether or not a translated work gets published.[7] One crucial factor is, as we know from research about culture specific items in Translation Studies, the relationship between source culture and target culture: how familiar is the source culture to the target culture? Are the two cultures related in any way(s)? Venuti underlines how by translating a cultural work written in a foreign language 'certain domestic values (are privileged) to the exclusion of others.'[8] He further explains:

> when translation projects reflect the interests of a specific cultural constituency [...] the resulting image of the foreign culture may still achieve national dominance, accepted by many readers in the domestic culture whatever their social position may be.[9]

Migozzi considers that what is of prime importance in the spread, geographically, of some narratives, works or genres is that the target culture should be able to recognise itself:

> the more national societies [...] are able to recognise themselves – in every sense – in these fictional mirrors, the more likely they are to welcome them and to metabolise them.[10]

Thus Migozzi emphasizes the importance of self-images while Venuti gives weight to the acceptance of foreign culture images. In both cases, however, what is at issue in increasing the likelihood of a successful transfer process is recognition: the target culture recognises itself, or the target culture recognises a picture of the other that it already holds.[11]

The self- and hetero-images held by the target culture play an important role in the transfer of cultural products, but successful transfer does not depend solely on the predisposition of the target culture. The source culture is, of course, also an important player in the spread of its own literature. The example of the funding provided for translations of *De helaasheid der dingen* by the Flemish Literature Fund is evidence of that. And it is not just source culture and target culture which have a role to play in this respect. As Espagne points out with his notion of 'Tiers impliqués' ('implicated third parties'), often intermediary cultures have to be taken into account.[12] This is illustrated by the role of the German translation of *De helaasheid der dingen*, which appeared only a year after the publication of 'the original' and then paved the way for other translations.[13] The Chinese translation in 2013, too, was an indirect translation via the English version a year before. In addition, the role of the global cultural network (where book as well as film won international prizes) and the way in which some works chime with the spirit of certain times[14] prove that it is necessary to look beyond binary oppositions of source and target cultures and to consider dynamic and changing interactions between the cultures involved.

Attention to contextual factors must be matched by attention to factors relating to the text itself. Apart from geopolitical, economic and cultural considerations, are some texts in themselves more apt to be accepted by other cultures? On the basis of his interest in popular and mass culture in Europe between 1830 and 1940, Migozzi also focuses on text-poetical or fictional criteria in order to explain the recurrence of some narrative characters and archetypes in a cultural-historical dynamic: he mentions the genre of the work (and whether the genre has a tradition (or not) in the receiving culture), its characters and their potential for becoming heroes or anti-heroes, and its affinity (or not) with topoi and iconic images at a given historical or political moment.[15] Research shows that film adaptation, too, accelerates the transnational circulation of some narratives by 'a supra-national homogenizing of genres since it adds to the power of the codes of cinematic narrative to override certain national traditions'.[16] Could, then, the genre of Verhulst's book as *Bildungsroman*, its alcoholic characters as universally recognizable anti-heroes and some iconic images of Belgian or Flemish culture explain the narrative's successful circulation? And what about the film adaptation and the transnational matrix of the story? Starting from his hypothesis that international success in the film industry cannot be directly correlated with the use of widely-known languages,[17] Cattrysse similarly states as the condition for the message which is to be translated, that 'it must function in an efficient way in an international context,' which generally speaking, according to him, 'has nothing to do with genre'.[18] Cattrysse harks back to Aristotle and his six levels of audience appeal, in which, next to plot, character, theme, spectacle and song (or music), language is 'clearly one aspect of a communicational whole'.[19] On the basis of this framework, he observes that American cinema, in a search for 'universals,' has from the beginning aimed to 'enhance maximal empathy from an international audience'.[20]

Against the background of his research into the way in which popular and mass culture move from place to place, Migozzi also believes that the universal is more fit for export than the local:

> exportability seems to be enhanced in the case of those narratives and narrative elements which have a *universal* dimension, in other words motifs, scenarios and heroes which are attractive to all kinds of audiences because of their deterritorialized narrativity, and which are cultivated or cultivable on foreign soil, in a manner of speaking.[21]

Migozzi goes on to say that for the original popular work to be translated it has to be 'cut loose from a national framing discourse' in the way, for instance, of works set in exotic places, such as 'the patriotic colonial novel' which, however, 'due to its over-reliance on a national interdiscourse, lends itself very badly to being exported'.[22] According to Migozzi, it is harder to transfer 'the genres and characters that are linked to a constraining territorial referentiality and/or to a cultural or political communal complicity [...],' that is, 'culturally codified'.[23] How can the transfer of locally-bound aspects of a narrative, and of culture-specific elements, be reconciled with the importance of the universal, which is the hallmark of the popular success of multimedia adaptation and translation, if we are to believe Cattrysse and Migozzi?

The author and academic Tim Parks bemoans the era of the Dull New Global Novel, deliberately written with the aim of being internationally successful.

> What seems doomed to disappear [...] is the kind of work that revels in the subtle nuances of its own language and literary culture, the sort of writing that can savage or celebrate the way this or that linguistic group really lives. [...] Writing in the 1960s, intensely engaged with his own culture and its complex politics, Hugo Claus apparently did not care that his novels would require a special effort on the reader's and above all the translator's part if they were to be understood outside his native Belgium'.[24]

For his part, Parks is convinced that 'culturally coded' novels require a special effort on the part of the 'foreign' reader, and especially the translator. But in his opinion this should not prevent novels from having a successful international career.

From the point of view of the transmission and comprehensibility of culture-bound elements, and the possible degree of opacity or difficult interpretation for a target reader, *De helaasheid der dingen* can be called a culturally coded novel, but it has had a successful international career, as book and as film. Does this mean that within the eight language areas which make up the corpus used here, the target culture has a high level of familiarity with the book? That, for example, Flanders and Belgium have a cultural image abroad which the book fits in a recognizable way? Or does it mean that the culturally-bound details of the novel were not seen as important, or not seen as culture-specific? Perhaps the decisive factor was the existence of universal features of the book, such as its genre as a *Bildungsroman* or its themes of alcoholism and neglect? Or is it that the translation and adaptation processes transferred the culturally-bound elements to a new cultural anchor ('a code switch'), substituting typically Polish or South Korean elements for typically Flemish ones? Our research question relates to this matter: how was the local, Flemish interpretation of the book – not as a given, fixed identity but as a language-embedded and perceived characteristic of the book – transferred across geographical and linguistic boundaries (via translation) and across media boundaries (via film adaptation), giving rise to transformations of the novel?

How have book translators and audiovisual translators rendered the meanings, connotations and historical-social values that are inseparable from the regional features of the work? In what follows, we examine the culture-bound linguistic usage and the culture-specific elements in *De helaasheid der dingen* as quintessential manifestations of the text's cultural anchoring. We investigate what happens to these on a textual level in the course of translation and adaptation and how they figure in the critical reception of the novel and its translations and adaptations.

THE FLEMISH CHARACTER OF THE SOURCE TEXT

Before we explore the treatment of linguistic usage and culture-specific elements in translations of *De helaasheid der dingen* and in the (translated) film version of the book, we must first examine the way in which these elements are handled in the source text itself and how their treatment is reflected in the critical reception of the book.

As far as the linguistic aspects of the book are concerned, *De helaasheid der dingen* contains a certain amount of non-standard language. Verhulst uses idiosyncratic, but also regional or local Flemish dialect words which diverge from standard Dutch in various ways – geographically, stylistically, sociolinguistically, in terms of register, and in terms of politeness. Examples of this lexis are 'mazout', which is generally used in Belgium, but not the Netherlands, to mean 'heating oil', but which in Belgium can also refer to a mixture of beer and Coca Cola, as it does in the novel; 'nonkel', a Flemish word for 'uncle' ('oom' in standard Dutch); and 'poepen', meaning 'to screw' (in the sexual sense) while in standard Dutch the word means 'to defecate'. To the average reader in the Netherlands, the text as a whole comes over as 'Flemish' rather than as standard Dutch. Verhulst, however, suggests that this view is flawed:

> What I notice, and this is not a criticism, is that Dutch people very often think that a word is not Dutch. If I then say that the word is in the [standard Dutch dictionary] Van Dale, they are sometimes unnerved. There is a huge group of words in Dutch which Dutch people think are Flemish dialect, but that is absolutely not the case.[25]

The writer emphasizes that he really did write his book in Dutch and not some other language. He goes on to quip that the translation rights are available to purchase: 'They're welcome to translate it into Dutch. I'm very curious to see what a translation would look like, I'd like to read it.'[26] This discussion points up the difference between on the one hand the objectively defined distribution and acceptability of linguistic forms and linguistic variants and on the other hand the sociolinguistic perception of these forms and variants by different user groups (education, social background, social class, age group).

Apart from the 'Flemish' character that these linguistic features contribute to the book, *couleur locale* is also evoked by the introduction of culture-specific realia. Thus we find the Aalst carnival, which is famous in Flanders for its parade of men dressed as women and for the excessive amount of alcohol consumed in the course of the event. Another example is the name of the village in which *De helaasheid der dingen* is set. Although fictive, the name Reetverdegem has a rich Flemish coloration. First, various places in Flanders have names which end in the suffix -degem or -gem. Second, the stem of the word, 'reet', which means 'arse' in vulgar usage, not only replicates the name of a genuine village, Reet, but also evokes associations with the so-called 'anal triangle'. This is a geographical area in Flanders which is located between three places, Reet, Aartselaar and Kontich, whose names have scatological associations: 'aarts-' recalls the word 'aars', which means 'arse', and 'kont' means 'bottom', 'backside'. In Flemish consciousness this area is associated with marginalization. Locality-bound realia turn up not just in the text but also in the paratext. Thus a sansevieria houseplant (often called 'mother-in-law's tongue') adorns the book jacket of the Dutch-language edition of *De helaasheid der dingen*. This plant can be seen in numerous front windows not just in Flanders but also, for example, in Wallonia. For many Flemish, and indeed Belgian, readers, this plant is a very familiar image.

Both Flemish and Dutch critics have interpreted the novel as a typical Flemish book. They situated it in the well-known genre of roots novel, which for some critics, especially Dutch ones, was a source of irritation. Representative in this respect is the following comment from literary critic Max Pam in the Dutch newspaper *De Tijd*:

> Can we finally have an end to Louis Paul Boon clones? [...] We reformed Dutch love reading that sort of folklore and the Flemings have no scruples in keeping us supplied with what we want. [...] it seems to me that it would be much better for Flemish literature if they just buried Louis Paul Boon.[27]

Not everyone shares the 'regional' interpretation. The literary criticism appears to be even more stereotyped than the genre that is under criticism, as appears from a (self-) mocking reaction from the Flemish writer Herman Brusselmans:

> [...] in this way it is a typically Flemish, indeed a typically Belgian book. Where else than in Belgium can the characters in a book express their own national character in such a manner? Nowhere else! I would go further; I find it the most Belgian book since the creations of Louis Paul Boon.[28]

The Dutch writer Ilja Leonard Pfeijffer was one of the few critics who drew on a wider, more international range of comparisons, reading the book more as a 'portrait of the artist as a young man'.[29] It is interesting that Verhulst himself said in an interview that in his eyes, his characters, with their drink problems, are not representative of Flemings in particular.[30] However, this viewpoint is not acknowledged in the critical reception of the book.

In what follows, we examine, on the basis of selected examples from the aforementioned case studies in the eight language areas studied, whether and how the view of *De helaasheid der dingen* as a 'Flemish' novel, which predominates in Flanders and the Netherlands, persists when *De helaasheid der dingen* travels abroad in three forms: as book translation, as film adaptation and as translated film.

THE FLEMISH CHARACTER OF THE BOOK TRANSLATIONS

While Verhulst insists that he wrote *De helaasheid der dingen* in a legitimate form of Dutch, it is nevertheless evident that the language of the book presents a challenge for its translators. The Italian translator, Claudia di Palermo, several times asked Verhulst for advice, which, she says, saved her 'from a number of blunders'. The Japanese translator, Saki Nagayama, enlisted the help of Luk van Haute, a Flemish translator who translates from Japanese. It is interesting that these two translators took very different approaches in their treatment of the 'Flemish' language usage and the associations that it evokes. The Italian translator judged that the dialect in *De helaasheid der dingen* 'is not absolutely essential, as, for example, is the case in *Die gore klerezooi in de Via Merolana* [*That Awful Mess on the Via Merolana*] by C.E. Gadda'. She decided to standardize the dialect, prioritising the general literary quality of the work. She comments on this shift:

> At least, in my opinion, although something is necessarily lost, the power and expressivity of Verhulst's prose is preserved. That came through in many Italian reviews, which found the language very lively and colourful.[31]

The Japanese translator, on the other hand, decided that her translation should preserve the distinction between the 'Flemish' usage and the standard Dutch usage. Therefore, after discussions with the publisher, she used the Kansai dialect of Japanese which she herself had spoken in her youth. In other words, regional usage was translated by regional usage. The effect of this choice is, according to the translator herself, that 'the characters in the Japanese edition appear a little less raucous [...] because the Kansai dialect sounds softer than the original Flemish dialect'.[32] This translation choice, which adds a Japanese regional colouring to the translation, with a result that the associations evoked are less crude and non-standard than those of the non-standard Dutch in the source text, is explained in the translator's afterword.

The realia, too, were handled in quite different ways by different translators. In the eight language areas that have been studied, the South Korean and Japanese translators opted for a source-text oriented approach. In the case of the Japanese edition, the translation of realia was explained in the afterword. In the

Figure 1. Book cover of the Japanese translation by Saki Nagayama of Verhulst's *De helaasheid der dingen.* (Tokyo: Shincho sha, 2012)

Figure 2. Book cover of the Korean translation by Suah Bae of Verhulst's *De helaasheid der dingen.* (Seoul: Open Books, 2011)

Korean version, translated via the German, Suah Bae found a suitable translation for many realia, despite the limited familiarity of South Korean readers with Flemish culture. In rare cases an explanatory footnote was added. According to Peeters, who studied the process of this translation, Bae did not want the South Korean reader to lose the feeling that s/he was reading a Belgian book: 'In her opinion, occasional words or activities that are incomprehensible to a South Korean form part of the attractiveness of the book and the pleasure in reading it.'[33]

The question is, then, whether the translation, given the lack of available hetero-images and the emphasis on the difference from the target culture (self-images), had a chance of success (in the sense of popular culture, as Migozzi understands it). Even if the publisher could play on a certain amount of recognition of the culture (cf. infra) with beer bottles on the jacket flap, the low sales may confirm the hypothesis that the combination of a lack of hetero-images and a wide gulf between source culture and target culture seriously threatens the chances of success of a translation.

The Italian translator chose to orient her translation of realia towards acculturation, prioritizing the readability of the Italian. As a result, in translating some realia or culture-specific jokes, she opted for 'solutions that are easier for the Italian reader to understand'.[34] When it came to the names of people

Figure 3. Book cover of the Italian translation by Claudia Di Palermo of Verhulst's *De helaasheid der dingen* (Roma: Fazi editore, 2009).

and places, however, she chose to retain the original names of, for example, pubs, and the original names of characters, because otherwise 'people and places in Flanders would suddenly have Italian names'.[35]

The translation strategies of the above-mentioned translators into Italian, Japanese and South Korean led them to carry over into the target text, to varying degrees, in their representation of linguistic usage and/or of realia, the Flemish coloration of the source text. Under these circumstances it is not surprising that the critics of their translations focus to some extent on a locally-bound, source-text oriented interpretation of the text. Thus Italian critics drew comparisons between *Il purtroppo delle cose,* the Belgian singer Jacques Brel and the Dutch painter Hieronymus Bosch. In South Korea, too, the novel was presented to readers (such as there were – only 1,300 copies were sold) as a locally-bound document: the publishers encouraged this by putting pictures of beer bottles on the front jacket flap, which accords with the Korean image of Belgium as a beer country. Nevertheless, in general, the culture gap between the novel and the South Korean public is not so great, according to Peeters, because of the tolerant attitude to excessive consumption of alcohol in South Korean business life. So while at first sight low availability of hetero-images suggested that readers would be unlikely to be able to establish connections between the source text and their own culture, the intersection of a self-image with the hetero-images that do exist resulted in a more universalising interpretation.

We hear a similar story from the Japanese and the Italian translators, albeit with more emphasis on the importance of self-images for the chances of success. Claudia di Palermo is reluctant to class *De helaasheid der dingen* as a typically Flemish book: 'the setting is of course very regional, but if one makes the necessary changes such a family can be found anywhere.'[36] Because of the social environment portrayed and the grotesque humour of the book, di Palermo sees similarities with an Italian locally-bound work, namely the classic film *Brutti, sporchi e cattivi* directed by Ettore Scola, thereby confirming that the recognition of the self-culture plays an important role in the reception of a book in translation, and how, in the presence of that recognition, the novel can count on a more global, universalizing interpretation.

The Japanese translator, too, remarks that there exists a drinking culture in Japan. She goes a step further in the identification of a self-image by suggesting that in a way, *De helaasheid der dingen* could be seen as a typical Japanese book. She says that the book evokes a typically Japanese feeling (*Yagatekanashiki*) which begins with laughter and becomes sadness or melancholy. Verhulst's writing, via the work of his Japanese translator, is seen by Japanese readers as close to their own culture.

THE FLEMISH CHARACTER OF THE FILM ADAPTATION

Shifts with regard to local colouring are also evident in the film adaptation of the book. In *De helaasheid der dingen* the dialogues between characters are written in a constructed language that evokes dialect. The dialect used has no written variant, so Verhulst has no choice but to create a literary language which conveys the idea that the dialogues are in dialect, even though the language used is not real dialect.[37] The use of lexical clues, especially (see above), helps to create this suggestion. The rest of the book is written in a high-flown, ironic register. This is the voice of the narrator, who in this manner establishes a distance from the 'characters' (including himself). In the film, we have to do with a dramatic or mimetic (showing) mode of representation, and thus mainly spoken language. The dialogues are therefore more prominent in the film than in the book and are spoken in dialect. From a quantitative point of view, the film is thus more explicitly regional. However, the director retains the voice of the narrator by introducing a voice-over in the frame story in which the boy has become a writer looking back on his youth. This frame story voice uses a register that is more or less literary. In the film version of the book, the distance between past and present, between the two social milieus, between the two 'I's (experiencing and narrating) and thus between dialect and standard language (literary register or not) is magnified.

If we look at the realia in the film adaptation, we can see two shifts. The main character in the novel has the same name as the author, Dimitri Verhulst. In the film, however, he is called Gunther Strobbe: the indication of the autobiographical has gone. This makes sense given that a film is a group production and in this manner breaks away from the author of the book. Only the fact that the protagonist becomes a writer alludes to the autobiographical character of the work.[38] Overall, however, the film contains far more locally-coloured realia than the book does. A director has to fill in all the details left unspecified in the book: every interior, every view of a village, every vehicle, etc. A book leaves the work of interpretation largely to the reader's imagination, whether or not that imagination is informed by local knowledge. The film is also entirely located in Flanders, although it depends on the familiarity of the viewer with the Flemish landscape and Flemish villages whether she or he recognises the location as Flemish or rather as 'not home' (without being specific). There are also a good many linguistic clues: names on signs and buildings, books, newspapers etc. in Dutch (for example the road sign bearing the name Reetveerdegem) all anchor the film in its locality (and are not translated in an audiovisual translation of the film). So from time to time we see pages from the story that Gunther is writing, an early sign that he is going to become a writer. We see Gunther working at his typewriter and then we get to see what he is typing: a written version of the scene that we are watching. Other details, too, point to a Flemish culture-bound context: at a certain moment, Gunther's cousin is seen reading a novel by Louis Paul Boon, a Flemish writer reference to whom was used by the critics (see above) to categorise Verhulst's book even more firmly as a 'backwoods' novel.

If we consider the reception of the (Dutch language) film, we find that the reactions to the character, locally-bound or not, of the film are comparable with the reactions to the book. Karin Wolfs sums the film up as 'a metaphorical self-analysis of Flanders' and refers to Brueghel. Marc Holthof sees in the film (and not in the book) 'sure enough […] a remake of De Witte',[39] the iconic first-ever Flemish film, which provided the initial impetus for the Flemish film industry. Holthof's review shows the same irritation that was evident in the critical reception of the book: he would like Flemish films to break free of that cramped Flemish frame. All in all, we can conclude that the Dutch and Flemish film critics have no doubt in classifying the film adaptation as Flemish, or even typically Flemish.

THE FLEMISH CHARACTER OF THE AUDIOVISUAL TRANSLATIONS

The film adaptation of *De helaasheid der dingen* has been distributed in, among other countries, France, Poland and Russia. Its showing in the three countries mentioned involved the use of three different audiovisual translation techniques: respectively, dubbing, subtitling and voice-over translation, in which the original soundtrack remains audible, but is voiced over by Russian actors using minimal intonation.

The play on linguistic registers between dialogue and narrator that characterises the original film is preserved in the French and Polish audiovisual translation. In the case of the French translation, against the background of a dubbing technique which in itself tends to favour the acceptability of the cultural product in the target culture, the gap between the reminiscing voice-over narrator and the characters in the main story is widened. The voice-over narrator speaks in a literary register that employs, for example, the *passé simple* and highly wrought syntax. The main characters, on the other hand, speak a language which, among other things, is coarser than that in the original film and which also retains certain (Flemish) words from the original soundtrack, which, however, will not be perceived as Flemish because they are used in French-speaking Wallonia as well as in Flanders, but which add a strong 'Belgian' colouring to the translated soundtrack. Examples are: 'allé pa' ('come on Dad'), 'manneke' ('man', 'fellow', but also an exclamatory interjection), but also the title motif 'helaas' (literally, 'alas').[40]

The Polish subtitlers also went to great lengths to reproduce the play of registers. They considered having the main characters speak in the Silesian dialect, but because this would call up unwanted associations with a coal-mining area decided against it. Instead, the uncles, who live on the margins of society, speak a jargon which recalls that of the rebellious urban youth of the eighties. (From a Polish perspective, Reetverdegem is more convincing as a town than as a village.)[41]

There is no trace of this sort of sophisticated intervention in respect of the language used in the Russian audiovisual translation: the dialect of the main characters is simply rendered in the standard language. So the Flemish threat 'ik draai hem, godverdomme, met zijn kloten in de gekaptmolen', which might be rendered as 'I'll fucking make mincemeat out of him, balls and all' turns up as: 'I'll make him into minced meat'.[42] The idiosyncratic voice of the frame narrator with its pretentions to literariness is also rendered in a 'neutral' standard usage, with a consequent narrowing of the gap between narrator and main characters.

The realia, too, are handled in different ways by the different audiovisual translations. The Polish subtitling shows a certain amount of naturalisation. This is already evident in the Polish title, *Boso al na rowerze* [Barefoot but on a bicycle], which carries an intertextual wink towards the social novel *Boso ale w ostrogach* [Barefoot, but with spurs] by the Polish author Grzesiuk. Another choice that results in naturalisation is the substitution of the names of Brazilian soap operas for those of the Austrian soap operas that feature in the film, Brazilian soaps being more popular in Poland.

In the Russian audiovisual translation, the Flemish colouring of the film is systematically neutralised by

Figure 4. Polish film poster of *De helaasheid der dingen* (Film: Felix van Groeningen)

the use of hypernyms to translate realia.[43] Thus Trappist beer (a quintessentially Belgian beer) is rendered simply as 'beer', as is (the drink) 'mazout'. Similarly a smurf (a quintessentially Belgian fictional being, available in toy form) becomes 'a toy'. These kinds of realia were given a more adequate translation in French, which is not surprising given that the frames of reference of the two cultures are more closely related to each other: Belgium and France are after all neighbours, with the French language as a common denominator.

The reception of the French film version of *De helaasheid der dingen*, unlike that of the Polish and Russian film versions, cannot be separated from the reception of the later book translation; the film adaptation paved the way for the reception of the novel and the favourable image of Verhulst in France. A noticeable feature of the interlinked receptions of book and film is the way in which the regional, culture-bound motif was interpreted: most critics linked the book and the film to Flemish hetero-images, or talked of them as typically Belgian phenomena. The French title *La merditude des choses* (literally 'the shititude of things'), whose scatological connotation Verhulst himself deplores,[44] in itself elicits associations with the so-called typically Belgian sadness and poverty which is the subject of the Dardenne brothers' films and of the popular Belgian documentary series *Striptease*.[45] For the French-speaking audience (in France and in Belgium), the cultural representation of the other in this instance involves a process of self-appropriation through the intertext provided in the receiving cultures by the well-known *Striptease* productions.

In Poland and Russia, the existing hetero-images of Belgium/Flanders did not play such an important role in the reception of the film. Quite the reverse, according to the Polish subtitlers, the film fits seamlessly into the Polish people's own history. The viewers would find it easy to understand the film because in Poland the nineties produced a lost generation from a socio-economic point of view, thanks to the turmoil of the transition from communism to capitalism. In Russia too, despite the imagological viewing instruction in the Russian title *Flamandskiye Natyurmorty* [Flemish Still Lives], the film was not seen as a document about Belgium or Flanders. In reviews on the internet regional associations were made at most with Europe, or with the Netherlands instead of Flanders or Belgium. One viewer wrote: 'This is a film about today's wild Europe, mired in madness', and another viewer wrote: 'an awful film about the awful life of awful 'Hollanders'. Nothing else to add. Worth watching if you like Holland and their lifestyle [there] in general'.[46] In a Russian context the film has thematic similarities with Russian films from the early years of the millennium, which also feature weak fathers with strong sons. At least according to Hashamova, this post-Soviet theme, which is, for example, developed by Zvyagintsev in *The Return*, should be understood as a collective longing for a return to patriarchal values after the turbulent nineties.[47]

CONCLUSION

In this chapter we have investigated, on the basis of the international and transmedial trajectory of Dimitri Verhulst's novel *De helaasheid der dingen*, how, and under what conditions cultural products may, or may not, arrive, break through and eventually become successful in other cultural communities and among global audiences more generally. We have examined how, in the course of the processes of translation and adaptation the narrative was transformed and, in whatever new shape or form, set off on its own trajectory, functioning in its own right in a new context. We therefore focused on a parameter which represented an important consideration in the translation of the book and film and the reception thereof, both in the source-language readership or audience and in other language areas and countries, namely the specific local or culturally-bound anchoring of the work. In a sense, our focus on the tension between culture-specific embedding and international circulation echoes a theme of the narrative itself: whilst the narrative, in the subtle nuances of its language, engages with the colourful way in which his family lives, the protagonist Dimitri uproots himself from the environment of his youth and thus translates himself: from dialect to the standard language, from uneducated, coarse language to literary language. He evolves at last into a writer. And yet the roots remain visible: distance and nostalgia both play a part in his memories of youth. The protagonist experiences the uprooting as alienation and loss, but also as a fresh chance; this is evident not only from the narrative but also from its international trajectory.

In order to accomplish research into the culture-specific embedding of *De helaasheid der dingen*, as book and as film, in eight different foreign cultures, it was necessary to have at our disposal specific knowledge of the target cultures. Translators and mediators have a larger cultural awareness with regard to their own target community, which facilitates the cultural transfer of narratives. The different sub-studies which were carried out within the framework of this research group, and which we brought together here, make it clear that this type of research is only possible in the form of teamwork. If not only researchers, but also translators, agents and authors are involved, you also need to take into account that all these different actors use different types of discourse, ranging from subjective to objective, from normative to neutral, from emotional and engaged to analytic. On top of this, all these actors have their own cultural representations, which also play a role.

Thus it became clear that the terms 'local', 'regional' or 'culturally bound' are neither objective nor stable, but are interpreted through the normative and imagological prisms of the socio-cultural group in question, and furthermore change each time a language boundary is crossed. What counted as local, and to what extent it counted as local, was very variable: what for one observer, researcher or critic was local was by no means always so for others. Moreover, the term 'local' can be interpreted differently and, as a consequence, may be seen as equivalent to 'regionally bound', or to 'Flemish', but in other cases may be seen as equivalent to 'Belgian' or even 'European'. This indicates the relativity of (the concept of) cultural specificity, since, as Ranzato rightly observes, all the people in a given community do not necessarily share the meaning of a given locution or reference that is supposed to belong to a foreign or to their own culture.[48]

Research into the manner in which a foreign work, especially one rich in culture-specific signs, can penetrate a receiving culture indicates that a number of different factors may exert a favourable influence. These include whether the target culture itself contains elements propitious to acceptance of the work (recognition of hetero-images and/or self images, for example, but also the capacity or the disposition of the translator or mediator to make its translation fit the new cultural environment), the mediating role of the source culture or an intermediary culture, the role of the global cultural network and its institutions, the historical and political period of production, distribution and reception, but also the original work itself, whose own textual, genre-related or thematic patterns or whose degree of rootedness in its 'place of production', as Pym says, in its own context of space and time,[49] may be more or less suited to attracting a universal audience. Last but not least, the film medium plays a decisive role in facilitating the transnational transfer of narratives.

We looked at how cultural specificity, in the way in which it is focused upon and discussed in the reception of *De helaasheid der dingen*, influences the manner in which a work may make inroads into a new target language area. In our approach, cultural specificity included on the one hand language and on the other hand culturally-specific elements. The case studies led to the conclusion that whether or not the 'cultural code' is retained in the book translation depends, on the textual level, to a very great extent on choices made by the translator (or before him or her the translator of the intermediary translation, as the French title based on the German translation shows) and on his or her evaluation of reader or audience attitudes. In some cases the book acquired, alongside the original 'cultural code', a new cultural colouring, as the Japanese example shows. Sometimes elements which at first sight seem typically Flemish or Belgian, such as the beer culture of Dimitri's early environment, were instead interpreted as universal or were seen as corresponding to self-images (as in the case of the motif of alcohol abuse). The audiovisual translation gives a mixed picture: for the French-speaking audience in France and in Belgium, which are culturally close to the community of origin, the Belgian character of the narrative was accentuated, while in Russia, the Flemish character as possible reception motif was not retained in the audiovisual translation, despite the title. The Polish audiovisual translators, for their part, gave a number of linguistic elements and realia a 'Polish' turn.

In the translation- and adaptation-strategies that were chosen, what seems to have determined the retention of culture-specific elements is the degree of (perceived) recognisability and familiarity from the point of view of the target culture. More generally, the translation of culture-bound language and culture-specific elements has to do with 'shared experiences'.[50] When the cultural specificity of the text is in close keeping with hetero- and/or self-images, there seems to be a greater chance that the text will achieve a certain amount of distribution, acceptance and even success in the receiving culture. Reception, it seems from our case studies, is also made more likely by a shift from a cultural specificity, whether or not it is perceived as such, to a universal interpretation.

However, the degree of distance between cultures could not be the only determining factor concerning the nature of the translation process and the reception of translations. That the process of the book translation was more source-language oriented, thus increasing the distance between the culture of origin and the receiving culture, as in the Japanese case-study, or that the translation was oriented towards acculturation and readability for the target audience, as in the Italian case-study, could not completely explain either the 'easy' or the difficult reception of the work.

But care must of course be taken in comparing the separate case studies not to be too quick to see patterns and principles. We should not lose sight of the personal, or of coincidence in the transfer process to certain target cultures. Maintaining a balance between research into individual cases and developing a more comprehensive framework for the transference of cultural specificity to other cultural audiences was one of the greatest challenges in a fragmentary panoramic study such as this.

NOTES

1 The title of this article has its origin in the title of the following review: G. Woodward, '*The Misfortunates* by Dimitri Verhulst. A gruelling tale of Belgian alcoholics is unexpectedly moving', in *The Guardian,* 22 March 2012. Our thanks go to Susan Reed for her correction of the parts of this text written in English, and to Susan Reed and Guido Latré for the translation of those parts of the text written in Dutch.

2 The languages into which *De helaasheid der dingen* was translated are Chinese, Danish, German, English, Estonian, Finnish, French, Hebrew, Hungarian, Italian, Japanese, Korean, Macedonian, Norwegian, Serbian, Slovenian and Spanish. For comparison with other Flemish novels, see the online *Translations Database of the Dutch Foundation for Literature,* http://www.letterenfonds.nl/en/translations-database.

3 This is also what Verhulst himself suggests as translation into English (O. Réthelyi, '"Altijd opnieuw ergens schrijver worden". Gesprek met Dimitri Verhulst', in *Filter. Tijdschrift over vertalen* 4 (2014), p. 5).

4 J. Collins, *Bring on the Books for Everybody: How Literary Culture Became Popular Culture* (Durham: Duke University Press, 2010), p. 18.

5 We use in this narrow sense of media transposition the term 'intermediality' as defined by Irena O. Rajewsky: 'here the intermedial quality has to do with the way in which a media product comes into being, i.e., with the transformation of a given media product (a text, a

film, etc.) or of its substratum into another medium. This category is a production-oriented, "genetic" conception of intermediality; the "original" text, film, etc., is the "source" of the newly formed media product, whose formation is based on a media-specific and obligatory intermedial transformation process.' (I.O. Rajewsky, 'Intermediality, Intertextuality, and Remediation: A Literary Perspective on Intermediality', in *Intermédialités : histoire et théorie des arts, des lettres et des techniques / Intermediality: History and Theory of the Arts, Literature and Technologies* 6 (2005), p. 51).

6 For the publication of these results, see S. Nagayama, 'Het ontstaan van Spijtige dagen. *De helaasheid der dingen* in het Japans', in *Filter. Tijdschrift over vertalen* 4 (2012), pp. 9-14.; Réthelyi, '"Altijd opnieuw ergens schrijver worden"', pp. 3-8; and the special online issue of *Filter. Tijdschrift over vertalen* on Dimitri Verhulst, http://www.tijdschrift-filter.nl/webfilter/dossier/verhulst.aspx (published in full online on 30 June 2015).

7 G. Sapiro, *Traduire la littérature et les sciences humaines: Conditions et obstacles* (Paris: La Documentation Française, 2012), p. 19.

8 L. Venuti, *The Scandals of Translation: Towards an Ethics of Difference* (London: Routledge, 1998), p. 71.

9 Venuti, *The Scandals of Translation,* p. 73.

10 '[...] les sociétés nationales [...] les accueilleraient et les métaboliseraient d'autant mieux qu'elles se reconnaîtraient – à tous les termes – dans ces miroirs fictionnels.' (J. Migozzi, 'EPOP import/export. De quelques hypothèses sur la circulation transnationale et transmédiatique des fictions de grande consommation en Europe (1840-1940)', in S. Delneste *et al.* (eds.), *Les racines populaires de la culture européenne* (Bern: Peter Lang, 2014), p. 20, translated by Susan Reed).

11 Leerssen also includes in this perception, next to self- and hetero-images, what he calls *meta*-images ('how a nation believes it is perceived by others'). See M. Beller and J. Leerssen (eds.), *Imagology: The cultural construction and literary representation of national characters. A critical survey* (Amsterdam/New York: Rodopi, 2007), p. 344.

12 M. Espagne, 'La notion de transfert culturel', in *Revue Sciences/Lettres* 1 (2013), http://rsl.revues.org/219.

13 Heilbron points out that from the eighties onwards, the German market, and more specifically, German translations of Dutch authors, and the success of these translations, has constituted an important pivot in the process of importing Dutch literature into France. (J. Heilbron, 'L'évolution des échanges culturels entre la France et les Pays-Bas face à l'hégémonie de l'anglais', in G. Sapiro (ed.) *Translatio: Le marché de la traduction en France à l'heure de la mondialisation* (Paris: CNRS Editions, 2008), p. 331.

14 Migozzi, 'EPOP import/export', p. 21.

15 See J. Migozzi (ed.), *De l'écrit à l'écran. Littératures populaires: mutations génériques, mutations médiatiques* (Limoges: Presses Universitaires de Limoges, 2000).

16 '(le) septième art, dont Matthieu Letourneux a pu montrer par exemple à quel point il contribuait à accélérer la circulation transnationale des récits d'aventures en induisant concomitamment une homogénéisation supra-nationale des genres puisqu'il contribue à faire prévaloir les codes du récit cinématographique sur certaines traditions nationales.' See the research of Matthieu Letourneux, quoted by Migozzi, 'EPOP import/export', p. 244. Translated by Susan Reed.

17 P. Cattrysse, 'Multimedia & Translation: Methodological Considerations', in Y. Gambier & H. Gottlieb (eds.), *(Multi)Media Translation* (Amsterdam/Philadelphia: Benjamins Translation Library, 2001), pp. 1-12.

18 Cattrysse, 'Multimedia & Translation', pp. 9-10.

19 Cattrysse, 'Multimedia & Translation', p. 10.

20 Cattrysse, 'Multimedia & Translation', p. 11.

21 'semblent bénéficier d'une prime narrative à l'exportation les récits et figures à dimension *universelle* [in Italics in the original text], autrement dit les motifs, scénarios et héros qui peuvent séduire des publics de tous ordres pour leur narrativité déterritorialisée, cultivés ou cultivables hors sol national en quelque sorte.' (Migozzi, 'EPOP import/export', p. 22, translated by Susan Reed).

22 'désarrimée d'un discours d'encadrement nationaliste, car le roman colonial patriotique se prête à rebours fort mal à l'exportation par sa trop grande dépendance à un interdiscours national.' (Migozzi, 'EPOP import/export', p. 22, translated by Susan Reed). This is what Finkel said about the translation of Culture Specific Elements in 1962: they 'stand out from the common lexical context, they distinguish themselves for their heterogeneity, and consequently they require a reinforcement of attention in order to be decoded.' See I. Ranzato, *Translating Culture Specific Elements on Television: The Case of Dubbing* (New York/London: Routledge, 2015), p. 53. See also A. Pym, *Translation and Text Transfer: An essay on the Principles of Intercultural Communication* (Tarragona: Intercultural studies group, 2010), p. 127: The more text 'presupposes its place of production, the more it is difficult to transfer it to another culture.' (quoted by Ranzato, *Translating Culture Specific Elements*, p. 58).

23 'les genres et les personnages [...] qui seraient liés à une référentialité territoriale contraignante et/ou à une connivence communautaire de type culturel ou politique [...]', i.e. 'culturellement codifié.' See Migozzi, 'EPOP import/export', p. 23, translated by Susan Reed.

24 T. Parks, 'The Dull New Global Novel', in *The New York Review of Books*, 9 February 2010.

25 'Wat mij wel opvalt, en dit is geen kritiek, is dat Nederlanders heel vaak denken dat een woord geen Nederlands is. Als ik dan zeg dat het gewoon in de Van Dale staat dan schrikken ze soms. Er is echt een gigantische groep woorden in het Nederlands waarvan Nederlanders denken dat het Vlaams dialect is, maar dat is helemaal niet zo.' (D. Verhulst in Réthelyi, '"Altijd opnieuw ergens schrijver worden"', p. 7, translated by Susan Reed).

26 'Ik zeg altijd aan Nederlanders die mij vertellen dat mijn boeken geen Nederlands zijn maar Vlaams dat de vertaalrechten te koop zijn. Ze kunnen het dan in het Nederlands vertalen. Ik ben zeer nieuwsgierig naar een vertaling, ik zou die wel eens willen lezen.' (D. Verhulst in Réthelyi, '"Altijd opnieuw ergens schrijver worden"', p. 7, translated by Susan Reed).

27 'Maar kan het eindelijk eens ophouden met die Louis Paul Boonklonen? [...] Wij, gereformeerde Ollanders, lezen dat soort folklore maar al te graag en de Vlamingen geven ons zonder scrupules telkens opnieuw waar wij om vragen. [...] voor de Vlaamse literatuur lijkt het me heel wat beter als ze Louis Paul Boon nu eens onder de grond stoppen.' (M. Pam, 'Laat duizend scheten waaien', in *De Tijd*, 3 February 2006), translated by Susan Reed.

28 '[...] aldus is het een typisch Vlaams jazelfs een typisch Belgisch boek. Waar anders dan in België kunnen de personages in een boek op zo'n manier hun eigen volksaard uitdragen?

Nergens anders! Sterker nog, ik vind het het Belgischste boek sinds de werkjes van Louis Paul Boon.' (H. Brusselmans, 'De dokter bellen van het lachen', in *NRC*, 19 January 2007, translated by Susan Reed).

29 I. L. Pfeijffer, 'Roman of kluwen van losse eindjes?', in *NRC*, 26 January 2007.

30 Réthelyi, '"Altijd opnieuw ergens schrijver worden"', p. 7.

31 'Tenminste, ik vind dat hoewel iets onvermijdelijk verloren gaat, de sterkte en expressiviteit van het proza van Verhulst goed overeind blijven. Dat was ook in vele Italiaanse recensies terug te vinden, die vonden de taal zeer levendig en kleurrijk.' See E. Brems, 'Twijfelen uit ervaring. Een gesprek met literair vertaalster Claudia di Palermo', in *Filter. Tijdschrift over vertalen* [special online issue on Dimitri Verhulst], http://www.tijdschrift-filter.nl/webfilter/dossier/verhulst.aspx (published in full online 30 June 2015), translated by Susan Reed.

32 'In mijn vertaling van *De helaasheid der dingen* heb ik in het nawoord ook toegelicht waarom de personages Kansai-dialect spreken; om het zware Vlaamse accent te onderscheiden van het beschaafd Vlaams-Nederlands, hebben de redactrice en ik besloten om het Kansai-dialect te gebruiken – het dialect dat ik in mijn jeugd zelf heb gesproken en goed beheers, zodat de gesprekken niet onnatuurlijk klinken. Omdat het zachter klinkt dan het oorspronkelijke Vlaamse dialect, lijken de personages in de Japanse editie wel iets minder luidruchtig. See Nagayama, 'Het ontstaan van *Spijtige dagen*', pp. 9-10, translated by Susan Reed.

33 'De voor Koreanen bij wijle onbegrijpelijke woorden of activiteiten maken volgens haar deel uit van de aantrekkelijkheid van het boek en het plezier tijdens het lezen zelf.' (N. Peeters, 'Verhulst in Zuid-Korea: lost in translation?', unpublished article), translated by Susan Reed.

34 'oplossingen die begrijpelijker zijn voor de Italiaanse lezer' (Brems, 'Twijfelen uit ervaring'), translated by Susan Reed.

35 'in Vlaanderen plekken en mensen plotseling Italiaanse namen hebben' (Brems, 'Twijfelen uit ervaring'), translated by Susan Reed.

36 'qua setting is het natuurlijk zeer lokaal, maar met de nodige verschillen kan zo'n gezin overal gevonden worden.' (Brems, 'Twijfelen uit ervaring'), translated by Susan Reed.

37 This is strongly reminiscent of what the linguist Guido Geerts wrote about the language of *Het verdriet van België*. His research led him to the conclusion that Claus' novel is a 'speech act' and not a linguistic 'reality'. On the one hand, the novel by Claus, especially the narrative passages, is unquestionably written 'in ordinary standard Dutch' ('in gewoon standaard Nederlands'). On the other hand, the language of Claus is obviously a contrived, artificially created language which no one speaks, but which clearly draws on sources including the West Flemish idioticon, Belgicisms and barbarisms, and which makes the book's construction particularly remarkable. Paradoxically, then, this consistent constructed language is 'a craftsman's toolkit, with which he creates a reality' ('een ambachtelijk instrumentarium, waarmee hij een werkelijkheid creeërt'). See G. Geerts, *Nederlands, een en veelzijdig: een selectie artikelen van Guido Geerts, hem aangeboden ter gelegenheid van zijn emeritaat* (Leuven: Universitaire Pers Leuven, 1995: p. 213, p. 217, p. 218, p. 222), translated by Susan Reed.

38 Verhulst commented on this in an interview: '[...] that the main character in the film was suddenly a writer. That was challenging for me.' ('[...] dat het hoofdpersonage in de film opeens een schrijver was. Dat was confronterend voor mij.'. See S. De Foer, 'Het is plezant

onafhankelijk te mogen denken', in *De Standaard*, 9 January 2016, translated by Susan Reed). In other words, in the profession of the protagonist Gunther Strobbe, we find the autobiographical stratum of the novel.

39 'warempel [...] een remake van De Witte', in M. Holthof, 'Felix van Groeningen. *De helaasheid der dingen*', in *Etcetera*, 119 (2009), p. 62, translated by Susan Reed.

40 See P. Boulogne, E. Brems and S. Vanasten. 'Van Reetveerdegem naar Trou Duc Les Oyes en Moskou. *De helaasheid der dingen* als (vertaalde) verfilming', in *Filter. Tijdschrift over vertalen* [special online issue on Dimitri Verhulst], http://www.tijdschrift-filter.nl/webfilter/dossier/verhulst.aspx (published in full online 30 June 2015).

41 M. Venken and K. Marcin Zalewski, '*Boso, ale na rowerze. De helaasheid der dingen* in Polen', in *Filter. Tijdschrift over vertalen* [special online issue on Dimitri Verhulst], http://www.tijdschrift-filter.nl/webfilter/dossier/verhulst.aspx (published in full online 30 June 2015).

42 In Russian: 'из него фарш сделаю', translated by Pieter Boulogne.

43 This is what Grit calls in Dutch 'kernvertaling' (literally: core translation). See D. Grit, 'De vertaling van realia', in H. Bloemen *et al.* (eds.), *Denken over vertalen. Tekstboek vertaalwetenschap*, (Nijmegen: Vantilt, 2004), pp. 279-286.

44 Réthelyi, '"Altijd opnieuw ergens schrijver worden"', p. 5.

45 It is interesting to note that Manu Riche, a documentary maker for *Striptease*, directed the 2015 film of *Problemski hotel* by Verhulst.

46 'это фильм о сегодняшней дикой Европе, погрязшей в безумства'; 'страшный фильм про страшную жизнь страшных голландцев. больше добавить нечего. смотреть стоит, если вам вообще нравится голландия и их образ жизни.' See 'Recenzii i otzyvy o fil'me "Flamandskie natjurmorty"', at http://films.imhonet.ru/element/1133266/opinions. Translated by Pieter Boulogne.

47 Y. Hashamova, *Pride & Panic. Russian Imagination of the West in Post-Soviet Film*. (Bristol/Chigaco: Intellect Books, 2007), pp. 116-120.

48 Ranzato, *Translating Culture Specific References on Television*, p. 54.

49 Ranzato, *Translating Culture Specific References on Television*, p. 58. See also footnote 18.

50 'The fruition of cultural elements is based on shared experiences [...]', Ranzato, *Translating Culture Specific References on Television*, p. 58.

BIBLIOGRAPHY

Beller, M. and J. Leerssen, *Imagology. The cultural construction and literary representation of national characters. A critical survey* (Amsterdam/New York: Rodopi, 2007).

Boulogne, P. and E. Brems, 'De internationale verspreiding van De helaasheid der dingen', in *Filter. Tijdschrift over vertalen* [special online issue on Dimitri Verhulst], http://www.tijdschrift-filter.nl/webfilter/dossier/verhulst.aspx (30 June 2015).

Boulogne, P., E. Brems and S. Vanasten, 'Van Reetveerdegem naar Trou Duc Les Oyes en Moskou. *De helaasheid der dingen* als (vertaalde) verfilming' in *Filter. Tijdschrift over vertalen* [special online issue on Dimitri Verhulst], http://www.tijdschrift-filter.nl/webfilter/dossier/verhulst.aspx (30 June 2015).

Brems, E., 'Twijfelen uit ervaring: Een gesprek met literair vertaalster Claudia di Palermo', in *Filter. Tijdschrift over vertalen* [special online issue on Dimitri Verhulst], http://www.tijdschrift-filter.nl/webfilter/dossier/verhulst.aspx (30 June 2015).

Brusselmans, H., 'De dokter bellen van het lachen', in *NRC*, 19 January 2007.

Cattrysse, P., 'Multimedia & Translation: Methodological Considerations', in Y. Gambier, and H. Gottlieb (eds.), *(Multi)Media Translation* (Amsterdam/Philadelphia: Benjamins Translation Library, 2001), pp. 1-12.

Clérigo dos Prazeres, S. C., '"Het Pruimenlied": "Het Kweeperenlied" of "De Garage van de buurvrouw"? Scheldtaal en (seksueel) suggestieve taal in een Portugese vertaling van *De helaasheid der dingen* van Dimitri Verhulst,' in *Filter. Tijdschrift over vertalen*, special online issue on Dimitri Verhulst, http://www.tijdschrift-filter.nl/webfilter/dossier/verhulst.aspx (30 June 2015).

Collins, J., *Bring on the Books for Everybody. How Literary Culture became Popular Culture* (Durham NC: Duke University Press, 2010).

Espagne, M., 'La notion de transfert culturel', in *Revue Sciences/Lettres* 1 (2013), http://rsl.revues.org/219.

De Foer, S., 'Het is plezant onafhankelijk te mogen denken', in *De Standaard*, 9 January 2016.

Geerts, G., *Nederlands, een en veelzijdig: een selectie artikelen van Guido Geerts, hem aangeboden ter gelegenheid van zijn emeritaat* (Leuven: Universitaire Pers Leuven, 1995), pp. 195-232.

Grit, D., 'De vertaling van realia', in H. Bloemen *et al.* (eds.), *Denken over vertalen. Tekstboek vertaalwetenschap* (Nijmegen: Vantilt, 2004), pp. 279-86.

Groeningen, F. van, *De helaasheid der dingen* (Lumière Cinema Selection, 2009)

Hashamova, Y., *Pride & Panic. Russian Imagination of the West in Post-Soviet Film.* (Bristol/Chigaco: Intellect Books, 2007).

Heilbron, J., 'L'évolution des échanges culturels entre la France et les Pays-Bas face à l'hégémonie de l'anglais', in G. Sapiro (ed.), *Translatio. Le marché de la traduction en France à l'heure de la mondialisation* (Paris: CNRS Editions, 2008), pp. 311-32.

Holthof, M., 'Felix van Groeningen. *De helaasheid der dingen*', in *Etcetera* 119 (December 2009), pp. 62-64.

Migozzi, J., 'EPOP import/export. De quelques hypothèses sur la circulation transnationale et transmédiatique des fictions de grande consommation en Europe (1840-1940)', in S. Delneste, J. Migozzi, O. Odaert and J.-L. Tilleul (eds.), *Les racines populaires de la culture européenne* (Bern: Peter Lang, 2014), pp. 15-26.

Nagayama, S., 'Het ontstaan van Spijtige dagen. *De helaasheid der dingen* in het Japans', in *Filter. Tijdschrift over vertalen* 4 (2012), pp. 9-14.

Pam, M., 'Laat duizend scheten waaien', in *De Tijd*, 3 February 2006.

Parks, T., 'The Dull New Global Novel', in *The New York Review of Books*, 9 February 2010.

Peeters, N., 'Verhulst in Zuid-Korea: Lost in Translation?', unpublished article.

Pfeijffer, I.L., 'Roman of kluwen van losse eindjes?', in *NRC*, 26 January 2007.

Rajewsky, I.O., 'Intermediality, Intertextuality, and Remediation: A Literary Perspective on Intermediality', in *Intermédialités : histoire et théorie des arts, des lettres et des techniques / Intermediality: History and Theory of the Arts, Literature and Technologies* 6 (2005), pp. 43-64.

Ranzato, I., *Translating culture specific elements on television. The Case of Dubbing* (New York/London: Routledge, 2015).

'Recenzii i otzyvy o fil'me "Flamandskie natjurmorty"', http://films.imhonet.ru., http://films.imhonet.ru/element/1133266/opinions/

Réthelyi, O., '"Altijd opnieuw ergens schrijver worden": Gesprek met Dimitri Verhulst', in *Filter. Tijdschrift over vertalen* 4 (2014), pp. 3-8.

Sapiro, G., *Traduire la littérature et les sciences humaines. Conditions et obstacles* (Paris: La Documentation Française, 2012).

Sapiro, G. (ed.), *Translatio. Le marché de la traduction en France à l'heure de la mondialisation* (Paris: CNRS Editions, 2008).

Ter Harmsel Havlíková, V., 'Godverdomse dagen in het godverdomse Praag', in *Filter. Tijdschrift over vertalen* [special online issue on Dimitri Verhulst], http://www.tijdschrift-filter.nl/webfilter/dossier/verhulst.aspx (30 June 2015).

Venken, M. and K. Marcin Zalewski, '*Boso, ale na rowerze. De Helaasheid der dingen* in Polen', in *Filter. Tijdschrift over vertalen* [special online issue on Dimitri Verhulst], http://www.tijdschrift-filter.nl/webfilter/dossier/verhulst.aspx (30 June 2015).

Venuti, L., *The Scandals of Translation: Towards an Ethics of Difference* (London: Routledge, 1998).

Verhulst, D., *De helaasheid der dingen* (Amsterdam/Antwerpen: Contact, 2006).

Woodward, G., 'The *Misfortunates* by Dimitri Verhulst. A gruelling tale of Belgian alcoholics is unexpectedly moving', *The Guardian*, 22 March 2012.

CHAPTER 17

June is Dutch Literature Month!

Online Book Reviewers and Their Role in the Transmission of Dutch Literature to the English-Speaking World

Suzanne van Putten-Brons,
Peter Boot (Huygens ING, Amsterdam, The Netherlands)

About twenty-five years ago Tim Berners Lee, a physicist working at CERN, the European Organization for Nuclear Research, introduced the World Wide Web. The World Wide Web is deeply influencing our ways of doing research, studying, making friends, socializing, shopping, and many other things. This article will discuss how the web also affects the international circulation of literature. Next to the institutions that are usually studied in this context, i.e. authors, publishers, translators, critics and professors, a new group is claiming a place in the literary field. This group of online book reviewers is a heterogeneous group of individuals about whom we know only very little. This article reports on a provisional study that we conducted in an attempt to get a better picture of the phenomenon.

The study was done within a larger project studying the Circulation of Dutch Literature (CODL), focussing on thirteen canonical Dutch-language texts.[1] Our interest in this study was specifically in international circulation, outside the Dutch-language area.

INCREASING DEMOCRACY?

The changes that the web is bringing about have often been hailed as an increase in democracy: the decreasing cost of publication creates a space where the public, what Jay Rosen called 'The People Formerly Known as the Audience',[2] claims a right to discuss and judge the output of the media industry, or, in our case, books. This democratization of the literary field is not always seen as a positive development. Web criticism has been vehemently attacked as the 'cult of the amateur',[3] as 'user-generated nonsense'[4] leading to 'The Death of the Critic'.[5]

Readers who want to share their opinions about a book can use any of the many alternative places that the Internet offers non-professional readers: book sellers' sites such as Amazon and its Dutch equivalent bol.com, book blogs, social network sites specializing in books such as Goodreads, lovelybooks.de and in the Dutch-language area for instance watleesjij.nu [what are you reading now], forum discussion sites, and of course general purpose social networks such as Twitter or Facebook.[6]

Not all book discussion sites are open to the general public. In the Netherlands, Recensieweb, 8weekly and deReactor.org are examples of 'closed' sites that have editorial boards and editorial polices, where people only write upon invitation. As they all publish in Dutch, they are of limited importance for the international circulation of Dutch literature, which was our main focus of interest in this study. We have looked at sites where access is unrestricted, and where the reviewers need have no professional training or experience. The changes that the existence of these sites brings with it are the subject of this article.

METHOD

In our study we looked at book discussion on some of the open sites, mostly on private weblogs. The study was done in the autumn of 2014. Criteria for the selection of bloggers were as follows: Since the study was undertaken as part of the CODL-project, the focus was on the discussion of books written by Dutch-language authors, either in Dutch or in translation. Since our interest was in the circulation of Dutch literature across the boundaries of the Dutch language-area, we selected non-Dutch reviews, and chose to limit ourselves to reviews in English. This does not necessarily mean that the bloggers or reviewers were native speakers of English, since many Dutch bloggers write in English to reach a wider public.

Earlier research into book bloggers has suggested they are usually well educated and sometimes have a day job working with books.[7] We wondered whether that would be the case for our reviewers as well. We asked about demographics (age, sex, education), about the motivation for writing about books, and about possible relations with the literary field, i.e. are the bloggers just 'general readers' or do they fulfil other roles in the literary field, perhaps as a consequence of their blogging.

After selecting appropriate candidates for the study, we searched the blogs for the information we needed to get a good grasp of bloggers' background and the reach of their blogs. Not all information could be found online, so a series of (email) interviews followed. Twenty-two of the fifty-one bloggers responded and were willing to give the information we asked for. For the remainder, we only have the information available on their blogs or sites.[8]

FINDINGS

Our initial search concentrated on reviewers who discussed a sizable number of books in Dutch, but in the final database we also added some people who wrote only one or two blog posts on Dutch books.[9] Most of the reviews appeared on single-person weblogs. Some bloggers post on a group blog; others use the book-based social networking site Goodreads.[10] Most weblogs are devoted solely to literature, but there are exceptions. Blogger Branko Collin posted only a few blogs on books; his usual subject is digital developments.[11] Iris of *Irisonbooks*[12] also writes about her young child. The blogger behind *Beauty is a sleeping cat* writes about 'books, movies, cats and other treasures', Susanne of *LibrarianLavender* also writes about cosmetics and fashion accessories. Some of the reviews appeared on the *Dutch Language Blog* of a language-learning institute.[13] One of the bloggers uses YouTube as her platform: Sanne Vliegenthart is a 'vlogger', a video blogger. Besides her job at a publishing company in Great Britain she has her own YouTube channel, *booksandquills*, where she posts weekly vlogs, mostly about books.[14]

What follows is some of the information we collected on these reviewers.

Gender. The majority of the bloggers is female (twenty-nine people), while seventeen of the bloggers are male. The gender of four reviewers is unknown, one blog was written by a couple, named Mary and Gerry.[15]

Age. Age is unknown for twenty-four persons. The others are spread equally over all age categories, as Figure 1 shows. Blogging is not necessarily, as sometimes thought, exclusively for the young. The person in his seventies is Stephen Durrant, a retired professor of Chinese literature, who writes on the Goodreads platform.[16] Some of the younger ones have started book blogging in their teens. Some bloggers (Sanne Vliegenthart, Nina of *J'adore Happy Endings*) regularly discuss literature for young adults.

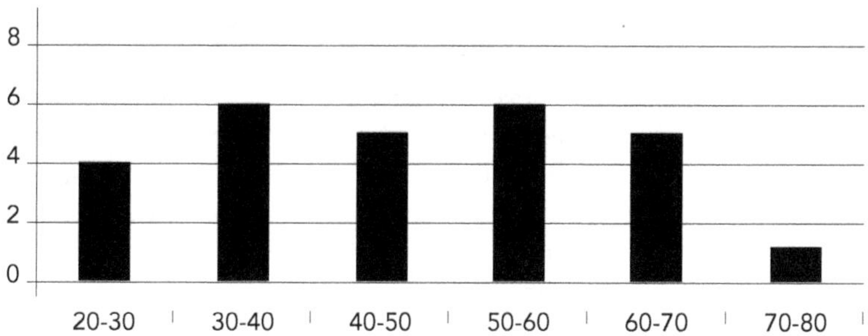

Figure 1. Age distribution of the book reviewers in this study

Education. Educational background was identified for only nineteen out of fifty-one participants. In this group, the majority has a university degree. At least three have a PhD. Clearly, the selection of people writing online is not random. A large group consists of students.

Occupation. Professionally, the reviewers are a diverse group: teachers, librarians, academics. Some work in ITC departments. Some are artists (actor, musician, documentary maker). Some describe themselves as writer or author, but what they write are usually magazine articles or website content. One reviewer was the author and publisher of a collection of stories, another wrote for television, yet another produced a book about people of Asian descent in Texas and there was an author of a series of books on computer programming. M.A. Orthofer (see below) wrote a book about his review site (The Complete Review).[17] There are reviewers who are also part-time publishers; there are (PhD) students, self-employed, unemployed or retired people. Many of them seem to have worked in multiple fields. Again, this is clearly a very literate and cultured group of people and it would be misleading to describe them as a bunch of 'ordinary readers'.

Relevant experience. Most bloggers turn out to have some form of experience in the literary field in the widest sense: any activity related to the production and transmission of literature. Sometimes this is a by-product of their profession, as in the case of teachers of literature and librarians. *Leeswammes* founded Book Helpline, an editing service for writers.[18] Experience in the literary field may also be a consequence of blogging activities, as when M.A. Orthofer (see below) was asked to participate in literary juries based on his online reviews.[19] Experience may also be the result of a side activity. Lisa Hill, for example, chairs sessions at a literary festival in Melbourne,[20] and Branko Collin, who works in IT, volunteers in his free time as a proof-reader for the Gutenberg project.

Link with the Dutch-language area. Why are the reviewers discussing Dutch books? Twenty-seven do not have a visible relationship with Dutch or with the Netherlands. Eighteen bloggers do have some sort of connection with the Netherlands, some are Dutch (eleven bloggers), another has a half-Indonesian ('Indo') father, others have lived in the Netherlands for a while, or picked up Dutch elsewhere. Oddly, we didn't encounter people from Flanders. Some of the Dutch reviewers are at least partially motivated by the desire to share their culture with the world and quite a few have lived in the UK for a long time. *Leeswammes*, who describes herself as bilingual, has both a Dutch-language and an English-language blog.

Reach. The number of people reached by the blogs varies, and depends on the bloggers' aims. Some use their blog mainly as a diary, a place to keep track of which books they have read and how they evaluated them. To them, followers are not very important. As Tim Patrick says in an interview, 'the site was designed for my own edification, and was not meant to be a large-scale discussion forum for these books. Therefore, the audience for the site is rather small.' Others use their blogs to get a message across. John Alvey, the person behind the huge website themodernnovel.org explained his idealism in these terms: 'My aim has been, at least partially, to introduce readers to books they might not otherwise be aware of and to promote authors who are worthwhile.'[21] *Little Dutch Book* blogs exclusively about Dutch literature, presumably with the intention of making the wider world read more of it.[22]

The blogs can reach their audience through multiple channels. A simple way of extending one's reach is cross-posting the reviews to Amazon, as Mary Whipple does.[23] Some blogs offer their readers the possibility of enrolling in a newsletter or following an RSS feed. The number of followers varies from thirty-one to 7500. Lizzy Siddal (see below) has 1300 email followers. The highest number was found at Simon Savidge's blog. He is a thirty-something writer and presenter at radio-shows on literature. The blogs' reach is also indicated by the number of readers' responses. Some bloggers accept no responses, but those who do reach an average of about twenty-five to thirty reactions, often the result of asking an explicit question of their readers. Simon Savidge, for example, concludes his review of *The Detour* by Gerbrand Bakker as follows:

> Have any of you read *The Twin* by Bakker? As I am desperate to read it now but am slightly worried that *The Detour* being a later book it might be more accomplished? Is that a bad/lazy assumption to make? I tell you what though, it is books like this that remind me I need to be a bit more like (the legend that is) Stu of *WinstonsDad* Blog and read much, much more translated fiction.[24]

Questions like these invite other readers to participate and to discuss certain books. In this case, eleven bloggers responded. One of them answers: '*The Twin* is a beautiful novel and one of my favourites and I have loaned my copy to all my bookish friends and it is getting quite worn as a result. So your assumption is unfounded and a very accomplished debut IMO so read it and know you are in for a treat.'

In some cases, the blogger-reader relationship becomes a sort of friendship, and the comment-facility becomes a means of cementing that friendship. On Nina's blog *J'adore Happy Endings*,[25] many commenters will say things like 'Great review Nina' or 'Thanks for sharing'.

Some bloggers expand the reach of their writings by means of a Twitter and/or Facebook account. This is sometimes amazingly successful: Sanne Vliegenthart has 14,000 Twitter followers, Orthofer 3900, Librarian Lavender 2800; for most the numbers are much lower. Sixteen bloggers have a

Facebook account connected to the blog. Other networks that allow people to connect are, for instance, Google (Nina of *J'adore Happy Endings* has 725 friends through Google Friend Connect, many of them book bloggers themselves), Bloglovin (she has 166 followers there) and NetworkedBlogs (Susanne of *LibrarianLavender* has 623 followers there).

It is interesting to see that some fragments of the community of bloggers around Dutch literature seem to be quite connected and solid. On the blogs we often encountered comments from other bloggers who were included in our study. The quote from Simon Savidge for example, mentions Stu of *WinstonsDad*, who is in our database as well. Many bloggers also refer to each other in their blog rolls, the list of blogs that they are reading. A name that keeps popping up is Iris, mentioned above, of *Irisonbooks*. Iris is twenty-six years old, female, PhD-student in religious studies and history. She is Dutch but blogs in English. In 2011, she initiated the Dutch Literature Month in June, an initiative to read and discuss on her blog a number of Dutch books.[26] A number of her blogging friends joined the initiative. Iris is a popular blogger. She discusses books from a variety of genres: nineteenth- and twentieth- century history, gender and postcolonial literature. She started blogging in 2010 and has built up a large group of followers, 2500 on her website and 2200 on Twitter. There is a considerable number of responses to her blogs, varying from ten to fifteen. She has clearly acquired a position as a mediator in the literary landscape.

Whatever these numbers may mean, publishers at least seem convinced that many bloggers have influence. Many bloggers receive review copies. One writes: 'Almost all publishers of literary fiction [...] approach me to review their new releases.'[27] This leads many bloggers to formulate more or less elaborate review policies, stating for instance (Susanne) 'I only write 5 star reviews. [...] If I don't like a book I won't review it.'[28] Iris writes: 'If I did not like a book, I will not lie about it, and so I might post a negative review. However, I do try to note why the book did not work for me, and for whom it might work.'[29] Many also report that publishers have used quotations from their blogs. Mary Whipple, a very prolific reviewer: 'Yes, my reviews have been quoted on publisher and author sites. Portions of reviews were published as blurbs on the book jackets.'[30]

CASE STUDIES

In the remainder of this article, we will show how some of the CODL-texts were discussed by our reviewers. In this study we did not encounter English-language reviews for the five books that date from before 1850,[31] nor for Herman Heijermans' *Op hoop van zegen* [*The Good Hope*]. However, Heijermans was discussed by Branko Collin, who liked his *Joeps wonderlijke avonturen* [Jack's Wondrous Adventures].[32] For the other books we have one or more reviews. Willem Elsschot's *Kaas* [*Cheese*] is discussed by Ad Blankestijn (see below), who describes it as 'a gentle, humorous story of small-time ambition faced with too grand an opportunity, told with brisk efficiency'.[33] Four reviewers discussed W.F. Hermans' *De donkere kamer van Damokles* [*The Dark Room of Damocles*]. Fleur of *Fleur in her world* notes that 'it's a book to make you think, and go on thinking for some time after you've put it down'. Lisa Hill is one of those that discuss Hella Haasse's *Oeroeg* [*The Black Lake*] and judges that 'it captures the pain and bewilderment of a cross-cultural friendship that cannot survive the war of independence'.[34] Annie M.G. Schmidt's *Minoes* [*The Cat Who Came In off the Roof*] is praised by many: 'I am very grateful to Annie M.G. Schmidt for writing this book and I wish she was still here to write lots more.' And: 'This is a tried and true Dutch classic that stands up to the test of time. I loved the unique friendships and the heartwarming story.'[35] Dimitri Verhulst's *De helaasheid der dingen* [*The Misfortunates*] is discussed twice. Tom Cunliffe is shocked by 'the level of debauchery' in the 'fairly cultured European nation' of Belgium but also writes 'the author frequently launches off into lyrical prose which adds a layer of unexpected beauty onto this terrible world'.[36]

For two of the CODL-texts we will discuss how our reviewers discussed them: Multatuli's *Max Havelaar* and Louis Couperus' *De Stille Kracht* [*The Hidden Force*].

Max Havelaar

Max Havelaar is one of the most important novels written in Dutch, published in 1861. It tells the story of its protagonist Max Havelaar, an alter ego of the author, as a colonial administrator in the Dutch East Indies. Havelaar tries to make his superiors act against the abuses of power that produce suffering among the indigenous people, but he is fired instead. The book tries to elicit indignation amongst the Dutch public about the system of colonial administration. *Max Havelaar* has been discussed by five very different bloggers in our collection: Jeannette Lambert, M.A. Orthofer, Ad Blankestijn, Iris and Tim Patrick.

Tim Patrick used his blog, *The Well-Read Man*, to keep track of a project he set up for himself. During the project, Tim Patrick becomes a well-read man by reading and reviewing fifty classical or otherwise important texts. *Max Havelaar* is one of them. Patrick formulates the reason he chose *Max Havelaar* for his list of fifty books as follows:

> I included *Max Havelaar* in the project after narrowing down a list of several thousand books to just the fifty that I would read. I tried to create a sample that represented the entire set of thousands of books, and *Max Havelaar* helped to bring international balance to the collection.

Patrick opens his short review with a blunt statement: 'You've never heard of *Max Havelaar*. [...] There are some good reasons for that. [...] The third, and most important, is that it deals with some European drama from over a century ago.' Patrick's view of his audience is clearly that it does not have a very sophisticated literary taste. Later in his review he writes: '*Max Havelaar* is the *Uncle Tom's Cabin* of the nineteenth-century Netherlands.' And: 'While Multatuli does tend to simplify the entire argument, *Max Havelaar* is nonetheless an influential and important book that had a significant impact on world affairs.'[37]

Jeannette Lambert's discussion of the book is much more personal than Tim Patrick's. Lambert is a jazz vocalist and poet, and one of the founders of a website called www.imho-reviews.com. The IMHO acronym is here resolved as 'In My Hysterical (and not the usual 'humble') Opinion'. The website contains reviews from a number of different commentators. Lambert wrote 105 posts on this website, varying from reviews of book to those of Jazz music. The site is no longer maintained: 'It was a project a friend and I started before reviews became so common directly on book selling websites like Amazon themselves. [...] As the format and technology changed, we stopped writing and moved on to pursue other activities.'[38] She now maintains a Pinterest board for translated Dutch literature.[39] Some of the Dutch books she read because of her background: 'I feel obliged to read all books relating to World War II in Indonesia, as part of my identity crisis.'[40] She often mentions her Indo father in her reviews on Dutch books. 'Identity' is a frequently used keyword on the site. In the interview she mentions that she now gets recommendations from Facebook groups for Dutch books targeted at people of Indo descent.

Her *Max Havelaar* review is appreciative of the historical accuracy of the book:

> I was also happy to get such sharp insight into the workings of the Dutch East Indies, as so many of the Indo-related novels I have been reading seem to assume we know all about it. Max Havelaar behaves so exactly as my Indo father often does that I felt I learned a lot about my family as well. No wonder everyone in Holland has to read this book in school![41]

M.A. Orthofer is the creator of the website www.complete-review.com. Started in 1999, the site is quite large; it contains reviews of almost 3500 books from all over the world.[42] Orthofer has 3700 followers on Twitter. In 2013, the list price of the copies he received was $ 7600, which shows that publishers expect him to have some influence on the reading public. Orthofer has described in a short book the history of his site and his opinions of reviewing.[43] His original aim was to provide information about books and link this to reviews elsewhere, but he found that many books went unreviewed and therefore decided to create his own reviews. He argues that, while over the last years print coverage for new books has declined rapidly, the diversity and accessibility of online reviews make up for the loss.

In the category 'Dutch Literature' one can find reviews on books from thirty-nine different authors, varying from Dutch classics like Multatuli and Couperus to contemporary authors like Charles den Tex and Arnon Grunberg. Not unlike Tim Patrick, Orthofer writes about Multatuli that 'his reputation doesn't exactly precede him in the Anglo-Saxon world'.[44] His *Max Havelaar* review of more than 2100 words is unusually long for an online review. Orthofer concludes: '*Max Havelaar* is a book of its times that has (somewhat surprisingly) nevertheless transcended them. The parts perhaps now outshine the whole, but it is still well worthwhile.'[45]

Iris is the blogger mentioned before who initiated Dutch Literature Month. She also provides on her site a brief list of translated Dutch literature. During Dutch Literature month she reviewed *Max Havelaar*, 'because of its importance in Dutch colonial history'. Iris says she 'was prepared to find it boring, and slow, and very detailed but not all that interesting.' 'But I think I underestimated this novel.'[46] As shown by the thirteen responses, her review caused some of her followers and peer-bloggers to read the book and write about it. One of them is Emma, French, who responds:

> I read this one too during this month of Dutch literature. I thought it was insightful. He was ahead of his time. As far as I know, there is no equivalent in French literature (at least not with the same fame) and there were probably many similar things to say about French colonization in Algeria, Indochina or Africa. I also think it's important to have read this book to fully understand Hella S. Haasse. I made the mistake to read one of her books before reading Multatuli and I would have enjoyed her book a lot more if I had read *Max Havelaar* first.[47]

There is one other blogger in our study who wrote a review of *Max Havelaar*: Ad Blankestijn, who lives and works in Japan. Under the motto 'Art makes life, makes interest, makes importance,' Blankestijn writes about literature and other arts on his blog *Splendid Labyrinths*. His review of *Max Havelaar* ('a book that will not shut up, even today') describes extensively the political circumstances behind the novel.[48] This blog is clearly not a diary. The novel is mentioned in another place on his blog as well: Blankestijn provides a list of ten important Dutch books that are available in translation. His comment there: 'the passionate novel that harshly woke up Dutch society in the nineteenth century.'[49]

These five reviewers are very different in their motivations for reading and writing: the well-read man mostly working on his own development; Jeannette Lambert working through her identity crisis; Orthofer, perhaps the most careful reviewer, for whom the review site itself is probably the main motivation; Iris for whom reading is perhaps mostly a social event, and Ad Blankestijn for whom the book is an occasion for teaching. The most influential bloggers are

Iris and Orthofer. But for all of them, the fact that they chose to read *Max Havelaar* shows that the book still has canonical status; Iris says that she 'was prepared to find it boring, and slow' but she acknowledges the power of the work. When they conclude, as Blankestijn does, that '*Max Havelaar* is a book that will not shut up, even today,' they do reconfirm that canonical status. The fact that they are recognizable persons may lend extra credibility to their voices. As Orthofer writes:

> As sources of predominantly personal opinion, the reviews written in the first person, the majority of review-focused book blogs seem to offer something that much print review coverage does not: readers sharing what are entirely their own, often visceral, reactions to books [...] [T]hese reactions often exude a fundamental honesty and the kind of intimate reaction that appears to appeal to readers. [...] [B]ook blogs, where reviews by (usually) one person are collected in one location, can establish identities – and find followers, of a sort – fairly easily.[50]

The Hidden Force

De Stille Kracht (1900) is an important novel by Louis Couperus first translated into English by Alexander Teixeira de Mattos as *The Hidden Force* (1921). A colonial administrator is brought to his demise by the limitations of his rational approach in dealing with indigenous resentment as well as by the troubles in his own home. The book is often seen as a prediction of the ultimate failure of the colonial system. In our study, we came across seven blogs that discussed works by Louis Couperus, four of them about *The Hidden Force*. Two of them are part of a joint discussion in 'Dutch Literature Month': both Lizzy Siddal and Iris (see above) posted a blog in which the two discuss elements of the book. It is quite interesting to see how they interact: the blogs are a report of a conversation, either online or in real life, in which they talk about expectations and reading experiences. The other two who discuss the book are Ad Blankestijn ('Couperus sniffed out the decay and final doom of the Dutch empire in the East Indies') and Orthofer ('Couperus has a fine touch in taking what seems absurd and making a believable figure with it').[51] Here we focus on the discussion between Lizzy Siddal and Iris.

Lizzy Siddal is a pseudonym of someone in her fifties. She discusses Dutch books on her blog as she did Dutch as a subsidiary subject during her studies in German. The two women have different reasons for choosing this novel. In their first exchange of thoughts, published on Lizzy Siddal's blog,[52] Lizzy says: 'This harks back to my student past – 2 years of studying Dutch language and literature. If asked which were my favorite Dutch novels, I would reply *The Darkroom of Damocles* and *The Hidden Force*.' Iris chose the book because it is most famous for its depiction of the Dutch colonial system.

In discussing how they evaluated the book, they come to speak about the differences in translation. They see the number of Malay words in the original and in the more modern English translation as an important factor. In the English translation, also available in the Gutenberg Project, most of these are translated, which made it easier to read than a more recent translation. The second exchange of thoughts has a more profound tone[53] as they ask themselves whether *The Hidden Force* is a timeless classic.

Iris answers as follows:

> *The Hidden Force* treads a fine line on several counts. On the one hand it can be viewed as a timeless classic that gives voice to themes of oppression and resistance in the form of a story about a man's career and his wife's love life. It is also very much a turn-of-the-century novel that both appeals to nineteenth-century literature and foreshadows developments in the twentieth century, as you mentioned earlier. And it is a novel of its time in its use of some colonial motifs and its prose and style. All are elements I appreciated for what they were, though they never led to me loving the book.

Lizzy replies:

> Well said. I agree with all of that. I would like to add though that it's very much a slow burning book that benefits from this kind of in-depth analysis. I think it also retains its relevance in today's climate of Western intervention. I suspect that's why there's a new film on the way.[54]

This online discussion, while certainly not a common case, vividly illustrates Iris' network. It also illustrates the point made earlier: all of the bloggers are to some extent persons who relate on a personal level to their readers. Unlike the usual literary critic, most bloggers have their own platforms from which they speak about books as well as about other aspects of their lives. Bloggers are friends rather than authorities. While being counseled about books by like-minded friends has been deplored by many as limiting one's development,[55] listening to these friends, as we see here, doesn't necessarily mean a menu of easy reading.

CONCLUSIONS

In this contribution, we have investigated a number of non-traditional online book reviewers and discussed some of the characteristics of the sites and their creators. Our study was confined to people writing in English about (translated) Dutch works. We saw that with respect to sex and age they are a diverse group. Some of them have a professional, educational or other link to the literary field, but others have not. They are usually well-educated. About one-third have a special relationship with Dutch, Dutch-language areas or Dutch history. Some of them form, to some extent, a coherent group. While we have by no means identified all online writers discussing Dutch literature in English, this is not as yet a very large group. Although the number of people reached by the blogs is hard to quantify, it is clear some of them have large audiences, either on the blogs themselves or through mailing lists, Twitter feeds, Facebook or other social media channels.

There are a number of ways in which these reviewers differ from traditional critics. As noted, one of the attractions of their writing is their personal style.[56] They do not get their authority, such as it is, from a social institution (such as a large newspaper or a university). The reviewers with their own weblogs are in a sense small entrepreneurs, competing on their own for attention from readers. Though most are well-educated, their education was not necessarily oriented towards literature. This may explain why (for some) their interest is wider than the 'higher' literature to which traditional critics usually limit their attention.

Turning to the books under discussion, most of the attention goes to recent literature. However, *Max Havelaar* and *The Hidden Force* are more than a century old and are apparently interesting enough for our group of reviewers. Both books are set in the Dutch East Indies. Some reviewers chose them because of this, or out of a general historical or a family interest. Others were influenced by the status of these works as Dutch or, indeed, international classics. In selecting these titles, they are of course reconfirming that classic status. Even when they did not enjoy the books that much, they mention that they are glad or proud that they did read them.

All in all, the presence of responses on the blogs, the existence of networks of bloggers, the large numbers of followers over different channels (mail, Twitter, etc.), suggests online reviewers may already be, or are about to become, a force to reckon with. The more popular among them certainly have acquired some influence on the circulation of (Dutch) literature.

NOTES

1 See the introduction to this volume.

2 J. Rosen, 'The People Formerly Known as the Audience', http://archive.pressthink.org/2006/06/27/ppl_frmr.html.

3 A. Keen, *The cult of the amateur: How today's internet is killing our culture* (New York, Doubleday/Currency, 2007).

4 O. Bendel, 'User-generated Nonsense. Literaturbesprechungen von Laien im Web 2.0', http://www.heise.de/tp/artikel/30/30206/1.html.

5 R. McDonald, *The death of the critic* (London, New York: Continuum International Publishing Group, 2007).

6 P. Boot, 'Towards a Genre Analysis of Online Book Discussion: socializing, participation and publication in the Dutch booksphere', in *Selected Papers of Internet Research* IR 12.0(2011). http://spir.aoir.org/index.php/spir/article/view/18.
7 A. Steiner, 'Personal Readings and Public Texts: Book Blogs and Online Writing about Literature', in *Culture unbound* 2 (2010) 28, pp. 471-494.
8 For reasons of time, we were not able to do an exhaustive search for online English-language reviews of Dutch literature. We did not, for instance, inspect the Librarything or Shelfari sites.
9 We provide a link for the blog the first time that it is mentioned. Blog names are italicised.
10 https://www.goodreads.com/.
11 http://www.tekstadventure.nl/branko/blog/.
12 http://irisonbooks.com/.
13 http://blogs.transparent.com/dutch/.
14 https://www.youtube.com/user/booksandquills.
15 http://www.ourbookreviewsonline.blogspot.nl.
16 https://www.goodreads.com/user/show/1457001-stephen.
17 M.A. Orthofer, *The Complete Review. Eleven Years, 2500 Review* (aestheticsofresistance/press, 2010), http://www.complete-review.com/main/CRbook.htm.
18 https://leeswammes.wordpress.com/about/.
19 http://rochester.edu/College/translation/threepercent/?id=7482.
20 https://au.linkedin.com/in/lisa-hill-4871a737.
21 Interview.
22 https://littledutchbook.wordpress.com/. There are no indications at all as to who is writing this blog. It might be an institutional site.
23 Interview. Whipple reviewed on Amazon long before she had her own blog. She is a 'Hall of Fame' Amazon reviewer (http://www.amazon.com/gp/pdp/profile/A319KYEIAZ-3SON/ref=cm_cr_dp_pdp), whose reviews were voted as helpful more than 30.000 times.
24 https://savidgereads.wordpress.com/2013/09/18/the-detour-gerbrand-bakker/.
25 http://jadorehappyendings.blogspot.nl/.
26 There is also a German Literature Month, hosted by Lizzy Siddal (see below) and Caroline (no surname known) of *Beauty is a sleeping cat* https://beautyisasleepingcat.wordpress.com/2015/12/01/final-giveaways-and-looking-back-on-german-literature-month-2015/. And there is 'Paris in July', with the aim 'to celebrate our French experiences through reading, watching, listening to, observing, cooking and eating all things French.' See http://bookbath.blogspot.nl/2011/05/paris-in-july-2011.html. Theme-based readalongs are a common feature of the book blogosphere.
27 Interview.
28 http://www.librarianlavender.com/search/label/Review%20Policy.
29 http://irisonbooks.com/review-policy/.
30 Interview.
31 Hadewijch's *Liederen*, *Elckerlijc*, Joost van den Vondel's *Lucifer*, Betje Wolff and Aagje Deken's *Sarah Burgerhart* and Hendrik Conscience's *De leeuw van Vlaanderen*.
32 http://www.tekstadventure.nl/branko/blog/2007/11/joeps-wonderlijke-avonturen.
33 http://splendidlabyrinths.blogspot.jp/2013/04/cheese-1933-by-willem-elsschot-book.html.

34 http://anzlitlovers.com/2014/01/11/the-black-lake-by-hella-s-haasse-translated-by-ina-rilke/.
35 http://www.goodreads.com/book/show/1795353.Minoes.
36 http://acommonreader.org/2012/01/05/review-the-misfortunates-dimitri-verhulst/.
37 http://wellreadman.com/2011/10/19/review-max-havelaar/.
38 Interview.
39 https://www.pinterest.com/nettecollect/dutch-literature-in-english/.
40 http://www.imho-reviews.com/opinion/88_0_1_0_C/.
41 http://www.imho-reviews.com/opinion/8_0_1_0_C/.
42 http://www.complete-review.com/main/absite.html.
43 M. A. Orthofer, *The Complete Review*.
44 http://www.complete-review.com/reviews/niederld/multatuli2.htm.
45 http://www.complete-review.com/reviews/niederld/multatuli.htm.
46 http://irisonbooks.com/2011/06/12/max-havelaar-by-multatuli-eduard-douwes-dekker/.
47 https://bookaroundthecorner.wordpress.com/2011/06/27/max-havelaar-by-multatuli/#comments.
48 http://splendidlabyrinths.blogspot.nl/2014/03/max-havelaar-or-coffee-auctions-of.html.
49 http://splendidlabyrinths.blogspot.nl/2014/03/ten-masterworks-of-dutch-literature.html.
50 Orthofer, *The Complete Review*, p. 85.
51 http://splendidlabyrinths.blogspot.nl/2014/03/the-hidden-force-by-louis-couperus.html, http://www.complete-review.com/reviews/niederld/couperl3.htm.
52 https://lizzysiddal.wordpress.com/2012/06/18/the-hidden-force-louis-couperus-part-one-what-a-difference-the-translation-makes/.
53 http://irisonbooks.com/2012/06/19/the-hidden-force-by-louis-couperus-part-two-or-is-it-a-masterpiece/.
54 At the time there were plans for the book to be made into a movie by Paul Verhoeven.
55 'But if we only listen to those who already share our proclivities and interests, will not the supposed critical democracy lead instead to a dangerous attenuation of taste and conservatism of judgment?' McDonald, *The death of the critic*, p. 12.
56 'Even though a book blog is about literature, the personalized tone is necessary to attract readers. A de-personalized blogger without passions leaves no impression, and tends to have few visitors.' Steiner, 'Personal Readings and Public Texts', p. 488.

BIBLIOGRAPHY

Bendel, O., 'User-Generated Nonsense. Literaturbesprechungen Von Laien Im Web 2.0', http://www.heise.de/tp/artikel/30/30206/1.html.

Boot, P., 'Towards a Genre Analysis of Online Book Discussion: Socializing, Participation and Publication in the Dutch Booksphere', in *Selected Papers of Internet Research* IR 12.0 (2011).

Keen, A., *The Cult of the Amateur: How Today's Internet is Killing our Culture* (New York: Doubleday/Currency, 2007).

McDonald, R., *The Death of the Critic* (London/New York: Continuum International Publishing Group, 2007).

Orthofer, M.A., 'The Complete Review. Eleven Years, 2500 Reviews', (Aestheticsofresistance/Press, 2010).

Rosen, J., 'The People Formerly Known as the Audience', http://archive.pressthink.org/2006/06/27/ppl_frmr.html.

Steiner, A., 'Personal Readings and Public Texts: Book Blogs and Online Writing About Literature', in *Culture unbound* 2: 28 (2010), pp. 471-494.

INDEX

www.ingramcontent.com/pod-product-compliance
Lightning Source LLC
Chambersburg PA
CBHW070545310726
48982CB00004B/837
* 9 7 8 9 4 6 2 7 0 0 9 7 0 *